Notable Sussex Women

580 Biographical Sketches

Helena Wojtczak

Notable Sussex Women: 580 Biographical Sketches
Copyright © Helena Wojtczak 2008

A CIP record for this publication is
available from the British Library
ISBN 978–1–904–10915–0

Published 2008
The Hastings Press
PO Box 96 Hastings TN34 1GQ
books@hastingspress.co.uk
www.hastingspress.co.uk

Book design by the author
Printed by TJI, Padstow, England

Hastings Press

FRONT COVER detail from a map of Sussex by cartographer F.S. Weller FRGS, published
by William Mackenzie, c1895.

REAR COVER PHOTOS *upper row* Mary Allen, suffragette and pioneering policewoman;
Vesta Tilley, music hall entertainer; Matilda Betham-Edwards, author and Francophile;
Hilda Leyel, philanthropist and herbalist; *lower row* Vivien Leigh, actress; D.K.
Broster, novelist; Madeleine Masson, author; Fay Compton CBE, actress.

ABOUT THE AUTHOR Helena Wojtczak is indubitably a woman of
Sussex: born in the West, she was raised in Brighton and lives in the
East. Among her five previous books are *Women of Victorian Sussex:
Their Status, Occupations and Dealings with the Law 1830~1870;* and
Railwaywomen: Exploitation, Betrayal and Triumph in the Workplace.
In 2007 she won the David St John Thomas Trust Award and Silver
Cup for Self-Publishing and its Non-Fiction Book of the Year Prize.

CONTENTS

Introduction

Acknowledgements   4
Notes on this book   4
Prologue   5
Putting notable women into context   7
Book statistics   14
Honours and awards   15
Index of notable women   17
Index of places   23
Index of plates   25

Biographies

WEST SUSSEX   27
Illustrations   102

BRIGHTON & HOVE   119
Illustrations   174

EAST SUSSEX   183
Illustrations   262

Appendix   285

Abbreviations and glossary   287
Educational establishments   289
Suffrage societies   293
Wartime organisations   295
Wartime medical organisations   297
Peacetime medical establishments   299
Miscellaneous women's organisations   301

NOTES ON THIS BOOK

Notable Sussex Women exists to record and commemorate the lives of 580 individuals whose names have never before appeared together in one place. It makes no claim to be loftily academic but aims to be both informative and accessible. Authors of collections of this kind must choose their own inclusion criteria, laying themselves open to criticism by those who, had they written the book, may have chosen otherwise. My criteria were decided after research and consultation. They are: birth, death, or residency of more than two years, although in ninety per cent of cases it was over five. Princess Amelia is the sole exception and was included because of the enormous impact her visit made upon the sleepy village of Worthing. Living persons are excluded, and Angela Thirkell and Millicent Fawcett, though they have Brighton buses named for them, are omitted as they were not residents. Each biography is of necessity concise and if a subject's connection with Sussex was limited to birth, education, death or under five years' residency, is correspondingly abbreviated, but a decision was made to include them because locals may find this information interesting. Academic-style referencing has been consciously omitted in a deliberate attempt to keep this book to a reasonable length and uncluttered by thousands of footnotes. Details of parentage, husbands and children have been kept to a minimum in favour of giving more space to the subjects' achievements and to their connections with Sussex including, wherever possible, their street addresses. Where subjects lived in more than one town they are listed where their residency appears to have been longest. What is often referred to as Sussex has since 1189 comprised the two counties of West and East Sussex and (since 1997) a unitary authority, the City of Brighton and Hove. These divisions provide a neat way of parcelling the book into three sections of roughly similar length. Towns are alphabetical within chapters and women are alphabetical within towns.

Errors and omissions are inevitable in a work of this breadth and corrections and additions are welcome. Please send them to books@hastingspress.co.uk or PO Box 96, Hastings TN34 1GQ. Additional relevant historical material can be found on our website www.hastingspress.co.uk.

To avoid repetition within the text, organisations, acronyms and abbreviations are explained and described in detail on pages 287–301. Figures in square brackets throughout the book refer to the numbers of pages upon which further related information may be found.

SOURCES AND ACKNOWLEDGEMENTS

My main sources were biographical works; *The Oxford Dictionary of National Biography;* press reports, features and obituaries; old phone books; Elizabeth Crawford's *The Women's Suffrage Movement: A Reference Guide*; *Who's Who*; the census; the British Library newspaper archives, www.copac.ac.uk and Lexis Nexis. All photographs of buildings are by the author, except as indicated. Cuttings from *The Times* are reproduced under licence from News International. The anonymous poem *A Woman's Sphere* on page 6 is from the *Englishwoman's Review*, 1st September 1875.

For providing facts or suggesting names I thank Amanda Waring, Val Brown, Richard Cheffins, Doreen E. Woodford, Paul Vallely, Kate McLintock, Diana Crook, Terence T. Quirke Jr, Jennifer Kloester, Helen Shipley, Chris Ravilious, Fred Reeve, Leigh Lawson, Geoff Meggitt, Jon Wynne-Tyson, Andrew Holmes-Siedle, Greg Rickford, Tom Dufty, Tilly Vacher, Neil Rogers-Davis, Mimi Colligan, Elaine Murphy, Andy Grant, Martin Snow, Arabella McIntyre-Brown, the Bailiffscourt Hotel, Mary Sheppard and Sister Carmel. Special thanks to Val Brown for checking details of medical women and establishments and for providing photos, to Maria Skrzypiec for being the first to read an early draft and to Adrian Hancock for his generous help with taking new and repairing old photographs.

PROLOGUE

One sex is habitually overlooked when inhabitants and officials of towns and counties look for eminent or otherwise interesting former residents to claim as their own. Not one woman graces the list of 'Notable Inhabitants' on Worthing Borough Council's website, nor is any member of the female sex included on the list of 'Famous ex-Residents' on the *Hastings & St Leonards Observer* website. No woman's name appears on any of the six commemorative plaques in Worthing. Arun District Council honours only one woman (and eighteen men) on its blue plaques; similarly, Eastbourne's plaque ratio is one female to eighteen males. West Sussex County Council has erected thirty-four plaques; only one is for a woman. This pattern is repeated in county guides and similar publications.

And yet, as this book amply proves, there is no shortage of notable women connected with Sussex, women who were considered sufficiently eminent to warrant entries in the *Oxford Dictionary of National Biography,* to deserve obituaries in the national press, who were the subject of published biographies, whose books sold in their tens of thousands, who were household names in their day, pioneers in their field, or whose achievements were recognised with awards, medals, honours and even damehoods.

Some are still in the limelight. Switching on the radio at random times, I have in the past year heard the voices of Mabel Constanduros, Jo Douglas, Gladys Morgan and Marjorie Westbury on Radio Seven; chanced upon feature articles about Barbara Bodichon, Anita Roddick, Annie Besant, Hertha Ayrton, Frances Wolseley, Vesta Tilley, Elizabeth David, Princess Beatrice and Emily Wilding Davison on Radio Four, where Gert & Daisy appeared in a feature on female comedy duos, Madeleine Masson's biography of Christine Granville was recommended as 'A Good Read' and Georgette Heyer's *Arabella* was the 'Book at Bedtime'. On TV, I saw a play about Fanny Cradock on BBC4 and footage of her appeared in a comedy show. New biographies of Princess Beatrice, Anna Jameson and Fanny Cradock were published in the past year, one of Georgette Heyer is in the pipeline and Marie Belloc Lowndes's *The Lodger* is again being adapted for the big screen. Last month, Catherine Cookson DVDs were given away free with the *Daily Mail*; today a new exhibition of Linda McCartney's photography opens. During a visit to Cowes I spotted new housing named for Princess Beatrice. Books by more than a dozen of the authors within have been reprinted in the past seven years after being out of print for over half a century. Recordings of over two dozen singers and actresses in this book have been uploaded within the past two years to the website Youtube.com, including some born in the nineteenth century such as Gracie Fields, Florrie Forde, Binnie Hale, Elsie Randolph, Edna Best, Ruby Miller and Clara Butt. Thorough research would doubtless reveal many more examples of continued interest in notable Sussex women, many of whom died decades ago.

Not every woman within these pages warrants anything so grand as a blue plaque; but they are worthy of attention for their contribution to society, the arts and sciences and the great struggle for women's emancipation; for rebelling against the narrow destiny set for women; for their audacity in invading men's spheres of public and professional life. In many cases these biographical sketches tell of women's refusal to stay within the confines of 'woman's sphere'. This expression was once in common usage; it described the man-made boundaries imposed on women, restrictions within which they were expected, usually obliged and often coerced, to conduct their lives. Rather than being omitted and ignored when plaques are awarded and lists compiled, it could be argued that notable members of the female sex deserve more, not less, recognition than their male counterparts for their achievements because they operated within a framework of sexual prejudice and met resistance and obstruction when stepping outside of their sphere.

A Woman's Sphere

" The philosophers seem to know that hard work never unsexes a woman: only wages can do that."—Mrs. Swisshelm.

'Tis a beautiful thing, a woman's sphere!
I have pondered the question for many a year,
And have reached a conclusion that's perfectly clear—
    That it's not the trade that a woman's in,
    The dirt or the weariness, toil or sin,
    It is only the money or rank she may win
        Which will lift her up out of her sphere!

'Tis a beautiful thing, a woman's sphere!
She may nurse a sick bed thro' the small hours drear;
Brave ghastly infection, untouched by fear,
    But she mustn't receive a doctor's fee,
    And she mustn't (oh, shocking!) be called an M.D.,
    For if woman were suffered to take a degree,
        She'd be lifted quite out of her sphere.

'Tis a beautiful thing, a woman's sphere!
She may trudge through the snow, both far and near,
As a teacher for £25 a year.
    But she must not ask a Professor's name,
    To learn in a College she has no claim—
    Much knowledge adds nought to a woman's fame,
        It's but raising her out of her sphere.

'Tis a wonderful thing, a woman's sphere!
She may vote for Town Councillors, Schools, or Mayor,
And numberless Boards and bodies—that's fair.
    But one feminine vote would the Commons sink—
    It's presuming, even, in her to think
    That mankind is bound by a mutual link,
        And that woman is man's compeer.

'Tis a marvellous thing, a woman's sphere!
She may starve at her needle, with fast-falling tear;
She may hammer nails, or sell gin and beer;
But she shan't be a lawyer, or clerk at most,
Or take any nice little government post,
For the Law and Society'd give up the ghost,
    If she stepped so far out of her sphere.

It's a terrible thing, a woman's sphere!
She may part with all that her sex holds dear,
May bear the taunt and the curse and leer,
    To earn her bread and to fill her cup—
    But when hands are stretched out to keep her up
    Unspotted and free—oh! then we hear
        That a woman must keep to a woman's sphere.

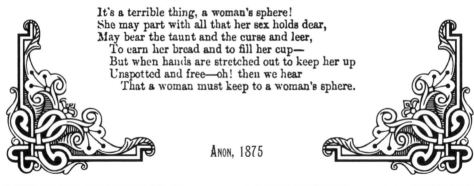

Anon, 1875

Putting notable Sussex women into context

As ninety-five per cent of the women featured within were born into the middle and upper-classes between the turn of the eighteenth century and the first decades of the twentieth century, this overview refers only to women of those classes and to that time period.

It began in childhood, when boys and girls became aware that one sex owned and ran the world and the other was clearly subordinate. Society was organised around the needs of men, who had assumed exclusive control of law and government and given themselves every possible advantage over women in the other crucial areas of society: education, occupation, inheritance, family life and religion. While a boy was raised to be independent and to take his place in society as a landowner, businessman, army officer, career professional or statesman, his sister was taught that her only 'career' would be that of wife and mother, whether or not that suited her. Girls' education was meagre (since teaching them beyond what they needed for domestic life was deemed pointless) and all universities were closed to them. While her brothers went to public school, a typical middle or upper-class girl was taught at home by an unqualified governess from whom she learned literacy, numeracy and 'ladylike' subjects. If lucky she might be sent to a ladies' seminary or finishing-school, but even there she was offered nothing academic or vocational. For example, Frances Power Cobbe attended Miss Poggi's 'Exclusive Establishment for Young Ladies' at 32 Brunswick Square, Hove, for two years (1836–8). The fee, £1,000, could have sent a boy to Oxford University for three years. Despite this, she found 'there was no solid instruction, no real mental training'.

Access to money, above anything else, is what gives a person autonomy and, until the mid-twentieth century, lack of it obliged dependence upon others, which brought with it obedience to their wishes. Both methods of acquiring money — inheriting it or earning it — were set up to severely disadvantage women. Property, businesses and wealth were passed from father to son; daughters received less or nothing. Noble titles also passed down the male line, denying women another source of power, influence or status. Nor was it possible for women to accrue wealth through employment. Until the late nineteenth century, the only career available to educated women was teaching infants or girls. Whether as governesses working in private houses, or as teachers in schools or seminaries, their wages were pitifully low. Some women with capital started a small business, typically educational,[1] but this rarely expanded beyond one establishment. Before 1882 married women were hindered in business because they could not enter into a business contract, sign a legal document, or sue a debtor (or anyone else) except with their husbands, giving the men in effect control of their wives' business matters.[2]

"Man is brought up to believe himself the all paramount, the most favoured; the one to whom power should be given and in whom command should be vested. Woman is brought up on a directly opposite principle. Thus the girl marries, believing herself her husband's inferior, and in turn transmits these doctrines to her children."

Lady Florence Dixie
(1855–1905)

"You bring up your girls as if they were meant for sideboard ornaments and then complain of their frivolity."

John Ruskin
(1819–1900)

"A girl in innumerable subtle, indirect ways is taught to mistrust herself. Ambition is held up to her as a vice — to a boy it is held up as a virtue. She is taught docility, modesty and diffidence. Docility and diffidence are of uncommonly little use in the business or professional world."

Lady Rhondda
(1883–1958)

Marriage, among other things, usually ended the employment of middle-class women. Except during the wars, from the 1890s until the 1950s state-owned or quasi-government organisations did not recruit married women and existing staff were forced to resign if they wed, regardless of their wishes, needs, rank, usefulness or length of service. This 'marriage bar' applied only to occupations which needed (at least a modicum of) education and had a career structure — char-ladies were safe!

By arranging inheritance in such a way as to prevent most women from coming into wealth, and by excluding them from lucrative employment, men gave themselves two paramount advantages: they kept most of the country's resources in male hands and forced women into involuntary dependence upon fathers, brothers and husbands.

Religion was a major influence on the lives of women. Home Bible-readings, compulsory church attendance and obedience to father, husband, Jesus and an all-seeing, all-powerful male God to whom one begged for mercy was the norm and those who disobeyed were the exceptions and were castigated as sinful.

Women's two roles in law and government were to obey the legislation men made and to pay the taxes that men levied and spent. The legal system was solely in the hands of male police, barristers, magistrates and judges and women were not even permitted to serve on juries.[3] Despite being the majority of the population they were excluded from local and national government and no woman could vote in parliamentary elections. The exclusion of women from the law-making process rendered them dependent upon men to change the system. As this required men to surrender their gender privileges, it often took decades of campaigning to persuade enough MPs to vote for a change in the law.

MARRIAGE AND MOTHERHOOD

Of those in this book only fifty-nine per cent (and only ten per cent of the senior academics) married, compared with over eighty per cent of the female population in general. Many intellectual women regarded marriage with a cynical rather than romantic eye, and with good reason, for it was a double-edged sword. A woman would increase her social status, become mistress of a household and the mother of children, but in exchange she gave up some of the most fundamental human rights.

Although men vowed 'With all my worldly goods I thee endow', in fact the very opposite was true. Until the law changed in 1870 and 1882, everything a woman owned, earned or inherited was the property of her husband from their wedding day.[4] This enormous transfer of power turned women into paupers dependent upon handouts from their 'lords and masters' and therefore subservient to them. A senior divorce judge even admitted that this was done in order to trap women within marriage. During the wedding ceremony all brides promised, within earshot of an ever-watching God they had been indoctrinated to fear, to obey their husbands. Passive submission to his sexual desires was a wifely duty, and the frequent childbearing and childrearing this inevitably led to further increased women's vulnerability and dependence upon men.[5] Children were (until 1925) the sole property of their father and, in the event of his death, their mother did not even have rights of guardianship until 1886.[7] The law gave fathers exclusive rights to make all decisions concerning their children's upbringing, and so the cycle began again when they favoured sons over daughters for education and inheritance.

No matter how disgruntled a woman might be with marriage in general and hers in particular, it was in her interests to keep it intact, because if provoked her husband might exercise his legal rights over her in full measure. Prior to 1870 separation left her destitute: her husband retained her income and inheritance, both current and future, unless she could get a divorce, which was expensive and difficult, especially as a husband's adultery was not sufficient grounds until 1923.[8] Unfaithfulness on her part gave her husband grounds for divorce, but as an adulteress she would be publicly disgraced (often in the national press) and might never see her children again. Until 1884 a spouse who left could be sent to prison for refusing to return;[9] until 1891 a husband could abduct his runaway wife, imprison her in his house and enforce his 'conjugal rights'[10] (marital rape was not illegal until 1991).[11]

STAYING SINGLE

Despite the enormous imbalance in the numbers of the sexes,[12] unless they entered holy orders, society viewed spinsters as objects of pity and ridicule, insultingly labelled them as 'surplus' (i.e. to men's requirements) and devised schemes to deport them. The most powerful women were wealthy widows and unmarried heiresses; however, in common with all other single women, to be considered respectable even they could not have a sex life, cohabit with a man or bear a child out of wedlock.

It was acceptable, however, to set up home with another woman, especially after the First World War, which killed or maimed millions of men of marriageable age. Although lesbianism was never illegal[13] it was taboo, driving lesbians to secrecy and leaving today's researchers to guess which cohabiting women were lovers and which were platonic friends. It is useful to bear in mind that our culture's obsession with frequent, lifelong sexual activity is a relatively recent phenomenon; previously it was normal for unmarried women to remain celibate throughout their lives, especially as 'decent' women were expected to have no sexual feelings.

"Marriage is for woman the commonest mode of livelihood, and the total amount of undesired sex endured by women is probably greater in marriage than in prostitution."

Bertrand Russell
(1872–1970)

Under exclusively man-made laws women have been reduced to the most abject condition of legal slavery in which it is possible for human beings to be held ... under the arbitrary domination of another's will, and dependent for decent treatment exclusively on the goodness of heart of the individual master."

Florence Fenwick Miller*
(1854–1935)

"'Tis less to be wondered at that women marry off in haste, for if they took time to consider and reflect upon it, they seldom would."

Mary Astell
(1668–1731)

"I think, therefore I am single."

Lizz Winstead
(1961–)

"A single woman is so free, so powerful."

Bessie Rayner Parkes*
(1829–1925)

From the mid-1700s a number of isolated individuals wrote about men's poor treatment of women as a class. Stirrings of more widespread discontent led to an organised movement that began around the mid-1860s and focused on education, employment and the vote [294]. From then, with the help of sympathetic male benefactors and MPs, women greatly improved their position in each of those three areas and by the 1890s there were several feminist newspapers (one of them edited by notable Sussex woman Florence Fenwick Miller) that teemed with news of women's achievements and campaigns. A large number of women in this book contributed to the changing status of their sex; either directly, by campaigning, or indirectly, by pioneering their way into male professions. Some of the most famous names in feminist history lived in Sussex.[14]

NOTABLE SUSSEX WOMEN

Notable Sussex women fall into three broad groups: over half were in the arts or sports, nearly a quarter were philanthropists or social reformers and the remainder were pioneers or professionals. A handful fell outside these categories and some belonged to more than one. About ninety per cent followed a profession or devoted their lives to a cause. The difficulties they encountered corresponded with how far they strayed from their 'sphere'.

Artists and sportswomen

Fifty-seven per cent of notable Sussex women were published writers or poets, exhibited painters or sculptors, professional musicians, well-known actresses or champion sportswomen. It comes as no surprise that this category is the largest, for the literary and performance arts were easier for women to enter than many other professions: no paper qualifications were needed and no governing body could prevent them from working in their chosen field. Every middle- or upper-class girl was taught to read, write and appreciate art, poetry and literature, and a good many learned to draw and paint, giving them the basic tools needed to become professional writers or artists, provided they had the necessary talent and could surmount the various obstacles.

Charlotte Brontë remarked that because women were generally confined to the home, most female novelists had limited life experience upon which to draw for storylines and characters, whereas male writers had seen something of the world. Furthermore, it was often difficult for women to obtain the peace and solitude required to think, plot

"What we ask is the removal of the aristocracy of their sex and the removal of the slavery of our sex."

Florence Fenwick Miller*
(1854–1935)

"Nature herself has decreed that woman ... should be at the mercy of man's judgement."

Rousseau
(1712–1778)

"Nature has given women so much power that the law has very wisely given them little."

Samuel Johnson
(1709–1784)

"I consider that women who are authors, lawyers, and politicians are monsters."

Pierre Auguste Renoir
(1841–1919)

"Ours is not a country which really encourages women, although our women have admirable records in every field they are allowed to try ... they are too often frowned out, made to feel intruders in a man's world."

Pearl Binder*
(1904–1989)

and write, because of the demand, criticised by Florence Nightingale, that women should be available to others at all times and must instantly abandon any hobby or pastime in order to amuse or serve them. Because they were usually dependent on their fathers, brothers or husbands, girls and women had to win the approval and goodwill of a man to secure not only the time and space in which to nurture their talents, but also the funds for materials and equipment. Girls blessed with a musical or artistic gift found it harder than boys to secure professional training, because they had first to obtain their fathers' permission (and funding) to engage a private tutor or attend a specialist college. It was therefore easy for men to prevent their daughters from pursuing anything they considered 'inappropriate' for the female sex or wasteful to spend money on something she would abandon upon marriage. For her own sake, a father could not condone activities that might make his daughter unmarriageable. Being seriously absorbed in developing an artistic, literary or musical talent would deter potential husbands: most men wanted a wife who would give him, his household and his children her undivided attention, not one wrapped up in her own pursuits.

Women who overcame the many obstacles and became professional writers or painters were aware of undercurrents of prejudice against women in the arts, which is why some invented a male pseudonym and others concealed their gender by using only their initials or remaining anonymous.[15]

A good many middle-class girls were taught to dance, sing and play the piano, but only as 'accomplishments' — something acquired for the pleasure of others in a domestic setting and certainly not for financial gain or public performance, which were thought vulgar. Many budding performers met with parental disapproval because it was not respectable for a girl to make a living on the stage. While a dignified Shakespearean thespian, a matronly, operatic contralto or a concert pianist would rise above suspicion, female entertainers in comedy, variety, pantomime, music hall and the circus were thought to have 'loose morals'. Indeed, their peripatetic, unchaperoned lifestyle was highly conducive to serial romances and sexual adventures. In addition, the profession was overcrowded and many struggling actresses resorted to casual prostitution to survive periods of unemployment.

In several respects female performers were a century ahead of their time: those at the pinnacle of their profession earned ten, even twenty times the average working woman's wage; they were the only women of their era to reveal their legs or to wear men's clothing in public; they generally retained their maiden names after marriage

"Women are never supposed to have any occupation of sufficient importance not to be interrupted ... They have accustomed themselves to consider intellectual occupation as a merely selfish amusement, which it is their 'duty' to give up for every trifler more selfish than themselves."

Florence Nightingale
(1820–1910)

"A woman must have money and a room of her own if she is to write fiction."

Virginia Woolf*
(1882–1941)

"For most of history, Anonymous was a woman."

Virginia Woolf*
(1882–1941)

"Alas! a woman that attempts the pen / Such an intruder on the rights of men / Such a presumptuous Creature, is esteem'd / The fault, can by no virtue be redeemed."

Countess of Winchilsea
(1661–1720)

"People find out I'm an actress and I see that 'whore' look flicker across their eyes."

Rachel Weisz (1971–)

and continued with their careers while raising children; many had extramarital affairs and divorced and remarried (sometimes more than once) when that was rare among — and considered scandalous by — the general population.

Few competitive sports were open to women, who were hampered by long skirts and corsets, by the cultural ideal of woman as passive and delicate, and by physicians' insistence that strenuous sports could cause infertility, a serious threat in a social climate where childbearing was seen as every woman's raison d'être. It was acceptable for women to compete (in a 'ladylike' fashion) at archery and croquet, and towards the late nineteenth century at lawn tennis, golf and cricket, ladies' tournaments taking place from the 1890s, when the first women's hockey and football teams were formed. Sports requiring revealing costumes were completely unacceptable until the 1920s.

Philanthropists, social workers and reformers

This category makes up twenty-four per cent of our notable women. Like their male counterparts, those who inherited wealth always helped those less fortunate by founding or supporting educational, medical and welfare establishments. Many middle-class spinsters received a small income from their family, which left them free to devote their lives to unpaid social work or public service. Some came to see reform as the only lasting way to cure society's ills, which in some cases drew them outside of philanthropy and into the very male world of politics, where they met the greatest opposition when attempting to get votes for women [293].

Pioneers and professionals

Twenty-two per cent of notable Sussex women were either the first of their sex to achieve something or followed careers that were considered the province of men. Compared with philanthropists or artists, theirs was the hardest struggle and involved overcoming various hindrances, which might include inadequate education, parental opposition, social disapproval, official obstruction and, in some cases, legal obstacles. Careers required serious study and self-confidence, but girls were raised to be modest and were cautioned to hold themselves back because being 'too clever' would scare away a potential husband. Furthermore, eminent physicians issued dire warnings that sustained intellectual study was beyond women's abilities and would lead to infertility.

The rare and lucky girl who managed to obtain both funds and paternal consent for higher education still had to find an establishment that would admit members of her sex: until the late nineteenth century universities and medical schools were strictly for men. Through personal philanthropy special colleges for women were opened, starting with Queen's College and Bedford College in

London in the 1840s. In the 1870s the London School of Medicine for Women was founded and degree examinations at the University of London were opened to women; at Cambridge, Girton and Newnham women's colleges were established and their students were admitted to Tripos examinations at the university from 1881, by which time Oxford also had two women's colleges: Lady Margaret Hall and Somerville [see p289]. All began as small, privately-owned, exclusive establishments attended by a tiny minority of highly privileged young ladies. By 1910 there were just over a thousand female students at 'Oxbridge'; however, Oxford refused to grant a degree to any woman until 1920, while Cambridge held out until 1947. Initially tutors at ladies' colleges were men; there were no suitably-educated women to take their places until the 1870s.

By the end of the nineteenth century teaching girls was no longer the only career open to educated women. There were several thousand trained and qualified nurses, over 100 physicians[6] and a few dozen government-appointed 'lady inspectors' of factories, schools, workhouses or workshops. During the First World War women's branches of the army, navy and air force were formed, and nurses serving in army hospitals at home and abroad proved themselves capable of working under dangerous conditions and of dealing with wounded soldiers. This created new career opportunities for educated women, not only as servicewomen and military nurses but as officers and chiefs of the Women's Auxiliary Army Corps, the Women's Royal Air Force, the Women's Royal Naval Service and Queen Alexandra's Imperial Military Nursing Service [see p297].

Although employed in the very lowest-grade office jobs from the 1870s, and as clerks and secretaries from about 1910, women rarely held senior positions in business until the late twentieth century. Each male bastion was eventually conquered, initially by the efforts of individual pioneers, although legal-minded women were assisted by legislation such as the Sex Disqualification (Removal) Act 1919, which allowed them to train and work as solicitors and barristers and to serve as magistrates. Although many public-sector workers won equal pay in the 1950s, real equality in the workplace did not begin to be possible until after the implementation of the Equal Pay Act 1970 and the Sex Discrimination Act 1975.

FOOTNOTES

* The author of this quote is a notable Sussex woman.
1. Typical women's businesses were shops catering mainly to a female clientele, e.g. milliner, dressmaker, and employment agencies for servants.
2. The Married Women's Property Act 1882 gave wives the right to enter into legal contracts.
3. Women in the public gallery were usually told to leave court during rape or other sexual assault cases.
4. There were a few exceptions: the very wealthy could obtain a prenuptial legal settlement, but it required the consent of the fiancé; a wife owned her paraphernalia (e.g. her clothing) and although her husband owned the rental income from her property he could not sell it. The Married Women's Property Acts became law in 1870 and 1882. The first gave wives ownership of their earnings and inheritance up to £200. The second gave wives control of all their property and made them liable to support their children and husbands.
5. There was no woman-controlled contraception or legal abortion until the 1960s.
6. Three of the first five qualified female physicians appear in this book: Elizabeth Blackwell [224], Sophia Jex-Blake [236] and Frances Hoggan [135].
7. The Guardianship of Infants Acts 1925 and 1886.
8. By 1857 only four British women had ever obtained a divorce, which required an Act of parliament. The 1857 Matrimonial Causes Act enabled divorce via the courts, allowed women to retain their property after divorce and restored the legal rights they had enjoyed as spinsters.
9. The Matrimonial Causes Act 1884.
10. A test case in 1891, known as the Jackson Abduction Case, or the Clitheroe Case, ended this right.
11. A husband's exemption from prosecution from rape of his wife was ended by the Law Lords in 1991.
12. In 1891, for example, women outnumbered men by 900,000.
13. Male homosexuality was illegal until the Sexual Offences Act 1967.
14. Madame Bodichon [193], Emily Davies [39], Florence Fenwick Miller [165], Elizabeth Blackwell [224], Sophia Jex-Blake [236], Emily Wilding Davison [96], Anna Jameson [137], Mary Richardson [227] and Margery Corbett Ashby [201].
15. Twenty-two of the writers and painters in this book used a male or genderless pseudonym or published as 'Anon'.

Book statistics

Just over one-fifth (21 per cent) of the notable women were born in Sussex, of whom seven per cent also died here. Over half died here but were not born here, and just over a quarter (27 per cent) lived part of their lives here but were born and died elsewhere. The vast majority were born during the reign of Queen Victoria (1837–1901). The total number of philanthropists, artists and pioneers exceeds 100 per cent because some women belonged to more than one category. Percentages are rounded up or down to the nearest whole number.

COUNTY		
West Sussex	207	36%
Brighton & Hove	164	28%
East Sussex	209	36%
CATEGORY		
Philanthropists/reformers	140	24%
Artists/sportswomen	331	57%
Pioneers/professionals	128	22%
CONNECTION WITH SUSSEX		
Born in county	80	14%
Died in county	302	52%
Born and died in county	40	7%
Resided only	158	27%
MARITAL STATUS		
Married	345	59%
Never married	235	41%
YEAR OF BIRTH		
1688–1800	29	5%
1801–1900	531	92%
1901–1948	18	3%

HONOURS AND AWARDS

A total of 137 — nearly a quarter — of the women in this book received honours from the monarch or the Red Cross. Except for military nursing awards and the rarely-given OM (founded in 1902, there have only ever been eight female recipients) there was no honour available for the monarch to bestow upon women until the Order of the British Empire was introduced in 1917. The Order of the Bath dates from 1725 but was closed to women until 1971. The CVO was inaugurated in 1896 but women were ineligible until 1936. The RRC and ARRC were introduced in 1893 as an award for military nurses, for either a specific act of bravery or for distinguished and lengthy service. The Most Venerable Order of St John of Jerusalem is an ancient royal order of chivalry that recognises outstanding service to the sick. It is awarded to chiefs rather than nurses.

The table lists honours in order of precedence and includes only those referred to in the text. Some women received several in the same order (for example OBE, followed later by DBE); only the highest is included.

	HONOURS FROM THE SOVEREIGN OR RED CROSS	
LG	Lady Companion of the Most Noble Order of the Garter	1
CB	Companion of the Most Noble Order of the Bath	1
CVO	Commander of the Royal Victorian Order	1
OM	Order of Merit	1
GBE	Dame Grand Cross of the Most Excellent Order of the British Empire	6
CH	Companion of Honour	1
DBE	Dame Commander of the Most Excellent Order of the British Empire	38
CBE	Commander of the Most Excellent Order of the British Empire	24
OBE	Officer of the Most Excellent Order of the British Empire	36
MBE	Member of the Most Excellent Order of the British Empire	15
BEM	British Empire Medal	1
GCStJ	Dame Grand Cross of the Most Venerable Order of St John of Jerusalem	1
-	Dame Chevalière of the Most Venerable Order of St John of Jerusalem (pre-1888)	1
LGStJ	Lady (formerly Dame) of Grace of the Most Ven. Order of St John of Jerusalem	3
CStJ	Commander (Sister) of the Most Venerable Order of St John of Jerusalem	1
RRC	Royal Red Cross	2
ARRC	Associate of the Royal Red Cross	3
-	Polar Medal	1

In addition to the above, four notable Sussex women were appointed (non-hereditary) baroness in their own right and one was elevated to countess. Ten were magistrates, seven were MPs, two were deputy lieutenants, one was a Lord-Lieutenant and one a High Steward. Two received the rare Florence Nightingale Medal, founded in 1912 and awarded to nurses of exceptional courage and devotion. Eight women received twenty war decorations between them, including three Croix de Guerre, one British Army Military Medal for bravery in battle on land and one Lloyd's War Medal for Bravery at Sea. Several won awards and medals in arts, crafts, science, literature, music and chess.

Index of notable women

Abram, Annie 121
Acton, Eliza 188
Aiken, Joan 70
Aiken, Mary 244
Alcock, Vivien 94
Allan, Elizabeth 153
Allen, Mary 223
Amelia, HRH Princess 94
Anderson, Frances 258
Anderson, Jean 205
Angell, Helen Cordelia 60
Angus, Peggy 219
Appleton, Honor 153
Arncliffe-Sennett, Maud 66
Ash, Maie 121
Ashby, Dame Margery Corbett 201
Ashford, Daisy 231
Askey, Anthea 94
Asquith, Lady Cynthia 85
Atkins, Vera 259
Attwell, Mabel Lucie 205
Aylward, Florence 245
Ayrton, Hertha 63
Bagnold, Enid 171
Bagot, Lady 153
Bailey, Mary Barbara 54
Baird, Edith 121
Baird, Lilian 121
Baker, Marjorie 55
Bannerman, Kay 154
Barber, Margaret Fairless 55
Barge, Gillian 223
Barker, Cicely 85
Barker, Mary 122
Barker, Valerie 41
Barnett, Dame Henrietta 154
Barrett, Rachel 47
Bath, Countess of 122
Batten, Mollie 67
Baxter, Lizzie 170
Baxter, Violet 169
Bayly, Ada 206
Beatrice, HRH Princess 32
Beck, Edith 42
Beck, Ellen 42
Beckett, Fanny 246
Bell, Vanessa 214

Bennett, Anna 122
Bennett, Jane 87
Bentley, Hendrina 207
Benzie, Isa 246
Besant, Annie 246
Best, Edna 155
Betham-Edwards, Matilda 224
Betts, Annie 60
Binder, Pearl 122
Bird, Ruth 61
Black, Clementina 123
Blackburn, Jessy 207
Blackwell, Elizabeth 224
Blake, Catherine 47
Blunt, Lady Anne 92
Bodichon, Barbara Leigh Smith 193
Bond, Jessie 94
Bondfield, Margaret 124
Bonnell, Sadie 257
Bonner, Hypatia 42
Boothby, Louisa 246
Bowerman, Elsie 247
Boyle, Eleanor 124
Boyle, Helen 155
Brackenbury, Hannah 155
Braddon, Mary 124
Braden, Norah 91
Braid, Hilda 125
Brassey, Annie 195
Brassey, Sybil 195
Brigden, Zoë 125
Brilliant, Fredda 92
Brooking, Dorothea 240
Broster, D. K. 196
Brown, Dame Beryl 231
Bruce, Mary 189
Bryer, Rose 125
Buckley, Arabella 125
Buckley, Dame Ruth 238
Burges, Caroline 188
Butt, Dame Clara 82
Buxton, Dame Mildred 68
Byng-Stamper, Frances 233
Byron, Lady 126
Cameron, Violet 95
Campbell, Dame Janet 126
Capper, Mabel 247

Carlyle, Florence 199
Carson, Kitty 156
Carter, Angela 207
Cartwright, Frances 156
Chamot, Mary 258
Chart, Ellen Nye 126
Cheshire, Dame Mary 208
Clarke, Anna 127
Clement-Jones, Vicky 46
Clewes, Dorothy 186
Coates, Edith 95
Cobden-Sanderson, Anne 57
Cogan, Alma 95
Cohen, Elsie 127
Cohen, Julia 76
Coleridge-Taylor, Avril 253
Collcutt, Grace 128
Collier, Mary 65
Collins, Dolly 225
Coltman, Constance 189
Colvin, Dame Mary 76
Compton, Fay 156
Compton-Burnett, Dame Ivy 157
Connelly, Cornelia 248
Conolly, Louisa 50
Constanduros, Mabel 90
Conti, Italia 128
Cook, Eliza 60
Cookson, Dame Catherine 225
Cooper, Diana 29
Cooper, Joan 231
Cooper, Joyce 34
Copeland, Ida 256
Corbaux, Marie 157
Corbett, Marie 202
Cornforth, Fanny 83
Cornwell, Alice 157
Costa, Margaret 248
Costello, Louisa 128
Coules, Mary 95
Cowdray, Annie 88
Cowdroy, Charlotte 96
Cox, Constance 128
Crabbe, Pauline 129
Cradock, Fanny 222
Creak, Edith 158
Crisp, Dorothy 186
Cropper, Anna 87
Crouch, Anna 129

Croudace, Camilla 96
Cumming, Primrose 253
Cunliffe, Mitzi 129
Currie, Mary [Violet Fane] 188
Curtis, Dame Myra 38
Damm, Sheila van 90
Dane, Clemence 69
Dannemann, Monika 254
Dare, Phyllis 158
David, Elizabeth 241
Davids, C.A.F. 258
Davies, Emily 39
Davies, Marjorie 196
Davies, Olwen Bowen 69
Davies-Colley, Eleanor 70
Davies-Colley, Margaret 70
Davison, Emily Wilding 96
Dawson, Margaret Damer 159
Deane, Edna 172
de Banzie, Brenda 172
de Fonblanque, Florence 44
Dehn, Olive 198
Delafield, E. M. 121
Denington, Baroness Evelyn 159
Denman, Gertrude 32
Dick, Kay 129
Dickinson, Maud 139
Dillon, Carmen 159
Dillon, Una 159
Dodge, Mary 256
Dors, Diana 43
Dorset, Catherine 34
Douglas, Jo 80
Dowding, Muriel 160
Dowson, Mary 56
Doyle, Dame Jean 200
Drummond, Victoria 203
Dudeney, Alice 232
Dunne, Mary 43
Durham, Frances 29
Eardley, Joan 61
Ebsworth, Dame Ann 96
Edwards, Monica 244
Elliott, Charlotte 130
Elliott, Janice 69
Elwood, Anne 37
Emery, Winifred 235
Emmet, Baroness 29
Esdaile, Katharine 92

Evans, Margiad 257
Eyre, Marjorie 83
Farjeon, Eleanor 230
Farrell, Kathleen 131
Field, Mary 96
Fields, Dame Gracie 256
Fiennes, Virginia 72
Fiennes, Jini 39
Finlay-Johnson, Harriet 81
Finnis, Valerie 199
Fisher, Cicely Corbett 202
Fitzherbert, Maria 131
Flatman, Ada 208
Fletcher-Moulton, Sylvia 187
Flower, Eliza 230
Forde, Florrie 77
Fox, Angela 44
Fox, Dame Evelyn 231
Francis, Ann 82
Franklin, Lilian 61
Freeman, Flora 160
Fremantle, Anne 192
Frere, Mary 248
Frost, Eunice 232
Froud, Ethel 173
Fullerton, Lady Georgiana 79
Fullerton, Mary 236
Gadd, Renée 161
Gammans, Annie 62
Garnett, Constance 132
Garnett, Eve 233
Garrett, Agnes 75
Garrett, Rhoda 75
Garson, Mary 132
George, Muriel 132
Gibbs, Maria 132
Giberne, Agnes 208
Gilbert, Mary Ann 208
Gilbert, Olive 161
Gildersleeve, Virginia 185
Ginesi, Edna 74
Gipps, Ruth 228
Gleitze, Mercedes 133
Gluck 83
Glyn, Elinor 173
Godden, Rumer 244
Godwin, Fay 241
Goffin, Cora 204
Goldie, Grace 133

Goldsmid, Louisa 209
Goodbody, Buzz 214
Goodman, Julia 133
Gordon, Mary 199
Gore, Margot 97
Gostling, Frances 96
Grace, Harriette 161
Gregg, Hilda 209
Gregory, Alice 186
Grice-Hutchinson, Marjorie 210
Guthrie, Kathleen 134
Gwilliam, Freda 218
Gwynne-Vaughan, Dame Helen 86
Hadland, Selina 249
Haigh, Emily 97
Hale, Binnie 188
Hale, Cicely 63
Hall, Marguerite Radclyffe 245
Hammond, Gertrude 97
Harper, Allanah 133
Harrison, Annie Fortescue 43
Harrison, Isabella Darent 249
Hart, Edith Tudor 134
Harvey, Kate 257
Harvey, Rosalie 254
Harvie-Anderson, Betty 45
Harwood, Isabella 226
Haslett, Dame Caroline 87
Hay, Mary Cecil 46
Haydon, Florence 190
Heald, Nora 84
Hengler, Jenny 233
Herbert, Louisa 134
Herringham, Christiana 204
Hessel, Phoebe 134
Heyer, Georgette 80
Hicks, Joyce 237
Higginson, Eleanor 35
Hiller, Dame Wendy 190
Hillyard, Blanche 73
Hilton, Daisy 134
Hilton, Marie 135
Hilton, Violet 134
Hodgson, Geraldine 135
Hoggan, Frances 135
Hollond, Ellen 250
Holmes-Siedle, Rosa 136
Hopkins, Ellice 136
Hornby, Mary Louisa 98

Horsfield, Agnes 222
Howard, Elizabeth 136
Howard-Gibbon, Amelia 30
Howells, Ursula 71
Howitt, Mary 226
Hubbard, Louisa 66
Hughes, Alice 98
Huntingdon, Countess of 137
Hutchins, Bessie 210
Impey, Mary 239
Inglesby, Mona 190
Ingpen, Joan 137
Irving, Ethel 190
Ison, Leonora 250
Jackson, Ada 191
James, Cornelia 161
Jameson, Anna 137
Janes, Emily 226
Jennings, Gertrude 49
Jex-Blake, Katherine 53
Jex-Blake, Sophia 236
Johnstone, Hilda 39
Jones, Mabel 162
Joseph, Helen 45
Kahan, Barbara 61
Kaye, Carol 138
Kaye, M.M. 241
Kaye-Smith, Sheila 239
Keary, Annie 210
Keevil, Gladice 38
Kelly, Fanny 138
Kenealy, Annesley 170
Kenealy, Arabella 171
Kent, Elizabeth 138
Kimmins, Dame Grace 197
Kingsford, Anna 250
Kinsley, Joy 39
Lamb, Winifred 67
Lancaster, Eva 251
Lanchester, Edith 162
Lane, Grace 163
Lane-Claypon, Janet 254
Lawrence, Dorothy 139
Lawrence, Millicent 139
Lawrence, Penelope 139
Lawrenson, Mary Ann 139
Layton, Dorothy 218
Leigh, Vivien 192
Leighton, Clare 62

Leighton, Margaret 39
Leinster, Duchess of (Emily) 50
Leinster, Duchess of (Vivien) 139
Leslie, Doris 47
Lessore, Thérèse 243
Levy, Amy 163
Leyel, Hilda 78
Lidiard, Victoria 163
Lister, Eve 140
Littler, Blanche 164
Löhr, Marie 140
Lomax, Emma 140
Longford, Elizabeth 229
Lonsdale, Dame Kathleen 191
Lopokova, Lydia 215
Lord, Henrietta 35
Lowndes, Marie Belloc 80
Lucas, Caroline 233
Lupino, Ida 164
Lynch, Theodora 66
Macfarlane, Susan 164
Macpherson, Annie 165
McCall, Annie 75
McCall, Rosemary 210
McCarthy, Lily Lambert 213
McCartney, Linda 240
McDougall, Grace 251
Mclennan, Margo 42
Mairet, Ethel 204
Mantell, Mary Ann 234
Manton, Jo 45
Marion, Kitty 222
Marryatt, Florence 140
Martindale, H. 141
Martindale, L. (Dr) 141
Martindale, L. (Mrs) 141
Mason, Agnes 252
Mason, Charlotte 98
Masson, Madeleine 37
Matheson, Hilda 259
Matters-Porter, Muriel 252
Maude, Joan 234
Maxse, Dame Marjorie 187
Mayne, Olga 69
Melhuish, Sarah 259
Mellon, Harriot 142
Menges, Isolde 165
Menges, Kate 165
Merrifield, Mary 142

Meynell, Alice 52
Meynell, Esther 205
Meynell, Viola 53
Mildmay, Audrey 220
Miller, Florence Fenwick 165
Miller, Lee 238
Miller, Ruby 40
Mills, Lady Dorothy 143
Moir, Margaret 48
Montefiore, Dora 226
Moore, Decima 143
Moore, Eva 144
Moore, Jessie 144
Mordan, Clara 191
Morgan, Gladys 99
Morgan, Gwenda 71
Morrison, Frances 71
Morten, Violet Honnor 244
Mould, Elizabeth 35
Muggeridge, Kitty 253
Muir, Willa 200
Mukle, May 44
Mullins, Gwen 51
Murray, Hilda 62
Murray, K.M. Elisabeth 57
Muspratt, Helen 145
Musson, Dame Ellen 211
Mutrie, Annie 145
Nagle, Florence 51
Neagle, Dame Anna 145
Neal, Mary 63
Neale, Elizabeth 54
Needham, Violet 216
Nesbit, Edith 218
Nevill, Lady Dorothy 73
Newmarch, Rosa 99
Nicks, Jennifer 145
Noakes, Daisy 145
Norfolk, Duchess of 31
Normanton, Helena 146
North, Katherine 82
North, Marianne 227
O'Keeffe, Adelaide 40
Owen, Rosamund Dale 99
Oxenham, Elsie 100
Paget, Dame Rosalind 36
Pannett, Juliet 30
Panter-Downes, Molly 146
Parkes, Bessie Rayner 79

Patterson, Sheila 166
Patton-Bethune, Florence 38
Peacock, Elizabeth 41
Pearsall, Phyllis 77
Peck, Winifred 211
Pemberton, Muriel 252
Penson, Dame Lillian 146
Pery, Dame Angela 198
Petre, Diana 147
Petre, Maude 86
Philipson, Mabel 53
Phillips, Mary 166
Phipps, Emily 211
Pickard-Smith, Kathleen 219
Piozzi, Hester Thrale 147
Plesch, Honoria 147
Polini, Emélie 77
Poole, Sophia Lane 100
Porter, Annie 171
Poulton, Diana 58
Powell, Erica 148
Powell, Margaret 166
Powell, Muriel 68
Powys-Lybbe, Ursula 203
Pragnell, Valerie 100
Pragnell, Vera 89
Pratt, Anne 46
Price, Nancy 59
Priestley, Eliza 89
Pugh, Mavis 40
Pye, Brenda 194
Quennel, Joan 74
Randolph, Elsie 30
Reckitt, Eva Collet 61
Redmond, Moira 35
Rennie, Belle 237
Rhondda, Viscountess 148
Richards, Audrey 67
Richardson, Dorothy 100
Richardson, Ethel 213
Richardson, Mary 227
Rivett-Drake, Dame Jean 167
Rivière, Joan 167
Robins, Elizabeth 56
Robinson, Sarah 213
Robson, Dame Flora 148
Roddick, Dame Anita 64
Rogers, Sunny 149
Rose-Innes, Jasmine 189

Rowden, Diana 221
Rowlands, Patsy 167
Rutherford, Dame Margaret 255
Sackville, Lady Margaret 260
Sackville, Lady Muriel 260
Salt, Dame Barbara 255
Saunders, Edith 149
Scarborough, Ethel 52
Sedgwick, Amy 149
Settle, Alison 85
Sewell, Anna 150
Sewell, Mary 150
Shackleton, Edith 84
Sheail, Nellie 41
Shelton, Anne 255
Sheridan, Clare 192
Sieveking, Isabel 228
Smiley, Lavinia 87
Smith, Charlotte 33
Smith, Hannah Whitall 48
Solomon, Georgiana 211
Spurgeon, Caroline 185
Stanley-Wrench, Mollie 75
Stitch, Wilhelmina 167
Stone, Elizabeth 101
Stone, Jean 188
Stopes, Charlotte 101
Strachey, Ray 48
Streatfeild, Noël 212
Strong, Patience 255
Sutcliff, Rosemary 88
Sykes, Ethel 230
Talbot, Dame Meriel 68
Taylor, Charity 55
Taylor, Mentia 168
Taylor, Margaret 150
Temple, Joan 192
Terry, Dame Ellen 259
Tetzel, Joan 214
Thompson, Dorothy 229
Thorne, Isabel 234
Thornton, Edna 101
Tilley, Vesta 168
Tiltman, Marjorie 73
Todd, Margaret 237
Troubridge, Una 245
Tryon, Lady Dreda 91

Tullis, Julie 221
Turner, Dame Margot 169
Turner, Minnie 150
Turner, Winnie 194
Tutin, Dame Dorothy 49
Underhill, F.O. 255
Unwin, Jane Cobden 58
Valiente, Doreen 151
Verrall, Margaret 151
Vyner, Margaret 198
Walker, Sheila 81
Ward, Barbara 65
Ward, Emily 36
Wardroper, Sarah 31
Waters, Doris 85
Waters, Elsie 85
Watson, Edith M. (Miss) 60
Watson, Edith M. (Mrs) 101
Webb, Mary 253
Wedgwood, Dame Veronica 185
Weldon, Georgina 216
Wellesley, Dorothy 261
Wentworth, Baroness 93
Wertheim, Lucy 151
Westbury, Marjorie 217
Whistler, Anna 228
White, Amber Blanco 49
White, Antonia 203
White, Beatrice 212
Wilberforce, Octavia 152
Wilkinson, Dame Louisa 201
Willard, Barbara 240
Willis, Olive 152
Wilson, Enid 201
Wolpe, Margaret 235
Wolseley, Viscountess 220
Wood, Anne 43
Woodhead, Grace Eyre 152
Woodhouse, Violet Gordon 242
Woolf, Virginia 243
Wyndham, Ursula 71
Wynne-Tyson, Esmé 76
Yavorska, Lydia 168
Yeldham, Florence 194
Young, Monica 229
Zangwill, Edith 46
Zimmermann, Agnes 212

Index of Places

Alciston 185–6 (265)

Aldrington 121

Aldwick 29

Alfriston 186 (206, 219, 267)

Amberley 29–30 (72, 212, 230)

Angmering 30 (232)

Arundel 30–32

Balcombe 32 (110, 225)

Barcombe 186–8

Battle 188

Beauport 188–9

Beddingham 189 (220)

Bexhill 189–192 (144, 170, 192, 218, 222, 223, 228, 231, 235, 260, 277)

Bignor 33–4 (41, 58, 102)

Blackboys 192

Bognor Regis 34–36 (29, 38, 132, 139)

Bolney 36–7

Bosham 37 (91)

Brede 192–3 (245)

Brightling 193–4

Brighton 121–153 (188, 190,191, 192, 202, 203, 205, 206, 209, 213, 216, 217, 218, 219, 220, 222, 225, 226, 231, 232, 233, 236, 243, 245, 250, 252)

Burgess Hill 37–8

Burpham 38 (112)

Burwash 194

Buxted 194 (254)

Catsfield 195–6 (261)

Chailey 196–7 (68, 187, 239)

Chelwood Gate 198

Chichester 38–41 (31, 33, 34, 35, 37, 50, 57, 58, 63, 65, 66, 67, 68, 74, 76, 89, 90, 98, 152, 156, 218, 222, 289)

Chiddingly 198 (213, 233)

Clayton 41 (234)

Climping 41–2

Cocking 42

Colgate 42 (80)

Coleman's Hatch 198–9

Coneyhurst 42–3 (106)

Crawley 43 (88, 93)

Crawleydown 43–4

Crowborough 199–201 (152, 227, 233, 256)

Cuckfield 44 (151)

Danehill 201–3 (279)

Ditchling 203–5 (41, 54, 188, 122, 264, 275)

Duncton 44–5 (111)

Durrington 45

Easebourne 45 (49, 68)

Eastbourne 205–212 (5, 49, 61, 72, 122, 147, 194, 200, 202, 219, 222, 230, 231, 241, 242, 243, 244, 248, 255, 270, 293)

East Dean 45–6 (206, 208)

East Grinstead 46 (29, 32, 92, 142, 201, 202, 243, 262, 279)

East Hoathly 213

East Preston 46–7 (165)

Ewhurst 213

Fairlight 213–4 (249)

Fairwarp 214

Falmer 214

Faygate 47

Felcourt 47

Felpham 47 (107)

Fernhurst 48–9 (59, 63, 109)

Firle 214–216 (243, 244)

Fittleworth 49

Forest Row 216 (142, 243)

Framfield 216–7

Frant 218 (34, 212)

Friston 218

Furners Green 218 (142)

Glynde 219–220 (194, 254)

Glyndebourne 220–1 (172)

Goodwood 50–1 (31, 108)

Graffham 51–2 (72)

Greatham 52–3 (85, 205)

Groombridge 221

Hadlow Down 221–2

Hailsham 222 (212, 247)

Hartfield 222–3 (56, 187)

Hassocks 53–4

Hastings 223–8 (5, 57, 78, 80, 87, 100, 126, 188, 189, 190, 193, 195, 212, 222, 239, 241, 246, 247, 249, 250, 251, 252, 253, 259, 260, 263, 273, 278)

Haywards Heath 54–5 (60, 61, 87, 150, 153, 172, 197, 232, 240, 301)

Heathfield 228–9 (152)

Henfield 55–7 (41, 128, 152, 299, 300)

Heyshott 57–9 (41)

High Salvington 59 (100)

Horsham 60–1 (43, 45, 55, 74, 88, 197)
Horsted Keynes 61 (91, 142, 202)
Houghton 61–2 (53)
Hove 153–169 (7, 30, 80, 83, 123, 125, 128, 131, 137, 138, 141, 142, 146, 148, 149, 151, 152, 168, 169, 174, 187, 204, 226, 240, 243, 257, 299)
Hurst Green 229–30 (253)
Hurstpierpoint 230 (232)
Iping 62
Keymer 62
Kingsley Green 62–3
Lancing 63 (150, 169, 170, 171)
Laughton 230
Lewes 231–5 (112, 187, 194, 197, 213, 219, 236, 240, 242, 243, 262)
Little Common 235
Littlehampton 63–5 (30, 39, 41, 105, 189)
Lodsworth 65
Lower Beeding 66
Madehurst 66
Maresfield 236 (217)
Mark Cross 236–7 (264)
Mayfield 237–8 (80, 217, 248, 268)
Midhurst 66–8 (33, 51, 88, 186, 220)
Milland 67–8
Muddles Green 238 (272)
Netherfield 238
Newhaven 68
Newick 239 (197)
Newtimber 68–9
Northiam 239 (192, 208, 245)
Nutbourne 69
Nutley 240 (136, 256, 261)
Ovingdean 169 (146)
Partridge Green 69
Peasmarsh 240
Pendean 69–70
Pett 241
Petworth 70–2 (152)
Pevensey 241 (97, 211)
Polegate 241 (187)
Portslade 169–70
Preston 171 (141)
Pulborough 72–3 (70, 86, 205)
Rodmell 243 (233, 234)
Rogate 73–4
Rotherfield 243
Rottingdean 171–2 (54, 127, 131, 175)
Rowfant 74

Rudgwick 75
Rustington 75
Rye 244–5 (70, 139, 206, 259, 263)
St Leonards 245–53 (61, 124, 138, 160, 195, 212, 214, 223, 226, 228, 239, 272, 275, 276, 294)
Salehurst 253
Saltdean 173
Sandhurst 253
Seaford 253–5
Sedlescombe 255
Selsey 75–6
Sharpthorne 75
Shermanbury 76–7 (56)
Shoreham-by-Sea 77 (81, 100, 128, 154, 169)
Shripney 78
Slindon 79–80 (65, 102, 103)
Slinfold 80–1
Sompting 81–2
South Harting 82
South Stoke 82
Southease 255
Southwick 82 (149, 243)
Steyning 83–5 (107, 135)
Storrington 85–7 (34, 53, 58, 90, 188)
Stunts Green 255
Sullington 87 (53)
Tangmere 87
Telscombe Cliffs 256
Three Bridges 87–8
Ticehurst 256
Turners Hill 88 (45, 108)
Uckfield 256–7 (30, 41, 202)
Upper Hartfield 257–8
Wadhurst 258
Walberton 88–9
Warnham 89 (61, 200)
Washington 89–90 (104)
West Burton 90
West Chiltington 90–1
West Grinstead 91 (203)
West Hoathly 91 (137, 198)
Whiteman's Green 235
Winchelsea 258–9 (157, 271)
Withyham 259–61
Woodmancote 92 (57, 152)
Worth 92–3 (88, 96)
Worthing 94–101 (5, 14, 35, 40, 45, 55, 59, 60, 81, 84, 85, 86, 110, 128, 148, 149, 150, 156, 165, 166, 236)

INDEX OF PLATES

First section, between pp128-9

1. Elsie Bowerman
2. Dame Dorothy Tutin
3. Maie Ash
4. Phyllis Dare
5. Matilda Betham-Edwards
6. Elizabeth Allan
7. Madeleine Masson
8. Dame Flora Robson
9. Gluck
10. Fay Compton
11. Lady Denman
12. D.K. Broster
13. Vivien Leigh
14. Eva Moore
15. Grace Lane
16. Margaret Leighton

Plate credits

D.K. Broster, St Hilda's College archives; Elsie Bowerman, Wycombe Abbey School archives; Gladice Keevil, Greg Rickford; Dolly Collins, Shirley Collins MBE; Agnes Zimmermann, St Agnes Church, Eastbourne; Madeleine Masson, Merrick Rayner; Matilda Betham-Edwards, Hastings Library; Lady Denman, the Women's Institute; Mother Mary Garson, the Grace and Compassion Benedictines; Hilda Leyel, Peter Leyel; Viscountess Wolseley, Hove Library; Zoë Brigden, the Marlinova Collection; HRH Princess Amelia, a memorial engraving by J.S. Agar from a miniature painted by Ann Mee (whose husband, incidentally, permitted her to paint only female subjects).

All other plates were sourced from unattributed postcards, cigarette cards, publicity and studio shots or are of unknown provenance, except as indicated on their captions.

Second section between pp256-7

17. Dame Ellen Terry
18. Agnes Zimmermann
19. Mary Chavelita Dunne
20. Mrs Martindale
21. Marguerite Radclyffe Hall
22. Zoë Brigden
23. HRH Princess Beatrice
24. Dolly Collins
25. Cora Goffin
26. Lydia Lopokova
27. HRH Princess Amelia
28. Viscountess Wolseley
29. Alice Dudeney
30. Ray Strachey
31. Maud Arncliffe-Sennett
32. Emily Davies
33. Rosamund Dale Owen
34. Mabel Constanduros
35. Mother Mary Garson
36. Virginia Woolf
37. Elsie Randolph
38. Diana Petre
39. Elinor Glyn
40. Kitty Marion
41. Binnie Hale
42. Hilda Leyel
43. Nancy Price
44. Rt Hon. Margaret Bondfield
45. Victoria Lidiard
46. Decima Moore
47. Marie Löhr
48. Dame Anna Neagle
49. Dame Gracie Fields
50. Clare Sheridan
51. Edna Best
52. Ethel Irving
53. Edna Thornton
54. Vesta Tilley
55. Elsie and Doris Waters
56. Muriel George
57. Brenda de Banzie
58. Ida Lupino
59. The Hon. Ursula Wyndham
60. Daisy and Violet Hilton
61. Marie Corbett
62. Fanny Cradock
63. Winifred Emery

WEST SUSSEX

Charlotte Smith

ALDWICK

LADY DIANA COOPER née Manners; Viscountess Norwich (1892–1986) actress and author.

Her mother was married to the Marquess of Granby (later, 8th Duke of Rutland) but her biological father was writer Henry Cust. She was educated at home in London by governesses, lived the life of a débutante and was judged the most beautiful woman in England. Photographs of her appeared in dozens of publications and her parents hoped she would marry the Prince of Wales. WWI saw her as an unqualified VAD nurse. Afterwards, she edited the magazine *Femina*, appeared in two silent films, married Alfred Cooper, had a string of lovers and toured the UK, USA and Europe for two years as Madonna in a revival of *The Miracle*. Her earnings paid her husband's election expenses and he became an MP.

Through the 1930s and 1940s her home was West House, Barrack Lane, Aldwick, a smallholding that was a gift from her mother. She did not maintain a London residence, but stayed at the Dorchester Hotel when visiting the capital. She appears to have been rather a road menace: twice arrested in 1941 for motoring offences, she was fined firstly 30s, then £3.12s 6d by Bognor magistrates (who also summonsed her during the war for 'wasting bread'). She wrote with great affection of her Sussex home in *The Light of Common Day* (1959, reprinted 1979), the second part of her three-volume autobiography.

In the late 1940s she lived mainly in France, where her husband was British Ambassador to Paris and she his glamorous society hostess, and where they were friends of the Duke and Duchess of Windsor (Edward and Mrs Simpson). When, in 1952, her husband was raised to the peerage as Viscount Norwich of Aldwick she retained her own name. He died the following year. After thirty-two years of widowhood she died in London, leaving a son, John Julius Norwich.

Further reading: Ziegler, P. (1981) *Diana Cooper: A Biography.* [Related image p115.]

FRANCES DURHAM CBE (1873–1948) pioneering civil servant.

One of eight children of a surgeon, she was born in Aldwick. She became one of the first women to be an inspector and organiser of technical classes for women and trade schools for the LCC Education Committee, and served on the Board of Education from 1908 to 1913. In 1915 she entered the civil service as chief woman inspector in the Insurance and Unemployment Department of the Board of Trade and the following year was promoted to assistant secretary, one of the first two women to reach that rank.

During WWI she organised women's services in the army, munitions and agriculture and was appointed CBE in recognition. She campaigned for equal pay and equal opportunities and was president of the Committee of Higher Women in the Civil Service.

AMBERLEY

BARONESS EMMET JP, MP née the Hon. Evelyn Rodd (1899–1980) politician.

The daughter of Baron Rennell of Rodd, she was born in Cairo and educated at Lady Margaret Hall and in Europe, where she became fluent in Italian, French and German. In 1923 she married Thomas Addis Emmet and two years later they bought Amberley Castle, once the manor house of the Bishops of Chichester. Widowed in 1932, she raised four young children alone, bred cattle and carried out major restoration works on the castle.

Having served on the LCC since 1925, she became a member of West Sussex County Council and county organiser for the WVS. In 1936 she became a magistrate and chairman of the children's and matrimonial courts. The great Indian stateswoman Mrs Pandit stayed with her during an official visit in 1954.

After three years on the Conservative Women's National Advisory Committee, in 1955 she was elected MP for East Grinstead, a seat once held by the husband of Marie Corbett [202]. To the left of the Conservative Party, she is best remembered for her commitment to women's rights and for pressing her party to include women's issues in its manifesto. She supported equal pay, separate taxation of married women and the admission of peeresses to the House of Lords. In 1965 she was elevated to a life peerage as Baroness Emmet of Amberley and served as deputy speaker of the House of Lords from 1968 to 1977, the first Conservative woman to sit on the Woolsack.

Baroness Emmet died at home and her memorial service was held at St Margaret's, Westminster. In 1981 the castle was sold and is now a hotel. Her daughter Penelope married Hugo Money-Coutts, the great-great-great-great grandson of Thomas Coutts, husband of Harriot Mellon [142]. [Related image p115.]

ANGMERING

JULIET PANNETT MBE, FRSA née Somers (c1911–2005) artist.

A niece of artist Kathleen Watson, she was born in Hove and as a child drew shepherds, cab drivers, rabbit-catchers and a Pyecombe crookmaker. She attended Wiston's School, Brighton, won a four-year scholarship to Brighton College of Art then taught physical training at Buckwood Grange School, Uckfield. In her spare time she sketched local characters for Sussex newspapers and magazines, including sportsmen from Sussex County Cricket Club and Brighton and Hove Albion.

She married Captain Maurice Pannett in 1938 and had two children (both were to become artists). In the late 1940s she sketched for the *Illustrated London News* (which gave her a reserved seat in the press gallery of the House of Commons) and many other publications, and received commissions to create portraits of musicians, artists, statesmen, lawmen, soldiers, intellectuals and royalty (including the Queen and Princes Edward and Andrew). Altogether, over 1,000 people sat for her. She was the artist on inaugural flights for several airlines, including Qantas, Trans Canada and El Al, and taught on P&O cruises. After living in Gloucestershire and Surrey she returned

to Sussex in 1964, buying Pound House, Roundstone Lane, Angmering, where she created a studio and taught art classes.

Appointed MBE in 1993, she was elected to the Society of Graphic Artists and the Pastel Society, was a Fellow of the Royal Society of Arts and an Honorary Freeman of the Worshipful Company of Painter-Stainers, whose Gold Medal she won in 1995. She died in Rustington. Twenty-two of her portraits are at the NPG and a Juliet Pannett Trophy is awarded each year in Sussex.

Further reading: Pannett, J. and Vreeland, V. (2006) *My Colourful Life.*

ELSIE RANDOLPH (1904–1982) musical-comedy actress, singer and dancer.

Her career began in the provinces when she was twelve and spanned stage, screen, radio and television over an extraordinary eight decades, a quarter of which was spent in a stage partnership with Jack Buchanan. She rose to fame in the 1920s, playing leads in West End shows in her native London and was never out of the limelight until she gave up acting in 1946 after marrying Vernon Page. She returned to the stage in 1953 and worked for another twenty-eight years. Cast by Hitchcock in two films forty years apart, in her seventies she played Lady Colefax in the 1980 TV series *Edward and Mrs Simpson*. Her final appearance was in a television drama in 1981. She lived in later life in Angmering, but died in London. [Related plate 37.]

ARUNDEL

AMELIA HOWARD-GIBBON (1826–1874) artist.

The daughter of the illegitimate son of the 11th Duke of Norfolk, she was born in Littlehampton. Her family lived in British Guiana for a while then settled in Arundel, where her father became mayor in the 1840s. She was privately educated, studying French, German and art in Paris and Stuttgart.

Her family moved to Brixton, London, whence she emigrated to Ontario, Canada. During the 1860s she became well known for her watercolour portraits and sketches.

She returned to London in 1873 to claim her inheritance from her uncle, was suddenly taken ill and died, aged just forty-eight. Her body was returned to Sussex and buried at St Nicholas's churchyard, Arundel.

In 1966 her most comprehensive work, *An Illustrated Comic Alphabet*, created in 1859, was published as a book by the Oxford University Press in Toronto and an annual prize for illustration of children's literature published in Canada, the Amelia Frances Howard-Gibbon Illustrator's Award, was created in 1971.

THE DUCHESS OF NORFOLK LG, CBE née Strutt; Lavinia Mary Fitzalan-Howard (1916–1995) owner-trainer of racehorses.

The daughter of the 3rd Baron Belper, she was born in Nottingham. In 1937 she married Sir Bernard Fitzalan-Howard, the 16th Duke of Norfolk and the Queen's representative at Ascot. At the coronation in 1937 she held the canopy above the Queen and in 1953 substituted for Queen Elizabeth II during the coronation rehearsals.

She became one of the most knowledgeable women in the equestrian world. As well as an owner and breeder she was a hunter and a point-to-point rider. In 1975 she became the first female steward at Goodwood, and trained racehorses at a time when Jockey Club licences were withheld from women [see Florence Nagle, 51]. Her horses 'Moon Madness', which won the St Leger in 1986, and 'Sheriff's Star', which won the Coronation Cup at Epsom in 1989, were trained at the Castle Stables in Arundel.

Upon marriage she had become, at the age of just twenty-one, mistress of Arundel Castle, with its 150 rooms. Twenty years and four daughters later, with no son to inherit the castle or the title, her husband built Arundel Park, a Georgian-style house some distance away, to be his family's home after his death; however, the duchess preferred it to the draughty old castle and so they moved in at once.

She supported 150 charities, favouring those for the disabled, and was president of the National Canine Defence League 1969–75. She was appointed CBE in 1971.

Widowed in 1975, she developed and secured the future of the family's private cricket ground as a memorial to her late spouse and succeeded him as Lord Lieutenant of West Sussex (the first non-royal woman so honoured), a post she held until 1990. That year, three years after the Queen altered the statutes to admit women, she became the first Lady Companion of the Most Noble Order of the Garter (LG), the oldest order of chivalry. During the procession, wearing a floor-length gown under her robes, she tripped in the quire, suffering a much-publicised nosebleed.

She died at Arundel and her memorial service was held at the cathedral. Her eldest daughter, Lady Anne Fitzalan-Howard, inherited the fifteenth-century Scottish Lordship of Herries of Terregles, but the Norfolk title and Arundel Castle passed to another branch of the family.

SARAH WARDROPER née Bisshopp (1813–1892) pioneer nursing administrator.

Born in Westburton, she married Dr Woodland Wyatt Wardroper FRCS in Chichester in 1840 and they settled at Maltravers St, Arundel, where he had a medical practice. When he died in 1849 she was left with four small children and very little money. She moved to the High Street and in 1854, when her youngest was eight, and applied successfully for a position as matron at St Thomas's Hospital, London, moving to nearby Penton Place, Lambeth, with her three sons (her daughter had married and gone to India, where she was to die aged twenty-nine).

In 1860 Florence Nightingale opened her pioneering Training School for Nurses at St Thomas's and selected Mrs Wardroper to be its superintendent. She and two sons moved into staff quarters at the hospital.

She remained as superintendent for thirty-three years, during which time the hospital moved from the Borough to Surrey Gardens, thence to its present site. She was highly respected and the success of the nursing school was attributed to her 'wonderful energy' and 'unsparing and sympathetic devotion'. Under her administration, 500 nurses were trained, of whom fifty became matrons and superintendents.

In his fifties her son Walter married widow Louisa Pearless and moved into her home, Uplands, Ship Street, East Grinstead, three doors from The Cottage, home of his spinster (paternal) aunts. When she retired, aged seventy-nine, Mrs Wardroper moved into Uplands and died there five years later.

In 1894 the Archbishop of Canterbury unveiled a memorial to her on the south wall of the chapel at St Thomas's Hospital. It is in the form of a panel embedded in terracotta with an image of the Good Samaritan and a sick man and is inscribed 'To the memory of Sarah Elizabeth Wardroper, a faithful servant of God and man, the working leader in a great reform, quietly and peaceably pursued, by which the care of the sick took its right place as a high and holy calling that enlists the noblest qualities of heart and mind, and turns to efficient use the intelligence, refinement and devotion of good women'.

BALCOMBE

HRH PRINCESS BEATRICE GCVO, GBE, VA, CI, RRC Princess Henry of Battenberg (1857–1944) composer, editor, translator, and Governor of the Isle of Wight.

The youngest child of Queen Victoria and Prince Albert, her widowed mother permitted her marriage to Prince Henry of Battenberg only if they lived with her at Osborne House on the Isle of Wight. By 1896 she was a widow with four small children. She took over Prince Henry's positions as Captain-General and Governor of the island and was appointed Governor of Carisbrooke Castle, as well as becoming the Queen's (unofficial) private secretary.

In 1917 she resumed her former name of Princess Beatrice, and in 1919 her nephew George V appointed her GBE for serving as president of the Isle of Wight British Red Cross Society. She was created a Lady of Justice in 1884, then Dame Grand Cross, in 1926, of the Order of St John of Jerusalem, and a Dame Grand Cross of the Royal Victorian Order in 1937.

Princess Beatrice played piano to professional standard and was a published composer. She inherited her mother's private journals, which she edited, archived and published in her own handwriting. This daunting task took thirty years to complete and in 1931 the 111 volumes were placed in the Royal Archives at Windsor Castle. She translated extracts from the diary of her great-grandmother, Augusta, Duchess of Saxe-Coburg-Saalfeld and published them as *In Napoleonic Days* (1941).

After many years living between Kensington Palace and Osborne House, she moved in with her niece Alice, Countess of Athlone, at Brantridge Park, Balcombe, where she died. She was buried at Windsor, but was exhumed and reinterred in 1945 beside her husband at Whippingham, Isle of Wight. Brantridge Park was offered for sale in 1974 and by 1982 had been split into twenty-four timeshare apartments. A former government building in Cowes, IOW, for which she laid the foundation stone, has lately been developed into luxury apartments that bear her name.

Further reading: Dennison, M (2007) *The Last Princess.* [Related plate 23; image p110.]

GERTRUDE, LADY DENMAN GBE née Pearson (1884–1954) head of the WI and WLA.

Born in London, the daughter of Viscountess Cowdray [88], she was raised on her parents' Sussex estate. After briefly studying economics and philosophy, at nineteen she married Thomas, 3rd Baron Denman, and when in 1911 he was appointed Governor-General of Australia she became First Lady. Sydney's Lady Denman Ferry was named in her honour (it now sits in retirement in Lady Denman Museum), as was Lady Denman Drive in Canberra, for which city she performed the official naming ceremony in 1913. After having two children she left her husband in 1914 and settled in Sussex.

She worked for her family's Cowdray Trust and other charities, and served on the executive of the Women's Liberal Federation. As owner-manager of Balcombe Place estate, she ensured that her cottagers had piped water and sanitation (luxuries at that time). As president of the women's section of the Poultry Association, she described countrywomen as 'the salt of the earth'. In 1930 she founded the Associated Country Women of the World, which currently has a membership of nine million in over seventy countries. From 1917 she served as chairman of the National Association of Women's Institutes, seeing their role as training women to be citizens and improving their knowledge and social status. She held the post until 1946, and in 1948 the Women's Institute Residential College was named for her.

Although contraception was highly controversial, she believed it could improve women's lives and so in 1930 she co-founded the Family Planning Association, serving as its chairman for the rest of her life (her children and grandchildren continued this work). She served on the council of the Eugenics Society, was president of the Ladies' Golf Union and a trustee of the Carnegie United Kingdom Trust. Dame Meriel Talbot [68] praised Lady Denman's 'fine powers of leadership' and described her as 'the ablest chairman — man or woman — that I have ever served under'.

At the outbreak of WWII she was appointed chief of the women's branch of the Ministry of Agriculture and became involved with the rebirth of the Women's Land Army, defunct since WWI. As its (honorary) director she allowed her home, Balcombe Place, to be used as its administrative headquarters and worked relentlessly for the welfare of her 51,000 'Land Girls'. When the government declined to extend to them the benefits conceded to women in the police, civil defence and armed services, Lady Denman resigned in protest.

Appointed CBE in 1920, DBE in 1933 and GBE in 1951, in 1947 she joined the campaign for peeresses to be admitted to the House of Lords. [293] She died in London and her memorial service was conducted by the Bishop of Chichester at St Mary's Church, Balcombe. Her ashes were scattered at Balcombe Place, which was sold at auction soon after her death and is now a residential care home.

Further reading: Huxley, G. (1961) *Lady Denman*. [Related plate 11.]

BIGNOR PARK

CHARLOTTE SMITH née Turner (1749–1806) poet and novelist.

The sister of Catherine Dorset [34], she was born in London into a wealthy family. Her mother died when she was three and she grew up at Stoke Manor, Surrey, moving at age ten to Bignor Park. Here she developed a love of Sussex that inspired her later poems about the South Downs and Beachy Head. She was well-educated at schools in Chichester and Kensington, and from twelve was taught by residential governesses.

At fifteen she was forced to move to London, for she was married off to Benjamin Smith (she later described the event as 'being sold like a legal prostitute') and by sixteen had borne the first of her twelve children. The marriage was unhappy. She was anti-slavery but her husband's income derived from inherited slave labour in Barbados and to survive she had to help him with the business. Moreover, her husband was addicted to gambling and was unfaithful and violent towards her.

Her father-in-law, who died when she was twenty-seven, left his enormous fortune in trust for her children, but the will was contested and the money not released for thirty-seven years, by which time she and many of her children were dead (Dickens is thought to have used her story as the model for the excessively protracted Jarndyce legal case in *Bleak House*).

Her husband was imprisoned for debt in 1783 and while (voluntarily) serving part of the seven months' sentence with him she wrote and self-published *Elegiac Sonnets and other Essays*, having it printed at Chichester. She negotiated his release and spent her earnings on his legal expenses. To evade his creditors they absconded to Dieppe, where she earned money by translating French literature into English. They returned to Sussex in 1784, living at Woolbeding House, north-west of Midhurst.

Elegiac Sonnets saw good sales (by 1800 it was in its ninth edition and filled two volumes), which prompted her to publish in her own name. Her next works were accepted by a publisher, from whom she extracted advances, and were commercially successful. Making claim to her childhood gentility she styled herself 'gentlewoman-poet Charlotte Smith of Bignor Park'.

In 1787 she left her husband and supported her numerous children by producing a novel a year for five years. Her first, *Emmeline, the Orphan of the Castle* (1788), quickly sold 1,500 copies and was into a third edition before the year was out. One of her recurring themes was women's poor status in the English legal system and, indeed, she was extremely lucky that her ne'er-do-well husband did not claim her earnings, which he was entitled to do under English law (he was later to die in a debtors' prison). To avoid his creditors she moved to Chichester, then in 1791 to Brighton, in 1793 to Storrington, then to Bath, Exmouth, Weymouth, Oxford, London, Frant and Elstead, before settling at Tilford, Surrey.

In all she produced eleven novels, three volumes of poetry, four educational books, a natural history of birds and a history of England. Her *Conversations Introducing Poetry*, a compilation for children, included works by her sister Catherine. One of the most popular writers of her day, she was admired and satirised by Jane Austen, praised by William Wordsworth, applauded by Thomas Paine and was the toast of supporters of the French Revolution. Some of her books were funded by public subscription and the list of sponsors reveals that many eminent persons — such as the Archbishop of Canterbury and the Duchess of Cumberland — held her work in high esteem. Samuel Coleridge credited her with reviving the English sonnet.

In August 1786 *The Times* incorrectly announced her death. She actually died twenty years later and was buried outside St John's Church, near her family's seat of Stoke, Surrey. Her son Lionel was knighted and became Governor of Barbados and then of Jamaica. Her most famous novel, *The Old Manor House*, was most recently reprinted in 1987.

Further reading: Fletcher, L. (1998) *Charlotte Smith, A Critical Biography*. [Related images pp28, 102, 116.]

CATHERINE ANN DORSET née Turner (c1753–c1816) children's writer.

The sister of Charlotte Smith [above], she grew up at Stoke Manor, Surrey, then at Bignor Park from age seven. In 1779 she married army captain Michael Dorset, had a son and daughter and was widowed in 1805. The following year she sold her interest in Bignor Park and nothing is known of her residency after this date.

In 1804 at least eleven of her poems appeared anonymously in her sister's book *Conversations Introducing Poetry*. Her poem *The Peacock 'at Home'* (a sequel to William Roscoe's *The Butterfly's Ball and the Grasshopper's Feast*) was published anonymously in 1807 (the 1809 edition revealed her identity), sold 40,000 copies in its first year, and was into its twenty-eighth edition by 1819. It was reprinted posthumously in 1849 and a facsimile of the original edition was issued in 1883. She also wrote *The Lion's Masquerade* (anonymous, 1807), *The Lioness's Rout* (1808) and *Think before you Speak* (1809). Her memoir of her sister appeared in Walter Scott's *Miscellaneous Prose Works* (1827). [Related image p102.]

BOGNOR REGIS

JOYCE COOPER (1909–2002) swimming champion.

The daughter of English parents, she was born in Ceylon and was inspired to take up competitive swimming at the age of sixteen after seeing Vera Tanner (of the 1924 Olympic team) swim at Eastbourne. She became one of Britain's most successful swimmers, at first surviving on a small allowance from her parents, which she supplemented by working as a seamstress and a ballroom dancing teacher.

She won nineteen Amateur Swimming Association championship races, held all the British freestyle records, earned many international and Olympic (1928 and 1932) medals and was world backstroke champion in 1932. She married a Mr Badcock, with whom she raised a family. She lived in Bognor and died at St Richard's Hospital, Chichester.

ELEANOR HIGGINSON JP née Ellis (1881–1969) suffragette.

A socialist and schoolteacher, she married chemist Arnold Higginson, had five children and opened a pioneering health food shop in Preston, Lancashire. After becoming secretary of the local branch of the WSPU, in 1914 she went to London to take part in an attempt to get a suffrage deputation to the King. During the struggle she was handled so violently by the police that she was left black-and-blue. In protest at the monarch's refusal to receive the deputation her group went on a devastating window-smashing raid and she was arrested (with sixty-seven others). All were sentenced to four months inprisonment, but none served the full stretch. In Holloway she went on hunger-and-thirst strike and was dealt with under the Cat and Mouse Act [294]. During her second imprisonment she was so ill they released her after three days.

After the war she became a magistrate and member of Preston Council. Widowed in 1938, for fifteen years from 1954 she lived in Bognor with another former suffragette, Beth Hesmondhalgh. She died at St Richard's Hospital, Chichester.

HENRIETTA FRANCES LORD (1848–1923) translator.

A barrister's daughter, she attended the University of London, then Girton, where she befriended Hertha Ayrton [63]. By the 1880s she was a member of Manchester suffrage society, a poor law guardian for Lambeth, a theosophist, a psychic researcher and a Christian Scientist.

At the age of fifty-six she married linguist Edward Williams, and after living in London, Kent and Chicago (where she owned a magazine, *Woman's World*) they settled at 3 Field Row, Chandos Road, Bognor. She learned Norwegian and German to a very high standard and became the first person to translate Ibsen's *The Doll's House* and *Ghosts*, and Froebel's *Mothers' Songs*. In addition she wrote two books on Christian Science, which were reprinted in 1986 and 2005. Her translation of *The Doll's House* was reprinted in 2007.

ELIZABETH ANNE MOULD FRSL née Williams; Lady de Sodington Blount (1850–1935) writer and scientist.

Born into comfortable circumstances in London, she enjoyed an excellent private education. She married Sir Walter de Sodington Blount Bt. and had four children (including Mary Corisande and Eva Apollonia). By 1891 she and her family had settled at 29 Queen's Park Road, Brighton. In 1893 she founded the Universal Zetetic Society, appointed herself its president, wrote for and edited its journal, and in 1898 published a novel, *Adrian Galileo*, the heroine of which was a crusading zetetic. She believed the earth was flat, something she proved conclusively in 1904 after carrying out experiments at Old Bedford Level, a canal in Cambridgeshire with a long, straight section. She hired a photographer to take a picture of a sheet hung across the canal six miles away. The result confirmed that there is no curvature of the earth. She proudly published the photographs and wrote some jubilant flat-earth songs.

A Fellow of the Royal Society of Literature and of the Society of Antiquaries, and president of the Society for the Protection of the Dark Races in England, she was a public speaker and essayist on the topics of biology, vegetarianism, science and religion. She also wrote several books, including *The Origins and Nature of Sex* (1923), which was among the first books to mention eunuchs and hermaphrodites.

The Blounts' address in 1914 was St Edmund's, Christ Church Road, Worthing. Widowed in 1915, she lived between London and Bognor for at least ten years. Aged seventy-three she married forty-year-old Stephen Morgan and moved to Hayling Island, Hampshire, where she died.

Further reading: Mitchell, J. (2002) *Eccentric Lives and Peculiar Notions.*

MOIRA REDMOND (1928–2006) actress.

The daughter of an actress and a stage manager, she was born in Bognor Regis. She enjoyed a forty-year theatrical career, starting out as a Windmill girl [see Sheila van Damm, 90] and appearing on the stage (*Titus Andronicus, The Winter's Tale,*

Vanity Fair); in films (*Doctor in Love, A Shot in the Dark*) and on TV (*Dixon of Dock Green, The Sweeney, The Avengers, I, Claudius*).

Her final appearance was in 1997 in *The Wingless Bird* by Catherine Cookson [225]. She was a founder-member of the Actors' Company and toured South America for the British Council. She married and divorced twice, and died in London.

EMILY WARD née Lord (1850–1930) founder of the Norland Institute.

Although born in Derby she was raised in London where, after working as an infant teacher, she studied the progressive educationist Froebel and became a lecturer for the Froebel Society. At twenty-six she founded Norland Place (infants') School in Holland Park, west London. In 1891 she married Walter Ward, with whom she adopted three children (from one family).

At the time children's nannies were untrained, so Mrs Ward decided to set up a college for those who wished to enter that profession. Her stated aims were twofold: to improve the care of children and to create a new career for women. Though the venture was ridiculed by her friends, the Norland Institute opened in 1892 with five students and within months was oversubscribed, though the fees were high and only middle-class girls were accepted. Students were trained not only in childrearing skills but in deportment and speech. Under her leadership the Norland Institute flourished, becoming the model on which all future nursery-nurse training was based.

At the beginning of the new century the Wards moved to The Dutch House, Campbell Road, Bognor. In 1908 they bought a corner property of flats, Field House, in nearby Gloucester Road, which they let by the week as holiday accommodation for Norland nannies. They lived awhile in London, then returned to Bognor in 1919. Widowed in 1924, Mrs Ward gave a stained glass window in memory of her husband to St John's Church. She died at her home of three years, Sudley Lodge, Upper Bognor Road, and her funeral was held at St John's.

The Norland Institute is still thriving, though it is now based in Bath, and yearly fees are over £20,000. Norland nannies are highly sought-after by aristocrats, celebrities and millionaires all over the world.

BOLNEY

DAME ROSALIND PAGET DBE, ARRC (1855–1948) leader of midwifery reform.

The child of a well-to-do family, she was born in Liverpool. She wanted to train as an artist, but her parents opposed her, so she took up nursing instead, becoming one of the first middle-class ladies to perform what was then rather a disreputable and low-status job. After gaining her midwifery certificate she joined the Matron's Aid Society and was its leading light for the next forty-four years, transforming it from a small, dull club into a thriving centre of reform, with lively meetings and prestigious speakers; she also edited its journal, *Nursing Notes*. The society later became the Royal College of Midwives.

Miss Paget was at the forefront of the movement that turned midwifery into a respectable career, while at the same time improving women's experience of childbirth. She qualified in massage which, like nursing, was considered rather seedy, worked hard to transform it into a profession for properly-trained practitioners and co-founded what is now the Chartered Society of Physiotherapy.

In 1890 she was appointed chief of Queen Victoria's Jubilee Institute for Nurses, became a travelling inspector and was awarded its Gold Badge. She spent twelve years working strenuously for a Midwives' Act, which was passed in 1902. During WWI she was inspector of nurses for the Red Cross VAD hospitals.

An active member of the Central Midwives' Board, she was admired for missing only one meeting in twenty-two years. She attended many official enquiries and conferences and campaigned tirelessly for midwives' welfare. She forged links with other women's organisations, including the NUWW, and joined the women's suffrage movement: in 1908 she marched with twenty midwives under a beautifully-embroidered silk banner depicting Florence Nightingale. (Her cousin and close friend, Eleanor Rathbone, was president of the NUWSS and later became an MP.)

In 1919 the Rosalind Paget Trust was set up to improve the status, education and wellbeing of midwives. By 1935, the year she was appointed DBE, she was living with her sister Mrs Dorothy Bolton at Colwood Park, Bolney, a magnificent, twelve-bedroomed mansion with ninety acres of land. Dame Rosalind died there, aged ninety-three.

BOSHAM

MADELEINE MASSON née Levy (1912–2007) writer.

Born in South Africa, the daughter of a French banker, at eighteen she married forty-year-old Baron Renaud Marie de la Minaudière and adopted one of his middle names as her surname. Living among Bohemian writers and artists in Paris she studied history and philosophy at the Sorbonne, where she earned a PhD, and art and humanities in Munich. During WWII she was about to leave France when she was recruited by the French Resistance to run messages and help escapees. In peacetime she worked as a reporter, feature-writer and a columnist in South Africa and Paris, where she contributed to a literary magazine, for which she interviewed many English writers, including Enid Bagnold [171].

Following a divorce she married Captain John Rayner and had one son. In 1963 they bought Dolphin Cottage, 15 Moreton Road, Bosham, and after living between there and London for a decade settled in Sussex permanently. She founded one of the first public relations firms in the UK and for nine years wrote a monthly column in the *Chichester Observer*.

Between 1936 and 1978 she wrote thirty-seven books, encompassing novels, cookbooks, a pictorial history of nursing, memoirs, biographies, plays, filmscripts, two translations from French and the story of her life in France, *I Never Kissed Paris Goodbye*. Her best-known work is a biography of SOE agent Krystyna Skarbek, alias Christine Granville. In 2004 she sold the film rights, becoming, at ninety-two, the oldest author ever to sign such a deal. The book was reprinted by Virago in 2005; the film has yet to be released. She worked into her nineties, appearing on BBC Radio Four's *Woman's Hour* in 2004, and was working on a biography of Baroness Orczy when she died, at Lordington Park Nursing Home, New Barn Lane, Chichester. She was interred at Bosham Old Burial Ground. [Related plate 7.]

BURGESS HILL

ANNE KATHARINE ELWOOD née Curteis (1796–1873) traveller and writer.

The daughter of Edward Curteis, future MP for Sussex, she was raised at Windmill Hill. She married Major Charles Elwood and in 1825 travelled overland with him to India. They took their time, savouring all the sights, arrived in Egypt a year later, took two more months to reach Bombay by sailing to Luxor and crossing the desert by camel. They returned in 1828 by ship, going via Ceylon, the Cape of Good Hope and St Helena, and made their home at Clayton Priory, where they were looked after by a plethora of residential domestic servants and joined the Sussex Archaeological Society. He became a JP and a deputy lieutenant of Sussex and she adapted her travel diaries into a book.

Believing herself the first English woman to have travelled by land to India (in fact, Eliza Fay had made the journey, though via Suez, in 1779), in 1830 she published (as 'Mrs Colonel Elwood') the two-volume *Narrative of a Journey Overland from England, by the Continent of Europe, Egypt, and the Red Sea to India*, which contains fascinating accounts of how she, as a Western woman, was received and her observations of daily life in India. Of her only other work, *Memoirs of the Literary Ladies of England from the Commencement of the Last Century* (1842), *John Bull* magazine commented: 'A more attractive production in the eyes of the fair sex could hardly be imagined'. It was used to help compile the *Dictionary of National Biography* and copies can still be found, though priced at over £1,000. [Related image p113.]

(ANNE) FLORENCE L.M.B. PATTON-BETHUNE (1864–1894) equestrian and novelist.

The only daughter of General Patton (he added 'Bethune' by Royal Licence in 1882), she was born in Somerset and lived most of her life at Clayton Priory. Nicknamed 'Pussie', she became well known in Sussex as a daring and accomplished horsewoman. Her sporting novel, *Debonnair Dick,* was published in 1892 and she had just submitted *Bachelor to the Rescue* to her publisher when, at the age of thirty, she was killed in a road accident in Hyde Park, London, when her tandem (a two-wheeled carriage drawn by two horses) collided with a brougham (a four-wheeled carriage drawn by one horse). The book, which was about a dog, was published eight weeks after her death. Her brother Douglas inherited Clayton Priory. [Related image p113.]

BURPHAM

GLADICE KEEVIL MBE (1884–1959) suffragette.

Educated at the Frances Mary Buss School in her native London, she worked as a governess in France and the USA, then for five years from 1907 as a paid organiser for the WSPU, responsible for suffragette activities in the West Midlands. (Her branch obtained a vote for one woman, Lois Dawson, by listing her on the electoral roll as 'Louis'.) She served as a national organiser and branch secretary in Birmingham and as a public speaker there and in London, being one of the chosen few to be given the rank of 'platform captain' at rallies in Hyde Park, London, and Heaton Park, Manchester. Arrested during a protest in London in 1908, she served six weeks in Holloway alongside Mrs Pankhurst and others, for which she received the Holloway brooch (the WSPU equivalent of the Victoria Cross).

Later that year while the premier was giving a speech in Birmingham she daringly approached the stage and asked him about votes for women. She was forcibly ejected, amid hisses and boos, but popped up just moments later in the orchestra pit, provoking guffaws of laughter from the audience, and continued to address Mr Asquith while the stewards scrambled to expel her again.

In 1912 her health broke down from exhaustion. She married Leslie Rickford in 1913 and moved with him to India, where she lived for thirty years, had three sons, and was appointed MBE in 1924 for services to the Bombay Girl Guides. Returning home in the 1940s they lived at Dickdene, Houndean Rise, Lewes, and in the 1950s at Warre House (now Frith House), then Wall Cottage, Burpham, where she ended her days. [Related images p112.]

CHICHESTER

DAME MYRA CURTIS DBE (1886–1971) senior civil servant and college head.

Leaving her birthplace, Sunderland, her family moved to Winchester and she was educated there and at Newnham. After working as an assistant editor on the *Victoria History of the Counties of England* she worked her way up the ranks of the civil service. During WWI she was recruited to the War Trade Intelligence Department, and in the 1920s and 1930s served on several government committees and in children's welfare. For this work she was appointed CBE in 1942 and DBE in 1949.

Retiring from the civil service at fifty-five she began a new career. She was elected principal of Newnham, where she helped to shape history by successfully negotiating for its students (all women) to be admitted as full members of Cambridge University in 1948. In 1952 she was the first woman elected to the university's Council of the Senate, and was chair of the Women's Appointments Board. Another committee she chaired managed to persuade the university to open a third women's college (New College) because Newnham and Girton were heavily oversubscribed.

During the 1950s she lived with Irish-born historian Professor Constantia Maxwell (1886–1962) at Little Baker's Cross, The Hill, Cranbrook, Kent. After her friend died she moved to 5a Northgate, Chichester, where she lived for nine years before moving into a nursing home in Bognor, where she died.

EMILY DAVIES (1830–1921) co-founder of Girton College.

Although born in Hampshire she grew up in Chichester, where her father was a vicar and ran a school. The family lived briefly in France in 1836, then at Ashley, near Chichester, until 1840, when they moved to Gateshead. She later became a close friend of Barbara Leigh Smith Bodichon [193], with whom she campaigned for the vote and for higher education for women. Their greatest achievement was founding Girton College for women in 1869, now part of Cambridge University.

At seventy-six she led a women's suffrage delegation to parliament and at eighty published *Thoughts on Some Questions Relating to Women*. She died in London, where she has a blue plaque. Her book *Higher Education of Women* was reprinted in 1988.

Further reading: Bennett, D. (1990) *Emily Davies and the Liberation of Women*. [Related plate 32.]

JINI FIENNES née Jennifer Lash (1938–1993) novelist and painter.

Born in Chichester, she grew up in India and Kent, wrote her first novel, *The Burial*, at nineteen, following it with five more and an autobiography. Her final work, *Blood Ties*, published posthumously in 1998, was described as 'precise and vivid, a novel which probes every exposed nerve of family feeling and family hell'. Although less well known as a painter, her artwork was widely exhibited. In 1962 she married Mark Fiennes and raised seven children (most of whom are now famous) and built or renovated fifteen consecutive homes. She died in Wiltshire.

Further reading: Fiennes, J. (1991) *On Pilgrimage* (autobiography).

PROFESSOR HILDA JOHNSTONE (1882–1961) medieval historian.

Educated at the University of Manchester, the city of her birth, in 1906 she became one of the first women to gain an MA. She lectured in medieval history until 1922, save for a break during WWI when she worked at the War Trade Intelligence Department.

For twenty years from 1922 she was chair of history at Royal Holloway College and in the 1930s protested against the marriage bar [8]. Between 1912 and 1961 she wrote fourteen books, including two short histories of Britain and biographies of Edward of Carnarvon, Edward I and Oliver Cromwell. She translated *The Annals of Ghent* from Latin (1951, reprinted 1985), and contributed chapters to several books with multiple authors.

Retiring in 1942, she settled in Chichester and was emeritus professor of history at the University of London (which had subsumed Royal Holloway). Between 1948 and 1951 she was honorary archivist to the Bishop of Chichester and consultant on ecclesiastical archives to the records committee of West Sussex County Council. She died at Littlehampton, and her papers were donated to Royal Holloway.

JOY KINSLEY OBE (1932–2004) pioneer prison governor.

Raised in Chichester, she attended Chichester High School for Girls, then trained as a nurse, midwife, psychiatric nurse and social worker. She entered the prison service in 1966, was promoted to governor of Holloway in 1982 and became, in 1985, the first woman governor of a male prison (Brixton). Later she was the first female inspector of male prisons.

MARGARET LEIGHTON CBE (1922–1976) actress.

Leaving her native Worcestershire at sixteen she joined the Old Vic theatre company in London. She performed with the greatest names including Laurence Olivier and Noël Coward, and won several awards including the Tony (twice) and a BAFTA. In the 1970s she lived somewhere near Chichester with her third husband Michael Wilding (his fourth marriage) in a cottage known locally as 'Vodka Villa'.

A year after being appointed CBE, her final stage appearance took place in 1975, in *A Family and a Fortune* by Ivy Compton-Burnett [157]. Suffering with multiple sclerosis, she appeared in a wheelchair. She died shortly afterwards in Chichester, aged just fifty-three. [Related plate 16.]

RUBY MILLER (1889–1976) actress.

A popular 'Gaiety Girl' on the West End stage, hers was the legendary shoe from which a besotted man drank champagne. After her first husband, Lieutenant Samson, was killed during WWI she declined proposals from two earls and a viscount to marry classical musician Max Darewski, who died just five months later. Her tragic love life was matched by her troublesome finances: she was bankrupted three times in seven years. In 1921 she had debts of £2,300 and assets, 'wearing apparel, £4' — in other words, the clothes she stood in.

Despite everything, she rose from chorus girl to musical comedy farceuse to Shakespearean and Shavian actress, in a career spanning over half a century, which included writing, adapting, producing and theatre management. She worked with all the top stars of her generation and, remarkably, made gramophone recordings as far apart as 1929 and 1966.

She spent the 1950s and 1960s giving lecture tours in which she spoke of her career in showbusiness. Under the name Madame Max Darewski she wrote two books of autobiography: *Believe Me or Not* (1934) and *Champagne From My Slipper* (1962). She died at her home, 8 Cawley Road, Chichester.

ADELAIDE O'KEEFFE (1776–1865) writer.

She was born in Dublin to actor parents who had a stormy relationship and parted acrimoniously. In 1781, as the law allowed, [9] John O'Keeffe took his five children to London and refused to let their mother see them for the rest of her life. He gained considerable fame in London as a dramatist and writer of farces, and was able to send his sons to Oxford University. He sent Adelaide to a convent, but removed her when she was twelve because he had lost his sight and needed her at home as his housekeeper, amanuensis and copyist.

Miss O'Keeffe also had literary talent. Some of her poems appeared in the 1804/5 two-volume anthology *Ann and Jane Taylor's Original Poems for Infant Minds*. Her first novel, *Llewellin*, was published when she was a teenager, but her second, *Patriarchal Times*, written in her twenties,

did not appear in print until she was thirty-five. It was well-reviewed and was followed by *Zenobia, Queen of Palmyra* (1814) and *Dudley* (1819).

In 1815 she and her father moved to Chichester, where to support them both she worked as a governess for fifteen years. Their finances improved when his plays were revived and they left in 1830 and settled in Southampton, Hampshire, where he died three years later. In 1839 she was living in Surrey but by 1841 was back in Sussex, this time in Montague Street, Broadwater, Worthing.

Her father was the most-produced dramatist of the 1830s, but while his farces played to packed West End theatres, she, by this time his sole heir, was scraping by on the breadline. She spent years fruitlessly campaigning to be paid the royalties due on his work; she appealed to the House of Commons and even wrote to Queen Adelaide, who generously gave her £200 from her own purse. After enlisting the help of other influential aristocrats, in 1834 Miss O'Keeffe was granted a civil-list pension of £50, which she considered woefully inadequate and publicly advocated that authors be paid annual state grants. She wrote several more books and collections of poems, but the income they generated was small. Her final novel, *The Broken Sword, or a Soldier's Honour, A Tale of the Allied Armies of 1757*, was published in Southampton in 1854. Soon afterwards she moved to Brighton, her final home, where she died.

MAVIS PUGH (1914–2006) actress.

The daughter of a solicitor, she was born in Surrey and educated in Kent. She spent many years performing on the stage, toured the music halls in a double-act with Hugh Paddick, and appeared in two films. She married John Clegg in 1959 and at the age of sixty unexpectedly found a new career playing dotty, upper-class ladies in TV sit-coms. She appeared in *It Ain't Half Hot Mum* (in which her husband played the posh pianist), *Dad's Army*, *Hi-de-Hi!*, *You Rang, M'Lord?*, *Sorry!*, *Are You Being Served?*, and *Fawlty Towers* (she asked for sausages for her pampered Shih-tzu dog). She retired to and died in Chichester.

NELLIE SHEAIL (1911–2006) musician.

Born in Heyshott, she grew up in nearby Bignor and Sutton. Her parents were amateur violinists who worked as farm manager and housekeeper for Lord Mersey on his estate, Bignor Park.

She played organ accompaniment at the village church until one day, aged twenty-six, she took the bus to Chichester Cathedral and, uninvited, rather audaciously asked the organist for lessons. Four years of tuition later she was appointed his assistant, almost certainly the first woman ever to fill such a position. Among her many recitals was the first British performance of Poulenc's *Organ Concerto.*

She gave up the post in 1955 when she married the Revd Morris Maddocks, the future Bishop of Selby, and moved into a rectory in Yorkshire, where she installed a magnificent Henry Willis pipe organ. Upon retirement they decided to return to Sussex and settled at Cathedral Close, Chichester, where she died.

CLAYTON

ELIZABETH PEACOCK (1880–1969) artist.

Her birthplace is unknown. She lived as a spinster semi-invalid cossetted by her family until she was thirty-six, then escaped in 1916 by enrolling in a textile weaving workshop run by Ethel Mairet [204] at Stratford-Upon-Avon. She moved with the Mairets to Ditchling in the early 1920s, where she met Molly Stobart, a wealthy spinster and self-published poet who became her lifelong companion. Miss Stobart's family built a house for the two women on Ditchling Road, Clayton, calling it Weavers.

Here Miss Peacock founded her own workshop, and her beautifully-designed textiles were purchased by many eminent persons including King Faisal of Egypt and famous fashion designer Elsa Schiaparelli. In 1931 she was commissioned to weave a sequence of eight banners for Dartington Great Hall, each one decorated with symbols of a trade carried out there; these remain among Dartington's great treasures. From 1940 to 1957 she taught weaving. After her death her works were displayed in two public exhibitions.

Further reading: Harrod, T. (1999) *The Crafts in Britain in the Twentieth Century.*

CLIMPING

VALERIE BARKER Mrs Arkell-Smith (1895–1960) sexual impostor.

She grew up in Surrey, where her father taught her fencing, boxing and cricket. At her ladies' schools she would sometimes dress as a boy and put on a false moustache. During WWI she was a VAD nurse. She married Harold Arkell-Smith but left him and instead lived with Ernest Pearce-Crouch. They had two children and ran Bailiff's Court Farm, Climping, but his drinking and laziness led to their parting, each taking one child. In 1922 she met Elfrida Emma Haward (b1896) of 8a Beach Road, Littlehampton, an assistant in her father's chemist shop at 15 High Street. Mrs Arkell-Smith pretended that she was a widowed single father masquerading as a woman. In 1923, calling herself Sir Victor Barker, Bt., DSO and wearing a man's suit and her ex-boyfriend's war medals, she booked into the Grand Hotel, Brighton, and ordered a wardrobe of gentleman's attire. Days later, she and Miss Haward were married at St Peter's Church and stayed locally while 'Sir Victor' acted with the Brighton Repertory Company. After living in Andover, London, Uckfield and Staffordshire, Miss Haward tired of the nomadic life and returned to her family in Littlehampton in 1927. 'Sir Victor' lived in London with a 'common-law wife', hired a valet, was shaved daily by a barber, founded a war veterans' club and swaggered about in a military uniform, recounting wartime anecdotes. She was described as 'the finest type of officer and gentleman anyone could wish to meet'.

Money troubles led to bankruptcy, exposure, sensationalist press coverage, a well-publicised trial, and nine months' imprisonment for the illegal marriage. She later held many short-term jobs and in 1934 was working in Henfield as 'John Hill'. She appeared as a circus attraction — 'The

Man-Woman' — and sold her story to the gutter press. She died, impoverished and forgotten, in Suffolk.

Further reading: Collis, R. (2001) *Colonel Barker's Monstrous Regiment: A Tale of Female Husbandry.* [Related images pp16, 111.]

COCKING

HYPATIA BONNER JP née Bradlaugh (1858–1935) writer.

Born in London, when her parents separated she and her mother moved to her grandparents' house on the Causeway, Cocking, when she was twelve. She left at nineteen to join her father Charles in London, where he and Annie Besant [246] were on trial for obscenity after publishing a pamphlet advocating birth control.

She studied political economy at City of London College just before it placed a ban on female students. Unusually for a woman, she taught chemistry and mathematics at the Department of Science and Art and four of her lectures were published in 1881 as *Chemistry of the Home.*

She wrote and lectured widely on subjects such as secularism and the blasphemy laws, about which she wrote a book, *Penalties upon Opinion.* Her other works included a biography of her father and a collection of children's stories. She owned and wrote for the *National Reformer* and was later editor of *The Reformer,* campaigned for votes for women and served on the executive of the Women's National Liberal Federation. She was a magistrate from 1921 to 1934. Her marriage to Arthur Bonner produced two sons, one of whom died young.

Further reading: Bonner, A. (1942) *Hypatia Bradlaugh Bonner.*

COLGATE

MARGO MCLENNAN née Eileen McMenemy (1938–2004) dancer, skater, actress and first woman celebrant of gay marriages.

Trained at the Italia Conti Academy of Theatre Arts [128] and Streatham Ice Rink, in the 1950s she was a cabaret dancer at the Dorchester Hotel, then a skating prodigy in *Humpty Dumpty on Ice* and other shows. In the 1960s, as Margo Mayne, she was an actress on the West End stage, screen and television, and appeared on magazine covers and in TV adverts. In the 1970s she became a soap-opera star, appearing in *Prisoner: Cell Block H* as an inmate, returning in 1981 as prison officer Parsons.

She married Tony Doonan, had a daughter, Nicola, and divorced in 1969. Her second marriage, to Rod McLennan, led to her living in Australia, where in 2001 she was licensed by the government as a marriage celebrant. In this role she became the first woman in the world to marry homosexual couples. Near the end of her life she lived in Colgate, where she died.

CONEYHURST

ELLEN BECK (1845–1940) and **EDITH BECK** (1847–1930) farmers and feminists.

The Beck sisters grew up in a Quaker family and left their Middlesex home about 1903, when they were both middle-aged, to buy and run Duncan's Farm, Coneyhurst. They were to live there until their respective deaths.

They were vegetarians, supporters of animal welfare and, above all, feminists. Since the 1870s Edith had supported the New Hospital and in 1889 they and their mother had signed an early women's suffrage petition. In 1907 they joined the WSPU and over the years donated several large lump sums to its support, as well as the proceeds of the farm produce they sold from stalls at suffragette events in London and elsewhere. By this time they were already in their sixties, and were obliged to abstain from acts of violence; however, they eagerly took part in rallies, marches, demonstrations and deputations to parliament, and Edith was arrested for obstruction on Black Friday [294], though she was later discharged.

They were both members of the TRL and in 1912 withheld their taxes. That year, they travelled to London to join the tail-end of the women's rights march from Edinburgh to London, organised by their Sussex friend and neighbour Mrs de Fonblanque [44]. They are known to have harboured suffragettes on their estate: for example, Harriet Kerr, general manager of the WSPU headquarters in London, stayed at Hook Cottage for a few weeks in 1913 to recuperate after a traumatic spell of imprisonment during which she went on hunger strike and was force-fed. After British women won the vote, in the 1930s the sisters were members of the WFL and the International Franchise Club.

Ellen left over £100,000, the equivalent to over £4m today. Her bequests attest to her passions: the New Sussex Hospital for Women, Christ's Hospital Girls' School, Billingshurst Women's Institute and 'other charities for the benefit of women'. [Related image p106.]

DIANA DORS née Fluck; Mrs Hamilton; Mrs Dawson; Mrs Lake (1931–1984) actress.

Known as the 'blonde bombshell', she was born in Swindon and studied at LAMDA. She notched up over a hundred film and TV credits, song recordings and guest appearances in her thirty-seven-year career. In spring 1958 she bought Palmer's Farm in Coneyhurst, a half-timbered, Elizabethan property with six bedrooms, a thirty-foot games room, a heated swimming pool, three staff cottages and fifty-six acres. She caused quite a stir when shopping in Horsham and Billingshurst, drawing enormous attention with her flashy American car. She married three times and had two children, who were raised by their father in the USA. She died in Berkshire. Palmer's Farm, which she bought for £12,000 and sold two years later for £25,000 has lately changed hands for £1.5m.

CRAWLEY

MARY CHAVELITA DUNNE pseudonym George Egerton; Mrs Melville; Mrs Clairmonte; Mrs Golding Bright (1859–1945) writer.

The daughter of an Irish soldier and a Welshwoman, she was born in Australia and nicknamed 'Chav'. She was educated privately, travelled by ship to Chile, then to Wales and Ireland. Under the pseudonym 'George Egerton' she wrote two plays that were produced in the West End, four volumes of short stories and *Rosa Amorosa,* a collection of love letters that was described in *The Times* as 'a mixture of flabby sentimentalism and raging self-consciousness'. George Bernard Shaw described her as 'intolerably loquacious'.

While working as companion to the Hon. Mrs Whyte-Melville she eloped with her employer's husband to Ireland, where they were shot at by Miss Dunne's father and wed in 1888 amid huge public outrage, for it was his third marriage after one divorce and one annulment for bigamy — shocking behaviour for a clergyman. They moved to Norway, where he died. She learned Norwegian, read Ibsen and Strindberg and took a lover, Knut Hamsun, whose novel, *Hunger,* she translated in 1899. She had numerous other affairs as well as two more impulsive marriages, was widowed twice more. Her only child, George Egerton Clairmonte, was killed during in action WWI, aged just nineteen.

In 1936 she helped found the Irish Genealogical Research Society and served on its council. In later life she lived in Sussex and died in poverty at Ifield Park Nursing Home, Rusper Road. [Related image plate 19.]

ANNE WOOD (1907–1998) singer and opera manager.

Born in Crawley and educated in Wiltshire, she trained as a singer and enjoyed a successful career as a contralto in oratorio, concert, recital and broadcasting. She became artistic director of the English Opera Group, founded Phoenix Opera and was its general manager for ten years, and taught singing at the Guildhall School of Music. She died in London.

CRAWLEYDOWN

ANNIE FORTESCUE HARRISON Lady Arthur Hill (1851–1944) composer.

The daughter of an MP, she was born in India and lived at Down Park, Crawleydown, from 1865, when her father built the mansion. In 1877 she married Colonel Lord Arthur Hill of Wakehurst Place, Ardingly, a recently widowed army officer with a baby son, and had one daughter (exactly nine months after the wedding). In 1881 he adopted as his company's regimental march *In the Gloaming,* a ballad whose tune she wrote during their engagement. It became one of the most popular songs of its day, selling 140,000 copies of sheet music in nine years in countries across the globe.

Using her maiden name she composed popular, light, sentimental music including *The Elfin Waltzes, Our Favourite Galop, Let Me Forget Thee* and *In the Moonlight.* She provided the music (and her mother-in-law, the Dowager Duchess of Downshire, wrote the words) for two operettas: *The Ferry Girl,* which was performed in London at the Gallery of Illustration, the Savoy Theatre and the Gaiety Theatre, and *The Lost Husband,* which played at London's Opera Comique in 1886. Widowed in 1931, she died in Berkshire.

CUCKFIELD

ANGELA FOX née Worthington (1912–1999) autobiographer.

The daughter of Lucy, who inspired Noël Coward's famous song *Don't Put Your Daughter on the Stage, Mrs Worthington,* she was born in Kent. Her mother's husband was a GP, but it was an 'open secret' that her biological father was dramatist Frederick Lonsdale. She married theatre producer Robin Fox and had three sons: Edward and James are famous actors while Robert is a producer. Her life with them inspired her to write two humorous, though sometimes caustic books, *Slightly Foxed by my Theatrical Family* (1986) and *Completely Foxed* (1989).

She lived between a posh London home at Eaton Square and Ockenden House, Cuckfield, moving in later life to a nearby cottage, Buntings, where she died.

MAY MUKLE (1880–1963) cellist.

A child prodigy, she was born in London to a master organ-builder who invented the world's first juke box. She began playing the cello at the age of four, made her first public solo appearance at nine and by age eleven was earning enough to support herself. Entering the RAM at thirteen, she won every cello prize, gained her ARAM at seventeen and performed until the age of eighty. With her rich-toned Montagnana cello that was a gift from an anonymous donor, she travelled extensively all over the world and was the first female cellist to achieve an international reputation. She co-founded a female chamber group (The English Ensemble) and performed at suffrage fundraising concerts. During WWII she founded the MM (Mainly Musicians) club at Oxford Circus, London, which she ran for twenty years. She lived in Sussex in later life and died at Cuckfield. The May Mukle Prize is awarded annually to a cello student at the RAM.

DUNCTON

FLORENCE DE FONBLANQUE née Sparag-napane (1864–1949) suffragist.

The sister of Mrs Arncliffe-Sennett [66], she was born in London and educated in Brussels and Brighton. She became a minor actress until she married actor Robert de Fonblanque (later Marquess of Juliers, Comte de Hautserve and Comte de Fonblanque). The couple settled at The Cottage, Duncton, and she dedicated herself to the women's movement.

She served on the committee of the West Sussex branch of the Conservative and Unionist Women's Franchise Association and joined the NUWSS and WSPU. In October 1912 she organised a march from Edinburgh to London to highlight women's issues including the sweated trades, 'white slavery' (i.e. prostitution) and suffrage. After making speeches to an assembled crowd of about 1,500 suffragists, feminists and other well-wishers, five women walked the four hundred miles in five weeks, holding meetings and collecting signatures on a petition for votes for women at every town en route. Suffrage literature, the ever-growing petition and their luggage followed in a van driven by a sixth woman. Hundreds more joined them once they reached north London, including the Beck sisters [42] and Israel Zangwill [46]. In central London they were met by four thousand supporters with banners who marched with them to 10 Downing Street to present the petition to the Prime Minister (who wasn't at home).

After the march she founded the Qui Vive Corps of Suffragists, whose HQ was 60 West Street, Horsham. Miss M.E. Byham was treasurer and Miss A.N. Roff of Easebourne was honorary secretary. She intended the corps to be deployed wherever any suffrage action was taking place. Wearing brown and green uniforms, cockades and specially-designed badges, they met every Saturday to march to another town and hold a meeting there to promote the suffrage cause; they once marched to Turners Hill and took tea with Viscountess Cowdray [88].

Mrs de Fonblanque died at home and was buried at Duncton churchyard, where her headstone proclaims her the 'originator and leader' of the march. This was specified in her will, and reveals her pride in her contribution to the woman's cause.[Related image p113.]

DURRINGTON

BETTY HARVIE-ANDERSON OBE, TD, DL MP, PC Baroness Skrimshire (1913–1979) politician.

A Scotswoman, during WWII she was chief commander of a mixed heavy anti-aircraft brigade with the ATS and received the Territorial Decoration. After the war she became leader of Stirlingshire County Council, was appointed OBE, then served as MP for Renfrewshire East for twenty years, becoming a privy councillor and the first woman deputy chairman of the Committee of Ways and Means (known as the Deputy Speaker), a post she held from 1970 to 1973.

In 1960, at the age of forty-seven, she married John Skrimshire, a consultant heart specialist for the NHS in the Worthing district, but she retained her name. They divided their time between Durrington Farmhouse, Pond Lane, Durrington, and her ancestral estate in Scotland. She retired from parliament in 1979, was created Baroness Skrimshire of Quarter, took her seat in the House of Lords, and died just one week later at Worthing Hospital.

EASEBOURNE

HELEN JOSEPH née Fennell (1905–1992) white anti-apartheid campaigner.

Born at Crescent Lodge, Easebourne Lane, she studied at King's College, London and in 1927 went to India to teach the children of governors and white colonials, moving to South Africa in 1930, where she was briefly married to Billy Joseph. She came home during WWII to serve in the WAAF, but otherwise spent the rest of her life there, campaigning against apartheid.

One of the country's greatest freedom fighters, in 1956 she led a protest march of 20,000 black women. She was a fearless and outspoken critic of the regime, was tried for treason and imprisoned for four months at the age of seventy-two, and was kept under house arrest for eleven years (1962–71 and 1982–4) for being a threat to state security, Revered in black townships and a close associate of the Mandelas, she received the highest honour of the African National Congress, the Isithwalandwe-Seaparankoe Medal. She died in Johannesburg.

EAST DEAN

JO MANTON (1919–1997) biographer.

Leaving her native Hertfordshire she studied at Girton and became the youngest ever TV producer for BBC Schools. She married, but left her husband to set up home with Robert Gittings in a Sussex house below Blackdown. It was built of mud and had squirrels inhabiting the attic. They married in 1949 and spent the next forty years in Sussex, living at Dodds Cottage, East Dean. It was once an outhouse to a larger house, which they had sold, and was converted with a £1,000 literary prize won by her husband.

She took a full part in village life, sang in the choir at Chichester and wrote several books for children, including two collections of Greek and Chinese legends, and a number of biographies, including those of Mary Carpenter and Elizabeth Garrett Anderson [299]. With her husband she compiled full-length biographies of the second Mrs (Thomas) Hardy, Dorothy Wordsworth, and Claire Clairmont and the Shelleys. After a stroke in 1993 she was obliged to spend the rest of her life in a nursing home.

EAST GRINSTEAD

VICKY CLEMENT-JONES MB, BCH, MRCP née Yip (1948–1987) founder of BACUP.

She was born in Hong Kong but moved with her family to 127 Imberhorne Lane, East Grinstead, in 1957, living there for ten years. She showed academic brilliance at an early age, shone at Nôtre Dame Convent School and went up to Girton, where she read archaeology, anthropology and medical science, earning a first-class honours degree, the Elizabeth Walter prize, the Pfeiffer graduate scholarship and the Raemakers prize. She married in 1973 during her clinical training at St Thomas's Hospital, London, where she qualified MB, BChir in 1974 and MRCP in 1976. She won a bursary to study the body's response to pain and devised a radioimmunoassay.

In 1982 she was diagnosed with ovarian cancer. This led her to found in 1984 the British Association for Cancer United Patients. She died in London and was cremated at Croydon. BACUP grew to be the largest and most successful organisation of its kind; it helps over 100,000 people annually.

ANNE PRATT (1806–1893) botanical writer.

Born in Kent and educated at Eastgate House School, Rochester, she gained considerable fame for her books *The Field, the Garden, and the Woodland* (1838), *Wild Flowers* (1852), which was published in individual sheets for hanging up in classrooms, and *The Flowering Plants and Ferns of Great Britain,* published in five volumes from 1855 and considered the best botanical work of the period.

At the age of sixty she married John Pearless and lived in his home town of East Grinstead for two and a half years. Nothing is known of her later life. [Related image p116.]

EAST PRESTON

MARY CECIL HAY (1840–1886) novelist.

The daughter of a clockmaker, she was born in Shropshire and raised in Chiswick and Cornwall. Between 1873 and 1886 she wrote fifteen romantic novels and several collections of short stories; these were widely read in the UK, the USA and Australia. As was common in the nineteenth century, her works appeared as serials in magazines before being published as books.

Her popularity declined, as did her health and, in the 1880s she, her mother and her sisters moved to Bay Trees, East Preston, where she died after a long illness. All her books are now long out of print, but copies of her most famous work, *Old Myddelton's Money* (1874) are still available secondhand.

EDITH ZANGWILL née Ayrton (c1879–1945) novelist, suffragette and peace campaigner.

Although of English parentage, she was born in Japan. Her mother, Matilda Chaplin Ayrton MD [one of the Edinburgh Seven, see Sophia Jex-Blake, 236], died when she was four and she was sent to Sussex to live with an aunt until, when she was ten, her father married scientist Hertha Marks [63], who raised her. After studying at Bedford College, she married novelist Israel Zangwill. In 1903 they bought a nine-bedroom house, Far End, Sea Lane, East Preston, where they raised their three children. Their early married life was devoted to the women's suffrage movement; both were members of the NUWSS, then the WSPU, and her husband joined Mrs de Fonblanque's march [44]. Her novel *The Call* (1924) was dedicated 'To all those who fought for the Freedom of Women' and is about a scientist — clearly, her stepmother — who joins the militant suffragettes.

Widowed in 1926, during the 1930s she became involved in the peace movement, and was chairman of the Women's International League Disarmament Campaign Committee and treasurer of the Women's Peace Crusade. She was still living at Far End in 1936, but died in Edinburgh. Her six published novels are now unavailable; her husband's remain in print. [Related image p113.]

FAYGATE

RACHEL BARRETT (1874–1953) suffragette.

A Welsh-born science teacher with a BSc from the University of Aberystwyth, she joined the WSPU in 1906, becoming an organiser, public speaker, and editor of *The Suffragette*, its weekly newspaper. In April 1913 she was arrested on conspiracy charges and sentenced to a month's imprisonment. She went on hunger strike and was released, re-arrested and released twice more under the Cat and Mouse Act [294]. While out on licence for the third time she was smuggled into the WSPU HQ, from where she secretly edited *The Suffragette* for five months. When the offices were raided by the police she went to Edinburgh, lived under the name Miss Ashworth, and published the paper from there.

Miss Barrett and her life companion Ida Wylie were close friends of the lesbian novelist Miss Radclyffe Hall [245], whom they supported during the trial of her book in 1928. She died at Carylls Nursing Home, Faygate.

FELCOURT

DORIS LESLIE née Oppenheim; Lady Fergusson Hannay (1891–1982) novelist.

The daughter of a prosperous tobacco merchant, she was born in London. At fifteen she wanted to be an actress but her father forbade it; she defied him by winning a scholarship to the Guildhall School of Music. Shortly after her acting début at the Old Vic she married, but was widowed shortly afterwards. Abandoning the stage she took up writing and produced sixteen popular novels and seventeen biographies, including the lives of Chopin and Richard II. She wrote all her books in longhand and insured her hand for a large sum.

She was married three times, to actor John Leslie, to R. Vincent Cookes and, in the 1930s, to Harley Street physician Sir Walter Hannay, but retained her first husband's name throughout her life. During WWII she lived in London, where she was wounded while serving as an ARP warden; later she lived in Hertfordshire. Widowed in 1961, she converted to Roman Catholicism, moved to Devon, and began to breed and show English bulldogs and to keep bees.

In 1970 the Catholic Women's League voted her Woman of the Year for Literature and her work gained a wider audience when BBC TV adapted and broadcast her 'Peridot' series of novels. In later life she lived in Felcourt. She died at the Royal Sussex County Hospital in Brighton. [Related image p116.]

FELPHAM

CATHERINE BLAKE née Boucher (1762–1831) printer, engraver and artist.

Taught to read and write by her husband William, she assisted him in producing his famous illuminated books, printing and hand-colouring the plates and stitching the volumes into paper wrappers. She printed intaglio engravings and worked on the illustrations for William Hayley's *Life of William Cowper*, very unusual work for a woman at that time. The Blakes lived in William Hayley's cottage in Felpham for three years; leaving in 1803 with rheumatism and respiratory complaints they returned to their native London, vowing never to return. The cottage is now called Blake's House and the street is now Blakes Road.

Rendered penniless by widowhood, she was obliged to work as a housekeeper, supplementing her income by selling her husband's work, completing several of his unfinished projects, including his watercolour illustrations to Bunyan's *Pilgrim's Progress,* and drew and painted her own compositions. Some of her work is now at the Fitzwilliam Museum, Cambridge. She died in London and was buried in Bunhill Fields.

Further reading: Ackroyd, P. (1996) *Blake.* [Related image p107.]

FERNHURST

HANNAH WHITALL SMITH née Whitall (1832–1911) evangelical preacher and author.

She and her husband Robert Pearsall Smith were born in Philadelphia, USA, and had two daughters and a son (four others died young). During the 1870s they addressed large religious meetings in various towns in England, Switzerland and Germany, and she co-founded the Women's Christian Temperance Union. In 1875 both spoke at a ten-day Christian Convention at the Pavilion and Dome in Brighton, where Mrs Smith was described as the 'special feature'. One day she addressed two all-female audiences each numbering over two thousand; among them was Lizzie Baxter [169]. Owing to a sex scandal involving her husband they cut short their visit and returned to the USA. In 1887 they returned to England and moved into the fourteen-bedroom Friday's Hill House, Fernhurst, home of their daughter Mary Costelloe, the mother of Ray Strachey [below]. (Mary remarried, becoming Mrs Berenson, and wrote three travel books.) Their other daughter Alys, a close friend of Helen Boyle [155], married the philosopher Bertrand Russell, whom she had met at the house. Mrs Smith was still at Friday's Hill House in 1891 and is assumed to have lived there at least a decade. Widowed in 1898 and wheelchair-bound in her later years, she died in her son's house at Oxford, her home since 1906.

She wrote at least a dozen popular books on religious matters. *The Christian's Secret of a Happy Life* (1875) went into over a hundred editions and is still in print today. Collections of her writings and letters have been published since her death, some of them edited by her granddaughter [below].

Further reading: Parker, R. A. (1959) *The Transatlantic Smiths*; Strachey, R. (1914) *A Quaker Grandmother*. [Related image p109.]

RAY STRACHEY née Rachel Costelloe (1887–1940) writer.

The granddaughter of Hannah Whitall Smith [above], she was born in London and raised at Friday's Hill House. After studying mathematics at Cambridge and electrical engineering at Oxford, in 1911 she married civil servant Oliver Strachey, with whom she wrote *Keigwin's Rebellion* (1916). Her sister Karin married Adrian Stephen, brother of Vanessa Bell [214] and Virginia Woolf [243].

She founded the Society of Women Welders, was parliamentary secretary of the NUWSS, chairman of the wartime Women's Service Employment Committee and head of the Women's Employment Federation. After working as political secretary to Nancy Astor, the first female MP, she stood unsuccessfully in three general elections. She wrote biographies of eminent women, memoirs, novels and history. Her most famous work was *The Cause* (1928, reprinted 1988), a valuable overview of the women's rights movement since 1792. She broadcast on BBC radio on 'Women and Work' and 'Building a House'.

Friday's Hill House was given up by her family in 1904, so when she returned to Fernhurst in 1921 she bought nine acres of land and built a house of pisé de terre (rammed earth). She named it Copse Cottage but it is known to this day as the Mud House. She installed an 80ft x 30ft pool (where she swam in the nude), and acquired WLA clothing — corduroy breeches, boots and a straw hat — to wear around her estate., where Virginia Woolf was a frequent visitor. She died in London from complications arising from a minor operation. Lady Astor heard of her death during an official luncheon with, among others, Caroline Haslett, [87] and all those present stood for a one-minute silence. [Related plate 30; image p109.]

MARGARET, LADY MOIR OBE née Pennycook (1864–1942) amateur engineer and philanthropist.

Nothing is known of her early life in Scotland until 1887, when she married (later, Sir) Ernest Moir, a colleague of Weetman Pearson [see Lady Cowdray, 88]. She called herself an 'engineer by marriage', because for many years she accompanied her husband on inspection visits to his civil engineering projects, taking a keen interest in their construction. She visited the Forth Bridge and became the first woman to walk through the Dartford Tunnel.

By 1911 the Moirs had two teenage sons (one was killed in WWI) and lived at Whitehanger, Marley Common, a twelve-bedroom house with a tennis court on its forty acres, until 1929, her husband becoming Baron Moir of Whitehanger in 1916. During WWI she founded the Weekend Relief Scheme to give female munitions workers weekends off, while their work was performed by well-to-do volunteers. She trained in the rough turning and boring of 4.5 shells and 18lb shrapnel and undertook to perform weekend shifts as a lathe operator for six months. She was also secretary and treasurer of the National War Savings Committee she organised the sale of bonds.

Lady Moir was appointed OBE in 1919, and in the 1920s raised funds for hospitals and held office in many organisations that benefited women. Most notably, she co-founded and was (for four years) president of the Women's Engineering Society, working alongside Caroline Haslett [87], and from 1935 she was its treasurer. She organised a simplified engineering course for women at a number of polytechnics, gave receptions at her London home to honour the pioneer female aviators and with Lady Denman [32] and Margaret Bondfield [124] supported a scheme to provide affordable flatlets for single working women. She was also a member of the Six Point Group [301].

Widowed in 1933, Lady Moir lived between Buckinghamshire and London. Her obituary in *The Times* was written by Caroline Haslett. Whitehanger later became a nursing home.

FITTLEWORTH

GERTRUDE JENNINGS (1877–1958) play-wright.

The daughter of the editor of the *New York Times*, she was a minor actress before achieving fame for writing a series of immensely popular, one-act comedy plays, which were broadcast on radio and staged in West End theatres and village halls (she once unsuccessfully sued the WI for infringement of copyright). A reviewer in *The Times* commented: 'She could create

the atmosphere, thicken the suspense and lead up to her climax as though she had three acts at her disposal'. Her play *A Woman's Influence* was particularly popular amongst members of the AFL.

She lived for at least thirteen years (1937–50) at The Knoll House, Sandy Lane, Fittleworth. Some of her plays, notably *Five Birds in a Cage*, *Between the Soup and the Savoury,* and *The Bathroom Door* (set in Eastbourne), are still performed today.

DAME DOROTHY TUTIN DBE (1930–2001) actress.

A musically talented child, she wanted to be a pianist but was steered into acting by her father. Although her second choice, her career lasted half a century. She trained at RADA in her native London, made her stage début in 1949 playing Princess Margaret in *The Thistle and the Rose* and first appeared on screen in *The Importance of Being Ernest* (1952). After joining the RSC she developed a gift for playing challenging Shakespearean roles. Although the stage was said to be her métier, she also played over forty television roles. She was highly acclaimed by all the leading drama critics, was nominated for a Tony and four BAFTAs and won the *Evening Standard* and the Olivier awards, yet she was seldom satisfied with her performance and was unnecessarily self-critical.

Appointed CBE in 1967 and DBE in 2000, she was married to actor Derek Waring and both her children became actors. She lived at 7 The Old School, School Lane, Fittleworth, and died at King Edward VII Hospital, Easebourne. [Related plate 2.]

AMBER BLANCO WHITE née Reeves (1887–1981) socialist-feminist writer.

The daughter of the feminist writer Maud Pember Reeves, she was born in New Zealand but lived in England from age ten. She studied in France and at Newnham, where she achieved a double first in moral sciences in 1908 and befriended Ray Strachey [48]. Like Dorothy Miller Richardson [100] she was made pregnant by the writer H.G. Wells (a married friend of her parents) when she was twenty-one, and was provided with a hideaway by Elizabeth Robins [56]. Wells arranged a hasty marriage of convenience to lawyer George Blanco White before the child was born in late 1909. She had two more children and lived between Hampstead and Bedham near Fittleworth for most of her married life.

During WWI she worked for the ATS and the Admiralty, and was headhunted by Winston Churchill for a post at the Ministry of Munitions. She was appointed to the Whitley Council of the Board of Trade but her contract was terminated because she was a married woman. She lectured in philosophy and psychology at Morley College, London, for thirty-seven years and was acting head for nearly two years from 1946. A member of the Fabian Society, she spoke against the marriage bar [8] and for equal pay.

She wrote four novels with feminist themes under her maiden name; her first was *The Reward of Virtue* (1911) and her best was *A Lady and her Husband* (1914). Her four non-fiction works, published in her married name, included *The Nationalisation of Banking* (1934) and *Ethics for Unbelievers* (1949). She also contributed a good deal of original material to H.G. Wells's book *The Work, Wealth and Happiness of Mankind* (1931), wrote book reviews for *Queen* and *Vogue* and articles for the *Saturday Review* and *Fabian News*. She edited *The Townswoman* (for the TG) and (with her husband) the *Woman's Leader*. In the 1930s she stood for parliament twice, as the Labour candidate for Hendon, but was unsuccessful. Widowed in 1966, she died in hospital in London.

GOODWOOD

DUCHESS OF LEINSTER née Lady Emily Lennox (1731–1814) grand multipara.

Her father, Charles Lennox, 2nd Duke of Richmond, grandson of Charles II by his mistress, became MP for Chichester at the age of twenty-one. He married a fourteen-year-old Dutch girl and they had twelve children. He gave each of his four daughters £10,000 (a magnificent sum), making them the most admired and privileged women in Britain. They were the subject of Stella Tillyard's 1995 book *Aristocrats*, which was adapted into a television mini-series in 1999 and released on DVD in the USA in 2006.

Lady Emily, a god-daughter of George II, was born and raised at Goodwood House and was married at fifteen to the Earl of Kildare, the richest man in Ireland, who became the Duke of Leinster in 1766. Her involvement with her husband's political machinations and scheming earned her the nickname 'the Queen of Ireland'. She played an important role in the development of his recently-built mansion, Carton House, near Dublin; in particular she is responsible for creating the Chinese Room and the famous Shell Cottage, which she had decorated with sea-shells from around the world.

After the death of her parents when she was twenty-one, she took in her younger sisters and raised them with her own nineteen children. Widowed in 1773, she eloped to France with her children's young tutor, William Ogilvie, with her ten youngest offspring in tow and pregnant by him with her twentieth. They married and three children were born of the union, bringing her total of live births to an impressive twenty-two. Having raised twenty-five children, she was a well-respected and oft-consulted authority on the subject, recommending a 'daily rattle' in a bouncing carriage during pregnancy.

Lady Emily died in London and her remains were deposited in the Lennox family vault at Chichester Cathedral. Carton House is now a 165-bedroomed hotel boasting a Lady Emily Suite. [Related images pp16, 108.]

LADY LOUISA CONOLLY née Lennox (1743–1821) mansion renovator and philanthropist.

One of the four daughters of the Duke of Richmond, she was born at Goodwood House. At the age of eight she was sent to live with her sister Emily [above] and at fifteen married the wealthy Thomas Conolly. She had no children of her own, but in middle age adopted her two-year-old niece, Emily.

She spent twenty-five years planning and directing the renovation and alteration of her husband's splendid Palladian mansion, Castletown House and its estate in Co. Kildare, the largest and grandest in Ireland. She installed an impressive new staircase, a print room and an eighty-foot long gallery, and had the extensive gardens redesigned (they boasted the biggest vine and the largest cedar in Ireland). A much-loved, hands-on philanthropist, she held fêtes for her servants and local people and hosted numerous charity receptions. She was patron of a myriad causes and in widowhood visited labourers' families in their cottages and built an industrial school for three hundred children, a church, workshops, breweries, bake-shops and a giant press for extracting oil from nuts. She designed every new building herself, using local materials, and where possible always gave work to local people.

Her funeral was attended by hundreds of admirers from all over Ireland. Castletown House now belongs to the government of Eire and is open to the public. [Related image p108.]

GRAFFHAM

GWEN MULLINS OBE née Elizabeth Gwendolen Brandt (1904–1997) artist and founder of Graffham Weavers.

Born into a wealthy family in London, she was taken to and from school in a chauffeur-driven car. A visit to Italy inspired her to study art, and later she attended the London School of Weaving. She married barrister Claud Mullins in 1925 and had three children. During WWII she was a volunteer at an occupational therapy unit, teaching ex-servicemen to weave and to bind books.

In 1948 her family moved to a house called Glasses, in Graffham. Here she founded a bookbinding group, then a village crafts' workshop, in former farm buildings at the end of her garden. She and her daughter Barbara taught pottery, spinning, dyeing, weaving, basket-making and woodwork. They ran week-long summer camps for children and in 1974 Barbara founded the Graffham Branch of the Association of Weavers, Spinners and Dyers. Mrs Mullins founded the Graffham Weavers, which unexpectedly grew into a thriving and profitable cottage industry. Local women became highly skilled and offered training courses; students arrived from art colleges in several countries. Graffham Weavers exhibited their crafts twice a year and received commissions from Worcester Cathedral, the Bishop of Ripon, and Exeter College, Oxford. Knotted, multicoloured rugs were Mrs Mullins's forte, and she exhibited them in London, Paris and Edinburgh.

She founded Craftsman's Mark, to supply spun wool to hand-weavers, and the Gwen Mullins Trust, to help young people set up their own craft studios and workshops. In 1971 she was involved with the establishment of the Crafts Advisory Committee (later the Crafts Council). One of the leading figures in the modern crafts movement, she was appointed OBE in 1975. She died at Midhurst.

FLORENCE NAGLE née Watson (1894–1988) racehorse trainer and feminist.

A baronet's daughter, she was born in Manchester and rebelled against authority at an early age. She held a driving licence at the age of fifteen and was expelled from her finishing school for hiring a car for an outing for which she had not gained permission. She married James Nagle against her parents' wishes, causing them to disown her, and from 1920 the couple bought racehorses and enjoyed some success; however, he gambled their money away and she divorced him in 1928.

In 1934, using an inheritance, she created a stud farm of her own in Berkshire, moving it to Westerlands, Graffham, in 1942. Her first horse, 'Sandsprite', came second in the 1937 Derby, following which she was in great demand as a trainer and notched up an impressive one hundred winners by 1966. Despite this the Jockey Club steadfastly refused to grant her a licence, simply because she was a woman. Her head lad was given a trainer's licence while she, the real trainer, was granted only a stable-lad's pass.

At the age of seventy-one, and at her own expense, Mrs Nagle took the Jockey

Club to the High Court, telling the press: 'I am a feminist and believe that things should be decided on ability and not sex'. She won the case, and she and Norah Wilmot (the Queen's horse-trainer) received their licences in 1966. Her first winner as a licensed trainer was 'Mahwa', which won the Lanes Stakes at Brighton in 1967. Within seven years seventeen women held licences; they had trained over 300 winners since Mrs Nagle had received hers.

She had bred Irish wolfhounds since the age of nineteen, and when she was eighty-three she sued the Kennel Club for sex discrimination in refusing women membership. This time, however, she lost. In 1971 she was the subject of a BBC TV documentary. She died at her home, Little Mayfield, Lordings Lane, West Chiltington. [Related image p114.]

ETHEL SCARBOROUGH (1880–1956) composer and social activist.

The daughter of a timber merchant, she was born in London and studied in Berlin and at the RAM. She became a prolific composer, producing orchestral and choral works, piano concertos, a symphony, piano music and song cycles. She was among the first women to conduct her own works, which she did between 1909 and 1925, when she became involved in Labour politics.

After presenting a petition containing 40,000 signatures asking the Board of Trade to reopen the steel works at Ebbw Vale, she stood for election against Aneurin Bevan and wrote and printed election songs. She participated in the famous Jarrow March against unemployment in 1936 and during WWII was chairman of Barnet Council. On the side she composed songs for BBC *Children's Hour*.

She died at Quiet Court, a very isolated cottage north-west of Graffham, where she had lived for some years. She had drawn up an extraordinary will: her sister could live in the house until her own death, then it was to be used by 'the Senior Woman Member of the Ministry of the Government in order that she may have a retreat in which to refresh her spirit, to learn of the trees and to listen greatly to herself'. In 1958 a court judged the gift 'void for uncertainty' because it was impossible to define 'senior', which might mean the oldest, the highest in rank, or the longest serving.

GREATHAM

ALICE MEYNELL FRSL née Thompson (1847–1922) poet, editor and suffragist.

Born in Surrey and raised in England, Switzerland, France and Italy, she converted to Roman Catholicism at nineteen. Her first collection of poetry was published as *Preludes* in 1875 and was well reviewed. Hordes of men fell hopelessly in love with her, and at thirty she chose one to marry: publisher Wilfrid Meynell. They had eight children in fourteen years and supported them solely from their literary earnings. As well as owning and editing *The Pen, The Weekly Register* and *Merry England* they wrote articles for top periodicals, including a weekly column in the *Pall Mall Gazette*. She produced six volumes of essays and several books, including one on Ruskin and another on Holman Hunt. In 1895 she was considered for the post of Poet Laureate and in 1914 was elected a member of the committee of the Royal Society of Literature.

Retaining a London residence, in 1911 the Meynells bought Humphrey's Homestead at Greatham, an eighty-acre estate with six houses. The estate became a literary Mecca visited by many well-known writers including Eleanor Farjeon [230] and Cynthia Asquith [85]. Other guests included Wilfred Blunt [see Lady Anne Blunt, 92] and her husband's niece, Esther Meynell [205].

Alive Meynell was a devoted feminist. She campaigned for the registration of nurses, was prominent in the Women Writers' Suffrage League and the NUWSS and once shared a speaking platform at the Royal Albert Hall with six other suffragists featured in this book. She died in London, where she was buried and where she has a blue plaque. Humphrey's is still in the Meynell family.

Further reading: Meynell, V. (1929) *Alice Meynell*. [Related image p16.]

VIOLA MEYNELL (1885–1956) writer.

The daughter of Alice [52] and cousin of Gerard, who married Esther Moorhouse [205], she was born in London and had written two novels by the time her parents bought Humphrey's Homestead in Greatham when she was twenty-six. She and her brother created self-published books by hand on the kitchen table; later he co-founded the Nonesuch Press with David Garnett, son of Constance [132]. When D.H. Lawrence lived with the family for six months in 1915, she typed his manuscripts; he later wrote *England my England,* a rather unkind story based on her family. After a few romances and a couple of broken engagements, she married Johnny Dallyn, a local farmer, had a son in 1922 and separated in 1929; as a Catholic, she could not divorce. She lived in London for six years, and in 1935 returned to Greatham to care for her widowed, elderly father. Her close friend Cynthia Asquith [85] moved to Storrington to be near her.

Viola Meynell was a reviewer, journalist and editor, wrote forty short stories and twelve novels, published a memoir of her mother in 1929 and of her father in 1952, and edited *The Letters of J.M. Barrie* (1942). Her masterpiece, *Follow Thy Fair Sun* (1935) was reprinted as *Lovers* in 1944 and her final novel, *Ophelia,* appeared in 1951. She died at home while working on a volume of collected stories, and was buried at the Catholic cemetery in Houghton. [Related image p116.]

HASSOCKS

KATHARINE JEX-BLAKE (1860–1951) classical scholar and college head.

A niece of Sophia Jex-Blake [236], she received an unusually superior education for a girl because, as one of the nine daughters of the headmaster of Rugby School, she was educated by its masters. She studied at Girton from 1879, spent a year teaching at Notting Hill High School, then returned to Girton as a classics lecturer. She was promoted to director of studies in classics, then to vice-mistress, and by 1916 was the mistress (i.e. head). By the time

she retired in 1922 the classics lecturers at six women's colleges (Girton, Newnham, Bedford, Royal Holloway, Somerville, and Lady Margaret Hall) had been her students. She conducted preparations for the college to receive its Royal Charter, retiring two years before the event and leaving a Jex-Blake Scholarship in her wake.

In the 1930s and 1940s she and her sister Henrietta, former head of Lady Margaret Hall, shared a home in Kent. She later moved to Nettlesworth, 76 Wickham Hill, Hassocks, where she died.

MABEL PHILIPSON MP née Russell (1887–1951) actress and politician.

Born into a working class family in south London, her mother died when she was eleven. Her father, a commercial traveller, opposed her desire to become an actress. Nevertheless, she rose from box office clerk to gaiety girl to musical-comedy performer to serious actress, despite losing an eye in a car crash that killed her first husband Stanley Rhodes in 1911, shortly after their wedding.

Her second husband, Hilton Philipson, became National Liberal MP for Berwick-on-Tweed in 1922. Owing to a fraud by his agent he was unseated and banned for seven years. She agreed to stand in his place, but would do so only as a Conservative candidate. She won with a much larger majority, snatching a seat the Liberals had held for thirty-six years and became the third woman — and the first actress — to sit in the House of Commons. The first, Nancy, Lady Astor, brought in a Bill prohibiting the sale of alcohol to minors; the second, Mrs Wintringham, had been recently widowed and therefore made no speeches. After Mrs Philipson's election this limerick did the rounds:

Lady Astor, MP, for sobriety
Mrs Wintringham; she's for propriety
Now Berwick-on-Tweed
With all speed has decreed
Mrs Philipson wins — for Variety!

Some people scorned her because they assumed that, as an actress, she was ignorant of politics, but her humble background gave her a special connection with her poor constituents and, as the mother of three children, she was particularly interested in the Adoption, Legitimacy and Guardianship of Infants Act that came before the House in 1927. She introduced the Nursing Homes Registration Act 1927 and asked some pertinent questions about the status of female civil servants. However, when forced to choose, she put party ahead of sisterhood and voted against women getting the vote at twenty-one (instead of thirty) because her colleagues believed it would be against party interests [293].

During her time in office she became the first woman member of the Air Committee and the first woman to join a parliamentary delegation to Italy, where she met both the Pope and Mussolini. She drew enormous criticism for performing in a musical in 1927 but nevertheless was offered the post of Minister of Health the following year. She would have been the first female cabinet minister, but declined the post because of her husband: since his ban was lifted he had twice tried and failed to get re-elected; she felt that taking promotion would damage his ego.

She stood down from her position as MP in 1929 and, returning to the West End stage, performed for five more years before retiring to spend the remainder of her life in Sussex. By 1935 she was living at Limberlost, Ockley Lane, Hassocks. Widowed in 1941, she moved in 1949 to 63 Westfield Avenue, Rottingdean. She died at Methuen Manor Nursing Home, 3 Harrington Road, Preston, Brighton, and her funeral was held at Ditchling parish church.

Further reading: Sleight, J. (1986) *Women on the March.*

HAYWARDS HEATH

SISTER MARY BARBARA VERNON BAILEY (1910–2003) creator of 'Bunnykins'.

As a child in Shropshire she sketched the wild rabbits around her home, was educated by a governess then boarded at Our Lady's Priory convent school at Haywards Heath. After training as a nurse she became a nun and teacher at the convent and was professed a canoness regular of the Lateran (Augustinian) Order in 1933.

In 1934 her father, general manager of Royal Doulton, asked her to create some rabbit illustrations for a proposed new range of children's tableware. The prioress permitted this, but reluctantly and with conditions: there must be no financial gain, and she must work in secret. After teaching six history lessons each day, and marking, she would work in her cell until late at night, drawing and painting by candlelight (the convent had no electricity). She depicted rabbits gardening, cuddling, picnicking, fishing, bathing, dressing, playing golf, dancing in the moonlight, riding on dodgems and cooking. Each piece was signed 'Barbara Vernon', to dissociate herself from her father.

Within a year her 'Bunnykins' tableware was all the rage among the middle-classes, the aristocracy and the royal families of Japan and Britain: Princesses Elizabeth and Margaret ate from Bunnykins plates. Her designs were so popular that Doulton ceased production of all other animal ranges. In five years she supplied over a thousand images, then other artists took over her work. The range continues today, though it is now manufactured in China.

In the 1970s the convent school was compulsorily purchased and the nuns moved to the Priory of Our Lady, Sayers Common, where she produced a series of children's prayer books. After she died, at Haywards Heath, a radio documentary called *The Bunnykins Business* was broadcast and Royal Doulton created a four-and-a-quarter-inch figurine to be sold in aid of her convent. The piece depicts Sister Mary Barbara as a rabbit in a nun's habit drawing at a desk by candlelight.

There are Bunnykins collectors' clubs and societies all over the world, which hold conferences and publish newsletters. Each original design signed by her is now a highly sought-after collectors' item.

MOTHER ELIZABETH NEALE (1822–1901) founder, Community of the Holy Cross.

She left her native Middlesex as a child and was raised by her widowed mother in Brighton, where she helped run a small orphanage for girls in the parish of St Paul's. In 1857 she established the Community of the Holy Cross, an Anglican sisterhood performing missionary work — including rescuing prostitutes — in the rough streets of London's East End.

In 1887 she wrote *Community of the Holy Cross: A Short Account of its Rise and History,* and the community built a convent at Haywards Heath, where she was mother superior until 1896. She died there and was buried, initially at St Wilfrid's churchyard, then reinterred in the community's burial ground in 1957.

DR (MAY DORIS) CHARITY TAYLOR née Clifford; Lady Taylor (1914–1998) pioneering prison governor.

A Surrey-born graduate of the LSMW, in 1942 she became the first female medical officer within Her Majesty's Prison Service when she was appointed at Holloway, the largest women's prison in Britain. She married Dr Stephen Taylor in 1939 and in 1945 became Britain's first female prison governor. They moved into staff quarters inside Holloway, where she raised three children. During her fourteen-year tenure she made numerous and pioneering improvements to prisoners' welfare, allowing them budgerigars, a goat and an aquarium, and introducing classes in first aid, literature and gardening. She also ended the inhumane practice of removing from their mothers any babies born in prison. Her worst experience was overseeing the execution of Ruth Ellis in 1955, the last woman hanged in Britain. In 1959 she became head and inspector of all women's prisons.

She was a member of the Suffragette Fellowship, many of whose members had once been prisoners in Holloway. She gave lectures on BBC radio and served on the General Advisory Council of the BBC from 1964 until 1967. Taking early retirement she lived for six years in Canada, where her husband, a Labour MP (and later, a life peer) had landed a job and where she was president of the Social Welfare Council (1968–71). They returned to Britain in 1973 and lived in Wales, where her husband died in 1988. Lady Taylor then moved to somewhere in Sussex and died at the Princess Royal Hospital, Haywards Heath.

HENFIELD

MARJORIE BAKER (1912–2004) photographer of Sussex life.

A butcher's daughter, she was born in Henfield and educated at Steyne School, Worthing, the town in which she later served her apprenticeship with London photographer Margaret Ellsmoor at her studio at Onslow House. Her career began in 1932 with a commission from Earl Winterton, MP for Horsham. In 1938 she bought a converted coach house in Park Road, Henfield, where she created a workroom, studio and darkroom that served as her workplace for the rest of her life.

She married Stephen Tidey in 1940 and while he was on military service continued her work, capturing images of servicemen and the WLA. After the war she had to employ four assistants to keep up with the demand for wedding and portrait photography. The couple had a house built adjacent to the studio, where she raised two sons and amassed a significant collection of images that documented the changes to family life, transport, architecture, carnivals, clothing, agriculture and industry over five decades.

When she retired, aged eighty-four, she and the curator of Henfield Museum set about cataloguing her work. She gained a wide audience when Horsham Museum used her images in a 2001 exhibition called 'Roadmender Country', after the book *The Roadmender*, written in Henfield by Margaret Fairless Barber [below]. This provoked widespread interest and a four-page spread appeared in *Country Life* magazine. Her photographs drew considerable praise and were described in the *Guardian* as 'masterpieces of technical, visual and dramatic art'. Thousands of her negatives are held at Henfield Museum for use in local events, while two hundred are at Horsham Museum. She died in Henfield.

MARGARET FAIRLESS BARBER pseudonym Michael Fairless; adopted name Dowson (1869–1901) religious writer.

The daughter of an attorney, she was born in Yorkshire and raised in Devon and Suffolk. She trained as a nurse and worked in the East End slums until her health failed (she was thought to have a weak spine), then took up writing under a male pseudonym. Increasingly physically infirm, she was adopted by Mary Dowson [below] and her husband, who cared for her for the remainder of her short life.

Her first book, *The Gathering of Brother Hilarius*, published the year she died, was a religious romance centering on the Black Death, but the work that brought her fame (albeit posthumous) was *The Roadmender* (1902), a popular and influential book that was reprinted thirty-one times in ten years, sold 250,000 copies in twenty years, was cited as providing a new philosophy of life to countless people and gave the nickname 'Roadmender Country' to the area between Horsham and the sea. She wrote it while living at the Dowsons' home, Mock Bridge House (later called Mercer's) between Henfield and Shermanbury. She died there and was buried at St James's churchyard, Ashurst, as Margaret Fairless Dowson. [Related image p110.]

MARY DOWSON MD née Tee; pseudonym William Scott Palmer (1848–1941) surgeon and author.

One of six children of a prosperous wool merchant, she was born in Yorkshire. In 1872 she married engineer Joseph Dowson, with whom she had two daughters (in 1874 and 1878). She studied at the LSMW and gained her LKQCPI in 1884. Two years later became the first female surgeon to qualify in Great Britain when, after four days of exams, she was invested by the Irish College of Surgeons in June 1886.

Living in Chelsea, London, she was lecturer in forensic medicine and hygiene at the LSMW, where she expounded her belief in holistic medicine, reminding students that patients were not 'a patchwork of signs and symptoms' but an organic whole.

She became interested in spiritual matters and the Roman Catholic modernist movement. In the 1890s she and her husband unofficially adopted religious writer Margaret Fairless Barber [above], who died just before finishing *The Roadmender*, written at Mock Bridge House, the Dowsons' second home near Henfield. Mary Dowson edited the final chapter and handled the book's publication. She later wrote several magazine articles and books under a male pseudonym, among them *An Agnostic's Progress* (1906) and *A Modern Mystic's Way* (1914), and co-wrote *Michael Fairless: Her Life and Writings* (1914, reprinted 1977) which was illustrated by her daughter Elinor. Widowed in 1940, she died at her home, Landhurst Shaw, Hartfield.

ELIZABETH ROBINS (1862–1952) actress, writer and feminist.

Born in the USA, she was educated at a ladies' seminary and, after beginning to study medicine, changed her mind and became an actress. She also wrote, under the names C.E. Raimond or Elizabeth Parks (a surname acquired by her brief marriage to George Parks, which was ended by his suicide). She moved to England in 1888, learned Norwegian, and by 1891 had become well known in theatrical circles for translating, producing and starring in the plays of Ibsen.

When she was in her mid-forties she left the theatre and joined the women's suffrage movement, to which she dedicated herself for several years. She was an activist within the AFL, served on the executive of the WSPU for five years from 1907 and was president of the Women Writers' Suffrage League. Although she would not participate in violent action, she took part in census resistance [294] and put her performance skills to good use as an effective public speaker for the campaign. She also wrote a related novel, *The Convert* (1907), a play, *Votes for Women!* (1907) and a suffrage history, *Way Stations* (1913). All royalties from the play were donated to the suffrage movement.

In 1909, using the profits from *The Convert*, she leased (and later purchased) Backset (later, Backsettown) a fifteenth-century farmhouse in a backwater of Henfield, discovered by her friend Mildred Buxton [68], and later acquired the surrounding fields to gain more privacy. She was visited by many suffragettes, including WSPU leading light Christabel Pankhurst, and met Octavia Wilberforce [152], a neighbour at nearby Woodmancote who was to be her close friend for forty years.

In 1927 she let the house to Dr Wilberforce and Dr Marjorie Hubert, who turned it into a convalescent home for women. She kept a rented flat in London but lived mostly at Dr Wilberforce's home, 24 Montpelier Crescent, Brighton, spending time also in the USA and, suffering long-term poor health, in various nursing homes. In the inter-war years Miss Robins took an active part in Henfield Women's Institute, served as chair of the board of directors of the New Sussex Hospital, was director of the feminist periodical *Time and Tide* and a vice-president of the Six Point Group. [301] A friend of Marie Belloc Lowndes [80] and Virginia Woolf [243], she continued to write, mostly under her own name, though her study of male-female relations, *Ancilla's Share: An Indictment of Sex Antagonism* (1924, reprinted 1976) was published anonymously.

When she flew to the USA for the final time at the age of eighty-eight, her travelling companion was Dr Martindale [141]. Two years later she died at 24 Montpelier Crescent. In her long life she had accumulated 102 packing cases of documents, twenty-five immaculate black hats and seventy volumes of diaries (the latter are now at the Elmer Holmes Bobst Library of New York University). Her book *The Magnetic North* was reprinted in 2006.

Further reading: John, A.V. (1995) *Elizabeth Robins: Staging a Life.* [Related images pp176, 300.]

HEYSHOTT

(JULIA) ANNE COBDEN-SANDERSON (1853–1926) social campaigner.

A daughter of radical MP Richard Cobden and sister of Jane [58], she was born in London but raised at Dunford House in Heyshott until she was twelve, when her father died and she was sent to boarding school. Her mother signed the 1866 suffrage petition and Barbara Bodichon [193] was a family friend. She married Thomas Sanderson and both took the hyphenated surname; they had two children.

She spent her life in the service of socialism, pacifism, feminism, vegetarianism and theosophism, campaigned for poor children and the unemployed, founded the Doves Press and was a member of the Labour Party. In the 1880s she gave a course of lectures on 'Openings for Women', detailing some unusual professions. In her fifties she joined the WSPU, then the WFL. She co-founded the TRL and led the famous Black Friday march [294]. Arrested three times, once with Dora Montefiore [226], she gave her occupation as 'worker for liberty'. Her imprisonment in Holloway, as the daughter of a highly respected and eminent statesman, brought huge publicity to the movement and shame upon the government.

In later life she was a poor law guardian in London, where she died. Sir Nigel Playfair (a resident of Hastings) founded the Anne Cobden-Sanderson Fund to continue her philanthropic work.

K.M. ELISABETH MURRAY FRHS (1909–1998) historian and archaeologist.

The niece of Hilda Murray [62], she was born in Cambridge, studied history at Somerville and gained a BLitt at Oxford in 1933; her thesis was published as *The Constitutional History of the Cinque Ports*. She went to the British School of Archaeology in Jerusalem and participated in excavations in Samaria. On her return she held various lecturing posts at Manchester University, Somerville and Girton. She published the *Kent Record Society Register of Daniel Rough* in 1945, contributed learned articles to academic journals and was a Fellow of the Royal Historical Society and the Society of Antiquities.

From 1948 she was principal of Bishop Otter College, Chichester. She moved in with her father at Heyshott and stayed in the locality for the next fifty years. Under her leadership the college changed radically, became co-educational, began an important collection of modern art and grew to accommodate 700 students. It is now part of the University of Chichester.

After retiring in 1970 she served on Chichester District Council (1973–87). As chairman of its Planning Committee (1979–82), she brought about the restoration of Pallant House and its development into an art gallery. She served on the Sussex Historic Churches Trust and the Society of Sussex Downsmen, and was chairman (1964–77) and president (1977–80) of the Sussex Archaeological Society. She helped organise excavations at Bignor and Fishbourne Palace and her love of nature led her to found the Downland Murray Trust to preserve a conservation area. Her semi-secret passion was her magnificent and elaborate dolls' house, for which she even wrote tiny books to place in its library.

At the age of nearly seventy she gained international renown for her book *Caught in the Web of Words* (1977), a biography of her grandfather Sir James Murray, founding editor of the *Oxford English Dictionary*. It took her five years to write and two to get published. Rejected by the Oxford University Press, it was later described as 'one of the finest biographies of the twentieth century', sold well and was reprinted in 2001.

She died at Pendean Nursing Home, Oaklands Lane, West Lavington, was cremated at Chichester and buried at St James's churchyard, Heyshott.

Further reading: Chichester Institute of Higher Education, Otter Memorial Paper no. 12 (1998) *Flints, Ports, Otters and Threads: a Tribute to K. M. Elisabeth Murray*.

DIANA POULTON (1903–1995) lutenist and biographer.

Born in Storrington (her maiden name is unknown), she studied at the Slade School of Fine Art and was taught the lute by Arnold Dolmetsch. She became one of the first professional lutenists of the twentieth century and performed on radio, at festivals, concerts and the V & A as both a soloist and in ensembles.

On the formation of the Lute Society in 1956 she was elected its chairman, and subsequently its president. In 1971 she was appointed the first professor of the lute at the RCM. She published books, sheet music and articles on lute technique and in 1972 wrote a biography of John Dowland. She married Thomas Poulton and from at least 1950 they lived at Laurel Cottage, Heyshott, a little thatched residence with beautiful gardens where she kept goats and made cheese. She died at Heyshott and her papers are lodged at the RAM.

(EMMA) JANE COBDEN UNWIN (1851–1947) social campaigner.

The elder daughter of radical MP and statesman Richard Cobden and sister of Anne Cobden-Sanderson [57], she was born in London and raised at Dunford House, Heyshott, until she was fourteen. From the 1870s she was an activist in the women's suffrage movement, serving as treasurer, delegate and speaker in various societies over many years. During the revival of the movement in the Edwardian era she joined the TRL and the WSPU, and served as honorary president of Brighton Women's Liberal Association and vice-president of the NUWSS.

She was one of the first three women elected to the LCC when it was created in 1889, but two years later, after a writ was filed by a Mr de Souza, her participation was deemed invalid because she was a woman. The controversy was widely reported and debated. (A century later her portrait, which hung for years in the LCC committee room, was cut from its frame and stolen.)

In 1892, at St James's Church, Heyshott, she married publisher Thomas Fisher Unwin, whose two brothers married sisters of Mrs Martindale [141]. They had a home in Kensington and another, Oatscroft, an eighteenth-century house in the grounds of her childhood home, which she had inherited. She presented Dunford House to the LSE in 1919. In 1923 she bought it back and sold it, and the LSE used the money to build its Cobden Library in honour of her father. She co-founded both the Cobden Club and Heyshott Working Men's Club and Coffee House, and devoted years to the complex task of sorting out her father's papers before donating them to the British Museum.

She was involved in campaigns concerning Irish Home Rule, the Boer War, strikers' wives, Arab women, Aborigines, and slavery. Widowed in 1935, she remained at Oatscroft, opening her gardens to the public each summer, until infirmity forced her to enter Whitehanger Nursing Home, Fernhurst [49], where she died. The University of Bristol holds her papers. Dunford House is now a YMCA conference centre.

HIGH SALVINGTON

NANCY PRICE CBE (1880–1970) actress, director, author and campaigner.

A Worcestershire lass, her desire to go on the stage was opposed by her father; however, while still at school she successfully auditioned for a Shakespearean role at the Theatre Royal, Birmingham. She married actor Charles Maude in 1907 and had two daughters. The couple separated and she bought Arcana, Heather Lane, High Salvington, where she lived from before 1914 until the 1960s, making friends with shepherds, gypsies and other locals including Margot Douglas, secretary of Worthing WSPU, who lived at The Cottage, Honeysuckle Lane.

By the 1920s she was established as a leading lady in the West End and had appeared in several films, both silent and 'talkie'. In 1930 she co-founded the Peoples' National Theatre, which staged eighty-two plays in twenty years. In one, *Whiteoaks*, she gave a 'shrewd and vigorous' performance with her parrot, Boney, perched on her shoulder. She was also a writer, director and producer of films and plays. In 1938 she directed Mabel Constanduros [90] in *The Shoemaker's Holiday* and she wrote and starred in the film *The Three Weird Sisters* in 1948. In addition she produced more than twenty books, which were popular and widely-read. One, *Ta-Mera*, was described as 'a brilliant novel ... full of the mysticism of Ancient Egypt'. She knew everyone in the theatrical and literary worlds and had friends in high places across Europe. She was acquainted with Queen Mary and Mussolini and once met Ethiopian Emperor Haile Selassie in a railway carriage.

Despite her busy career she found time to work on behalf of causes close to her heart: war charities, the blind, the countryside and animal welfare. In 1938 she founded the Downland Trust Appeal to raise money to buy The Sanctuary, almost sixty acres of rural land on the south-west slopes of High Salvington (including Honeysuckle Lane) to prevent its being sold to a house-builder. Using the catchphrase 'Save the Downs' she organised a fundraising variety matinée at London's Playhouse Theatre. Rather astutely, she invited Queen Mary, which meant she could charge handsomely for the tickets. Among the all-star cast were local residents Elsie and Doris Waters [84], former actor-manager Cyril Maude, widower of Winifred Emery [235] and Miss Price herself, reciting poetry that eulogised Sussex. A photograph of her presenting Queen Mary with a posy appeared in *The Times* the next day. The Duke of Norfolk agreed to attend a similar event at the Connaught Theatre, Worthing, which raised £1,000, and local people chipped in with small amounts; a taxi driver once pressed a half-crown into her hand 'for the fund'. She and Miss Douglas eventually raised £6,000, to which Worthing Council added £7,000, and the land was bought for £13,000.

During WWI she had served on a North Sea minesweeper; during WWII she was in her sixties and stayed at home. After a German Dornier bomber crashed near her house she invited the pilot (the sole survivor) in for coffee before handing him over to the authorities. Later he sent her a thank-you note.

She was appointed CBE in 1950 and, to mark her seventieth birthday, a seat bearing the inscription 'Tribute to Nancy Price CBE, actress, authoress, humanitarian' was unveiled on the Downs. After retiring in 1952, at the age of seventy-two, she edited a theatre magazine, *Pedlar's Pack*. She devoted herself full-time to her passion for animals, nature and the countryside, co-founded the Council of Justice to Animals and placed a memorial stone at Beach House Park to commemorate 'Warrior birds who gave their lives on active service 1939–45'. In 1957 she wrote *I Watch and Listen: A Book Mainly Concerned with the Courtship and Song of Birds.*

She died at 145 Rowlands Road, Worthing, where she had lived for at least five years, and her funeral was at the thirteenth-century church of St Mary the Virgin at nearby Clapham. Her papers are held at the West Sussex Record Office. Her daughter Joan Maude [234] became an actress. [Related plate 43.]

EDITH MARGARET WATSON CVO, CBE (1883–1953) pioneering civil servant.

The daughter of the surveyor to the Board of Trade, she was born in Birkenhead and joined the civil service as a typist in Whitehall. She made history in 1914 when she was summoned into the private office of Andrew Bonar Law, Secretary of State for the Colonies, to take dictation, work that hitherto had been reserved exclusively for men. In 1915 he promoted her to assistant private secretary, the first woman ever to hold that rank. She continued to serve him during his career as Chancellor of the Exchequer, Leader of the House, Lord Privy Seal and Prime Minister. About 1923 his successor Stanley Baldwin promoted her to private secretary, the highest position ever held by a female civil servant. She retained the post through the premierships of MacDonald, Chamberlain, Churchill and Attlee.

Appointed CBE in 1919 and Commander of the Royal Victorian Order (CVO) in 1937, she retired to The Cottage, West Way, off Salvington Hill, in 1945, where she died eight years later. She remains the only person to have been private secretary to six prime ministers.

HORSHAM

HELEN CORDELIA ANGELL (née Coleman) (1847–1884) artist.

One of twelve children of a physician, she was born in Horsham and grew up in North Street. Her artist brother William employed her and their sister Rebecca to design and execute paintings on pottery.

In 1874 she married a man twenty-four years her senior, with whom she lived in an opulent house in Kensington, looked after by plenty of servants. She became widely renowned for her watercolour studies of flowers, fruit and tropical birds. After her tragically early death, at the age of just thirty-seven, *The Times* described her as 'one of the most exquisite artists of our time', adding that she had surpassed even the great William Hunt. She was a member of the Watercolour Society, and some of her work is held at the V & A.

ANNIE BETTS (1884–1961) apiculturist.

She was born and raised in Surrey, educated at Farlington House Ladies' School, Haywards Heath, and took an external BSc with the University of London. During WWI she undertook aeronautical research on variable pitch airscrews and joined the Royal Aeronautical Society.

She became highly knowledgeable in the field of apiculture, about which she wrote 145 articles. From 1929 she edited *Bee World* magazine, establishing it as the English-speaking world's leading journal on the subject. She also published several short books: *Practical Bee Anatomy: with Notes on the Embryology, Metamorphoses and Physiology of the Honey Bee* (1923) and *The Diseases of Bees: Their Signs, Causes and Treatment* (1951). From 1935 for many years she lived somewhere in Horsham, but died in Surrey.

ELIZA COOK (1812–1889) poet, balladeer and magazine publisher.

She came to Sussex at the age of nine and was raised on a farm in St Leonard's Forest near Horsham. As an adult she returned to her birthplace, London, cropped her hair, wore men's clothes, drank beer and wrote passionate poems to American actress Charlotte Cushman. Her work was published in magazines and her first volume of poetry, *Lays of a Wild Harp*, appeared in 1835. At first she published as 'E. Cook', but after much public acclaim admitted she was a woman.

Her poems and ballads brought fame on both sides of the Atlantic and her magazine *Eliza Cook's Journal* began publication in Fleet Street in 1849, achieving a circulation of 50,000 before ceasing production in 1854. In its pages she called for more educational and employment opportunities for women and for working class people of both sexes.

In 1864 she was granted a civil-list pension of £100 a year 'in consideration of her literary labours both in poetry and prose'. Copies of *The Poetical Works of Eliza Cook* (1870) are still available secondhand. [Related image p16.]

JOAN EARDLEY (1921–1963) artist.

Born in Warnham, she was raised on her family's dairy farm somewhere near Horsham, but was taken to be raised elsewhere after her father's suicide in 1928. After studying at Goldsmiths' College, London, she attended Glasgow School of Art and spent the rest of her life in Scotland. She was elected an Associate of the Royal Scottish Academy in 1955 and a full Academician in 1963. She died in Glasgow. Her beautiful landscapes and seascapes can be seen at the Tate, the Scottish National Gallery of Modern Art and municipal galleries across Britain.

LILIAN FRANKLIN OBE (1882–1955) FANY commandant.

Of wealthy means, she joined the FANY in 1909 and by 1914 was running the organisation jointly with Grace Ashley-Smith. In 1916 a female convoy was formed at Calais under her command to take food and clothing to men on the front line and to transport the dead and wounded. This work was performed in highly dangerous conditions, sometimes under shell-fire. At the end of each day, hungry and exhausted, they slept in tents on the beach. Noted for her courage and unflappable spirit, she was mentioned in dispatches, received Belgian bravery awards and was appointed MBE in 1918 and OBE in 1933. She died at her home, 94 Rushams Road, Horsham.

Further reading: Beardwood, L. (1997) *FANY at the Western Front.*

HORSTED KEYNES

RUTH BIRD (1899–1987) historian.

Her association with Sussex began at age ten, when she was sent from her birthplace, London, to Elstree Grange boarding school in Eastbourne, where she spent eight years. Excelling in the public examinations, she attended Bedford College for five years, gaining a first-class BA with honours and an MA with distinction. She became intensely religious, committing herself to a nun-like existence bordering on poverty, and dedicated her life to teaching and writing history. She co-authored entries on the villages of Humberstone and Knighton for the *Leicestershire Victoria County History* and wrote *The Turbulent London of Richard II* (1949).

From the age of sixty-four she lived in semi-retirement in Horsted Keynes, where she edited the writings of a former rector of St Giles's Church, which were published as *The Journals of Giles More* (1971). She was co-writing a history of the village when she became ill. She died in hospital in Haywards Heath and her ashes were buried in St Giles's churchyard.

BARBARA KAHAN OBE née Langridge (1920–2000) children's welfare worker.

Her father was the stationmaster at Horsted Keynes, where she was born in the station house. She read English at Newnham and social sciences at the LSE and in 1955 married child psychiatrist Dr Vladimir Kahan. She dedicated fifty years of her life to children in care, becoming chair and vice-president of the National Children's Bureau, president of the Association of Children's Officers, deputy chief inspector in the Children's Department of the Home Office and assistant director of social work service. She wrote a number of influential reports, co-authored the 1991 Staffordshire 'Pindown' report, and wrote several books including *Growing Up in Care* (1979). Appointed OBE in 1990, she left her money to a trust to support children in care.

HOUGHTON

EVA COLLET RECKITT (1890–1976) founder of Collet's bookshops.

A member of the family who owned the Reckitt–Colman business empire, she was born in Yorkshire. Around 1901 she and her parents moved to St Leonards, where she joined the Church Socialist League. During WWI she worked in London as a factory welfare officer then for the Labour Research Department. She took a BA in philosophy at University College, became a part-time lecturer, an executive member of the Labour Research Department and editor of its journal, and served on the executive of (the left-wing) Plato Films.

In the 1920s she bought a cottage, The Hollow, Houghton, and joined the Communist Party, remaining an active member for the rest of her life. She was under constant surveillance by MI5: her post was intercepted; her phone calls were monitored; her London homes were routinely searched. National Archives file KV2/1369-1375 of 1929 reveals that, after a quarrel about politics, one of her Houghton neighbours reported Miss Reckitt for 'subversive activities', prompting the Sussex Constabulary to search her home. The file includes a hand-drawn map showing the location of the cottage, to illustrate how its isolation made it unsuitable for constant covert surveillance.

In 1934, using her inheritance, she co-founded the Eva Collet Trust, and Collet's Bookshop at 66 Charing Cross Road. Her primary aim was not to make profits but to encourage, promote and distribute socialist and communist books. Between 1934 and 1976 she also opened a folk record shop, a Russian shop, a Chinese shop, a handicrafts centre, a library supply service, a worldwide export service, the Penguin Bookshop and several more branches of Collet's. By 1975 the business was grossing £2.5m.

The Hollow was her home for about fifty years; she also maintained a pied à terre in London. She died at the Royal Free Hospital, Hampstead, and was cremated at Golders Green. Branches of Collet's closed down one by one and the business went bankrupt in 1993.

IPING

ANNIE GAMMANS FRSA, MP née Paul; Lady Gammans (1898–1989) politician.

Her early life was spent in Hampshire, where she was born, educated and married. She spent some years abroad because her husband was a colonial civil servant; later he became a Conservative MP and while he served as postmaster-general she took care of his constituency work.

He became a baronet in 1955, and when he died two years later she stood in his place, becoming the seventy-first woman to be elected an MP, bringing the number of female MPs to twenty-seven (out of 603). Her limited education and knowledge, coupled with her disinclination to debate, meant she made little mark in parliament or in her constituency of Hornsey, London, and she stood down in 1966.

She retired to her home, Fitzhall, Fitzhall Road, Iping, where she died a millionairess. Her portrait photograph by Bassano is held at the NPG.

KEYMER

CLARE LEIGHTON (1898–1989) engraver.

The daughter of two writers, she was born in London and privately educated until she was seventeen, when the family moved to a rented cottage in Keymer. At first she studied locally, at Brighton College of Art, but moved later to the Slade School of Fine Art and learned wood-engraving at the Central School of Arts and Crafts.

She taught art until the 1920s, when she began to support herself by selling her illustrations to newspapers and magazines for use in books and as prints. In 1930 she gained first prize at the International Engravers' Exhibition at the Art Institute of Chicago and afterwards illustrated several books she had authored, including *Country Matters* (1927) and *The Farmer's Year* (1933). She lived in Buckinghamshire for a while then became a citizen of the USA, where she spent the rest of her life.

KINGSLEY GREEN

HILDA MURRAY (1875–1951) philologist and academic.

A daughter of lexicographer Sir James Murray and aunt of K.M. Elisabeth Murray [57], she was born in London and raised in Oxford. She worked with her father, sorting and alphabetising entries and collecting statistical details for his *Oxford English Dictionary*. As a home student at the university she graduated with first-class honours in English language and literature.

She published the Middle English poem *Erthe upon Erthe* (1911) and an edition of five Aesopian fables by the Scottish poet Robert Henryson (1930).

For sixteen years she was lecturer in Germanic philology at Royal Holloway College, then director of studies and lecturer at Girton, where she was vice-mistress from 1924 until 1936, when she retired and settled with her mother and sister at Sunnyside, Kingsley Green. She died in hospital at 9 College Lane, Chichester and was buried in Fernhurst Cemetery.

LANCING

HERTHA AYRTON née Phoebe Sarah Marks (1854–1923) electrical engineer.

Born in Hampshire, she was sponsored by wealthy women, including Louisa, Lady Goldsmid [209] and Barbara Leigh Smith Bodichon [193], to study maths at Girton. In 1885 she married Professor Ayrton, a widower with a little girl, Edith — who later became Mrs Zangwill [46] — and had a daughter with him, whom she named Barbara Bodichon Ayrton. She joined the suffrage movement in 1872 and became vice-president of the NUWSS.

She constructed a sphygmomanometer (pulse recorder) and invented and patented a line divider. She was the first woman to experiment on the electric arc, about which she wrote a book, and in 1899 was the first woman elected to the Institution of Electrical Engineers. Although she won the Royal Society's Hughes Medal she was, as a married woman, ineligible for membership.

In middle age she joined the WSPU, marched in processions and took part in deputations. Her London home was used for convalescence by Emmeline Pankhurst and other leading suffragettes recovering from the effects of hunger strikes and force feeding. A member of the TRL, she laundered WSPU money and harboured forty suffragettes on census night. She donated most of the money left to her by Mme Bodichon to the WSPU and similar organisations.

During WWI she patented anti-aircraft searchlights and arc lamp technology, and invented the Ayrton Fan, over 100,000 of which were used in the trenches in WWI to dispel poison gas. She died of blood poisoning at a friend's home, New Cottage, North Lancing, after being bitten by an insect. Two years after her death her friend Ottilie Hancock endowed the Hertha Ayrton Research Fellowship at Girton College. [Related image p16.]

LITTLEHAMPTON

CICELY HALE (1884–1981) suffragette.

A doctor's daughter, she was born in London and educated by governesses. For six years she served as information officer for the WSPU, organising stewards for rallies and helping to typeset the outlawed *Suffragette* newspaper in various secret locations [see Rachel Barrett, 47]. When the vote was won she spent sixteen years as a social worker and nine years as a journalist on child-care matters for *Woman's Own*. For twenty years she was division secretary of Arun Valley Girl Guides.

She cohabited with women friends all her adult life; firstly Elizabeth Gordon, then with 'one of the pioneer policewomen' (unnamed). From 1934 she lived at 42 South Terrace, Littlehampton, spent a few years in Oxford, then returned to live at 40a South Terrace until 1953, when she moved to 10 Southlands Court. In 1973, aged eighty-nine, she published *A Good Long Time*, a memoir of her part in the women's suffrage movement, and suddenly found herself in great demand by television and radio, schools and societies to talk about the campaign. Copies of her autobiography are available secondhand.

(CLARA) MARY NEAL CBE, JP (1860–1944) folk-dance revivalist and social reformer.

A native of the West Midlands, where she studied economics at Birmingham Ladies' College, her family moved to Bournemouth, Hampshire. She read about the conditions of the poor in London and at twenty-eight joined the Methodist West London Mission to help underprivileged girls. There she met Emmeline Pethick (later Lady Pethick-Lawrence), with whom in 1895 she founded the Espérance Girls' Club and, in 1897, a dressmaking and tailoring co-operative, Maison Espérance, employing young women at fair wages. In 1900 she established the Green Lady Hostel in East Street, Littlehampton, as a holiday home for the workers. It was purchased on a mortgage in the names of the Hon. Lily Montagu (a Jewish philanthropist) and Emmeline Pethick, and accommodated sixty working-class London girls at a time for a fortnight's holiday. The railway company helped by giving each girl a reduction of 7s 6d off the fare.

Miss Neal formed the Association for the Revival and Practice of Folk Music (later the Espérance Guild of Morris Dancers). She obtained songs from Cecil Sharp, dance steps from William Kimber and tuition from a troupe of traditional dancers. Soon her girls were performing publicly and teaching all over Britain.

In 1906 she took the minutes at the inaugural meeting of the London branch of the WSPU, held at the home of Sylvia Pankhurst, whose mother Emmeline had founded the organisation. Elizabeth Robins [56] was also present. Mary Neal served on the national committee of the WSPU, started a branch at the Espérance Club and joined the United Suffragists and the TRL. Already in her fifties, she took no part in militant activity, though she was noted for her 'witty and racy' speeches. She also wrote articles for *Votes for Women*, *The Times*, the *Pall Mall Gazette* and the *Observer*.

The Earl of Lytton's daughter, Lady Constance, gave the Espérance dancers a massive donation of £1,000 in 1908 and was invited to Littlehampton, where she met the leading lights of the WSPU. She became one of the most famous suffragettes: the imprisonment and force-feeding of the daughter of a highly-respected and noble statesman brought unprecedented publicity to the movement and ignominy upon the government. The hostel, its garden and the historic meeting were depicted in the 1974 TV series *Shoulder to Shoulder*.

In 1910 Cecil Sharp and Mary Neal fell out: he felt she was popularising folk dancing without observing historical

accuracy; moreover he disapproved of his sister Evelyn's involvement with the suffragettes and resented his dances being used in their events. He excluded the Espérance Club from his book on morris-dancers (about which Miss Neal later wrote two volumes of her own). When she and her troupe arrived in the USA to fulfil a busy programme of engagements they discovered he had cancelled them and in her absence from England he stole her domestic bookings. Their feud continued until the war started in 1914, with angry letters appearing in the national press.

During WWI she worked as a pensions administrator then devoted herself to raising her adopted son, Anthony MacIlwaine. In 1925 they moved to 31 St Flora's Road, Littlehampton; by 1940 they had moved to Green Bushes, Rustington. She was a magistrate for twelve years and a member of the Howard League for Penal Reform. Her CBE in 1937 was for services to the folk song and dance revival. In 1940, aged eighty and in fear of being bombed in her south coast home, she accepted an invitation to stay with the Pethick-Lawrences in Surrey and remained for four years. She died at Shere and was cremated in Woking. In Islington there is a women's Morris side named New Espérance in her honour and she has two blue plaques in Littlehampton. Her *Espérance Morris Book* can be bought secondhand for around £60. The Green Lady Hostel is now the Ormsby Centre. [Related images pp105, 114.]

DAME ANITA RODDICK DBE née Perella (1942–2007) founder of the Body Shop.

She was born in Littlehampton to an Italian-Jewish immigrant family who ran various catering enterprises including a café at 17 Surrey Street. Her parents divorced in 1950 and her mother married her ex's cousin who, she later discovered, was her biological father. She attended St Joseph's Convent and Maude Allen Secondary Modern, where she later taught English and history. She worked in Paris and Geneva and visited Africa, the Far East and the Pacific.

In her mother's club at Littlehampton she met Gordon Roddick. She had a daughter and was expecting another when they married. They opened a restaurant called Paddington's and an eight-bedroom hotel, Woodlands Corner, in St Winefride's Road. While her husband spent two years riding on horseback from Buenos Aires to New York, to support herself, the children and the mortgage, in 1976 Mrs Roddick opened a toiletries shop, The Body Shop, between two funeral directors at 22 Kensington Gardens, Brighton. The potions were concocted in her kitchen and were made of natural ingredients not tested on animals. She sold half the business to raise money for a second shop, in Chichester. When her husband returned, he took over the finances and suggested franchising. The business went public in 1984 and by the nineties she was the fourth richest woman in Britain, with 2,100 outlets in fifty-five countries.

Mrs Roddick became equally famous for campaigning for the environment, Fair Trade, pacifism and human rights. She was involved in hundreds of causes, including the Chichester-based charity Children on the Edge. She resigned as chief executive and sold The Body Shop to the multinational L'Oréal for £625m, of which she and her husband received £130m. This money, plus another £50m of her own, was destined for charitable causes via her Roddick Foundation (founded 1990), whose HQ was at Watersmead Business Park, Littlehampton, home also of her manufacturing plant.

Appointed OBE in 1988 and DBE in 2003, she lived at Highfield House, Baycombe Lane, Slindon, and died in St Richard's Hospital, Chichester. She left nothing to her daughters, preferring to give all her wealth to charity and letting them make their own way in the world.

LODSWORTH

MARY COLLIER (*bap* 1688–1762) poet and early feminist.

Born and raised in Lodsworth, she was taught to read and write but, when her mother died, leaving her to support her infirm father, she worked as a labourer. She left Sussex in her thirties after her father died, crossing the border to Hampshire, where she scraped a living as a brewer and laundress in Petersfield. Reading a poem called *The Thresher's Labour* by Stephen Duck, she was incensed at his assertion that rural women had an easier life than men. In 1739 she self-published a riposte in poem form: *The Woman's Labour: an Epistle to Mr Stephen Duck*, which, she said, was intended 'to call an Army of Amazons to vindicate the injured sex'.

Aged sixty-three she took a post as housekeeper at a farm in Alton, Hants. Shortly before her death she self-published *Poems on Several Occasions*, supported by public subscription, the preface to which contains all that is known about her life.

Further reading: The University of Saskatchewan, Canada, has lately published the whole of *The Woman's Labour* on its website.

BARBARA WARD Baroness Jackson of Lodsworth (1914–1981) journalist and economist.

Raised as a Roman Catholic, she was born in Yorkshire and studied at Somerville, graduating with first-class honours in politics and economics. During WWII she assisted Jewish refugees and worked for the Ministry of Information, then became assistant editor of *The Economist*. She lectured in many countries and wrote several books on politics and economics, including the influential *Home of Man, Spaceship Earth* and *Rich Nations, Poor Nations*. The recipient of a clutch of honorary degrees, fellowships and awards, in 1971 she became the first woman to address a synod of Roman Catholic bishops. She was a regular on the radio programme *The Brains Trust* and a governor of the BBC.

She married Robert Jackson, but did not take his name, nor the title Lady Jackson when he was knighted in 1956, the year their son was born; they separated in 1973. She retired to The Pound House, Lodsworth, and was appointed DBE in 1974, being raised to the peerage as Baroness Jackson of Lodsworth in 1976. She died at home, her requiem mass was held in the local Roman Catholic church and she was buried in the local parish graveyard.

LOWER BEEDING

LOUISA MARIA HUBBARD (1836–1906) women's campaigner.

She was brought to Sussex from her birthplace, Russia, at the age of seven and lived at Leonardslee for most of her life; her father demolished and rebuilt the mansion in 1855. In 1876 her sister Marion married Sir Edmund Giles Loder, who bought the Leonardslee estate from his in-laws in 1889 and developed the beautiful gardens, now owned by the National Trust.

Louisa Hubbard was of independent means, but she spent a lifetime campaigning on behalf of middle-class women who were obliged to work for a living but found no careers open to them and ended up filling lowly positions as governesses. In 1873 she founded a teacher-training facility in Chichester on the site of a former men's college. Bishop Otter's Memorial Training College for Ladies was intended to meet the demand for schoolmistresses which followed the 1870 Education Act. Later she founded the Women's Emigration Society and in 1889 Court Work and Leisure, a sickness-insurance society for working women. She also helped to establish the NUWW in 1895 and was the major benefactor of the Gentlewomen's Employment Club.

She published many related books, such as *Work for Ladies in Elementary Schools* and *A Guide to All Institutions for the Benefit of Women*. She edited *Work and Leisure* magazine, the *Women's Gazette* and *The Handbook of Women's Work*, later called *The Englishwoman's Yearbook* [see Emily Janes, 226]. These influenced attitudes towards career women and spawned many societies for teaching, nursing, gardening, midwifery, emigration and ecumenical work. To solve the problem of where career women might live, dine and socialise in London, in the 1880s she supported the Ladies' Dwellings Company Ltd. A close friend and ally of Rosalind Paget [36], in 1881 she founded the organisation that later became the Royal College of Midwives. At the time, midwifery was not considered 'decent' and she regretted having to use the term 'midwife', because: 'It would be so awkward if we used it just when the fooman came in to put on the coals'. Years ahead of her time, she wanted women to hold official positions within the church, and published *Anglican Deaconesses: Is There No Place for Women in the System?*

Her hobby was landscape painting and in the 1880s she wrote *The Beautiful House and Enchanted Garden* and *Where to Spend a Holiday*. During a visit to Austria she became ill, and died there. *The Times* called her 'a most earnest worker in the interests of her sex' and Edwin Pratt wrote a book about her.

Further reading: Pratt, E.A. (1898) *A Woman's Work for Women*.

MADEHURST

MRS HENRY LYNCH née Theodora Foulks (1812–1885) writer.

Her wealthy family owned the Dale Park estate, where she was born and raised. Nothing is known of her early life, but by the age of thirty-two she was living in Kingston, Jamaica, where she married. After her husband's death in 1845 she moved to London and enjoyed a twenty-year writing career writing hymns, poems, social history, travel-guides and novels.

Her novels feature Jamaican society in the final years of slavery and the early years of emancipation. Her best-known work was probably *The Cotton Tree, or Emily the Little West Indian* (1850). Although highly regarded in her time, after her death, which occurred in London, her works soon went out of print and she has been forgotten.

MIDHURST

MAUD ARNCLIFFE-SENNETT née Sparagnapane (1862–1936) actress and suffragette.

The sister of Florence de Fonblanque [44], she was born in London and became an actress under the name Mary Kingsley. She married Henry Arncliffe-Sennett in 1898 and together they ran her family's firm, G. Sparagnapane, manufacturers of Christmas crackers and wedding cake ornaments. Because the men she employed had a vote but she, the boss, did not, she joined and financially supported many suffrage societies. A popular speaker, she joined several deputations and, through her firm, once supplied 7,000 rosettes free of charge to suffrage marchers. She founded the Northern Men's Federation for Women's Suffrage and was twice arrested: once on Black Friday [294] and once for smashing a window at the *Daily Mail*. After three hours in Holloway her fine was paid by the newspaper's owner, Lord Northcliffe, to avoid bad publicity. She accompanied the coffin of Emily Wilding Davison [96] by train to Morpeth.

During WWI she wrote *A Manifesto on Venereal Disease* and campaigned vigorously against the Contagious Diseases Acts. In later life she was involved in the Midhurst–Haslemere Anti-Vivisection Society. She died at her home, Eversheds, Midhurst, and was buried at Woking in Surrey. Her husband arranged the posthumous publication of her autobiography and donated her suffrage scrapbooks to the British Library. A painting of her as Joan of Arc, patron saint of the suffrage movement, whom she had once played in *Henry VI*, is on display at the Swan Theatre, Stratford.

Further reading: Arncliffe-Sennett, M. (1938) *The Child* (autobiography). [Related plate 31.]

MOLLIE BATTEN OBE, JP (1905–1985)
academic, and religious activist.

A draper's daughter, she gained a BSc in chemistry and another in economics and became a nationally-recognised pioneer in the training of social and youth workers. She served as a magistrate in Birmingham, joined the Ministry of Labour, and in 1942 was appointed to the Manpower Services Board, involved in the conscription of women for war work, for which she was appointed OBE.

She read theology at Oxford, gaining her third bachelor's degree and obtaining an MA at almost fifty. A staunch member of the Anglican Group for the Ordination of Women, she protested about the 'apartheid' that she said 'operated against women' at that time: 'Women are second class citizens in business, in the church, and often in law … what can you do about it? Make a fuss and you're called a feminist'.

She became the first female lecturer at Oxford University Business Summer School and was later appointed principal of William Temple College (a Christian business school) where she raised eyebrows by smoking a pipe during lectures.

After retiring in 1966 she moved to Guillards Oak House, Midhurst, in 1969. She became active in the dioceses of Chichester and Portsmouth, served as chairman of the Chichester constituency Labour Party and wrote five lengthy essays on religious matters for *The Times*. She died at Midhurst Cottage Hospital.

DR AUDREY RICHARDS CBE (1899–1984)
social anthropologist.

A university lecturer and founder the African Studies Centre at Cambridge University, she wrote several books, including *Economic Development and Tribal Change* and *East African Chiefs,* and was the first female president of the Royal Anthropological Institute (1959–61) and the first woman elected to the British Academy (1967). Taken ill in Sussex while staying with her sister, she died at the King Edward VII Hospital, Midhurst. A lecture was established in her name at Oxford University and her book *Hunger and Work in a Savage Society* was reprinted in 1985.

MILLAND

DR WINIFRED LAMB (1894–1963) classical archaeologist.

The only child of future MP Edmund Lamb, she was born in London into a wealthy, Roman Catholic family whose home from before 1919 was Borden Wood House, a large country estate off Cook's Pond Road, Milland. She was an exceptional scholar at Newnham, and after graduating in classics in 1917 she worked for naval intelligence during WWI.

After the war she became the first female archaeologist in Anatolia, highly respected for her Greek and Turkish excavations. On her return she became the first female keeper of Greek and Roman antiquities at the Fitzwilliam Museum in Cambridge. As well as museum catalogues she wrote *Greek and Roman Bronzes,* which became the standard work on the subject, and *Excavations at Thermi in Lesbos*. In 1940 she received her PhD from Cambridge.

During WWII she worked for the BBC, sustaining serious injuries when a V-2 rocket hit her London flat. After the war she returned to live at Borden Wood House permanently. She died at Easebourne Cottage Hospital and was buried at the Catholic cemetery at Midhurst.

NEWHAVEN

MURIEL POWELL MBE (1889–1972) founder of Searchlight.

Nothing is known of her life until she was forty-four, when she resigned from her job as matron of Chailey Heritage Craft Schools, Marine Branch, at Tidemills, Bishopstone, which she had held since 1924 [see Grace Kimmins, 197]. She spent her life savings of £14 on a bungalow next to Newhaven battery, where she founded Searchlight Cripples' Workshop. She shopped at the markets in Brighton, returning with the materials to manufacture jam and toffee, which inmates helped to make and pack for sale. When wartime rationing precluded this she switched to handicrafts and chair caning.

In 1951 a second building was opened by the Duchess of Norfolk [31], who became a patron, and Searchlight received a visit from the Queen in 1962. Nothing is known of Miss Powell's latter years. Searchlight now has a day centre and three residential houses accommodating forty-seven persons.

NEWTIMBER

DAME MILDRED BUXTON GBE, JP née Smith; Countess Buxton (1866–1955) philanthropist.

A daughter of the governor of the Bank of England, in 1896 she married widower Sydney (later, Earl) Buxton MP. In 1914 they moved to South Africa, where he was Governor General. Their only son was killed in action in WWI, and in his honour they founded a children's hospital in Cape Town, donating £5,000 of the £6,000 costs.

The Lady Buxton Centre in Cape Town was named for her and she was appointed GBE in 1919 for charity work. Returning to the UK in 1920, they settled at Newtimber House. Lady Buxton carried out charity and public work, serving as a magistrate and as chairman of the New Sussex Hospital for Women and Children and of the Society for the Overseas Settlement of British Women.

In 1935 she gave Newtimber Hill (150 acres of downland) to the National Trust. She died at home, leaving one daughter; another had died in 1923.

DAME MERIEL TALBOT DBE (1866–1956) women's welfare worker.

Born in London, the granddaughter of Baron Lyttelton, her great aunt was married to Gladstone, the Prime Minister, her uncle was the Bishop of Southwark and her father was an MP for forty-two years. One sister married the Bishop of Chichester, another became Countess of Antrim, while one brother was a judge. Though she had no need to earn money she worked for charities then served for fifteen years as secretary to the Victoria League (founded in 1901 to promote a closer union between the different parts of the British Empire), which took her to several Commonwealth countries.

During WWI she became the first female inspector at the Board of Agriculture, then director of the women's branch of its Food Production Department, where she was involved in organising the WLA. One of her main concerns was to ensure that WLA members maintained high moral standards, and she wrote several reports on the subject, but accepted that military-style discipline was unattainable, since the women worked for private employers. After the war she stayed with the Ministry of Agriculture as adviser on women's employment and held several other public appointments. She was intelligence officer of the Overseas Settlement Department and a member of several government committees, dealing with subjects as diverse as police, headmistresses, and the BBC (where she was on the Central Appeals Advisory Committee) and served as chairman of the London Council for the Welfare of Women and Girls. She combined a high sense of public duty with feminism and deep religious feelings. Always ready to publicly defend her sex from any suggestion that they were inferior to men, she was described as having 'a brilliant brain, sparkling conversation and a spirit that burned like a flame'.

She was appointed OBE in 1917, CBE in 1918 and DBE in 1920. In the early 1930s she convalesced at Backsettown but by 1939 she was living at Newtimber Lodge, where she died. She was buried in the Talbot family churchyard at Markbeech, Kent, and her Commonwealth travel journals (1909–11) are held in the Centre for Kentish Studies. [Related images pp115.]

NUTBOURNE

OLGA MOSLEY MAYNE CBE (1885–1942) chief commander, ATS.

The daughter of General Sir Eric Mosley Mayne of the Indian Army and cousin of Sheila Walker [81], she was born in Hampshire and raised in Somerset and Surrey. During WWI she went to Italy, where she organised clubs and canteens for soldiers and sailors, and in 1918 was appointed OBE for this work.

In the 1930s she moved to Shorts Farm, Nutbourne, her home for the rest of her short life. In 1938 she was among the first women to enlist in the newly-formed ATS. She was immediately appointed an officer and during WWII rose swiftly to the rank of chief commander and was appointed CBE. She was killed on active service in 1942 and was buried in Leicestershire.

PARTRIDGE GREEN

JANICE ELLIOTT (1931–1995) author.

Born in Derby and raised in Nottingham, she read English at St Anne's College, Oxford, graduating with a BA in 1953. She was a journalist on *House and Garden* and *The Sunday Times*, a book reviewer for the *Sunday Telegraph*, and the author of twenty-two novels, five

children's books and a collection of short stories, encompassing fantasy, social realism, myth and modern history. Her first book was *Caves with Echoes* (1962); her last, *Figures in the Sand* (1994).

She lived with her husband Robert Cooper in a sixteenth-century cottage at Partridge Green, where she wrote on an old manual typewriter, occasionally gazing out at her pond and beloved quince tree. In the mid-1980s she moved to Cornwall, where she died, leaving her papers to the University of Exeter.

PENDEAN

CLEMENCE DANE CBE née Winifred Ashton; stage name Diana Cortis (1888–1965) artist, actress and writer and **OLWEN BOWEN DAVIES** (1899–1986) writer.

Miss Ashton was born in London and educated in Germany, Switzerland and the Slade School of Fine Art. She dabbled in art — her bronze bust of Ivor Novello still graces the Theatre Royal, Drury Lane — and was an actress for two years, but writing was her forte. In a highly-successful, fifty-year literary career, under the pseudonym Clemence Dane she produced feminist essays, literary criticism, short stories, detective fiction, anthologies, novels, plays for the stage, radio, TV and films and a factual book about Covent Garden.

Her 1921 stage play *A Bill of Divorcement* was adapted for film three times between 1922 and 1940. *The Moon is Feminine* (1938), a novel, was set at 11 Marine Parade, Brighton. Her screenplay *Fire over England* (1937) starred Flora Robson [148] and Vivien Leigh [192]. She shared an Academy Award with Anthony Pélissier [son of Fay Compton, 156] for the screenplay for *Vacation from Marriage* (1945). Critic St John Ervine called her 'the most distinguished woman dramatist' and she was appointed CBE in 1953. Her final work, a novel titled *Bonfire*, was published posthumously in 1981 and her first novel, *Regiment of Women* (1917), was reprinted in 1995 as part of Virago's 'Lesbian Landmarks' series.

Miss Dane was in the 1920s a member and vice-president of the Six Point Group [301] and in the 1930s served as president of the Society of Women Journalists. She lived for forty years with Welsh-born Olwen Bowen Davies, a writer of children's stories that were very popular in print and on radio during the 1920s and 1930s. Their main residence was in London but they also kept a country home, firstly in Kent then, from the late 1950s, at The Caravans, Pendean Lodge, Dunford Hollow, Pendean. Miss Davies remained there for ten years after Miss Dane's death (at her home in London) then moved to Shropshire, where she died.

PETWORTH

JOAN AIKEN (1924–2004) writer.

A daughter of American poet Conrad Aiken [see Mary Aiken, 244], she was born in Jeake's House, Mermaid Street, Rye. Her father left when she was a baby, her mother remarried and the family moved to Farrs, a house in Sutton, near Pulborough. At twelve she went to boarding school in Oxford, where she wrote her first novel at sixteen. Two years later her first short story was published and another was broadcast on BBC radio's *Children's Hour*. Working in various research, editing and copy-writing jobs in London, she wrote in her spare time, producing novels, poetry, plays and short stories, fairy and folk tales, history, fantasy and horror. This brought a steady income, the *Manchester Guardian* Award, the Edgar Allen Poe Award and the Lewis Carroll Shelf Award. *The Winter Sleepwalker* (1994) is often cited as her best work, and is one of the most beautifully-illustrated children's books. *The Wolves of Willoughby Chase* (1962) was adapted into a film in 1988. To help other authors she wrote a manual: *The Way to Write for Children* (1983).

She married Ronald Brown in 1945, had two children and lived in Lewes. After being widowed in 1955 she moved to the seventeenth-century former inn White Hart House, High Street, Petworth. In 1977 she married American painter Julius Goldstein and they bought The Hermitage, a Grade II listed house in East Street,

Petworth, where she wrote about twenty of her ninety-two books. (Her husband lived between Petworth and New York, where he taught art, giving her plenty of time alone to write.) She died at home, just two days after posting the typescript of *The Witch of Clatteringshaws* to her publisher. [Related image p263.]

ELEANOR DAVIES-COLLEY MB, BS, FRCS (1874–1934) surgeon and co-founder of the South London Hospital.

The sister of Margaret [below] she was born at Hilliers, Petworth, the home of her mother's parents, the Turners. Her family had homes in Chester, at 36 Harley Street, London, and at Borough Farm, Pulborough. Her grandfather, father and two brothers were surgeons, and after performing voluntary work among the East End poor she studied at the LSMW, graduating MB, BS, in 1907 and obtained her MD in London in 1910. In 1911 she was the first woman to pass the examination of the Royal College of Surgeons in London.

She became senior obstetrician at the New Hospital and co-founded (with eminent surgeon Maud Chadburn) the South London Hospital for Women and Children, where she was honorary surgeon for twenty-two years. She was also surgeon to the Marie Curie Cancer Hospital, obstetrician at the Elizabeth Garrett Anderson Hospital and co-founder of the Medical Women's Federation. She lived with Maud Chadburn for twenty-five years. Their home was at 16 Harley Street, where Miss Davies-Colley died.

MARGARET DAVIES-COLLEY (1878–?) artist and suffragette.

The sister of Eleanor [above] she was born at Hilliers, Petworth and raised in Chester and London. A member of the WSPU, in 1909 she was arrested with twenty-nine others, including the national treasurer and Mary Allen [223] for causing a disturbance at Downing Street. She gave her occupation as artist and her address as Borough Farm, Pulborough, her family's fourteen-bedroom country house. She was sentenced to a month in Holloway, but whether she served the term is not known. Nothing more is known of her life.

URSULA HOWELLS (1922–2005) actress and founder of the Herbert Howells Society.

The daughter of the well known church music composer Herbert Howells, she attended St Paul's School for Girls, where her father succeeded Gustav Holst as musical director. At the age of sixteen she was selected to play cricket for the England women's team, but became an actress instead. After playing many stage and film roles from her eighteenth birthday until her forties, she developed a talent for portraying elegant, upper-class English society ladies and became famous for such roles in the TV series *The Forsyte Saga*, in which she was watched by millions for half a year in 1967, and in the sitcom *Father, Dear Father*. At the age of almost eighty she played matriarch Kitty in *The Cazalets* and a posh lady in *Midsomer Murders*.

She married twice; firstly, in 1949, to Davy Dodd; secondly, in 1968, to film director Anthony Compton Pélissier, the son of Fay Compton [156]. Four years after her father's death in 1983, she founded the Herbert Howells Society and paid for many of his compositions to be recorded. Widowed in 1988, she moved to Petworth, where she was a keen supporter of the Petworth Festival.

GWENDA MORGAN (1908–1991) wood engraving printmaker.

The daughter of a shopkeeper, she was born in Petworth, where she spent all her life. After her father's death she lived with her stepmother Una for many years. Trained by Iain Macnab in the 1930s, she made a career engraving scenes of fantasy locations and illustrated ten books, including Grey's *Elegy*, Grimm's *Fairy Tales* and *A Little Place in the Country* by Marjorie Tiltman [73]. She was a member of the Society of Wood Engravers and a fellow of the Royal Society of Painter-Etchers. During WWII she was a member of the WLA and in 2002 Peter Jerome published in limited edition *The Diary of a Land Girl 1939–45*, which included thirty-one of her engravings.

The year she died her work was exhibited at the Duncan Campbell Fine Art Gallery in London. Twenty-one of her engravings are held at Worthing Museum and her work can still be bought at reasonable prices. Occasionally a secondhand copy of her 1985 limited-edition book *The Wood-Engravings of Gwenda Morgan* appears on the market for about £175.

FRANCES MORRISON née Cooper (1807–1898) socialist-feminist journalist and public speaker.

The child of an unwed farmgirl, she was born and raised in Petworth and from the age of sixteen lived with house-painter James Morrison. They moved to Newcastle and married five years later, when she was pregnant. By the 1820s she had a large brood and a paid job. Running a newspaper shop exposed her to radical ideas and soon she was writing anonymous articles for *The Pioneer* magazine, in which the Morrisons started the first women's page in any publication, co-authoring articles on women's rights, calling for equality both in pay and within marriage — pie-in-the-sky ideas at that time.

As a widow she became the first woman known to work as a travelling lecturer, speaking about female emancipation to large audiences crowded into public halls. She spoke particularly of women's economic dependence on men and how it often forced them into marriages that were cruelly oppressive. After apprenticing her eldest daughter to the tape-weaving trade she retired from public life in the 1850s, married a London pastry-cook and lived the rest of her days in obscurity.

THE HON. URSULA WYNDHAM (1913–1995) autobiographer and journalist.

The only daughter of the 5th Lord Leconfield, and distantly related to Dreda Burrell [91], she was born in London and grew up in grand houses in Northamptonshire and Leicestershire, where she was educated by governesses.

During WWII she worked in an aircraft factory and later as an unqualified nurse. After the war she lived with her parents in a mansion flat in London on an allowance of £150 a year. When she was thirty-five this was increased to £500, enabling her to set up a home of her own at Brown's House, Sutton, near the family seat of Petworth House, where her brother Lord

Egremont resided. In 1953 she moved to a cottage near Graffham and three years later bought (and named) Honeyway House, Petworth, her home for the rest of her life.

She raised herds of goats, and while they grazed the local hedgerows had ample time to read book on genealogy and social history. Back at her cottage she filled her time writing novels and a historical biography, but none was published. In the 1970s David Liddle, public librarian at Petworth, reproached her for scribbling comments in the margins of books mentioning the Wyndhams: 'Her defence was robust. She had a right and a duty to correct statements concerning her family. My response ... was that she should write her own book.' The first volume of her memoirs, *Astride the Wall*, was published in 1988. Despite being reviewed as 'lame material amateurishly presented' it was followed by *Laughter and the Love of Friends* in 1989. From 1992 she wrote for *The Oldie*, firstly on the 'Chattering Classes' page, then as its agony aunt. She was so candid about sexual matters that she once had to be censored by the editor. The column led to appearances on radio and features in newspapers.

A stick-thin, stiffly-upright, formidable figure with a military bearing, at times she terrified her friends, let alone her enemies. She 'relished the prospect of battle', said her obituarist, adding, 'With the manners of a county lady she combined the outlook of a bandit chief'. Although she claimed, 'I've left my background behind me' she was greatly affronted if anyone omitted her 'honorable' title. Her nephew, Lord Egremont, threw an eightieth-birthday party for her at Petworth House. She died in Petworth two years later. [Related plate 59; image p114.]

PULBOROUGH

VIRGINIA FIENNES née Pepper; Lady Twisleton-Wykeham-Fiennes (1947–2004) explorer and expedition organiser.

Born into a family that had owned and worked the Amberley chalk quarries for 300 years, she lived first at Crofters, Mare Hill, Pulborough before the family moved to River, near Tillington. At the age of nine she met Sir Ranulph Fiennes Bt., her twelve-year-old neighbour. After being educated at Arundale School, Pulborough, and Moira House School, Eastbourne, she married him at Tillington Church in 1970.

She became a deep-sea diver, then organised her husband's trip down the Nile by hovercraft, and the first trans-navigation of British Columbia by river. In a musquash swamp one night she was startled by a grizzly bear and shot through her own boot. She lived for two months in an Omani sheikh's harem as his (platonic) third wife, and arranged expeditions with Sir Ranulph to find the lost city of Ubar, which they located after twenty-six years of research.

Far from being the 'little wife at home', she was an accomplished explorer and base leader for expeditions in Africa, Arabia and the polar regions. She undertook the research for her husband's travel books and planned most of his thirty expeditions, finding sponsors and choosing teams, routes and schedules. In 1979 her long-held dream to circumnavigate the world via the poles was brought to fruition and became the benchmark for modern exploration. During the Transglobe Expedition she ran the radio stations at both poles, having trained at the Royal Aerospace Establishment and the WRAC Territorials. She set up 80ft radio masts, despite high winds and temperatures of minus fifty, and helped to save a group of scientists lost in Antarctica. Her Jack Russell, Bothie, was the first dog to travel to both poles and became Cruft's Pet of the Year. The expedition, which Prince Charles described as 'mad but marvellous', took three years; on their return they worked to pay the expedition's debts with lectures and selling Transglobe equipment, living on £50 a week.

She was the first woman invited to join the Antarctic Club and was the first to be awarded the Polar Medal, which she received from the Queen in 1987 in recognition of her research work for the British Antarctic Survey and Sheffield University (on Very Low Frequency radio propagation). In the 1980s they moved to Somerset and she became a hill farmer on Exmoor, raising pedigree Aberdeen Angus cattle, Black Welsh Mountain sheep and St John's Waterdogs. She died at Exeter.

Further reading: Fiennes, R. (2007) *Mad, Bad and Dangerous to Know*; Fiennes, V. (1987) *Bothie the Polar Dog*.

BLANCHE BINGLEY HILLYARD née Bingley (1863–1946) tennis champion.

Britain's first truly outstanding female tennis player, she was noted for wearing soft, white-leather gloves to ensure a firm grip on the racket. Her career spanned three decades; she competed in the first ladies' singles championship at Wimbledon in 1884, reaching the semi-finals, and subsequently played in thirteen finals, which remains a Wimbledon record, as does the fourteen-year time span between her first and last — she won the first of her six Wimbledon singles titles in 1886 and the last in 1900. She also won the Irish championships on three occasions and the German title twice. Married to one of the founders of the Lawn Tennis Association, she took two breaks of two years each for childbearing. Playing her final Wimbledon in 1913, aged forty-eight, she reached the semi-finals.

She died at Mare Hill, Pulborough, in her house, Greenford, which she named after her birthplace in Middlesex. [Related image p16.]

MARJORIE HESSELL TILTMAN née Hand (1900–1998) writer and journalist.

Born in Worcestershire, she was raised in Birmingham and London, trained as a journalist and landed her first job on *The Pictorial* magazine at the age of eighteen. In 1925 she married Hugh Hessell Tiltman and they bought a cottage in Coldwaltham, where she became devoted to cultivating the garden. She began to write on rural matters for magazines such as *Country Life* and *Good Housekeeping*, then tried her hand at fiction. Her first novel, *Quality Chase* (1939), was based partly on the early life of her father. Highly-praised, it was the *Evening Standard* Book of the Year and was dramatised on BBC radio.

Encouraged by this success she produced a further thirteen fiction and non-fiction titles, including the acclaimed *Cottage Pie* (1940), *A Little Place in the Country* (1944), illustrated by Clare Leighton [62] and *Goodbye to Lilley House* (1948).

For much of the time her husband, a foreign correspondent for the *Guardian*, worked in China and the USA, but when he moved to Tokyo in 1951 she joined him. However, she was so distressed by the social conditions in Japan that she returned after just a few months and bought The Court House, Rectory Lane, Pulborough, where she lived without him until her death. She left £100,000 to establish a literary prize in her name.

ROGATE

LADY DOROTHY NEVILL née Walpole (1826–1913) horticulturalist and author.

Known as Dolly, she was born in London, the daughter of the 3rd Earl of Orford. She married Reginald Nevill (later a JP and a deputy lieutenant of Sussex) with whom she had two children. As well as enjoying a London residence, she bought Dangstein House in about 1850 and opened in its grounds a school in which six poor girls were boarded, clothed and educated. She had three sons and a daughter and by 1861 employed thirteen resident servants (in later life she would join a national campaign to abolish the tax on servants).

One evening Lady Dorothy's crinoline caught alight as she stood near the drawing-room fire at Dangstein: 'In an instant I was in a blaze, but I kept my presence of mind, and, rolling myself in the hearthrug ... eventually beat out and subdued the flames. I was rather badly burnt about one of my arms, where the marks remain to this day ... None of the ladies present could do much to assist me, for their enormous crinolines rendered them almost completely impotent to deal with fire.'

A member of the Royal Horticultural Society, her garden became nationally famous and was described as the best in

England. She had seventeen hot-houses, employed thirty-four gardeners and was famed for her orchids, pitcher plants and other tropical species, including trees. She conducted successful trials using the ailanthus silkworm and in 1862 published her own translation of a French book about the history, rearing and management of the worm. She had pigeon-whistles imported from China and attached them to the tails of her many pigeons, creating a 'wind-orchestra' which, she said, resembled the sound of an aeolian harp.

Her interests were wide-ranging: she was a member of the women's movement and spoke at a great suffrage rally in London in 1893. She collected art, porcelain and snuff-boxes, judged cat shows, and was a leading society hostess. Miss Braddon [124] was her preferred novelist and wood-carving was her favourite hobby. She wrote several books on history, travel and her own memoirs, including *Mannington and the Walpoles* (1894), *Under Five Reigns* (1910) and *My Own Times* (1912).

She was already fabulously wealthy, and when her husband died in 1878 he left her an additional £2,000 a year (the equivalent of over £100,000 today). She sold the Dangstein estate and moved to London, where she died and has a blue plaque. Dangstein House was demolished and rebuilt in 1933. Of the original, all that remains is the basement, some garden walling, the school and the road name Lady Dorothy's Walk. Her daughter Meresia (1849–1918) was vice-president of the Ladies' Grand Council of the Primrose League of the Conservative Party.

Further reading: Nevill, D. (1906) *The Reminiscences of Lady Dorothy Nevill*. [Related image p113.]

JOAN QUENNEL MBE, JP, MP (1923–2006) politician.

Educated at Bedales, she served with the WLA during WWII. Her family home was Dangstein House, which she was later to inherit on the death of her father in 1966. While running her dairy and arable farms and an investment company, she served as a West Sussex county councillor (1951–61),

a governor of Crawley College, chairman of the Horsham Divisional Conservative Association and a magistrate.

She won the seat of Petersfield in 1960, becoming the seventy-sixth female MP. A woman who knew her own mind, during her election campaign she announced her support for physical punishment as a cure for juvenile delinquency, saying she saw nothing wrong 'with a good fourpenny one in the right place at the right time'. She was not afraid to publicly criticise Conservative Central Office about its administrative failings and she championed women's issues in the House of Commons. She stood down from parliament in 1974.

She died at St Richard's Hospital, Chichester, and was cremated. She left the Dangstein estate, comprising a mansion, twenty-three acres of gardens, a home farm, cottages, two houses and 370 acres of woodland, to the National Trust.

ROWFANT

EDNA GINESI (1902–2000) painter and designer.

Of Italian extraction, she was born in Yorkshire and studied at Leeds College, the Royal College of Art, and in Europe. In 1926, when she married fellow artist Raymond Coxon, sculptor Henry Moore was best man (his sketch of her is in Wakefield Art Gallery). She joined the Twenties Group [see Lucy Wertheim, 151] and worked as an artist for over seventy-five years, living for sixty years between her homes in London and Sussex, where in 1938 she established a studio at Old Rowfant Mill, Old Hollow. Her work ranged from detailed plant sketches to portraits and landscapes, though in later years her style became more abstract. One of her landscapes is titled 'Rowfant'.

She also enjoyed interior design and decorating and was passionately interested in botany. During WWII she drove ambulances. Her seventy-one-year marriage ended when her husband died at Rowfant, aged 100, in 1997. She also died there, aged ninety-eight.

RUDGWICK

ANNIE MCCALL MD (1859–1949) physician and promoter of maternity care.

The daughter of an insurance agent, she was born in Manchester. With her widowed mother's enthusiastic approval she studied medicine at the LSMW, qualifying LKQCPI in 1885. She later gained her MD from Berne in Switzerland. After studying obstetrics in Vienna, she returned to London, ran outpatients' clinics for poor women and opened Clapham School of Midwifery and a maternity hospital in 1889. The hospital was unique for giving priority to single mothers, who were usually excluded from charitable institutions on moral grounds. Later renamed the Annie McCall Maternity Hospital and long since demolished, it is commemorated in the road name Annie McCall Close. Her ideas were radical at the time: she advocated a special diet during pregnancy and a natural childbirth: she trained midwives to practise 'masterful inactivity', avoiding interference and forceps if possible. Her other specialisation was tuberculosis (which had killed her father) and she opened a small sanatorium at her home, Kings, in Rudgwick.

She was a suffragist, a committed Christian, an opponent of vivisection, and being deeply against alcohol was an activist in the London Women's Union of the Church of England Temperance Society. In 1909 she was elected to Lambeth Council and served on its health committee with Alice Gregory [186]. She died at home in Rudgwick and was buried in Holy Trinity churchyard. She left her London house to the United Temperance Council and most of her £92,000 estate to the LSMW to fund the Annie McCall Scholarship in Midwifery.

RUSTINGTON

AGNES GARRETT (1845–1935) and **RHODA GARRETT** (1841–1882) interior designers and feminist campaigners.

Rhoda was a clergyman's daughter from Derbyshire who had fallen on hard times; her cousin Agnes had two famous sisters: Elizabeth Garrett Anderson [299] and Dame Millicent Fawcett [293]. From 1867 Rhoda and Agnes were active in the LNSWS and later held office, spoke in town all over the UK in favour of women's rights and campaigned for the repeal of the CD Acts.

They trained as architects, although it was difficult to find someone who would accept female apprentices. In 1875 they established the first all-female design and decorating company, taught interior decoration and won many high-profile commissions for public buildings and private residences. Their popular book *Suggestions for House Decoration in Painting, Woodwork and Furniture* went into five editions in three years. They exhibited in Paris, at the Arts and Crafts Exhibition Society and at the Exhibition of Women's Industries. Rhoda became a member of the Royal Archaeological Society and the Society for the Preservation of Ancient Buildings.

The cousins lived together all their adult lives, between their two West End business premises and their thatched cottage, The Firs, at Rustington. Rhoda died of typhoid at their London home at the age of forty-two and was buried at the churchyard of St Peter and St Paul, Rustington. Agnes survived Rhoda by fifty-three years. She continued the business until 1905, served as a poor law guardian, campaigned for the revision of Indian marriage laws, was vice-president of the National Council of Women and of the National Council for Equal Citizenship. She died in London. Annie Swynnerton's portrait of her, painted in Rustington, is in Manchester Art Gallery.

Further reading: Anscombe, I. (1984) *Woman's Touch: Women in Design from 1860 to the Present Day.*

SELSEY

MOLLIE STANLEY-WRENCH FRHS née Louise Violet Gibbs (1880–1966) author, folklorist, journalist, essayist.

Educated at home in Oxfordshire, she wrote *Love's Fool* (1908) and seventeen other novels, one of which, *Burnt Wings* (1909), was adapted into a film in 1916.

She also wrote two volumes of *Stories of Famous Operas* (1924), edited a collection by female poets called the *Lyceum Book of Verse* (1931), and a number of cookbooks, uncluding *Bachelor Woman's Cookery* (1934). Cookery was to her an art form, and her literary dinners attracted the most famous writers of the day. For twenty-five years she wrote the cookery page of *Woman's Illustrated* and contributed short stories, serials, articles, recipes and verse to many popular magazines and newspapers. She was a member of the Women Writers' Club and PEN, and was a longstanding correspondent of Marie Stopes, daughter of Charlotte [101].

She married in 1902 and in 1917 had a daughter, Margaret, who became a poet, dramatist and translator. She lived at Medmenny, 5 Clayton Road, Selsey, certainly between 1927 and 1961, possibly longer. Widowed in 1951, she died in hospital.

ESMÉ WYNNE-TYSON née Ripper (1898–1972) actress and writer.

A member of a theatrical family, she became a child star in London's West End under the pseudonym Esmé Wynne, and later collaborated with Noël Coward on various productions. During the 1920s she wrote five novels; one, *Security*, was produced as a play in New York and London. She later became a Christian Scientist and a freelance journalist, edited *World Forum* magazine and wrote several books on philosophical, religious and spiritual matters, some in collaboration with J.D. Beresford. Her book *The Philosophy of Compassion* was described in the *Scotsman* as 'weighty erudition'.

She married Linden Tyson (both taking the surname Wynne-Tyson) and had a son, Timothy Jon, but separated when he was six. Having lived in Hampshire, in Brighton (until 1939) and later in Selsey, in later life she bought a modest, weather-boarded bungalow at 9 Park Lane, Selsey, where she became virtually a recluse, devoting herself entirely to writing. She died at St Richard's Hospital, Chichester.

Further reading: Wynne-Tyson, J. (2004) *Finding the Words: A Publishing Life*.

SHARPTHORNE

JULIA MATILDA COHEN née Waley (1853–1917) author and educationist.

Born into a Jewish family in London, she was educated at Queen's College and at twenty married Nathaniel Cohen. She conducted children's services at the West London Synagogue and wrote and edited several related books, including the *Infants' Bible Reader* (1897), *The Children's Psalm Book* (1907) and *Addresses to Children* (1922). She promoted vocational training for women, helped establish a domestic science course at Queen's College and was vice-president of the Domestic Training Home, Regent's Park. She served on the council of the college hall of residence for female medical students and on the committee of the Society for the Training of Jewish Teachers, and lectured in art history at the British Museum. Her most notable achievement was co-founding and presiding over the Union of Jewish Women. Widowed in 1913, she died at Courtlands, Chilling Street, Sharpthorne (where she had lived for at least nine months, possibly much longer) and was buried at Willesden Jewish cemetery.

SHERMANBURY

BRIGADIER DAME MARY COLVIN DBE (1907–1988) director of the WRAC.

The granddaughter of a baron and daughter of an army officer, she was born at Morley's House on the Shermanbury Grange estate, her family's home until 1936. She joined the FANY in 1938 and took a commission in the ATS during WWII, leaving Sussex forever. She commanded a Central Ordnance Depot ATS Group in Northamptonshire, and afterwards served in Germany and Northern Ireland, training female army officers. After a short time as deputy director of the WRAC, in 1957 she became director. In 1961 she led and was spokeswoman for the British contingent at the first conference of directors of the women's services of NATO countries, held that year in Copenhagen. A WRAC accommodation block in Hong Kong was named Colvin House in her honour (it was demolished in the 1970s).

Appointed OBE in 1947 and DBE in 1959, she became lady-in-waiting to the Princess Royal. In later life she lived in Rutland. She loved everything to do with equestrianism, was a keen fox-hunter and served for twenty-five years as a senior dressage judge.

SHOREHAM-BY-SEA

FLORRIE FORDE née Flora Augusta Flanagan (1875–1940) music hall artiste and producer.

Her forty-eight year career began at age seventeen, singing in music halls in her native Australia. In London in 1897 she signed a three-year contract and became known as 'the Australian Marie Lloyd'. She pioneered the audience 'singalong' with her classics *Down at the Old Bull and Bush, I do Like to be Beside the Seaside* and *It's a Long Way to Tipperary*. Between 1903 and 1936 she made 700 recordings on cylinders and discs, appeared in several films and broadcast on radio. She introduced the legendary duo Flanagan and Allen (the former adopted her maiden name) and produced their shows, as well as pantomimes.

She married twice, the second time in 1905 to Worthing art dealer Laurence Barnett, with whom she settled in Shoreham. Widowed in 1934 she moved to north London and continued to perform until the day she died, in Aberdeen. She was buried near her daughter's home at Streatham, south London.

PHYLLIS PEARSALL MBE, FRGS née Gross (1906–1996) creator of the A–Z.

The daughter of a mapmaker and an artist, she was born in London (the house now boasts a blue plaque). She boarded at Roedean until her father's cartographic company went bankrupt, then lived in France. At twenty she married an artist and lived in Europe before leaving him and returning to London.

Working as a portrait painter in the 1920s she was weary of getting lost while trying to find her way to her clients' homes using the only map available, the 1919 Ordnance Survey. She decided to create a proper street plan. For six years she worked for up to eighteen hours a day and walked 3,000 miles to catalogue the capital's 23,000 streets. When the plan was complete, no one would publish it. Using money earned from painting, and hiring only a draughtsman, she designed the pioneering, book-format layout herself, performed the proofreading and indexing, and had 10,000 copies printed under the imprint 'the Geographers' A–Z Map Company'. She took 250 copies in a wheelbarrow to W.H. Smith's, where they sold prodigiously. She continued to paint portraits and during WWII drew women performing war work in factories. By 1945 the A–Z was being printed in the Netherlands and flying home from there she was seriously injured in a plane crash which scarred her for life.

In the 1960s she moved the company to Kent, where it expanded, eventually producing plans of 159 British cities. She turned it into a charitable trust to ensure that it was never bought out, passed her shares into a trust for her employees, and continued as chairman and joint managing director for the rest of her life. She retired to Shoreham and wrote *Fleet Street, Tite Street, Queer Street* (1983), *Only the Unexpected Happens* (seven short stories, 1985), *Women at War* (1990) and her autobiography, *A–Z Maps: The Personal Story, From Bedsitter to Household Name* (1990). Brighton bus 883 is named for her.

Further reading: Hartley, S. (2002) *Mrs P's Journey: The Remarkable Story of the Woman who Created the A–Z Map.*

EMÉLIE POLINI (1881–1927) actress.

The daughter of a theatrical manager, she was born in Shoreham, almost certainly at 20 Brunswick Road, and christened Emily Adeline Polini. She became an actress on the London stage and toured with various theatrical companies, travelling to the USA and Australia. After marrying Harold Ellis in 1918 she settled in New South Wales and had a child. The couple separated and she returned to the stage. She died in the USA, leaving her estate to her sister in London, actress Marie Nares.

SHRIPNEY

MRS C.F. LEYEL née Hilda Wauton (1880–1957) lottery organiser and herbalist.

The daughter of a French master at Uppingham School, her ancestor Valentine Wauton married Oliver Cromwell's sister. Her mother hailed from Burpham in Sussex, and Hilda was born in London and educated at Halliwick Manor, Barnet. In her late teens she was a minor actress until 1900, when she married Carl Leyel, a prominent West End theatrical manager. She bore two sons by 1906 and lived in London, then Twickenham.

For at least twenty years she performed unpaid charity work, firstly by organising fancy dress balls and, in 1917, a grand tombola, launched at the Royal Albert Hall, to raise money for troops during WWI; prizes included a fur coat, pearls, and two acres of land. In May 1918 she founded the first charity shop, in London's West End. Rich ladies donated gold and silver items, which were either melted down or sold, in aid of the Red Cross. The shop raised nearly £70,000 in a year (worth £2.5m today).

In 1919 she developed and organised the Golden Ballot, a 5s lottery with 500 prizes (including cash, pearls, aeroplanes, houses, cars, public school fees, trips around the world, a servant for a year), which raised £256,000 (the equivalent of £7.3m today) for ex-servicemen and the Royal National Orthopaedic hospitals and paid for a 350-bed TB sanatorium to be built on a 300-acre site near Maidstone. When the prize-winners were announced in April 1920 Mrs Leyel was summonsed on twelve charges of contravening the 1823 Lottery Act and fined £40. Two years later she and two colleagues stood trial at the Old Bailey for similar offences under the Lottery Act and also the Betting Act 1853. This time, to keep within the law, Mrs Leyel had devised a game in which the public paid five shillings to enter a competition in which they had to guess the names chosen by her to form a fantasy government. The judge called her 'an exceedingly ingenious person', and the jury acquitted them. Although the trial established the legality of her scheme, in 1923 Mrs Leyel announced that she would organise no more and turned her attention to herbalism.

Since early life she had made an informal study of flowers, herbs and medicine, and from the mid-1920s made herbalism her full-time work. She was a fellow of the Royal Institution and an officer of l'Academie Francaise, which awarded her the Palme Académique of France in 1924. In 1927 she opened the Culpeper Houses, a chain of shops in London offering herbal medicines, foodstuffs and cosmetics, some with an upstairs room used for examining and diagnosing patients. She founded the Society of Herbalists (from 1977, called the Herb Society). In 1941 the Pharmacy and Medicines Bill almost outlawed herbalism, but her influential friends managed to get the bill modified (it was repealed in 1968).

Between 1925 and 1957 she wrote twenty books on cookery, diet and the use of herbs, of which several were in print long after her death, including *The Elixirs of Life* (1948, reprinted 2002), and edited Grieve's two-volume *A Modern Herbal* (1931, reprinted 1996). Her best known work, *The Gentle Art of Cookery* (1925, reprinted 1942, 1974, 2004), co-written with Olga Hartley, became a classic reference book for decades and greatly influenced Elizabeth David [241]. *Time* magazine called her 'Britain's greatest advocate of herbal medicine' and *The Times* called her 'a visionary of her time'. Her renowned library of herbalist books was placed on public exhibition and was described by Wilfred Blunt [see Lady Anne Blunt, 92] as 'one of the finest privately owned collections of this country'.

Widowed in 1925, by 1932 she was living at Shripney Manor, from where in 1938 she sent an angry letter to *The Times* complaining about having refugees being billeted on her. She died in London and her valuable library of books was divided: some went to the Herb Society, while 978 were auctioned at Sotherby's, raising over £21,000, which went to support the Culpeper shops, ten of which are still trading. Her daughter-in-law sold Shripney Manor in the late 1950s. [Related plate 42, image 116.]

SLINDON

LADY GEORGIANA FULLERTON née Leveson-Gower (1812–1885) author and philanthropist.

Born in Staffordshire, she was the granddaughter of the 5th Duke of Devonshire, and as a child had once sat on the knee of George IV. Her father was an ambassador and she grew up in St Petersburg, the Hague and Paris, where she had piano lessons from Liszt and became best friends with the Duchess of Angoulême, daughter of Marie Antoinette. In 1815 her father became a viscount and in 1833 the 1st Earl Granville.

In 1833 she married Captain Alexander Fullerton, an attaché in Paris, where they lived until 1841. Her literary career took off when she was thirty-two, with the publication of *Ellen Middleton*, a melodramatic murder story and the first of her eight novels, which all had Roman Catholic themes. Said to be the catalyst for several conversions, she became a Catholic in 1846. She also turned her hand to short stories, a play, poetry and biographies, including one written in French.

After the death of her only son she vowed never to buy or possess anything beyond necessities. She wore only black dresses and shawls and plain caps, and never bought gloves, because they cost half-a-crown (12.5p) that she would prefer to give to the poor. She donated all of her literary earnings to charity.

From the 1850s she and her husband lived at Slindon Cottage, where she could be near her friends the Duchess of Norfolk at Arundel and Lady Newburgh at Slindon House. As prominent members of high society they also kept a home in London's Park Lane. In 1878 they moved to Ayrfield, Bournemouth, Hampshire, a grand house where they had eight residential servants, including a butler and footman. She died at the house and was buried at Roehampton. Her nephew married Lady Rose Bowes-Lyon, sister of the late Queen Mother.

Madame Augustus Craven published a biography of Lady Georgiana, which was translated into English by H.J. Coleridge in 1888. [Related images pp103, 113.]

BESSIE RAYNER PARKES Mrs Parkes Belloc (1829–1925) poet and women's rights campaigner.

A granddaughter of scientist Joseph Priestley and cousin of Dr Blackwell [224], she was born in Birmingham. Her family moved to 6 Pelham Crescent, Hastings, when she was seventeen. There, she and Barbara Leigh Smith, later Mme Bodichon [193] educated themselves in art, literature, philosophy and politics and wrote feminist articles for radical journals. Later she wrote *Remarks on the Education of Girls* (1856) and *Essays on Women's Work* (1865) as well as two volumes of poetry, and also *Vignettes: Twelve Biographical Sketches* (1866).

In the 1850s she co-founded the first committee and petition to campaign against the poor legal position of wives. The petition supported a Married Women's Property Bill, which failed, but the campaign continued and achieved success in 1870. In 1858 she became part-owner and editor of the *English Woman's Journal*, a magazine focussing on education, emigration and employment. Its offices were used as a meeting place for mid-Victorian feminists, among them Lady Goldsmid [209], who became known as the Langham Place group. In 1866 she co-founded the committee that organised the first women's suffrage petition, which John Stuart Mill presented to the House of Commons. She served on the founding council of the WPPL, along with Frances Hoggan [135], Louisa Goldsmid and Mentia Taylor [167].

After marrying Louis Belloc (in 1867), moving to his native France and converting to Catholicism, she abandoned feminism and became estranged from Mme Bodichon. Early widowhood and bad investments left her impoverished and she struggled to raise her children. In 1889 her bankruptcy was announced in *The Times*. Some income was derived from writing the autobiographical works *In a Walled Garden* (1895, reprinted in 2004), *A Passing World* (1897) and her final collection of poems *In Fifty Years* (1904).

At the suggestion of Lady Georgiana Fullerton [above], in the 1880s she rented Slindon Cottage (now Dower House) and later downsized to Newlands on Church Hill, renaming it The Grange. Her address in 1911 was Gaston Cottage. She died at home and was buried within the grounds of St Richard's Roman Catholic church. Her son Hilaire and daughter Marie [below] became writers. Hilaire's connection with Slindon is kept alive; his sister and mother are all but forgotten. [Related images pp102, 103, 263.]

MARIE BELLOC LOWNDES (1868–1947) author.

The daughter of Bessie Rayner Parkes [above], she was born in London, spent two years at a convent school at Mayfield then lived with her mother in Slindon. Raised bilingual, she began to write about France, earning an income that helped support the family and send her brother to Oxford University, where his excellent education led to a lucrative writing career. He repaid his sister by becoming a fervent opponent of women's higher education, and while she was president of the Women Writers' Suffrage League he was the most prominent and vocal anti-suffragist of his day. In 1896 she married Frederick Lowndes of The Times editorial staff. They had a son and two daughters and led a busy social life that included visits to her close friend Alice Meynell [52] and to Number Ten, by invitation of her friend Margot Asquith, wife of the Prime Minister and mother-in-law of Cynthia [85].

Unlike her brother, her husband was an advocate of women's rights and used a £2,000 legacy to support her career. She wrote seventy books (each with a quill pen), including romance and crime novels, short stories, royal biographies and plays. Her best known work was The Lodger: A Tale of the London Fog (1913), about a couple who suspect their lodger is Jack the Ripper. This sold a million copies in twenty years and was adapted into a play, a Hitchcock film and an opera. The film of her novel Letty Lynton, a tale of love and blackmail, appeared in 1932.

In widowhood she wrote a four-volume autobiography In a Passing World (posthumous, 1948) while living between her home in London and that of her elder daughter Elizabeth Northcote, Countess of Iddesleigh, at Parfitts House, Longwater Lane, Eversley Cross, Hampshire, where she died. Her requiem mass was held in Westminster Cathedral. The Lodger and some of her other works were reprinted in 2003–5. Her daughter Susan edited and published The Diaries and Letters of Marie Belloc Lowndes in 1971. [Related image p116.]

SLINFOLD

JO DOUGLAS née Rickett; Mrs Doll (1926–1988) television producer.

As a wireless mechanic in the WAAF during WWII, she staged and appeared in forces' shows, later attending RADA, and was a stage and film actress under the name Jo Douglas. In 1955 she became the only female TV producer of light entertainment and in the 1960s was the only female producer at ATV, working on Emergency Ward 10 and The Arthur Askey Show. She later directed twenty plays and produced films. She retired in 1985 and died at her home, White Briars, The Street, Slinfold, survived by her husband and two sons.

GEORGETTE HEYER (1902–1974) novelist.

Born in Wimbledon, she devised her first historical story while staying at Hastings in 1919. She sent it to an agent and it was published when she was nineteen. She wrote romances and mysteries but is famous chiefly for her historical novels set in the Regency period. Sometimes slated by critics, they were nevertheless loved by the public and her royalties helped support her siblings after their father's death.

In 1925 she married Ronald Rougier. They lived in Tanganyika, Macedonia and London, then moved to Sussex in 1931, where they stayed for eleven years, living firstly at Southover, Colgate, where their son was born in 1932; then from 1934 at Blackthorns, Five Oaks Road, near Slinfold. In 1940 they moved to Steyning Mansions, King's Parade, Brighton, then in 1941 to 27 Adelaide Crescent, Hove. They returned to London in late 1942, where she lived the rest of her life.

While living in Sussex she wrote nineteen of her fifty-seven novels, including Regency

Buck, which she set partly in Brighton. Her work has remained in print for decades, has been translated into a dozen languages and adapted for the stage and TV. Her 1984 biography was written by the sister of Joan Aiken [70].

Further reading: Hodge, J.A. (1984) *The Private World of Georgette Heyer;* Kloester, J. (forthcoming) *Georgette.*

SHEILA WALKER CBE née Mosley Mayne (1917–2006) chief commissioner of the Girl Guides.

A cousin of Olga Mayne [69], she was born in Lahore (then India, now Pakistan). When her family came home they settled in Slinfold, where in 1924 she joined the local Brownies. She was a boarder at St Mary's Hall School, Brighton, where she became a Girl Guide. During WWII she was working as a secretary in London when her aunt's house, in which she was living, suffered a direct hit from a German bomber and she was buried in the wreckage and trapped for fourteen hours. She convalesced from her physical injuries and mental trauma at the family home in Slinfold. Here she met Captain Dawson, whom she married in St Peter's Church. They had two children, then he was killed in the war. After working abroad for ten years she married Owen Walker.

In the 1950s she started a new career in the Girl Guide movement, rising steadily through the ranks to become Commonwealth chief commissioner. In five years she travelled 200,000 miles around Britain and visited nine other countries. Appointed CBE in 1981, she retired from the Guides, moved to Northamptonshire and became vice-chairman of the Campaign for the Protection of Rural England.

SOMPTING

HARRIET FINLAY-JOHNSON Mrs Weller (1871–1956) pioneering schoolmistress.

Raised in humble circumstances, she qualified as a teacher through private study and received her certificate in 1894. At twenty-six she became headmistress of Sompting Village School, Loose Lane. There were 120 pupils, and she taught the fifty juniors, aged eight to fourteen. Her sister Emily, though six years her senior, was not certificated and so was placed in charge of the infants. Both sisters lived with their widowed mother in the adjoining schoolhouse.

Miss Finlay-Johnson completely revolutionised the school, introducing penpals in Canada and lantern-slide lectures. She collected a large library, to which she allowed her pupils free access, sent their work and news of their unusual activities to local newspapers and encouraged them to write letters to the press. Visits to fig gardens and grape houses, nature walks and countryside and seashore rambles, bee-keeping, gardening and cooking were added to the school day, but perhaps her most important innovation was the use of drama in teaching. Sompting children excelled at art, which drew praise from the chief inspector of drawing at the Board of Education, who also reported that the pupils had achieved the highest educational level he had ever encountered. By 1903, aged only thirty-two, Miss Finlay-Johnson was appointed to an advisory committee on West Sussex County Council.

At a time when most village parents took no part in their children's education, she developed an all-inclusive community spirit, inviting families to become involved in the school life of their children. A women's band was formed, while the menfolk produced a Shakespeare play and performed it at the Theatre Royal, Worthing, drawing praise from London critics and increasing the fame of the school, its unusual methods, and its headmistress.

Her marriage to the village wheelwright in 1910 obliged her to resign in accordance with the marriage bar [8]. The following year her groundbreaking book *The Dramatic Method of Teaching* appeared. It contained the appeal: 'Go forth, little book, from my halting pen, into the world of men and women of learning, knowledge, culture, and research! Tell them of the little school on the Sussex Downs where children and teachers lived for a space in the world of romance and happiness.' She lived in Sompting for the rest of her life, dying at Southlands Hospital, Shoreham. The former school is now a community centre.

SOUTH HARTING

KATHERINE NORTH née Hodges (1889–1982) wartime heroine.

An actress's daughter, she was born in Middlesex and raised at South Harting. She trained as a dancer but when WWI began she retrained as a motor mechanic and volunteered to drive ambulances for the SWH. Her unit, which included Elsie Bowerman [247] went to Russia to transport wounded Serbian and Russian soldiers to field hospitals. Her task was to drive primitive motor-ambulances across fields and along roads full of craters and deep mud, frequently under aerial bombardment. She spent most of the war suffering from hunger and fatigue and covered in mud and oil, but added a smattering of Russian and Serbian to her schoolgirl French and German. Later in the war she served with the Hackett–Lowther unit in France, performing arduous and dangerous work on the front line for the French Army. She received several foreign awards: the Croix de Guerre, the Medal of St George and the Order of St Stanislas.

Between the wars she married a photographer then, during WWII, in her mid-fifties, returned to her role as ambulance driver, this time in London during the Blitz. She worked for the Red Cross until 1968, then retired to South Harting. Her memoirs are held at the Leeds Russian Archive.

Further reading: Fawcett-Cahill, A. (ed) (1999) *Between the Lines: Letters and Diaries from Elsie Inglis's Russian Unit.*

SOUTH STOKE

ANN FRANCIS née Gittins, (c1738–1800) classical scholar and poet.

She was born and raised in South Stoke, where her clergyman father broke with convention by teaching her Latin, Greek and Hebrew, at which she attained great proficiency. She married the Revd Robert Francis and moved to Norfolk, where she lived the rest of her adult life. She became one of the few women of her era to be acknowledged as an outstanding classics scholar. Although she acknowledged that society believed it was 'an improper undertaking for a woman', she translated *The Song of Solomon* from Hebrew and published it, adding a preface of her own plus historical, critical and explanatory notes. This was followed by 'The Obsequies of Demetrius Poliorcetes: a Poem', again adding her own notes. In 1790 she self-published *Miscellaneous Poems, by a Lady,* followed by a ballad in 1798.

SOUTHWICK

DAME CLARA BUTT DBE (1872–1936) legendary contralto.

Henry Butt, the captain of a small ship, and his wife Clara were returning from Jersey, whence they had eloped, when she went into labour. They moored at the fishing village of Southwick, where baby Clara was born at 27 Adur Terrace on 1st February. They baptised her in the unusual, clam-shell font at the Wesleyan Methodist Church on 3rd April, then returned to Jersey, moving later to Bristol.

Young Clara trained as a singer, grew to six feet two by the age of seventeen and developed a deep and powerful voice that ranged from C below middle C to high B flat. It was said that 'she could pit her voice against the full power of the Albert Hall organ'. Elgar composed *Sea Pictures* especially for her and her recording of *Land of Hope and Glory* is still revered as the classic version. She married baritone Kennerley Rumford and had two children (one died young; the other took his own life). She was appointed DBE in 1920 for charity work during WWI. Owing to cancer of the spine her final recordings were made from a wheelchair. She died in Oxfordshire and commemorative plaques were placed on the buildings in which she was born and died. Both have since been demolished, but she has a blue plaque in London.

Further reading: Ponder, W. (1978) *Clara Butt.*

MARJORIE EYRE real surname Eyre-Parker (1897–1987) Savoyard.

Leaving her native Derby she studied at the RCM and, after a spell as a soprano chorister, from 1925 worked for the D'Oyly Carte New Opera Company, playing minor and major parts, and touring the USA. By 1929 she had retrained as a mezzo-soprano and played principal soubrette roles for the rest of her twenty-two-year career, during which she appeared on two D'Oyly Carte recordings. She married Chichester-born principal baritone Leslie Rands in 1926 and had a son. The couple retired to somewhere in the Sussex countryside in 1947, but returned to the stage in 1949 for a tour of Australia. In 1952 they starred in a week's charity run of *Merrie England* in Priory Park, Chichester.

By 1950 they were living at 9 Albany Villas, Hove, and by 1963 had moved to 23 Glebe Villas, Southwick. Miss Eyre was for some decades vice-president of the Gilbert & Sullivan Society. She outlived her husband by fifteen years and died in Brighton.

STEYNING

FANNY CORNFORTH real name Sarah Cox (1835–c1906) iconic model.

She grew up in Mouse Lane at her birthplace, Steyning, and attended the village school. After her mother and all her siblings died, she and her father moved in 1848 to 1 Railway Street, Brighton, where he worked on the railways. At age fourteen she entered domestic service, and later moved to London, where in 1856 she met pre-Raphaelite artist Dante Gabriel Rossetti and sat for him and for Edward Burne-Jones. She was married to Timothy Hughes, but after Rossetti was widowed in 1862 she lived with him for the rest of his life.

Rossetti painted her at least sixty times, in oil, watercolour, pastels and pencil, making hers one of the most famous faces on earth. It appears in dozens of internationally-famous paintings, including 'The Bower Garden', 'Found', 'Bocca Baciata', 'The Salutation of Beatrice', 'Lucrezia Borgia', 'Fair Rosamund', 'Medusa' and 'Aurelia,

Fazio's Mistress'. As well as being admired by visitors to major art galleries across the globe for 150 years, images of her have been reproduced on millions of prints, posters, greetings cards, postcards and books.

Her place and date of death are uncertain: a letter of 1905 states that she had been taken to 'somewhere near Brighton', possibly the home of her sister-in-law, who lived at The Turret, Hove.

Further reading: Walker, K.S. (e-book, 2006) *Stunner: The Fall and Rise of Fanny Cornforth.* [Related image p16.]

GLUCK FRSA née Hannah Gluckstein (1895–1978) artist and cross-dresser.

Born into the wealthy, dynastic, Jewish family that founded the J. Lyons & Co. catering and hotel empire, she attended St John's Wood Art School. She shocked her family by dressing and behaving like a man, smoking a pipe and opening doors for ladies. Generously provided for from the family trust, she lived in a luxurious house in Hampstead, was looked after by servants throughout her life, and had her suits, shirts and ties made by top couturiers.

Insisting on being known simply as Gluck, with 'no prefix, suffix, or quotes', she painted floral pieces, landscapes, self-portraits, her family, friends and lovers and designed and patented the Gluck frame, consisting of three stepped panels, making the painting appear to fade into the wall.

Her lovers included Constance Spry (florist to royalty) and socialite Nesta Obermer, whose many homes included The Mill House in Plumpton Lane, Plumpton, where Gluck stayed frequently from 1936, arriving from London in her hostess's chauffeur-driven Rolls Royce until she bought her own car. During the war she rented Miller's Mead, Plumpton, where she set up a studio and harangued and dismissed a long series of domestic servants.

During WWII she sketched local scenes, including an army canteen, women of the WI, and Edith Shackleton [84] working as a fire-warden. They met when Miss Shackleton attended an exhibition at Miller's Mead in 1942; later the pair enjoyed a week at the Beaufort Hotel, 21 Brunswick Place, Hove, and weekends at the Beach Hotel, Worthing. Despite this, Gluck was so possessive of Mrs Obermer that the latter ended the relationship, leaving Gluck devastated. Miss Shackleton invited her to stay awhile at the Chantry House, Steyning, the home she shared with her sister. Gluck's biographer records shrieking matches, friends staying away, servants resigning. The sister was driven out by 1946, selling Gluck her share of the house. Ten years later the Gluckstein family trust bought Miss Shackleton's share as well, making Gluck master of the house.

Her career flourished and the Royal Society of Arts awarded her a Life Fellowship in 1951. From 1953 to 1967 she spent one-third of her income and most of her time and energy on a campaign to improve the quality of artists' paints, and succeeded in obtaining official standardisation of pigments, oil and canvas. She continued to paint into old age, exhibiting at the age of seventy-five.

After thirty turbulent years Miss Shackleton moved out. Alone, Gluck receded from public view and became depressed. After she died her ashes were scattered in the garden of her studio at the Chantry House. Her painting 'Medallion', of herself and Nesta Obermer, was used for the cover of the Virago Press edition of the lesbian novel *The Well of Loneliness* [see Marguerite Radclyffe Hall, 245].

Further reading: Souhami, D. (2000) *Gluck.* [Related plate 9; image p107.]

NORA (SHACKLETON) HEALD (1881–1961) and **EDITH SHACKLETON (HEALD)** (1886–1976) journalists.

The two sisters, born in Lancashire, were by the 1920s among the most high-profile and respected female journalists of their generation. To preserve their individuality in professional life, Nora used their father's surname, Heald; Edith used their mother's, Shackleton (they were distant relatives of the explorer). In 1934 they bought the Chantry House at Steyning (living briefly at nearby Smuggler's Cottage while it was renovated). The estate included two cottages, which housed their domestic servants.

Throughout her working life Nora Heald stayed in London during the week, where she was a columnist on the *Daily Herald* and a writer for the *Sunday Despatch*, the *Daily Mail* and the *Daily Chronicle*. She made radio broadcasts in the 1920s and was editor of *The Queen*, then of *The Lady* from 1930 to 1953, where Stella Gibbons, author of *Cold Comfort Farm*, was her secretary. Her fashion writer was Alison Settle [85] who also moved to Steyning.

Miss Shackleton's name was well known to millions. She had been a suffragist and the first female reporter in the House of Lords; she wrote features for several daily and Sunday newspapers, for *The Lady* and for *Time and Tide*, a feminist magazine. She was the youngest-ever leader writer on the *Evening Standard*, and was the book reviewer and the 'witty and graceful' drama critic on the *Standard* and the *Daily Mail.* By the 1940s she was one of the highest-paid female journalists in the world and quotes from her reviews were proudly displayed on book jackets and advertisements. In her fifties Miss Shackleton had an affair with seventy-two-year-old poet W.B. Yeats, who had also been the lover of Dorothy Wellesley [261]. He visited frequently and wrote some of his final works at the Chantry House.

The sisters lived together in perfect harmony for fifty-eight years until their lives were torn apart in 1944 when Gluck [above] moved in. Miss Heald moved out in 1946 and lived for a few years in Wykeham Close, then at 106 High Street until at least 1957. Miss Shackleton endured a tempestuous relationship with Gluck for thirty years until, elderly and infirm, she moved into Homelands, a nursing home in Horsham Road, Cowfold, then to Carisbrook, 36 Goring Road, Steyning, where she died. Her ashes were buried in Steyning churchyard with those of her sister and mother.

The Chantry House bears a blue plaque in honour of W.B. Yeats, a mere visitor. Nothing records Miss Shackleton, Miss Heald, nor the artist Gluck who, collectively, lived there for at least eighty-two years. [Related images pp16, 107.]

ALISON TOWERS SETTLE OBE née Fuchs (1891–1980) journalist and editor.

Born in London, she attended Brighton & Hove High School and married a barrister in 1918. He died in 1925, and to support her two children she took up journalism. She was a regular contributor to *The Lady*, the *Daily Mirror* and the *Sunday Pictorial*, where she was in charge of the women's pages, was beauty editor at *Homes and Gardens*, director and editor of *Vogue* for eight years and fashion editor of the *Observer* for twenty-two years. She made many radio broadcasts from major fashion shows, wrote four books, was president of the Women's Press Club and a member of the Council for Art & Industry and the Council of Industrial Design. She won the Silver Medal of the Royal Society of Arts.

In the 1930s she lived between London and Kent, and from 1946 to 1971 at South Cottage, 6 Church Street, Steyning. She died at Worthing. The Alison Settle Archive at Brighton University preserves her papers on fashion, textiles, clothing and women's professional practice.

ELSIE WATERS OBE (1893–1990) and **DORIS WATERS OBE** (1899–1978) comedians.

The sisters, who were born in the East End of London, lived and worked together all their lives. Their brother, Jack Warner, was famous for being the eponymous 'Dixon of Dock Green' on TV, and they became internationally famous as the comical Cockney duo 'Gert & Daisy', much-loved characters whom they played in music halls, concerts, variety shows and films, on radio, television and gramophone records.

Their long and productive joint career began in 1927 and by the 1940s theirs was the most successful female double act on radio. They developed a completely new style of comedy by chatting to each other about their (imaginary) lives, friends and neighbours, and the world in general.

Doris died at their bungalow, Byfield, Goring Road, Steyning; Elsie ended her days at Downlands Rest Home, Laines Road, Steyning. The local museum holds a collection of 'Gert & Daisy' memorabilia. [Related plate 55.]

STORRINGTON

LADY CYNTHIA ASQUITH née Charteris (1887–1960) novelist and diarist.

The daughter of the 11th Earl of Wemyss, she was born in Wiltshire. At sixteen she met Herbert Asquith (whose father became Prime Minister in 1908); they became secretly engaged and married in 1910 against her parents' wishes. After WWI her shell-shocked husband could not work. To support her family, which included three sons, in 1918 she became secretary to the author of *Peter Pan*, Sir J.M. Barrie. They later became lovers, although he was twenty-seven years her senior. After he died in 1937, leaving her £30,000 (worth millions today), she moved to Sullington House, Washington Road, to be near her friend Viola Meynell [53] at Greatham. During her years with Sir James she had produced a series of ten anthologies and at Sullington began to write books, including ghost stories, royal biographies (notably those of Elizabeth I and the future Queen Mother) and a memoir of her former employer, *Portrait of Barrie*.

She was much admired for her dazzling good looks and her aristocratic blood, Enid Bagnold [171] and Angela Thirkell modelled novel characters on her, and some believe that her lifelong friend D.H. Lawrence modelled Lady Chatterley on her. In 1946 she moved to Bath and after her husband's death two years later settled in London, where she wrote *Haply I May Remember*, *Remember and Be Glad*, *Married to Tolstoy* and her *Diaries 1915–1918*, which were reprinted in 1987 and are considered her finest work. She died in Oxford.

Further reading: Beauman, N. (1987) *Cynthia Asquith*.

CICELY MARY BARKER (1895–1973) writer and artist.

A Surrey-born poet, children's writer, illustrator of books, postcards and greetings cards, and designer of religious memorial pieces and a triptych, she is best known for creating the famous Flower Fairies: ethereal, smiling children with butterfly wings. Although the children were idealised, the plants were botanically correct. She moved to Sussex in old age and, after living for some time in a nursing home in Storrington, died in Worthing Hospital.

Her paintings are now highly collectable, while the Flower Fairies are again becoming ubiquitous. Several of her fairy books for children were reprinted between 2002 and 2007, including a pop-up gift book, *How to Find Flower Fairies*, based on her work.

Further reading: Laing, J. (1995) *Cicely Mary Barker and her Art*.

DAME HELEN GWYNNE-VAUGHAN GBE née Fraser (1879–1967) mycologist, and head of the WAAC and WRAF.

Leaving her native London, she spent her childhood abroad and was educated by governesses and at Cheltenham Ladies' College. Against her family's wishes, in 1899 she became one of the first female students at King's College, London. She was awarded the Carter Medal and a BSc in botany; later she gained a DSc and a position as lecturer. In her spare time she performed voluntary work in girls' clubs and co-founded the University of London Women's Suffrage Society. In 1909 she became the first woman to head a department at Birkbeck College, London. She married paleobotanist David Gwynne-Vaughan in 1911, but was widowed just four years later and never remarried.

During WWI she was appointed chief controller of the WAAC. As head of female units in France she was responsible for 10,000 war-workers. In 1918 she took over leadership of the WRAF from Lady Rhondda, daughter of Viscountess Rhondda [148] and was the first woman appointed a military CBE; later she was raised to DBE, then GBE in 1929. In peacetime she was a professor of botany, the author of two books on fungi, and an unsuccessful Conservative Party candidate in the 1924 general election.

In 1939 she became the first director of the ATS, Army Branch, with the rank of chief controller, but did not do well and left two years later aged sixty-two. She returned to Birkbeck College as a lecturer until her retirement in 1944, after which she served on various military committees. She lived for three years at the RAF home at Sussexdown at Storrington, where she died. Her memorial service was held in the RAF church, St Clement Danes, London.

MAUDE DOMINICA PETRE (1863–1942) Roman Catholic critic and modernist.

The granddaughter of an earl, as a child she was exceptionally studious, read very widely, became fluent in French, Italian and Latin and a fervent Roman Catholic. She studied philosophy in Rome and in 1890 joined the Society of the Daughters of the Heart of Mary, an order of nuns who did not wear habits or live in convents. She became a local and later a provincial superior for England and Ireland, and had at least two (presumably consecutive) homes in Storrington: Mulberry House and Hespera Cottage.

Her involvement in modernism (which the Vatican tried to suppress) forced her to leave holy orders in 1908, and her home in Storrington, to the consternation of the Roman Catholic authorities, became a gathering place for modernists. She produced fourteen books and over ninety articles, and edited numerous essays by others. The Catholic Bishop of Southwark asked her to take an anti-modernist oath, but she refused. One of her works, (written as M.D. Petre) the *Autobiography and Life of George Tyrrell*, was even placed on the Roman Catholic index of forbidden books.

During WWI she served as a military nurse in France and England. She helped to establish a local branch of the Labour Party, served as chair of the municipal council for several years, founded a cottage hospital in Brewer's Yard, pioneered a local housing scheme and was president of the local WI. In the 1930s she lived at Erehwon, Cootham, Pulborough, but in 1939 she moved to London where, despite her advanced years, she took her turn fire-watching during the Blitz. She died in London and was buried in the churchyard of St Mary's, Storrington. Her papers are held Emory University, Atlanta.

LAVINIA SMILEY née Pearson (1919–1991) artist, author, and NT benefactor.

The granddaughter of Lady Cowdray [88] and niece of Lady Denman [32], she lived most of her life at Parham House, an Elizabethan mansion on a 4,000-acre estate that her father had bought in 1922 and restored. At St Peter's Church, Parham, in 1939 she married landowner Captain Michael Smiley of Shopwyke House, Chichester. They had three children. Her elder sister was to inherit Parham but in 1955 her father gave Lavinia Castle Fraser and its estates, and she continued his programme of complete architectural restoration. When in 1976 it was finished to perfection, the castle and its policies, with an endowment, were made over to the National Trust and it is currently one of its most-visited Scottish properties.

She was an artist and an author, and published a number of children's books, which she also illustrated. She wrote a memoir of her early years, *A Nice Clean Plate* (1981) and a biographical history, *The Frasers of Castle Fraser* (1989). [Related image p108.]

SULLINGTON

JANE (LOIS MARION) BENNETT (1915– 2007) WRNS officer and TES art editor.

The daughter of a GP, she was born in Billingshurst, where in the 1920s her family lived at Rose Hill. She was educated in Paris, Switzerland and Germany and in 1939 was recruited to the WRNS as a foreign language specialist to the commander-in-chief at Plymouth. By 1941 she was in charge of a team of linguists involved in reading Axis signals traffic and in 1942 was sent to the Intelligence Department at the Admiralty, where she became a first officer.

From 1945 she was employed on the *Times Educational Supplement,* becoming features editor in 1961 and from 1969 art editor, in charge of images. Under her influence the TES became attractive, lively, accessible and entertaining, owing to the increased use of photographs, cartoons and other illustrations, and during her tenure its circulation doubled to 90,000 by 1966. After retiring in 1975 she lived in Sullington, moving later to Wiltshire.

TANGMERE

ANNA CROPPER (1938–2007) actress.

Lancastrian Miss Cropper rose to fame playing challenging dramatic roles, often as haunted, mentally-ill characters in films, and on TV and radio during the 1960s and 1970s. Her performances drew excellent reviews and in later years she appeared in *Casualty, Midsomer Murders* and *Poirot*.

She married William Roache (Ken Barlow in *Coronation Street*) but divorced him in 1974. In later life she lived between Turkey and Tangmere, which she called 'God's little pocket' and where she died.

THREE BRIDGES

DAME CAROLINE HASLETT DBE, JP (1895–1957) engineer and electricity promoter.

The daughter of a railway signal fitter, she was born and raised at New Road, Three Bridges, and attended Haywards Heath High School. During WWI she became a secretary locally at the Cochran Boiler Company, but finding that such stereotypical women's work did not suit her she requested a transfer to the firm's boiler works in London. Most unusually, this was granted and she received a thorough training in engineering.

To encourage the use of electricity in the home she wrote articles (addressed mainly to women) in newspapers and magazines and edited the *Electrical Handbook for Women*, which went into six editions in her lifetime. She served on dozens of public bodies, travelled the world promoting the use of electricity and wrote many academic papers. She was the only female member of the British Electricity Authority on its inception in 1947 and served on its successors until her death.

A staunch feminist and campaigner for equal pay, she did much to open engineering to women, mentoring individuals who wanted to pursue it as a career. She founded the Electrical Association for Women in 1924, which reached a peak membership of 14,000. (By 2000 this stood at 4,000 and it closed down.) She was the first secretary of the Women's Engineering Society, edited its journal and was its president (1939–41). In 1949 she wrote *Problems Have No Sex* and in 1950 became president of the International Federation of Business and Professional Women. She was appointed a companion member of the Institution of Electrical Engineers and an electric-cable ship was named for her. She served on Crawley Development Corporation (set up in 1947 to plan and build the town) and as a magistrate.

Appointed CBE in 1931 and DBE in 1947, she died having never married her long-term boyfriend, engineer Fred Button. Her wish to be cremated by electricity was fulfilled at the City of London Crematorium, and her ashes were scattered in its grounds. After her death the Caroline Haslett Memorial Trust was established to provide scholarships for women in engineering. Haslett Avenue, Crawley, was named for her, and boasts a blue plaque on EDF Energy Networks' premises.

Further reading: Messenger, R. (1967) *The Doors of Opportunity: A Biography of Caroline Haslett DBE.*

TURNERS HILL

ANNIE, VISCOUNTESS COWDRAY GBE née Cass (1860–1932) philanthropist.

After leaving her native Yorkshire, she married Weetman Pearson MP, a building contractor who struck oil in Mexico. According to his biographer, in 1888 when he was building a railway in Spain, she 'went with him and shared the rough quarters, bad food, and exposure to all weathers'. He shared every detail of his business and political life with her; she made speeches and canvassed at his electoral contests and took care of the constituency business whenever he was away. He bought the Paddockhurst estate, near Worth Abbey, in 1894, when it was described in *The Times* as '1,900 acres, with a commodious mansion'. In 1909 he bought the 9,000-acre Dunecht Estate in Scotland as a gift for his wife.

She was president of the Horsham Suffrage Society and in 1912 shared a speaking platform with Clementina Black

[123] at the Royal Albert Hall. During WWI she was treasurer of the London unit of the SWH and in 1917 led the largest-ever deputation of women to the Prime Minister to demand votes for women. She was a patron of many charities, including the South London Hospital for Women [see Eleanor Davies-Colley, 70], donated an expensive London house, 20 Cavendish Square, to create a nurses' club and gave another property, worth £20,000, to a girls' club. Together the Pearsons donated £50,000 to Aberdeen's hospitals, the equivalent to millions today.

Her husband was raised to the peerage in 1910 as Baron Cowdray of Midhurst and became a viscount in 1917. On his death in 1927 she inherited his valuable house in central London and succeeded him as High Steward of Colchester, the first woman to fill such a role. She gave oak panelling, a lichgate and a memorial screen in his honour to St Leonard's Church, Turners Hill. Appointed GBE in 1931, she died at the Ritz Hotel, Paris, the following year. Her daughter Trudie became Lady Denman [32] and her granddaughter was Lavinia Smiley [87]. [Related image p108, 298.]

WALBERTON

ROSEMARY SUTCLIFF CBE (1920–1992) children's novelist.

Although born in Surrey, she grew up in Malta, where her father was a naval officer. A victim of Still's Disease (a form of juvenile rheumatoid arthritis), she used a wheelchair for most of her life. Her schooling was poor: her family moved house several times and her illness led to frequent hospitalisation.

At fourteen she enrolled in Bideford Art School, Devon, which she attended for three years. Following the advice of her tutors she took up painting miniatures, joined the Royal Society of Miniature Painters and exhibited at the Royal Academy. But her heart was not really in it, because she longed to write. In her mid-twenties she sent a book of Celtic and Saxon legends to the Oxford University Press. They rejected it but commissioned her to write something about Robin Hood. Her *Chronicles of Robin Hood*, and *The Queen Elizabeth Story* appeared in 1950. From then she wrote continuously, producing novels (five of them for adults), legends, radio scripts, plays and her autobiography, *Blue Remembered Hills*. She loved dogs and sometimes wrote them into her novels; a particular fan of Chihuahuas, she kept two, Pippin and Barbaby.

Miss Sutcliff spent the majority of her adult life at Flint Cottage, Yapton Lane, Walberton, where, after her father's death, she was dependent on paid carers. Although her hands were crippled with arthritis she wrote four drafts of each novel in longhand. Writing daily, from mid-morning till night, each of her works took about ten months to complete. Her thirty-seven books sold well and were placed on reading lists nation-wide, making her virtually a household name, and she narrated some of her writings for broadcast on BBC radio. She won the Carnegie Award, the *Boston Globe* Horn Book Award, the Hans Christian Andersen Award and the Phoenix Children's Book Award, was appointed OBE in 1975 and CBE in 1992.

She was still writing on the morning of her death, which occurred at St Richard's Hospital, Chichester. Her final work, *Sword Song*, was completed by her cousin, Anthony Lawton, edited by Jill Black and published posthumously in 1997. Her books are still popular and her King Arthur trilogy was reprinted in 2007.

WARNHAM

ELIZA, LADY PRIESTLEY née Chambers (1836–1909) public health campaigner.

One of the eight daughters of a publisher, she was born in Edinburgh. In 1856 she married gynaecologist and obstetrician William Priestley, a distant relation of Bessie Rayner Parkes [79]. They started life impoverished but soon prospered as he gained renown for his medical work.

Mrs Priestley, who had four children, also contributed greatly to public health,

though not for money. She served on numerous London committees such as the National Health Society and the Homes for Waifs and Strays, and was president of a number of organisations including the ladies' committee of the British Medical Association. She wrote many journal articles on health issues such as 'Winged Carriers of Disease' and 'The Penalties of Ignorance' and campaigned for the compulsory registration of midwives. She co-founded the Children's Hospital, where she promoted the modern methods of hygiene propounded by Pasteur and Lister.

Lady Priestley was appointed a Lady of Grace of the Order of St John of Jerusalem in 1894. Her husband, who delivered the babies of two of Queen Victoria's daughters, was knighted in 1893 and became an MP in 1896. Among their famous friends were Chamberlain, Millais and Dickens. The late 1890s saw them attending dinner parties at Number Ten and receptions at Buckingham Palace. In 1898 Sir William bought a posh residence in London's Mayfair, and Westbrook Hall, a seventeenth-century, timber-framed manor house near Warnham with fifty acres of land where they lived until their respective deaths.

Widowed in 1900, she published her autobiography *The Story of a Lifetime* in 1908, died the following year in London and was buried next to her husband in the churchyard of St John's, Warnham.

WASHINGTON

VERA PRAGNELL (1896–1968) alternative living pioneer.

The daughter of textile magnate Sir George Pragnell, she was born in London. During WWI she worked for the Red Cross and suffered the loss of her father and brother. She studied sociology, psychology and economics, became a mystical Christian socialist, bought a cottage in Haslemere, Surrey, and invited others to share her simple lifestyle there. Upon receipt of her inheritance she sold the cottage and in 1922 bought a large tract of land and two derelict cottages at

Heath Common, between Washington and Storrington, for £850. Here she established The Sanctuary, a self-sufficient commune where people of all classes, ages and beliefs could live together as a community. Although she did everything in the name of God and had a large cross erected, she did not insist the settlers practice any religion.

Miss Pragnell spoke of her project at Speakers' Corner in Hyde Park, London, and soon settlers began to arrive from all over the UK, including some from the East End slums, and set up home in caravans and tents. (One early resident was W.C. Owen, a well-known anarchist; another was Dion Byngham, formerly a leader in the Order of Woodcraft Chivalry.) She gave them plots of land upon which they began to build wooden shacks, to plant vegetables and to keep livestock. The Sanctuary had no electricity, and water was obtained from a well or rainwater-butts, but there were community events, concerts and dancing. Rumours that settlers frolicked naked and practised what was then called 'free love' did not destroy the commune; that was effected by people's selfishness and greed. At first, some settlers began to erect fences around their plots; then some died, and their heirs sold the land for large sums. The true communards became disheartened and left and the Sanctuary came to an end.

In 1927 Miss Pragnell married an artist, Dennis Earle, and the couple went to Tahiti for eighteen months. On their return, using the two cottages (long since knocked into one) they opened Sleepy Hollow, Longbury Hill, 'the little Downland country house hotel that is different', promising 'Beauty and comfort, courtesy and peace'. Their daughter Deirdre and Mrs Earle's mother Leonora, Lady Pragnell, lived with them.

Mr Earle built houses on the remaining plots, and the whole area is now covered by expensive, detached homes. Evidence of her experiment lives on in the private-road names Sanctuary Lane and Vera's Walk, where a timber shelter dedicated to her memory contains an explanatory plaque. [Related image p104.]

WEST BURTON

MABEL CONSTANDUROS née Tilling (1880–1957) comedian, scriptwriter and playwright.

Born in Walworth, south London, after working as her father's secretary she joined an amateur dramatic society and trained at the Central School of Speech Training. In 1906 she married an insurance broker and had two sons in 1908 (both died as babies) and a third in 1915. Writing sketches and short stories led her to join the BBC Radio Repertory Company at the age of forty-five. She became famous for creating the Buggins Family of Walworth, for which she wrote 250 scripts between 1925 and 1948, and at the beginning she also played all six characters, from the granny to the baby. Years later she created a second radio family: the Robinsons. She also wrote over a hundred plays, some with her nephew, and appeared on the West End stage, in films and on gramophone records.

Although it was her married name, she was always known as 'Miss' Constanduros. She left her husband by the late 1920s and moved with her teenaged son to Sussex, where she lived for about thirty years, at Pound Cottage in Rustington, then Prattenden in Bury, New Cottage in West Burton and lastly Five Oaks in West Burton. She played Mrs Buggins for the last time, aged seventy-six, when she opened Aldingbourne church fête. She died a year later at the Royal West Sussex Hospital, Chichester.

Further reading: Constanduros, M. (1946) *Shreds and Patches*. [Related plate 34.]

WEST CHILTINGTON

SHEILA VAN DAMM (1922–1987) rally driver and theatre owner.

She was born into a wealthy, Jewish family in London, where in 1944 her father Vivian inherited London's famous Windmill Theatre from his employer (Laura Henderson). She was a daring, sporty woman who especially enjoyed activities that were outside of the accepted behaviour for members of her sex. During WWII she served as a WAAF driver, trained privately as a pilot in peacetime and joined the WRAF Volunteer Reserve.

As a publicity stunt for her father's theatre Miss van Damm entered the 1950 Marylebone Cricket Club–*Daily Express* car rally as the 'Windmill Girl'. She won third place in the ladies' section and was invited to join an all-female crew for the 1951 Monte Carlo Rally. The winner of a ladies' prize in the 1951 RAC Rally and the 1952 Motor Cycling Club Rally, she once beat famous racing driver Stirling Moss and set a world record driving a prototype 137 Alpine sports car at 120mph. She competed in rallies around the world and won several more prizes, including the Coupe des Dames (the highest award for women) and the Coup des Alpes. After coming second in the 1956 Italian Mille Miglia race, having driven a Sunbeam Rapier 1,000 miles at an average of 66mph, she was featured in Sunbeam's newspaper advertisements.

She left the sport in 1956, became president of the Doghouse Club (for motor-racing wives) and of the Sunbeam Talbot Owners' Club, and wrote her autobiography, which she called *No Excuses*. In 1960 she inherited the Windmill Theatre and soon became renowned for booking up-and-coming young comedians such as Peter Sellers, Bruce Forsyth, Harry Secombe and Tony Hancock. But Soho was rapidly becoming too seedy for her taste and she sold the theatre in 1964 and wrote *We Never Closed: The Windmill Story* (1967).

She moved to Broadford Bridge Farm, West Chiltington, and with her sister Nona ran a small farm and stables. In later life she became a dedicated fund-raiser for the International Spinal Research Trust.

WEST GRINSTEAD

DREDA, LADY TRYON née Etheldreda Josephine Burrell (1909–2001) founder of Manor House School.

The daughter of Sir Merrik Burrell Bt. and a relation of Ursula Wyndham [71], she was born at Knepp Castle, which continued to be her home until marriage. In the 1920s she shocked everyone by setting off alone on a year-long journey around the world — not the 'done thing' for an upper-class young lady at that time. During her grand adventure she shot a crocodile in India, was arrested in Korea and made history by becoming the first woman to play polo in Iraq.

In 1939 she married Captain Charles Tryon (who later became Lord Tryon, Keeper of the Privy Purse and Treasurer to the Queen). They went to live on his inherited 2,000-acre country estate at Great Durnford, Wiltshire. The maintenance and repairs of the estate and its 109-roomed mansion were very costly. To raise funds, while he was serving in the war she founded a girls' boarding school on the premises, developed it into one of the best in Britain and ran it herself for fifty years. She had a great sense of humour, and arrived at the school for her eightieth birthday party dressed as Boadicea and riding in a 'chariot' — the side-car of a motorcycle.

She had a son and a daughter, and enjoyed horse- and dog-racing and keeping greyhounds. She was county commissioner for the Girl Guides in Wiltshire and served on the PNEU.

WEST HOATHLY

NORAH BRADEN (1901–2001) potter.

Born in Kent, she was a talented violinist who eschewed music school to study art at the Central School and the Royal College of Art in London. She specialised in ceramics and for many years worked and lived with fellow potter Katharine Pleydell-Bouverie in Berkshire, where they designed, created and fired many beautiful pieces that were exhibited in London galleries, drawing considerable praise.

She lived in Sussex for a quarter of her century-long life. Having moved to West Hoathly in 1936 to look after her mother (possibly at a house called Cobwebbs) she stayed until her mother's death in 1954. She returned to Sussex in 1994, when she entered Sailaway Retirement Home, Bosham, where she died seven years later. Examples of her work can be found in the V & A, the Fitzwilliam Museum, Cambridge, and many other collections.

KATHARINE ESDAILE née McDowall (1881–1950) art historian.

A niece of E. W. Benson, the Archbishop of Canterbury, her mother was a high school headmistress and her father was secretary of the Girls' Public Day School Trust. She was born in London, where she attended Notting Hill High School and later read classics at Lady Margaret Hall. In 1907 she married bibliographer Arundell Esdaile of Hazelwood Park, Horsted Keynes, future secretary of the British Museum, and had three children.

During WWI she ran an estate agency when its owners were called up to fight. She then worked for the architectural publishers Batsford and studied post-Reformation sculpture, making herself the leading authority in what had been, until then, a neglected subject. She had an indefatigable capacity for work and her notes on the churches she visited across Britain filled fifty notebooks. These were adapted into hundreds of scholarly and influential articles that appeared in a host of academic journals. In addition she wrote six books, including *English Church Monuments* (1946) and was a specialist on the sculptor Roubiliac. She wrote (as Katharine A. Esdaile or Mrs Arundell Esdaile) with what one reviewer described as 'infectious enthusiasm' and in 1928 received a Royal Society of Arts Medal.

From 1927 the Esdailes lived at Leams End, Highbrook Lane, a six-bedroomed house with six-and-a-half acres of land, and attended nearby St Margaret's Church. She died at the Queen Victoria Hospital, East Grinstead. *English Church Monuments* is easily available from secondhand bookshops. [Related image p103.]

WOODMANCOTE

FREDDA BRILLIANT FRSA (1903–1999) sculptor and author.

Born in Poland, her career began in the 1930s in Moscow and took her to Australia, India, the USA and England. Although primarily a sculptor, in the 1920s she had trained as an opera singer and during WWII performed with a touring theatrical company.

A member of the Society of Portrait Sculptors, her sitters included many eminent persons such as Molotov, Eisenstein and Nehru. When she arrived in France to sculpt Picasso he pinched her bottom, so she left and never spoke to him again. Her statue of Mahatma Ghandi, cross-legged and wearing a dhoti, was unveiled by Harold Wilson in 1965 in Tavistock Square, London, where it still enjoys pride of place.

Married to Herbert Marshall, she lived and worked at Hole Farm, Brighton Road, and The Barn Studio, East Kentwyns, Woodmancote, where she sculpted Duncan Grant [see Vanessa Bell, 214]. In 1966 she moved with her husband to the USA, where he was a professor of Soviet and East European studies. Returning in 1989, they fought and won a legal battle to reclaim their home from tenants, and installed a giant copy of her statue of Gandhi between the front door and her studio.

In the 1980s she wrote several books (*Biographies in Bronze, The Black Virgin, Truth in Fiction* and *Women in Power*) which are now out of print and unavailable. She died in the USA. Locals still remember her long, black dresses, tasselled shawls, brightly-coloured headscarves and fur coats, and the way she sang out loud in the streets. [Related image p16.]

WORTH

LADY ANNE BLUNT née King; Baroness Wentworth (1837–1917) breeder of Arab horses, traveller and author.

Her grandfather was Lord Byron, her mother the Hon. Ada Byron, her father William King, 1st Earl Lovelace, and she was raised and well educated by her grandmother Lady Byron [126]. Having a private income of £3,000 a year (worth £175,000 today) enabled her to study the arts and sciences at a high level: she learned four languages, was taught to draw by John Ruskin, and owned two Stradivarius violins, upon which she practised daily. In 1869 she married poet Wilfrid Scawen Blunt, who in 1872 inherited the 400-acre Crabbet Park estate, and other property; by 1898 they were living at New Place, Shipley (near Horsham) and in 1911 at Dragon's Green Rd, near Brooks Green, and Hillside, Worth.

Lady Anne was probably the first Western woman to cross the Arabian desert on horseback and the first to visit the Arabian Peninsula. She translated texts from Arabic to English for publication. She also wrote several books, including *Bedouin Tribes of the Euphrates* (1879, reprinted 2006) and *A Pilgrimage to Nejd, the Cradle of the Arab Race* (1881). Her watercolours were exhibited in Saudi Arabia, where the couple purchased Arab stallions and mares from sheikhs and shipped them to Crabbet Park, where they founded a world-famous private stud. A second stud was developed on their thirty-acre estate in Egypt.

Lady Anne had much misfortune in her life. Her many pregnancies resulted in a heartbreaking series of miscarriages, stillbirths and cradle-deaths, and just one surviving child, Judith [below]. Crabbet Park was targeted by burglars in 1881, and in 1887 she was injured and fell unconscious during a rowdy political meeting In Ireland at which her husband was arrested. He pursued numerous affairs (and even moved his mistresses into Crabbet Park), and so Lady Anne preferred to live in Egypt.

In 1906 the Blunts separated and the stud was divided: half went to Wilfred (at Newbuildings Place, Southwater) and half to Lady Anne (at Crabbet Park). She moved to Shaykh Ubayd, Egypt, remaining there for most of the rest of her life while Judith ran the stud in Sussex. In 1917 Lady Anne became the 15th Baroness Wentworth (in her own right), but died in Cairo later that year. Her journals are housed in the British Library in London.

Further reading: Winstone, H. (2005) *Lady Anne Blunt: A Biography.* [Related images pp116, 117.]

BARONESS WENTWORTH née Judith Blunt (1873–1957) horse-breeder and author.

The daughter of Lady Anne Blunt [above], she was born in London but spent much of her childhood in the Middle East. In 1899 she married the Hon. Neville Lytton (from 1947, 3rd Earl of Lytton) in Cairo and they moved to a house on her parents' Crabbet Park estate. He deserted her and their two children (they were to divorce in 1923). In 1904 her father gave her the estate and the famous stud. On her mother's death in 1917 she became the 16th Baroness Wentworth and her daughters inherited her mother's half-share of the Crabbet stud. However, her father repeatedly snatched horses and took them to Newbuildings estate. He dispersed the Cairo stud and sold some of the finest horses. She took legal action against him in 1920 and the court found in her favour.

For thirty-seven years Crabbet stud flourished in her hands. As a breeder she had few equals, combining knowledge with instinct, and ninety per cent of all Arabian horses in the world today carry lines to Crabbet bloodstock in their pedigrees. As well as breeding Arabs, she created a White Mountain pony stud and bred dogs: her toy spaniels won countless championships. She wrote *Thoroughbred Racing Stock and its Ancestors* (1938) and *The Authentic Arabian Horse and his Descendants* (1945, reprinted 1980) as well as works of poetry and a book on toy dogs. Unusually for a lady she played billiards and squash, but her great passion was real tennis, for which she had a superb court built at Crabbet Park, employing a resident coach, world champion Geoffrey Covey, to train her to championship level (though there was no ladies' competition). In gratitude she gave him Maidenbower and Frogshole farms and made him stud groom and farm manager.

After she died, in hospital in Crawley, the barony of Wentworth passed to her son. She bequeathed the stud farm to Mr Covey, but he had died a few days before her, so it passed to his son Cecil. Confronted with over seventy horses and a fat tax bill, he had no choice but to sell some. In 1970 work began on the M23, which completely bisected the property. The remaining horses were bought by breeders the instant he offered them for sale, and the legendary, century-old stud was no more, though its memory lives on in the modern street names Horseshoe Close, The Covey and Bridle Way. Crabbet Park House was turned into flats in 1963. A plaque commemorating Crabbet Park Stud is on nearby Gatwick Worth Hotel.

WORTHING

VIVIEN ALCOCK (1924–2003) writer.

She was born in Worthing, where she spent the first sixteen years of her life, leaving to study at the Oxford School of Art. During WWII she worked as an ambulance driver with the ATS in Belgium, France and Germany. Against the wishes of both sets of parents she married Leon Garfield in 1948 and they adopted a child in 1964. She worked as a commercial artist and assisted her novelist husband by giving him many plotlines. Only in mid-life did she begin to write novels herself. The first of her twenty books, *The Haunting of Cassie Palmer*, appeared when she was fifty-six; her last, *The Boy Who Swallowed a Ghost*, when she was seventy-seven. She spent her married life in London, where she died.

HRH PRINCESS AMELIA (1783–1810) populariser of Worthing as a resort.

The fifteenth child of the reigning monarch George III, she was born at Windsor Castle. She arrived at Worthing on 1st August 1798, aged fourteen, to improve her ailing health by bathing in sea water, which was then believed to have curative properties; the 120-strong Derbyshire Militia descended upon the town to serve as her personal bodyguard. On her birthday a week later local churches pealed their bells and royal salutes were fired offshore and by the militia; at night the sky was brilliantly illuminated.

Her stay, in a house at Montague Place, lasted for only six months, but it drew to the town the aristocratic, the fashionable and their followers. Their patronage over the next decades transformed Worthing from an obscure fishing village to a thriving resort. The female figure on Worthing's Coat of Arms is believed to be Princess Amelia, the teenaged girl who unwittingly changed Worthing irrevocably and forever. [Related plate 27.]

ANTHEA ASKEY (1933–1999) entertainer.

Just after her birth, in London, Miss Askey's father Arthur made his first BBC radio broadcast as a comic actor. As she grew up he shot to super-stardom and became a household name. During WWII the Askeys moved to Worthing and in 1944 bought a permanent home somewhere in Sussex, where they caught the gardener stealing their home-grown vegetables to sell to the local greengrocer!

Miss Askey was sent to boarding school on the Isle of Wight, where, aged twelve, she made her first stage appearance, and at fifteen she was cast as Violet Elizabeth in a radio adaptation of *Just William*. Although always working in her father's shadow, being his daughter had its advantages: her twenty-first birthday party, held at the Dorchester Hotel, was attended by the cream of British showbiz. During the 1950s she appeared, much of the time alongside her father, in plays, pantomimes, films and shows, and was a regular on *The Dickie Henderson Show*.

After marrying Bill Stewart in 1956 she retired from the limelight to raise her three children (a fourth died as a baby). In the 1980s she tried to revive her career but she was unknown to younger audiences and could obtain bookings only in panto and in provincial theatres, though she was the Worthing compère of the national talent contest *Search For a Star* [see Gladys Morgan, 99], appeared in a couple of panel shows and secured a small part in *The Darling Buds of May* in 1993. She died in a hospice in Worthing, a week before her planned wedding to pianist Will Fyffe.

JESSIE BOND (1853–1942) Savoyard.

Although born in London, she was raised in Liverpool, where she became firstly a pianist and then a contralto. She was married briefly (at sixteen) to a brutal man called Schöttlander and had a child that died in infancy. For the next twenty years she refused many proposals of marriage. From 1878 she appeared as a leading lady in the Savoy Operas for thirteen years, including a year touring the USA with *HMS Pinafore* and *The Pirates of Penzance*, and was highly regarded by W.S. Gilbert and Sir Arthur Sullivan, who wrote many parts especially for her. She was the original 'Tessa' in the Gondoliers, playing opposite Decima Moore [143], the first 'Casilda'. By 1890 she was earning £45 a week (worth

£2,500 today) and singing for the Prince of Wales at soirées and dinner parties.

W.S. Gilbert wrote that he would be 'distressed beyond measure' if she left, but she did so in 1891 and toured with a number of other companies until 1897, when she married Lewis Henry Ransome. She retired from public life, exhausted by overwork, although she was tempted out of retirement by revivals of the Savoy Operas in the late nineties.

Widowed in 1922, two years later she moved to Worthing, where she was to end her days. At first she entertained wounded WWI soldiers and sailors in local convalescent homes, then turned her attention to compiling her memoirs.

Further reading: Bond, J. (1930) *The Life and Reminiscences of Jessie Bond, The Old Savoyard, as Told by Herself to Ethel MacGeorge.* [Related image p16.]

VIOLET CAMERON real name Thompson (1862–1919) comic actress and producer.

Known for her startling blonde hair and gorgeous singing voice, her career as a West End actress lasted thirty-three years, during which she founded the Violet Cameron Opera Company, which toured the provinces and the USA. She was equally famous for her private life, which scandalised Victorian London. While married to Spanish baritone David de Bensaude she had an affair with the Earl of Lonsdale, a married man she met in Brighton in 1886. The furious actions of her estranged husband, including two years of incessant harassment, during which he twice smashed his way into her house, threatened her life and sued Lord Lonsdale for £10,000 damages, dragged all three names through the courts and was extensively reported not only by the gutter press but also in the broadsheets and magazines, where they were repeatedly and mercilessly lampooned in doggerel verse and cartoons.

After a divorce, Mr de Bensaude disappeared into obscurity, Lord Lonsdale returned to his wife, and Miss Cameron continued her stage career while raising her children (a boy by her husband; a girl by her lover). She died after a short illness at Holindale, Madeira Avenue, Worthing and was buried at Broadwater cemetery. Interestingly, her obituary in *The Times* misrepresents her as lifelong spinster while the Earl's obituarist claims he died childless.

EDITH COATES OBE (1908–1983) mezzo-soprano.

Born in Lincoln, she trained at Trinity College of Music and enjoyed a glittering stage career lasting forty years, becoming a leading lady of the Sadler's Wells Opera Company, where she was famed for her commanding presence and powerful voice. In 1933 she married actor, director, designer, manager and producer Harry Powell Lloyd. Appointed OBE in 1977, she died at her home in Worthing.

ALMA COGAN real name Alma Cohen (1932–1966) pop singer.

When she was a child her family left her native east London and moved to Worthing, where they initially lived above their shop in Warwick Street, then in a large house on the corner of Lansdowne Road and Downview Road. They later moved to Berkshire. Effervescent and glamorous, from 1952 to 1966 she made a large number of recordings, was the resident singer on a BBC radio show and was among the highest-paid female entertainers of her era. She died of cancer aged just thirty-four.

Further reading: Caron, S. (1991) *Alma Cogan: The Girl with the Laugh in her Voice.*

MARY COULES (1896–1957) journalist.

Her father was an editor (and later deputy chief) at Reuters news agency, where she joined him in 1917. Unusually for a woman, she became an expert on international affairs, specialising in French politics and spending half her forty-year working life in the Paris office, an employee of Roderick Jones, the husband of Enid Bagnold [171]. A woman in a what was then a man's world, she was described as being 'worth a man-and-a-half'. She was very proud to have been the only female journalist present at the Versailles Peace Conference in 1919. In her spare time she wrote adventure stories. She retired to Worthing, where she died.

CHARLOTTE COWDROY MBE (1864–1932) founder of Crouch End school.

She was born in London where, obeying her father, she studied at Stockwell Training College and taught at elementary level. Defying him she enrolled on a degree course, and so he terminated all financial support. In 1900 she opened her own school, which was soon attracting pupils from all over the world and grew into Crouch End High School and College, of which she was director-principal until her retirement. The school's ethos emphasised femininity and she caused controversy in 1921 by arguing that strenuous sports could adversely affect girls' reproductive ability.

She retired to and died in Worthing, having just completed her book, *Wasted Womanhood,* which was published a year after her death and included a biography of Miss Cowdroy by Marguerite Bennell.

CAMILLA CROUDACE (1844–1926) linguist and educationalist.

Her father's career having taken her to Kiev, Miss Croudace learned French, German and Russian. In 1856 her mother read in an English newspaper that young women could obtain higher education at Queen's College and immediately sent Camilla there. For several years she earned her living as a governess and schoolteacher before landing a position as lady resident at Queen's, where she became the dominant influence for the next quarter-century, devoted to the cause of women's higher education. She retired in 1906 and moved to Keith Cottage, Park Avenue, Worthing, where she died. She was buried at St Peter's, Lynchmere.

EMILY WILDING DAVISON (1872–1913) suffragette.

A Christian, socialist and feminist, she was born in London and educated by a governess. She worked as a teacher at Seabury School, West Worthing, for two years from 1896. Later she achieved first class honours in English at St Hugh's. A WSPU suffragette, the last of her many militant acts was to throw herself in front of the King's horse Anmer at the 1913 Derby [see Mary Richardson, 227]. She died of her injuries and was buried in Northumberland.

Further reading: Stanley, L. and Morley, A. (1988) *Life and Death of Emily Wilding Davison.* [Related image p16.]

DAME ANN EBSWORTH DBE (1937–2002) high court judge.

The daughter of a Royal Marines officer, she was educated at Notre Dame Convent in Worth, Portsmouth High School and Royal Holloway College. From 1962 until 1983 she was a barrister in Liverpool, then was appointed a circuit judge. She was nicknamed 'Foghorn' because her booming voice could be heard two rooms away. In 1993 she became the sixth female High Court judge (when there were 105 men) and later was the first woman appointed to the Queen's Bench Division of the High Court. This surprised her, because female judges were usually allocated family work, not serious crime cases.

Her work obliged her to reside in Liverpool for many years, but she retired to somewhere in Sussex, where she enjoyed her large garden. She died in Worthing, leaving £1m to the Institute of Child Health to fund a research chair in childhood epilepsy at Great Ormond Street Hospital.

MARY FIELD OBE (1896–1968) film producer.

Born in Wimbledon, she graduated from Bedford College with an MA. In 1926 she became a film director and, apart from making one comedy in 1931, spent her career producing hundreds of educational films for children, some of which she narrated herself. Over the years she came to be acknowledged as the world's leading authority on children's films. She was executive producer for J. Arthur Rank Children's Cinema Clubs, served on the British Board of Film Censors, was a Fellow of the British Film Academy, a judge of scripts for the British Film Institute and president emeritus of UNESCO's International Centre of Films for Children. She is chiefly remembered for her pioneering, award-winning films of nature in slow motion.

She married an older man in 1944 and was widowed in 1952, after which she carried out lecture-tours in Europe, Australia, New Zealand and India, and wrote many articles and several books about her work, including *Good Company* (1952). President of the British Federation of Business and Professional Women, she was appointed OBE for services to children's education. She died at Brimar Nursing Home, 27 St Botolph's Road, West Worthing.

MARGOT GORE MBE (1913–1993) pioneering military pilot.

Born and raised at Carclew, Brighton Road, Worthing, she moved to London and worked at Smithfield Market to finance her flying lessons. During WWII she was a flying instructor and in 1940 began ferrying new and repaired Tiger Moths between factories and airfields as a pilot in the women's section of the ATA. By 1941 she held the rank of captain, and was for four years commanding officer at Hamble-on-Solent Ferry Pool, in charge of pilots of both sexes. In 1943 she became the first woman to fly Halifax bombers and Boeing B17s.

Appointed MBE in 1945, two years later she was the first woman to enlist in the WRAF reserve. In peacetime she became a practitioner and lecturer in osteopathy and played golf at county level. She died in Oxfordshire.

FRANCES MARION GOSTLING née Parkinson (1860–1935) travel-writer, translator and photographer.

Leaving her native London in 1887, she married a physician and they settled at Barningham, Rowland's Road, Worthing. She wrote mainly about France and, unusually for a woman at that time, was an expert photographer and used her own work to illustrate her books. Best known for her 1909 book *The Bretons at Home*, she also wrote *Auvergne and its People* (1911, reprinted 2004) and translated two books by Breton writer Anatole le Bras. She died at Barningham, 40 Crescent Road, Worthing (now South Lodge Children's Centre).

EMILY HAIGH pseudonym Beatrice Hastings (1879–1943) writer and journal editor.

A South African by birth, she was educated at a boarding school in Pevensey. Having squandered a large inheritance, she rode horses in a Transvaal circus and worked as a showgirl in New York before arriving in Paris in 1914, where for two years she enjoyed a tempestuous, habitually (and mutually) violent, live-in relationship with the artist Modigliani, who painted her at least fourteen times. Described as a short-tempered, alcoholic bisexual, she had been married twice by the age of thirty, and once remarked that there were so many notches on her bed post 'she had nearly whittled away her bed'.

She was a journalist on a highbrow Parisian journal and later co-edited and contributed to *New Age* magazine. Using her pseudonym she wrote and published poems and stories, and essays on feminism and social reform. Settling in England in 1937 she wrote and self-published, under the imprint The Hastings Press, two small volumes called the *Defence of Madame Blavatsky*. She married a boxer called Lachie Thomson and lived at 4 Bedford Row, Worthing, where one day she was found dead, having asphyxiated herself with domestic gas. She stipulated in her will that no service be held and that her ashes be thrown 'down a hill, or in a field'.

Further reading: Gray, S. (2004) *Beatrice Hastings: A Literary Life.* Meyers, J. (2006) *Modigliani.* [Related image p110.]

GERTRUDE DEMAIN HAMMOND R.I. (1862–1953) watercolour painter and book illustrator.

The daughter of a clerk, she was born in London. She emulated her sister Christiana (also an artist) by studying at Lambeth Art School (1879–85) then at the Royal Academy Schools, winning a Silver Medal and the frieze-painting prize (worth £40). She was the first female student to win the RA prize for Decoration of a Public Building but declined to create a 16ft mural with life-size figures for the dining hall at Girton, as she found the task too physically daunting and time-consuming. Elected to membership of the Royal Institution, she exhibited there in 1891 (Empress Frederick of Germany purchased one of her paintings) and also in Paris, the USA and New Zealand. Interviewed by a journalist in 1891 she was adamant that she wanted her work judged against that of men, and did not exhibit in women-only shows. Between 1888 and 1925 she produced sketches for newspapers and periodicals and her best-known work, her illustrations of editions of Dickens, Bunyan, George Eliot and Shakespeare.

She married clerk Henry McMurdie in 1898 and had three daughters in ten years. During the 1930s they lived at 10 Christchurch Road, Worthing, then 36 Clifton Road; in the 1940s they moved to Kent. Posters of her work are still available.

MARY LOUISA HORNBY (c1836–1913) philanthropist and promoter of Braille.

The daughter of a clergyman, she was born in Liverpool, where she received a good education, becoming fluent in French and German. As a young woman she visited some very unusual places for a Victorian spinster, including Sinai and Bosnia, then became one of the first nurses to be trained at St Thomas's Hospital in London [see Sarah Wardroper, 31]. She was a district nurse in the Liverpool slums until 1870, then went abroad as a volunteer nurse during the Franco–Prussian War.

After learning Braille she organised the translation of nearly six thousand works of fiction and established a huge Braille collection, sending books for the blind to libraries in several countries. Throughout her life she took in many orphans, raising them at Woodhouse Street, Kirkdale, in the modest Liverpool community that was her base until infirmity brought her to a Worthing nursing home, where she died.

ALICE HUGHES (1857–1939) portrait photographer.

The daughter of a portrait painter, she was born in London, attended boarding-schools in Kent and Belgium then became personal assistant to her father. She learned photography in order to keep records of his paintings, progressed to photographing his clients, and in 1891 opened her own studio at their home in central London. Although she would photograph only women and children, within a few years she had become London's leading society photographer. Her portraits appeared in all the best magazines, and her sitters included Queen Alexandra and Queen Mary, as well as the mistresses of Edward VII.

In 1911 she sold her business and 50,000 negatives to a rival firm in order to set up in Berlin. She arrived there in 1914, but when WWI began a few months later she was forced to leave and in the process lost all her photographic equipment and personal possessions. She reopened in London the following year and in the early 1920s joined forces with Sir Charles Forbes to develop colour photography. In 1923 she wrote a memoir, *My Father and I*. She retired to Worthing in 1933 and died in Worthing Hospital six years later.

CHARLOTTE MASON (1842–1923) educationist.

Born in Wales, from 1864 she spent sixteen years in Sussex, ten at the Davison School in Worthing, becoming headmistress of the infants, and six as lecturer and vice-principal of Bishop Otter College in Chichester.

She wrote several geography books, including *The Forty Shires: their History, Scenery, Arts and Legend*, and was also a suffragist, but her greatest passion was for home-schooling. She taught in Yorkshire, then settled in Cumbria and wrote several more books, including *Home Education* (1886), which went into many editions. Concerned about the poor level of education given by governesses, she founded the Parents' National Education Union in 1888, edited its *Parents' Review* and was director of the Parents' School Union. She founded a training school for governesses at Ambleside, Cumbria, which became the House of Education.

She never retired, dying 'in harness' at eighty-one. Her name is still revered in the world of home-schooling, there is a Charlotte Mason Curriculum and a college in Lancaster was named for her. The PNEU became the Bell Educational Trust and still exists today.

Further reading: Cholmondeley, E. (1960) *The Story of Charlotte Mason*.

GLADYS MORGAN (1898–1983) comedian.

A Welsh-born soprano, her beautiful singing voice won her a part in a children's touring concert party; later she formed a musical trio then became part of Carrie Laurie's Juveniles, where she met comedian Frank Laurie. They married and formed a double-act as straight-woman and comedian, which became successful once they swapped roles. After forty years in revue and variety, she won a spot as resident comedian on a BBC radio show, *Welsh Rarebit*, broadcast from Cardiff. She dropped her phoney Lancashire accent in favour of her native one and had audiences rocking with laughter with her homely routines and songs. This led to invitations to appear at top variety theatres and on TV and radio and in 1956 she addressed the Women of the Year luncheon at the Savoy Hotel, representing women in broadcasting.

Nicknamed 'Funny Chops', her trademarks were a blazer and beret, a toothless grin and a ridiculously infectious, maniacal laugh. In the mid-fifties she appeared regularly on *The Frankie Howerd Show* and after she joined the cast of *Educating Archie* the need to be at the recording studio in London every Sunday prompted her to move the family in 1958 from the north of England to Salisbury Road in Worthing, where she lived for the next quarter-century. In 1959 she appeared on TV's *The Anne Shelton Show* [256].

Through the 1960s she topped the bill in summer variety shows and pantomimes, appearing in venues as diverse as Butlins and the London Palladium. She expanded her act to become 'Gladys Morgan and Family', comprising her husband, daughter Joan, son-in-law Bert Holman and the family dog. They completed five seasons in Australia and four sell-out summer tours of South Africa, where they had their own series, *The Morgans*, on Springbok Radio. She appeared with Bud Flanagan in the film *The Wild Affair* (1963) and took over from Anthea Askey [94] as the Worthing compère of *Search for a Star*, a national talent competition.

Mrs Morgan died in Worthing, and in 2007 BBC Radio Wales broadcast a special programme celebrating her life and work.

ROSA HARRIET NEWMARCH née Jeaffreson (1857–1940) writer and translator.

Born in Warwickshire, she devoted her life to promoting Russian and Czech music in Britain. She translated libretti into English, published articles, wrote some of the Russian entries for *Grove's Dictionary of Music and Musicians* and produced several books, including *The Russian Song Books* and *Music From Czechoslovakia.*

She lived in west London for most of her adult life, but ended her days at Percival's Hotel, Heene Terrace, Worthing. Her books about Henry Wood, Tchaikovsky and Sibelius are still in print.

ROSAMUND DALE OWEN (1846–1937) author, and founder of a community.

Her father was an author on spiritualism and a U.S. congressman (the town of Dale, Indiana, was named in his honour) and she was born at New Harmony, a utopian community in Indiana founded by her grandfather, Robert Owen. An accident at age twenty-five left her paralysed and blind; she recovered, but began seeing visions and hearing voices. She wrote *Duality: Male and Female Created He Them* and in 1882 began work on her magnum opus, *The Mediators*, a book that took forty years to complete and was never published. In 1888 she married mystic Laurence Oliphant, and settled in London, where he died three months later. She moved to a mystical community in Palestine, then established a socialist community at Haifa, Israel, but its austerity was so stringent that everyone left except a lawyer called Templeton, whom she married. He took his own life shortly afterwards.

She fought the Turkish Government for thirty years over ownership of a large tract of land at Esdraelon, where Armageddon, the final battle between good and evil, is destined to take place. Eventually it was conceded that she owned a small area around Haifa railway station. Back in England she wrote *My Perilous Life in Palestine* (1928), which is still available secondhand. She retired to The Haven, 201 Brighton Road, Worthing, where she died. [Related plate 33.]

ELSIE OXENHAM real name Elsie Dunkerley (1880–1960) author.

One of four sisters, each a lifelong spinster, she was born in Lancashire. Her family moved to Ealing, then to Farncombe Road, Worthing, in 1922 and she taught folk dancing in nearby villages and schools. Her father, who wrote novels under the pseudonym John Oxenham, took his girls on trips to Buckinghamshire, where Elsie was later to set her celebrated series of 'Abbey' books, adopting the pseudonym Elsie Oxenham. Her first novel appeared when she was twenty-seven and seven years later she hit on the formula which was to make her world famous. *Girls of the Hamlet Club* was the first of her forty-five 'Abbey' stories. In total she wrote eighty-seven novels in forty-three years.

When her mother died in 1925, she and a sister bought a house nearby. Her address in the 1950s was Inverkip, 45 The Glen, Worthing, while her sister Erica lived at Conifers, Heather Lane, High Salvington. She died at Marlposts Nursing Home, 1 Parkfield Road, Worthing, where she had lived for two years. There are Elsie Oxenham Appreciation Societies in four countries and some of her books are still in print.

Further reading: Godfrey, M. (2003) *The World of Elsie Jeanette Oxenham and her Books.*

SOPHIA LANE POOLE née Lane (1804–1891) travel writer.

A native of Hereford, aged twenty-five she married Edward Poole. They separated in 1842 and she, her two sons, her well-known Orientalist brother Edward Lane and his Greek wife went to Egypt for seven years. Unlike him, she was allowed access to the secret world of Egyptian women, and wrote about their lives in her book *The Englishwoman in Egypt*, written in the form of letters to a friend and serialised weekly from 1844 to 1846. This was intended to be a companion book to her brother's *Manners and Customs of the Modern Egyptians* (which has never been out of print since 1836). According to Jane Robinson, when Mrs Poole's 'highly popular accounts of a lady's life in Egypt were published back in London, they caused a mild sensation'

because of her descriptions of herself, 'A Christian wife and mother dressing up in Turkish "trousers" and visiting the city's harems ... and, worst of all, taking Turkish baths with the natives.'

Returning to England in 1849 she lived with her brother and his wife for the rest of her life, firstly at 25 White Rock, Hastings (1851) then at 1 Union Place, Broadwater, Worthing until 1876 (the census shows her as head of the household). Towards the end of her life she moved to Acton, then to her son's home in the staff quarters of the British Museum, where she died.

Further reading: Kararah, A. (2003) *The Englishwoman in Egypt.* [Related image p116.]

VALERIE PRAGNELL (1942–2006) artist.

Born in Shoreham and raised in Worthing, she adopted Scotland as her lifelong home and became one of Britain's most original artists. She used materials provided by nature: branches, twigs, straw, mud, moss, thorns, bark and leaves, often weaving them into basket-like sculptures. Her work attracted international acclaim, some was auctioned at Sotherby's and bought by the Metropolitan Museum of Modern Art in New York. Married with two children, she died in Scotland.

DOROTHY MILLER RICHARDSON (1873–1957) novelist and journalist.

A grocer's daughter from Berkshire, she lived with her family at 6 Victoria Terrace, Heene, Worthing, from 1880 to 1883, then moved to London. During a family holiday in Hastings in 1895 her mother committed suicide, then, early in her writing career she, like Amber White [49], became pregnant by H.G. Wells. She miscarried, suffered a nervous breakdown and recuperated on a farm somewhere in Sussex for five years until 1912. She wrote reviews, sketches, short stories, poems and factual pieces on a wide range of topics including literature, politics and dentistry. Her magnum opus, 'Pilgrimage', comprised thirteen volumes beginning with *Pointed Roofs* (1915) and ending with *March Moonlight* (1967). She pioneered the 'stream of consciousness' writing technique and was compared to James Joyce and Virginia Woolf [243].

From 1912 she lived between Cornwall and London, and in 1917 she married Alan Odle, an artist fifteen years her junior, whom she outlived by nine years. From 1954 she lived in a nursing home in Kent, where she died. Her body was donated to medical science and was buried two years later at Streatham Park cemetery, London.

ELIZABETH STONE née Wheeler (1803–1881) socialist-feminist novelist.

A native of Manchester, she wrote novels, children's fiction, social history and verse. Her novels exposed the truth about the harsh lives of working women. Her first, *William Langshawe, the Cotton Lord,* depicts the seduction of a working girl by the son of a rich mill-owner; her second, *The Young Milliner,* reveals the lives of seamstresses (one expires from overwork; another is forced into prostitution). The book criticises well-to-do women, in whose service seamstresses were exploited.

Her pioneering *The Art of Needlework from the Earliest Ages: Including Some Notices of the Ancient Historical Tapestries* (1840) criticised the patriarchal analysis of history, eulogising the needle as a civilised device superior to man's destructive sword, and was a plea for women's contribution to culture to be acknowledged. Her length of residence in Sussex is unknown, but her final book was published in Worthing in 1873, and in 1881 she was living with her sister at 7 Alfred Mews, Broadwater, Worthing, where she died.

CHARLOTTE CARMICHAEL STOPES née Carmichael (1840–1929) author and scholar.

The first woman in her native Scotland to obtain a certificate in arts (Edinburgh University did not then award degrees to women) she was an award-winning expert on Shakespeare; she wrote, among other related works, *The Bacon-Shakspere* [sic] *Question Answered.* She was also a passionate feminist, writing two related books: *British Freewomen: their Historical Privilege* (1894) and *The Sphere of 'Man' in Relation to that of 'Woman' in the Constitution* (1907).

She married in her forties and had two daughters (Marie was the youngest holder of a DSc and became famous as a pioneer of family planning clinics). Granted a civil-list pension of £50 a year in 1904, she died at Amatola Nursing Home, Shakespeare Road, Worthing. Four of her books on Shakespeare were reprinted in 2005.

EDNA THORNTON (1875–1964) singer.

A farmer's daughter, she was born in Yorkshire. She became a grande dame contralto with a booming but versatile voice that was used to great effect during her fifteen seasons at Covent Garden Opera House, her appearances at the Aldwych and Drury Lane theatres and during her tours of Commonwealth countries. Especially admired for her Wagnerian roles, she was famous not only for her prodigious volume but for her extraordinary memory: she could learn any operatic or oratorio role almost at a moment's notice. She retired at the age of forty-nine and settled somewhere in Worthing, where she died forty years later. Her recordings are still played on BBC Radio Three. [Related plate 53.]

EDITH M. WATSON née Wall (1888–1966) social activist.

The child of an unwed servant, she was born in Hackney workhouse and as a child helped her mother earn money by sewing buttons on shirts. She worked as a nursemaid in South Africa then became a captain in the Salvation Army, where she was almost raped by a fellow officer. Back in Britain she joined the suffragettes, wrote for the *Daily Herald* and *The Vote* and was imprisoned for chaining herself to the doors of Marylebone Magistrates' Court. She deplored the way female victims of assault were treated and spent three years publishing details of domestic violence and sexual abuse cases in a women's journal. During WWI she was the first woman to wear a police uniform when she joined the Women's Police Volunteers [295]. After marrying Ernest Watson she had a son in 1919, but the couple divorced in 1926.

She was for many years an activist in the Labour Party, helping to improve working conditions in mental hospitals, obtaining evidence clandestinely by disguising herself as a nurse. In the 1950s she was among the first to publicly criticise female genital mutilation. She died in a nursing home at 3 St Botolph's Road, Worthing.

The Grange, Slindon, former home of Bessie Rayner Parkes

Bignor Park, childhood home of sisters Catherine Dorset and Charlotte Smith

Leams End, West Hoathly, formerly the residence of Katharine Esdaile

The Dower House, Slindon, once home to Lady Georgiana Fullerton and, later, to Bessie Rayner Parkes

Vera Pragnell's memorial shelter at Washington

The inscription on the base of Ardingly memorial sign, erected in memory of Viscountess Wolseley, 'Citizen and Gardener of London' (meaning she was an elected member of the Worshipful Company of Gardeners).

Mary Neal, her Espérance Guild of Morris Dancers, and the
Green Lady Hostel at Littlehampton (from old photographs).

BY DIRECTION OF THE OWNER.
WITH POSSESSION OF THE RESIDENCE.
Coneyhurst, nr. Billingshurst.

WEST SUSSEX.

Billingshurst 2½ miles. Horsham 5 miles.

THE CHARMING OLD-WORLD RESIDENTIAL AND
AGRICULTURAL FREEHOLD PROPERTIES.
DUNCANS FARM—a XVIIth-Century Farmhouse.
Nine bed rooms, 1 dressing room, 2 bath rooms, hall, 3
reception rooms. Offices and outbuildings. Company's
water. Electric light from own plant.
Garages, farmery. Entrance lodge, drive. Charming
secluded gardens, orchard, kitchen garden and lands of
the home farm. In all about 44 ACRES.
HOOK FARM—A XVIth-Century Farmhouse.
Buildings, garden, orchard, an excellent modern cottage
and farmlands, in all about 59½ ACRES.
An enclosure of accommodation land of nearly 13 ACRES.
TOTAL AREA ABOUT 116 ACRES
and including the valuable standing timber.

The Beck sisters' home, Duncan's Farm, Coneyhurst, for sale in 1944 and (below) today

Blake's House, Felpham, once the home of Catherine Blake (from an old photograph)

The Chantry House, Steyning, once home to Nora Heald, Edith Shackleton and Gluck

Goodwood House, home of Emily, Duchess of Leinster and Lady Louisa Conolly (from an old photograph)

Paddockhurst, Turners Hill, former residence of Viscountess Cowdray and her daughter, Lady Denman

Parham House, the family home of Lavinia Smiley

Friday's Hill House, Fernhurst; home of Hannah Whitall Smith (seated, far left) and her granddaughter Ray Strachey (from an old photograph).

The Mud House, Ray Strachey's later residence

The grave of Michael Fairless Barber (Margaret Dowson).

4 Bedford Row, Worthing, home of Emily Haigh.

Brantridge Park, Balcombe, final residence of HRH Princess Beatrice.

Bailiff's Court Farm, once run by Valerie Barker

The Cottage, Duncton, former home of Mrs de Fonblanque

Gladice Keevil and her final home, The Wall Cottage, Burpham;
below is Dickdene, her home in Lewes (from an old photograph).

DANGSTEIN,

In the highly picturesque and favourite country between MIDHURST and PETERSFIELD, with a healthy sandy soil.

MESSRS. DANIEL SMITH and SON, are instructed to announce, that if not previously Sold by Private Contract being now prepared to treat for its disposal, the above delightful **FREEHOLD RESIDENCE** and **ESTATE** will be submitted to **PUBLIC COMPETITION** in the ensuing Spring. The proprietor has spared no expense in the erection and completion of the Mansion, which as an elegant and truly classical specimen of Grecian achitecture can scarcely be surpassed in a building of a moderate scale. Its interior arrangement and decorations are fully correspondent in rich taste and substantial comforts.

It is happily placed on a fine healthy eminence, amidst scenery of indescribable beauty, near the village church of Turwick, on the verge of an extensive tract of wild park-like heath land, and encircled by a compact little domain of 180 Acres in pasture, arable, and groves of oaks and arch intersected by varied walks, all sloping with south and westward aspects to the picturesque vale connecting the neighbouring towns of Petersfield and Midhurst, bounded by a bold and romantic portion of the South Down Hills.

Attached to the Mansion is an elegant and costly Conservatory, with Flower Garden and broad Terrace-walks, a capital walled Garden, with excellent Hothouses, &c., newly erected Stabling, Farm-buildings, and every requisite appendage for a country establishment.

HOUSES, &c., to be LET or SOLD.

TO BE LET, FURNISHED—August, September, and October,—NEWLANDS, SLINDON, ARUNDEL; four miles from Goodwood. Small house, six bedrooms, drawing, dining-room, and parlour; stabling for four horses, paddock, and small garden. Rent, £5 5s. a week for two months, including Goodwood-week. House can be viewed any time.—Apply Housekeeper, Newlands, Slindon, Arundel.

SUSSEX.—To be LET FURNISHED, August 1st, artistic COUNTRY HOUSE; 4 sitting rooms, 9 bed rooms (4 are small), 2 bath rooms; shady garden; croquet and tennis courts; small garage; main electric light, drainage, and water; 20 guineas weekly August, longer by arrangement.—Mrs. Zangwill, Far End, East Preston, near Littlehampton.

NEW PUBLICATIONS.

Narrative of a journey Overland to India, by Mrs. Colonel Elwood, two vols. octavo, Colburn and Bentley— A journey overland to India by a female is not a thing of every day occurance, and a production of much less merit than that of Mrs. Elwood, would ,from its novelty, sufficiently reward curiosity. We are glad to say, however, that these volumes are in every way interesting, and that they may be read by all classes with amusement and benefit.

OVERLAND JOURNEY FROM ENGLAND TO INDIA.—In the introduction to this interesting work, just published, giving an account of this arduous undertaking, Mrs. Colonel Elwood says, " I may safely declare that I am the only lady who ever travelled to India over land; and probably mine is the first journal ever kept by an Englishwoman in the Desert of the Thebais, and on the shores of the Dead Sea." The authoress underwent, indeed, many strange adventures in wild and perilous places, and her book may be considered perfectly unique.

Lady Dorothy Nevill's house, Dangstein, *Hampshire Telegraph*, 1844; Lady Georgiana Fullerton's house, Newlands, *Pall Mall Gazette*, 1889; Edith Zangwill, *The Times*, 1935; Katherine Elwood, *Derby Mercury* and *Brighton Gazette*, 1830; fatal accident to Florence Patton-Bethune depicted in the *Illustrated Police News*, 1884.

Woman, 83, accuses Kennel Club of sex discrimination

Mrs Florence Nagle, a breeder of Irish wolfhounds, yesterday asked an industrial tribunal to rule that the Kennel Club's insistence on male membership only is out of date. She has accused the club of sex discrimination.

Mr James Fox-Andrews, QC, said that Mrs Nagle, aged 83, of Petworth, West Sussex, applied for membership last December but was rejected because the club's constitution does not admit women. "In acting in this way the Kennel Club is guilty of sex discrimination of the most blatant kind. It is difficult to understand it in the 1970s", he said.

Breeders and exhibitors not members of the club were still subject to Kennel Club rules, Mr Fox-Andrews said. But the disciplinary committee comprised men who acted as judge, jury and prosecution.

"Women are subject to the authority of a body on which they have no chance of being represented. Throughout the world, bodies controlling dogs have modelled themselves on the Kennel Club, with one difference, the Kennel Club is unique in barring its doors to women."

Mrs Nagle told the tribunal it was essential for a breeder to be registered with the Kennel Club. "If you are not registered you cannot compete in shows. You cannot register pedigrees. People abroad do not want dogs without pedigrees."

Mrs Nagle, who has been breeding dogs since 1913, said two thirds of the people registered with the Kennel Club were women. But women had no say in the running of the club.

Mr Fox-Andrews said the Crufts Show last year raised £680,000 for the club, which he described as the "controlling body of dogdom". "It is really a case of taxation without representation for women, because it is they to a significantly large measure who pay the fees."

Mr Robert Gatehouse, QC, for the Kennel Club, asked Mrs Nagle if the club had always been a private club, a "male preserve", since it was formed in 1874. Mrs Nagle replied: "Yes, but that does not make it right."

The hearing was adjourned until today.

Woman loses action to join Kennel Club

Women have lost the fight to join the al-male Kenel Club but have been given support for another struggle before the Equal Opportunities Commission.

Mrs Florence Nagle, aged 83, of Petworth, Sussex, asked an industrial tribunal to find the members of the club guilty of sex discrimination. The tribunal ruled against her but criticized the club.

It said in its decision, given yesterday, that commission might well consider the club's attitude to women.

Mrs Nagle said: "We lost the case because the tribunal said I was not a person who made a living from dogs. But any woman who did that certainly would not have been able to take the club to court. It is a very expensive business.

Cuttings from *The Times:* Florence Nagle, June and July 1978; Ursula Wyndham, 1958; Green Lady Hostel (Mary Neal), 1909.

NUMBERING THE VILLAGE

TO THE EDITOR OF THE TIMES

Sir,—Allowing for the natural distaste of a rural community to being urbanized, numbers have much to recommend them. It is almost impossible to think of a really good name for a house; particularly one that will please everyone. While some will view with a sense of enchantment the name Flea Bank, there is a numerous class of genteel person who would rather live in the open than under such a domicile.

Surnames seldom sound well as house names; field names, though boasting the beauty of archaic allusion, can seldom boast anything else and, as a general rule, grate upon the ear.

There is a sad paucity of imagination when it comes to thinking of suitable house names—the endless crop of Rose Cottage, Holly Cottage, Walnut Tree Cottage that no English village is without—and the alternative of Dunroaming, Home Again does nothing to help the situation.

I speak from the heart as it has recently been my headache to name a newly built house. Every idea I had met with volleys of abuse from others. Their ideas found no favour with me.

Oh, for the peace of being given a number!

Yours faithfully,
URSULA WYNDHAM.
Honeyway House, Petworth, Sussex.

THE GREEN LADY HOSTEL, LITTLEHAMPTON.—The object of this hostel, which was established in 1901, is to place at the disposal of leaders of working girls' clubs, preferably in London, a suitable country house and staff for club holiday parties; it is also available for families and individuals, especially for solitary girls. The committee is unsectarian, and guests are welcomed from all Churches and creeds. A lady is in charge, but club holiday parties are managed (except as to household arrangements) by their own leaders. The hostel, which has accommodation for 50, stands in its fine old garden a few minutes from sea and station, and adjoins the open country. Increasing numbers of wage-earners have annually been received (last year the total was 425), and the committee are doing their best to keep the hostel within the reach of the lowest paid and therefore most needy wage-earner. They hope to make it self-supporting, and look for the days when every wage-earner will be able to pay cost of his or her holiday. That day is not as yet in sight; they cannot raise their prices, and so still need help. There is a small deficit to make up on the payments of visitors, and there are the winter expenses, repairs, and renewals. The committee ask for help to the amount of £500 to enable them to pay the balance of the purchase money and certain necessary expenditure, and assistance in making known to as wide a public as possible the objects and advantages of the hostel. Fuller information can be obtained from the hon. secretary, Miss Fraser, 16, Prince Edward's-mansions, Pembridge-square, W., or the lady superintendent, Green Lady Hostel, Littlehampton.

A WOMAN IN THE GOVERNMENT

TO THE EDITOR OF THE TIMES

Sir,—Yes, I agree with Princess Antoine Bibesco that the sooner we get away from saying we want "a woman" in the Government, or anywhere else, the better. Men seem to be irritated by the suggestion, which in itself is a pity. In any case it is approaching the question from a wrong angle.

When appointments are made surely one question only should be asked : "Who is likely to do the job in the best way ?." Any further comment, such as, "Oh, but she's a woman !" might be shown to be as foolish as to say, "Oh, but he's a man !"

The National Government has been brought into being largely through the common sense of many of my country-women. In making the appointments, major and minor, was any consideration given to the parallel capability of individual men and women ? That seems to be the point. If the question, "Who will do the job in the best way ?" had been fairly asked, I venture to think we should have had no correspondence on the subject or leading articles in *The Times*, for we should have had in the Government that most effective of all combinations, whether in the home or out of it, men and women working together—a truly National Government.   Yours, &c.,
MERIEL L. TALBOT.
Backsettown, Henfield, Sussex, Nov. 29.

TO THE EDITOR OF THE TIMES

Sir,—It is time the Government of our country took the women-power of the Empire into account. British women are in the front line and have proved not only their courage but their ability to rise to any and every emergency. When will the Government give the lead to authorities throughout the country and appoint women as well as men to executive posts ?

At present, if a man is available, no matter how inefficient, he gets the job. For example, billeting should have been a woman's job from start to finish. Now the problem of food is serious. It is essentially one which women understand and can handle. As the situation is at present far from satisfactory, let the Government get the women on to it. Their practical minds will solve many of the problems at present confronting the Ministry. Only by using the best possible material, both men and women, in the best possible way are we going to win this war.

The Government have not begun to appreciate the contribution the women of this country would make if brought everywhere in to counsel. This lack of vision on the men's side may become a tragedy.   Yours, &c.,
EVELYN EMMET.
Amberley Castle, Amberley, Sussex.

BRITISH WOMEN IN MALAYA

TO THE EDITOR OF THE TIMES

Sir,—Allow me to join Mrs. Spooner in paying tribute to the British women in Singapore. I saw, alas! very little of the rest of Malaya but I was in the island until four weeks before its fall and had opportunity to compare the energy and zeal of its women with those of many other countries, including America, Java, Australia, and London during the severest raids, and I can assure all those who believe stories of sloth and self-indulgent negligence that they are wrong.

The women, handicapped by a devitalizing climate, worked with exactly the same enthusiasm as we do in England. Never was there a suspicion of defeatism or any avoidance of hard work or responsibility. Work parties, clubs for Dominion soldiers, hospitals, and canteens were run by the women. The A.R.P. was reinforced by them, and the blood transfusion centre, started three years ago by a doctor, who was also a leader, was operated entirely by voluntary women—and nowhere in England have I seen it better organized or run. In Malaya, as here, the women in war are heroic, and there they had more to bear.
Yours faithfully,
DIANA COOPER.
West House, Aldwick, Bognor Regis, Sussex, July 29.

Letters to *The Times*: Dame Meriel Talbot (left) 1931, (below) 1953; Lady Diana Cooper, 1942; Baroness Emmet, 1941.

WOMEN AT THE WICKET

TO THE EDITOR OF THE TIMES

Sir,—To one who has enjoyed cricket all her life—and it is a long one—the article in *The Times* of August 13 is of unique interest. Members of the White Heather Club, of which I was an early member, accepted with true feminine docility from male relations and friends, including many scoffers, that women's physical make-up prevented them from throwing, and also that their game would always be inferior to that of men. Great was my surprise, therefore, and my delight, to see a girl save a boundary hit to the remotest corner of the Oval, and with ease and certainty return the ball full pitch into the wicketkeeper's hands.

I have by me two full columns in which your Cricket Correspondent reported the match at the Oval in 1937 between the women of England and Australia. He wrote: "It had been a great match to watch—a revelation of sustained efficiency." And again: "In every respect, in bowling, batting, and fielding alike there was a lesson to be learnt by men." It is refreshing to see gloomy prophecies blown sky high. Yours faithfully,
MERIEL L. TALBOT.
Newtimber Place, Hassocks, Sussex.

THE GENTLE ART OF COOKERY

By MRS. C. F. LEYEL and MISS OLGA HARTLEY

A new and original cookery book with 750 recipes. Not a "Mrs. Beeton," but a gay and witty book with all sorts of modern things in it. Read especially the chapters on:—Cold Supper Dishes; Sandwiches; and Cooking for Children. And just peep at the menu for a complete dinner from *The Arabian Nights*. "A book no properly constituted home should be without." *Morning Post*

7s. 6d. net.

*

CHATTO & WINDUS : 99 ST. MARTIN'S LANE, W.C.2

The Echoing Green
DORIS LESLIE

(Author of "Fools in Mortar," &c.) This brilliant author gives us in this story of Theo Van Tal, the daughter of a Jewish father and Gentile mother, a most fascinating study in feminine psychology. "Charming."—*Yorks Post.* "Plenty of interest."—*Evening News.* (3rd Imp.)

"Something exquisite and in its way perfect."

YOUNG MRS. CRUSE

By VIOLA MEYNELL, Author of "Modern Lovers," "Columbine," &c.   7s. 6d. net.
Queen.—"For all that novelists and critics are supposed to be jealous and ungenerous folk, there is no joy for them like coming upon a book that they would have given their right hand to have written. *Young Mrs. Cruse* is just such a book."

THE CHINK IN THE ARMOUR.

By Mrs. BELLOC LOWNDES, Author of "The Uttermost Farthing." Second Edition in the press. Crown 8vo, 6s.
"Mrs. Belloc Lowndes' new novel is a *tour de force*. Each step of the drama is skilfully drawn." —*Westminster Gazette.*

This Month will be published,
In Five Volumes, 12mo. price 15s. sewed,

E THELINDE ; or, The RECLUSE of the LAKE.
By CHARLOTTE SMITH.
Printed for T. Cadell, in the Strand:
Of whom may be had, by the same Author,
1. Emmeline ; the Orphan of the Castle ; 3d Edition, 4 vols. 12s. sewed.
2. The Romance of Real Life, 3 vols. 9s. sewed.
3. Elegiac Sonnets, 5th Edition, with Additional Sonnets, and other Poems, Embellished with Plates, 10s. 6d.

KNIGHT'S WEEKLY VOLUME.
This day,

T HE ENGLISHWOMAN in EGYPT; Letters written during a Residence in Cairo, in 1843 and 1844, with E. W. Lane, Esq. Author of "The Modern Egyptians." By his SISTER.
Volume One.
London: Charles Knight and Co. 22 Ludgate street.

THE BEDOUINS OF THE EUPHRATES

VALLEY. By Lady ANNE BLUNT. Edited, with a Preface and some Account of the Arabs and their Horses, by W. S. B.

"We have read Lady Anne Blunt's book with a kind of enjoyable amazement. . . . . We feel that a review can give but a faint idea of the varied interest of this book. It has matter for every reader. Here are humour, adventure, sport, information about things that are to most people altogether unfamiliar."—*Saturday Review.*

Vol. 1, *crown* 8vo, 7s. 6d.,

Adverts in *The Times*: Mrs Leyel, 1925; Doris Leslie, 1929; Viola Meynell, 1924; Marie Belloc Lowndes, 1912; Charlotte Smith, 1789. Sophia Lane Poole (credited only as E.W. Lane's sister), *The Examiner*, 1844. Lady Anne Blunt, *Pall Mall Gazette*, 1879. Sketches of Hannah Whitall Smith (left) and Anne Pratt, the *Women's Penny Paper*, 1889.

Lady Anne Blunt with her husband Wilfred Scawen Blunt in Egypt, engraving by S. Vuillier

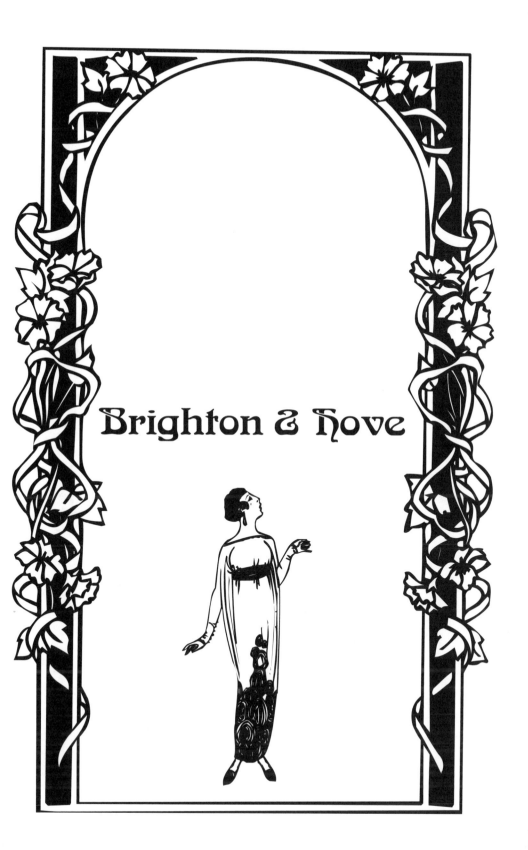

Brighton & Hove

ALDRINGTON

DR ANNIE ABRAM (1869–1930) historian.

Born in London, she read history at Girton but, as Cambridge would not award degrees to women, moved to the LSE, where she gained a doctorate in economics. She wrote several books, including *Social England in the Fifteenth Century* (1909) and *English Life and Manners in the Later Middle Ages* (1913) as well as many learned academic articles, including 'Women Traders in Medieval London'. She died at 12 Mansfield Road, Aldrington.

E.M. DELAFIELD JP née Edmée Elizabeth de la Pasture (1890–1943) writer.

Her father was the 14th Count and 3rd Marquis de la Pasture; her mother (Mrs Henry de la Pasture, later Lady Clifford) was a successful novelist and dramatist. She was born at 6 Walsingham Terrace, Aldrington, where her family lived for a short time. In 1900 her father bought Llandogo Priory and the family lived between London, Devon and Wales. When she was twenty-one her mother remarried and Edmée spent nine months in a convent in Belgium, an experience she was later to write about.

During WWI she was a VAD nurse and worked at the Ministry of National Service. Using the name E.M. Delafield she wrote five plays and forty books, encompassing travel, sketches, parodies, essays and fiction, of which over thirty were novels, beginning with *Zella Sees Herself* (1917) and ending with *Late and Soon* (1943). Once she was well-established, she was invited to judge literary prizes. Her series *The Diary of a Provincial Lady*, described as 'outrageously funny', appeared in the feminist magazine *Time and Tide,* became a series of bestselling books and was dramatised on BBC Radio Four.

She married land agent Major Dashwood, whom she gently lampooned in print. They lived in Malaya, then in 1922 settled permanently at Croyle House, near Kentisbeare, Devon. She had two children, was president of the local WI and served as a magistrate. She died at home and was buried in Kentisbeare churchyard.[Related image opposite.]

BRIGHTON

MAIE ASH (1888–1923) comedy actress.

Much admired for her beauty, she was born in London and made her West End début aged fourteen. Her early marriage to actor Stanley Brett produced a daughter but ended in divorce in 1913. She toured the UK playing a music-hall double act with her second husband, Fred Arnold (stage name Allandale) until 1921, when he died suddenly during a rehearsal in Birmingham. She moved to 24 Marine Parade, where she died of cirrhosis of the liver aged just thirty-five. She was buried in London. [Related plate 3.]

EDITH BAIRD née Winter-Wood (1859–1924) and **LILIAN BAIRD** (1881–1977) chess puzzle composers.

Edith was born in France and raised in Devon by a family of champion chess players. In 1880 she married a naval surgeon twenty-eight years her senior and lived in Northumberland, where her only child, Lilian, was born. From 1888 she became increasingly renowned for inventing chess problems. The first took her a hundred hours to devise, but the rest took about half an hour each, and they were published in newspapers and periodicals worldwide under the name 'Mrs W.J. Baird'. Dubbed 'the Queen of Chess', she won numerous awards, including the Sussex Chess Silver Medal for best three-move problem for three consecutive years. Her first compilation was published in 1902 as *700 Chess Problems*; this was followed in 1907 by a book of 300 problems 'enriched with Shakespearean quotations'; by that time she was the most famous female chess composer in the world and fans would come to Brighton just to meet her. Altogether, she composed over 2,000 problems; she was also adept at archery and both she and her daughter Lilian were talented painters and verse-writers.

By 1891 the family was living at 14 College Terrace, Brighton, where they remained for at least ten years. She was widowed in 1907 and in 1911 is listed at The Cottage, Hambrook, West Sussex. She died in Devon.

Lilian Baird, known as Lily, learned chess moves at the age of four and at eight her first puzzle was published in thirty periodicals. Hailed as a child prodigy, she won a trophy and gained the nickname 'The Infant Queen of Chess'. Her portrait appeared in magazines and fans wrote for her autograph. She excelled at nearby Portland House School, winning several prizes, but was dogged by ill-health and by her twenties had faded into obscurity. She married Captain Strong in 1910 and lived abroad. After WWII she returned to Brighton, living for many years at 14 Harrington Road. [Related image p16.]

MARY BARKER MBE (1907–1999) hand-weaver and artist.

Born in Somerset, she was the first woman to study textile industries at Leeds University, specialising in silk weaving, and in the 1930s designed fine Wilton carpets. During WWII she served as an officer in the WRNS, and in 1950 took over Ethel Mairet's teaching position at Brighton School of Art. Until 1959 she lodged with Mrs Mairet [205] at Ditchling; later she lived at 1 Harrington Road, Brighton.

Among her creations were elegant, gauze-weave stoles and scarves, abstract hangings in silk and wool, embroideries, hand-woven wallhangings, lithographs and paintings. She exhibited at London craft and weaving exhibitions, at the V & A and in Australia, New Zealand, the USA and Canada, where she also undertook lecture tours. For nearly half a century she was involved in the Guilds of Weavers, Spinners and Dyers, serving as journalist, secretary, chairman and president. In 1992 she was appointed MBE for services to hand-weaving, and died in Brighton seven years later.

Further reading: Barker, M. (1998) *Tangled Threads* (autobiography).

THE COUNTESS OF BATH née the Hon. Henrietta Johnstone; from 1767, Pulteney (1766–1808) philanthropist.

A baronet's daughter, she was born in Westminster and as a baby she and her father adopted her mother's maiden name. Through her mother she became the wealthiest woman in England when she inherited about £400,000 (worth £23m today) plus considerable landed property.

Her life was dedicated to good works and she was a generous benefactor who particularly favoured endowing schools and supporting nuns in French convents. In 1791 a piece of music ('Miss Pulteney's Fancy') was named for her. In 1792 she was created Baroness of Bath and was elevated to countess in 1803. In between she married General Sir James Murray of Claremont, who also adopted the Pulteney surname.

She died at The Steyne, Brighton, and was buried, after a breathtakingly ostentatious funeral, at Westminster Abbey. She had no children, so her titles became extinct and her fortune, which despite her philanthropy had grown to £600,000, she bequeathed to her cousin Elizabeth Fawcett (later, Pulteney). In 1818 the town of Henrietta in New York state was named for her.

ANNA BENNETT (c1750–1808) novelist.

She worked as a shopkeeper then a workhouse matron in her native Wales before moving to Surrey as the kept mistress of Sir Thomas Pye, an elderly admiral, by whom she had two children. After he died she wrote a series of best-selling novels, initially publishing as 'Anon'. Her first, *Anna Bennett, The Memoirs of a Welch* [sic] *Heiress*, dedicated to the Princess Royal, sold out on publication day, went into four editions and was translated into French. *The Beggar Girl and her Benefactors*, dedicated to the Duchess of York, was published in seven volumes in 1797. Coleridge called it 'the best novel ... since Fielding'. By 1806 she was a household name and her book *The Ghost of My Father* sold 2,000 copies on publication day. In later life she lived in Brighton, where she died. She was buried in London.

PEARL BINDER Lady Elwyn-Jones (1904–1989) author, artist and journalist.

She began life in humble circumstances in Lancashire, travelled extensively in Russia and China, studied art and fashion and trained in lithography at the Central School of Art. In the 1920s she moved to the East End, where she championed the

Pearly Kings and Queens, about whom she wrote a musical (*When the Summer Comes Again*); later writing another (*Down the Road*) about Victorian costermongers.

Her range of interests, talents and accomplishments was extraordinarily diverse and her life exceptionally productive. She presented an early television programme (on the history of fashion), broadcast on radio, wrote a biography, novels and children's stories (one was *Muffs and Morals*) and was also a journalist, sculptor, ceramicist, stained glass and graphic artist. She made stage costumes, designed a Pearly mug and plate for Wedgwood and twenty-two armorial windows for the House of Lords, lithographically illustrated Thomas Burke's book *The Real East End* and exhibited at Whitechapel Art Gallery. Her feature on the gaiety and charm of Brighton appeared in *Geographic Magazine* in 1963 and the following year she wrote *Treacle Terrace*, a children's novel about the twin evils of property speculators and crooked solicitors.

Known to her friends as Polly, she wore sweeping robe dresses in gorgeous, ethnic fabrics with harem trousers and pretty, flat sandals. She was as anti-high heels as she was pro-women; in 1961 she called for a woman to be secretary-general of the United Nations, as she believed this would bring about world peace. Aged thirty-three she married law student Frederick (later, Lord) Elwyn-Jones, who became an East End Labour MP, barrister, judge and eventually Lord Chancellor. They had a son and two daughters and lived at 2 St Margaret's Place, Brighton, in the 1960s, then at 17 Lewes Crescent, Kemp Town, until her death, taking a deep interest in local issues. A blue plaque on the latter commemorates both husband and wife. [Related images p180.]

CLEMENTINA BLACK (1853–1922) political activist and novelist.

A daughter of solicitor David Black, Brighton's Town Clerk and coroner, she was born at 58 Ship Street. After her mother died, Miss Black, then twenty-two, took care of her invalid father and her seven younger brothers. She wrote two novels: *A Sussex Idyll* (1877) and *Orlando* (1880) before she and her sister Constance [132] moved to London, where they mixed with political and literary figures including Eleanor Marx and Amy Levy [163].

In 1893 Miss Black suffered multiple personal tragedies. Her brother Arthur murdered his wife Jessie and baby son Walter at their home, 77 Goldstone Villas, Hove, before committing suicide; six months later her father died. She refused to marry, because 'The law denies to a married woman the freedom of action which more and more women are coming to regard not only as their just but also as their dearest treasure', but she adopted her late brother's surviving child, five-year-old Gertrude Speedwell Black.

She became active in the WPPL and, as its delegate to the 1888 TUC conference, moved the first-ever resolution for equal pay and inspired Annie Besant [246] to help the Bryant & May match workers. She co-founded the WTUA and for twenty years collected and publicised information on women's work in 117 trades. She was an active member of the Fabian Society and co-founded the Consumers' League. For years she travelled the country making speeches to persuade women to join trades unions. She supported the introduction of wages' boards to enforce a minimum wage and was an executive member of the Anti-Sweating League, working with Cicely Corbett Fisher [202] to organise conferences. She wrote several books related to labour, including *Married Women's Work* (1915, reprinted 1980) and continued to write novels, although the only one that met with success was *An Agitator* (1894), based on the trade union movement. Because women could not influence employment legislation without the vote, she became a fervent suffragist, inaugurating a declaration in 1906 that was signed by thousands. She became vice-president of the NUWSS in 1913 and edited *The Common Cause*.

In recognition of her unceasing endeavours on behalf of working women, in 1913 she was granted a civil-list pension of £75 a year. She died at her home in Barnes and was buried in East Sheen Cemetery. Brighton bus 658 is named for her.

RT HON MARGARET BONDFIELD CH, JP, MP (1873–1953) trade unionist and politician.

One of eleven children of a poor Somerset lacemaker, she bettered herself by becoming a pupil-teacher at the local school at the age of thirteen. At fourteen she arrived in Sussex to take up a job as an assistant in a colonial outfitter's shop, moving later to a milliner's in Western Road. She spent seven years in Brighton, becoming friends with the Martindale family [141].

She moved to London in 1894 and for a quarter-century was the most important woman in the trades union movement, holding many leading positions within a dozen organisations. She was the first woman to attend the TUC conference, the first on its General Council and its first female chairman. She was a suffragist during the Edwardian era, a pacifist during the war, and an activist in the Labour Party and the WTUL.

In 1923 she became the fifth woman to become an MP and the first female Labour MP. After losing and regaining her seat, she was the first woman in the cabinet and the first to be a Privy Councillor, serving as Minister of Labour from 1929 to 1931, when she again lost her seat.

A deeply religious woman, she worked unpaid for the YWCA and the National Council for Social Service for many years. She also wrote several books, including *Our Towns* (1934). Appointed Companion of Honour in 1948, she died in Surrey five years later. Brighton bus 619 is named for her.

Further reading: Bondfield, M. (1949) *A Life's Work* (autobiography). [Related plate 44.]

ELEANOR VERE BOYLE née Gordon (1825–1916) artist.

A native of Scotland, where her wealthy family owned Ellon Castle, she married the Hon. Revd Richard Cavendish Boyle, an earl's son and future Chaplain-in-Ordinary to Queen Victoria. Using only her initials E.V.B. she enjoyed a successful career illustrating children's books; the best known was *Child's Play* (1852), which went into several editions.

Later she wrote instructional books on horticulture, including *A Garden of Pleasure* (1895). As a widow she lived firstly in Buckinghamshire, then at 4 Holland Road, Brighton, where she died in her nineties, having outlived two of her four children.

MARY ELIZABETH BRADDON (1835–1915) novelist and playwright.

She was born into a middle-class London family. In 1839 her mother discovered her father's infidelity and left him, taking the children to live at Maze Hill, St Leonards, for four years. Mary Braddon later became an actress under the pseudonym Mary Seyton and supported her mother, who toured with her as chaperone. Between 1857 and 1960 she lived at 26 and later 34 New Road, Brighton, appeared at the Theatre Royal and wrote for the *Brighton Herald*.

She began to compose short stories and poems and, in 1860, with financial help from a male benefactor, left the stage to focus exclusively on writing. She took a job in London as an editorial assistant to her publisher, John Maxwell, whose wife was in an institution. Rather scandalously for that era, she (and her mother) moved in with him and raised his five children, to which she eventually added six more. They married in 1874, after his wife's death.

A pioneer of the 'sensation' genre, in 1862 she hit the jackpot with the serial (and later, novel) *Lady Audley's Secret*, which went into nine editions within the year. Between 1860 and 1913 she wrote ninety novels and five plays, enjoying great commercial success; however, her work was dismissed a 'populist trash' by George Eliot and caricatured by *Punch* magazine.

She died on her estate, Lichfield House, Richmond, Surrey, where there is a memorial to her in the local church. Her husband later developed the estate, naming the streets after her books. *Lady Audley's Secret* eventually sold millions, was adapted into a play and a film, and is still in print.

Further reading: Carnell, J. (2000) *The Literary Lives of Mary Elizabeth Braddon*. [Related images pp16, 178, 181.]

HILDA BRAID (1929–2007) actress.

Born in Northfleet, Kent, she trained at RADA, winning an award for diction. She joined the RSC at Stratford and appeared on the West End stage and in a few films. From 1963 she worked as a TV character actress in dozens of roles in dramas, soaps and comedies, including *Oliver Twist, Catweazle, Crossroads, Z Cars, Emmerdale, Brookside, Casualty, One Foot in the Grave, Man About The House* and *My Family*.

She became a household name in the 1970s for her role in *Citizen Smith*; later she played 'Nana Moon' in over 200 episodes of *Eastenders* until 2005, when she was seventy-six and had completed fifty years in her profession. An episode that focussed almost entirely upon her won the British Soap Award for Best Single Episode in 2006.

Married to actor Brian Badcoe (a B.P. Badcoe is listed at 10 Foundry Street, Brighton 1971-2), she had two children. In later life she helped raise funds for Alzheimer's charities. After a fall at home in 2006, she stayed for some months at Fairdene Lodge Nursing Home, 14 Walsingham Road, Hove, then moved in with her friend, theatre producer Brian Ralfe, at 6 Eaton Manor, The Drive, Hove. She died at the Royal Sussex County Hospital, Brighton, and was cremated at Woodvale.

ZOË E. BRIGDEN (1891–1983) aquatic entertainer.

The daughter of a Brighton tailor, she lived for at least thirty-eight years in Mighell Street, firstly at no. 21 and from 1903 at no. 2. Between 1915 and 1924 she was famous for performing dare-devil diving exhibitions, launching herself from a highboard on the West Pier, swimming from pier to pier and performing a unique 'wooden soldier' dive, plunging headfirst into the sea with her arms straight by her sides.

She gave up performing and, although unwed, had a son in 1925 and opened a hairdressing salon in Whitehawk. In the late 1930s she heroically rescued a small girl who was being strangled in a murder attempt by her father on the Downs behind East Preston Park. In later years Miss Brigden lived awhile in Seaford, then with her younger sister Adelaide at 92 Roedale Road, Brighton. [Related plate 22.]

ROSE EDOUIN BRYER (1844–1925) actress.

A member of a well-known theatrical family who toured as a troupe using the name Edouin, she was born at 24 Ship Street, Brighton. She first appeared on the London stage at age nine, playing Puck to great critical acclaim. In 1856 the family moved to Australia and later toured China, where she married theatre entrepreneur George Lewis in Shanghai in 1864. While raising at least seven children, the couple toured with their own travelling theatre, acting and producing Shakespeare and melodrama in India, South Africa, New Zealand, Australia and China. She sometimes played male roles, including Hamlet and Romeo. She returned to England in later life and died in Harrogate, having spent seventy-two years in the theatrical profession.

ARABELLA BURTON BUCKLEY (1841–1929) scientist and writer.

Her father was curate of St John the Evangelist, Brighton, from 1840 to 1843 and she was born in the town, christened at St Nicholas's Church and grew up at Ditchling Terrace until her family moved to London when she was about seven. Unusually well educated for a girl, for eleven years (1864–75) she was secretary to geologist Sir Roderick Murchison, during which time she became highly knowledgeable and personally acquainted with all the leading scientists of the day.

She lectured and wrote many articles and a few books on the natural and physical sciences. Her first publication, *A Short History of Natural Science* (1876) was commended by Charles Darwin and by 1884 she was described as 'one of the most learned ladies in England'. In middle age she married the elderly Thomas Fisher MD, but was soon widowed. She wrote seven more books, including *A History of England for Beginners* (1887) and *Moral Teachings of Science* (1891). She died in Devon. [Related image p181.]

LADY BYRON Anne Isabella Noel, née Milbanke; Baroness Wentworth (1792–1860) philanthropist.

Lady Byron was the estranged wife of the 'mad, bad, and dangerous-to-know' poet Lord Byron and a longstanding correspondent of Dr Elizabeth Blackwell [224]. She was born in Durham and co-founded a school in nearby Seaham. Her father changed the family surname to Noel in 1815, the year she married Byron. They separated in 1816 and in 1826 her daughter's maths tutor, co-operative movement pioneer William King, found a house for her in Brighton 'on the front near where Dr Russell had lived'. While there she was associated with Dr King in founding branches of the Co-operative Society in Brighton and also in Hastings, and lent part of her house as premises for a Mechanics' Institute. These ventures were typical of her philanthropy, which focussed on helping the ill-educated and underprivileged to improve themselves and on relieving people living in poverty and slavery. Her most notable achievement was perhaps the founding of the first industrial school, at Ealing Grove, near Fordhook, her house in Acton, near London, in 1834. In 1854 her address was 6 Pavilion Buildings; she later moved to 2 Tackleway, Hastings, living between there and her London residence until her death. She has a blue plaque in London.

Her daughter, the Hon. Ada Byron married Dr King. She was a mathematician and the first woman associated with the birth of computing. One of her three children was Lady Anne Blunt [92].

Further reading: Pierson, J. (1992) *The Real Lady Byron.* [Related image p16.]

DAME JANET CAMPBELL DBE, MB, MD, MS, JP (1877–1954) pioneering civil servant.

A bank manager's daughter, she was born in Brighton and lived at 172–3 North Street for at least twenty-five years. She attended Brighton & Hove High School for Girls and studied medicine at the LSMW. Joining the civil service she advanced through increasingly senior posts never before held by a woman, eventually becoming senior medical officer to the Ministry of Health and chief woman medical adviser to the Board of Education. During this time she was able to improve the lives of countless women by influencing policy regarding the provision of maternity and child welfare.

In 1924 her valuable contribution to public health was recognised with the DBE. However, as soon as she married Michael Heseltine in 1934 she was dismissed owing to the marriage bar [8]. She lived in Surrey, then Gloucestershire, where she served as a magistrate, and ended her days in London.

ELLEN NYE CHART née Rollason (1839–1892) actress and theatre owner-manager.

The daughter of a builder, she was born in London. She came to Brighton in the summer of 1865 to play Pauline in *The Lady of Lyons* at the Theatre Royal in New Road, where she met Henry Nye Chart, a similarly unremarkable actor, who was the theatre's proprietor and manager. He had taken it over in 1854, when it was insignificant and floundering, and turned it into a prominent and successful business. In 1864 he had formed a syndicate and bought the theatre for £7,500, later extended and renovated it, and leased 9 New Road as a scenery and prop store.

Miss Rollason married him in 1867 and had a son, Henry. They were partners in every sense of the word: a loving couple who not only acted together but shared the management of the theatre. When he died in 1876 he left her everything. Under her management the theatre flourished and she purchased 9 New Road as her residence. She presented the latest plays, operas and pantomimes, booked the top performers and introduced 'flying matinées' (London productions would bring their cast, scenery, props and costumes by train to Brighton, give a daytime performance and return to London for the evening show). Her innovations transformed the theatre into one of national importance. Nevertheless, every Christmas she gave a free pantomime for the inmates of Brighton workhouse and always took a bow at the end.

In 1889 she sold the theatre and house to the Brighton Theatre Royal Company

Limited for £43,000 and successfully negotiated for the right to live in the house till her death, and to be joint managing director of the company at a handsome salary of £415 a year.

She died at the Grosvenor Hotel, London, and was buried at Brighton & Preston Cemetery after an ostentatious funeral. Brighton bus 605 is named for her, and she haunts the theatre to this day as its celebrated ghost, the 'Grey Lady'. [Related image p16.]

ANNA CLARKE (1919–2004) novelist.

Of English parentage, she was born in Cape Town, South Africa, and educated in Canada and Oxford, (her family moved with her father's job as a professor of education). After gaining an external BSc in maths from London University, she worked as a secretary to various companies, including two publishers. In 1947 she married David Hackel (they divorced in 1957).

Moving to Brighton in the early sixties, she lived at 12 Franklin Road until at least 1972. She took a degree in English literature at Sussex, then became one of the first Open University students, studying the arts. She later gained an MA from Sussex for her research into Victorian publishing (and later wrote what was described as a 'beautifully ingenious, 1880s publisher's office murder tale').

Clinical anxiety, agoraphobia and claustrophobia forced her to give up work and she spent her days sitting in local parks, scribbling drafts of stories into notebooks. At the age of forty-nine her novel *The Darkened Room* was published, the first of her thirty-one books, which included a series featuring Paula Glenning, an English professor, as the heroine-detective. One novel, *Legacy of Evil* (1976), was set in Brighton. Three of her short stories were published in *Ellery Queen Magazine*.

Although she wrote specifically to make a living, her stories were highly praised as well-plotted and beautifully written. Her work was popular on both sides of the Atlantic and her final six books were published only in the USA. Her last novel was *The Case of the Anxious Aunt* (1996). She died in Brighton.

ELSIE COHEN (1895–1972) art house cinema pioneer.

As a sub-editor on *Kinematograph Weekly*, in 1919 she interviewed legendary film-maker D.W. Griffiths, who inspired her to open a cinema. In 1928 she hired a run-down, 600-seater in Great Windmill Street, London, where she opened the Palais de Luxe, the first art house cinema in Britain, and began screening foreign films. When, a year later, the building became the Windmill Theatre [see Sheila van Damm 90] Miss Cohen persuaded the owner of a cinema in Oxford Street to let her relaunch it as the Academy Cinema. She turned it into London's most prestigious continental film theatre, introducing British audiences to the work of Jean Renoir, Ingmar Bergman and Andrzej Wadja, among others. She founded a 'Junior Academy', showing films for children every Saturday morning, installed a manager and travelled around Europe in search of suitable films. In 1939 she successfully challenged an LCC ban on a film about Hitler. During WWII she closed the cinema and worked on the production of recordings for the troops. Her pre-war plans to open five similar cinemas in other major towns were not revived after the war.

She married a Dr Kellner but appears in phone books from 1939 to 1972 as Elsie Kellner, indicating his absence. From 1939 she lived at The Sheiling, 44 Cranleigh Avenue, Rottingdean, and from 1968 until her death at 13 Heathfield Avenue, Saltdean. She was cremated at The Downs, Bear Road.

GRACE MARION COLLCUTT (1875–1954) painter.

One of the six children of a prosperous architect, she was born in London, studied at Richmond School of Art and Slade School of Fine Art, then spent the rest of her life in Brighton, where she was a member of the Sussex Women's Art Club. Many of her paintings in both oil and watercolour were of Brighton scenes, including 'The Royal Albion Hotel', 'Charles Street', 'The String Shop' and 'Spring in the Old Steyne'. She exhibited at the Abbey Gallery and the Royal Academy in London.

She lived at 23 Old Steine with her brother, Arthur, who was a physician both in private practice and (in an honorary capacity) at St Mary's Home for repentant prostitutes. He died in 1933 and she lived the rest of her days at 11 Denmark Terrace. Brighton Museum holds a large number of her works.

ITALIA CONTI (1873–1946) founder of a theatrical academy.

She was born in London, but her family moved to Duncannon House, 20–21 Norfolk Square, Brighton, when she was a baby and her five siblings were born there. After her father died the family returned to London in 1881. She produced amateur shows by children and was inspired to become an actress by Ellen Terry [259], who paid for her tuition. She directed a play at the Savoy Theatre when she was just twenty-three and in 1911 opened a small stage school. She died in Dorset. Her school became world-famous as the Italia Conti Academy of Theatre Arts and is now accredited to offer degree courses.

LOUISA STUART COSTELLO (1799–1870) writer, painter, biographer and poet.

Sources differ as to her birthplace, but she was raised in Paris and supported her widowed mother by working as a governess, by painting and selling miniatures and by writing poetry. Her earnings enabled her brother to attend Sandhurst Royal Military Academy and supported him until his death in 1865. By the early 1830s she was living in Brighton, earning her living as a highly-skilled copyist of illuminated manuscripts (some are now in the British Museum).

Her book *Memoirs of Eminent Englishwomen* (1844), a collection of short biographies of aristocratic and royal women, was illustrated with her own engravings from portraits. *The Rose Garden of Persia* (1845) and *Memoirs of Anne, Duchess of Brittany* (1855) were also widely read and highly praised. Her three-volume novel *Clara Fane* (1848) was said to have 'sparkles of real cleverness'. She also wrote essays, short stories and travel books that exhibited her wide knowledge of history, art and literature.

Fame failed to bring wealth, however; in 1852 she was granted a civil-list pension of £75 a year 'in recognition of her merits as an authoress'. In the 1860s she retired to Boulogne, where she died. Some of her books were reprinted in 2005 and 2007. [Related image p181.]

CONSTANCE COX née Shaw (1912–1998) playwright.

She came to Sussex from her birthplace, Surrey, as a child and at eighteen wrote a farce for the Brighton Amateur Operatic Society. During WWII she was the postmistress at Shoreham-by-Sea, writing in her spare time while her fighter-pilot husband Norman fought (and died) in the war. Her first West End play was staged in 1942. She moved to Brighton and worked in her mother's tobacconist shop, wrote plays based on classic novels and served as chairman of the Sussex Playwrights' Club. After her adaptation of *Vanity Fair* became a hit in 1946 she took up writing full-time, creating original plays and adapting thirty classics for the stage, TV and radio, including works by the Brontës, Austen, Hardy, Wilde and Tolstoy; she also wrote some episodes of the *Forsyte Saga*. Her adaptations of the works of Charles Dickens were the first ever shown on TV. She won the prestigious American Screenwriters' Guild Award and the Television and Screenwriters' Award. Widely credited for pioneering the practice of shrinking huge classics to fit the requirements of the small screen and thereby introducing them to an audience that never read books, conversely she was criticised by some for dumbing-down great works of literature for a mass audience of TV viewers.

She lived at 12 Widdicoombe Lane, Brighton, in the 1950s, moved in 1961 to 120 Shandon Road, Worthing, then to 2 Princes Avenue, Hove, where she lived from 1969 until at least 1984. She died in Henfield. The Sussex Playwrights' Club offers a Constance Cox Memorial Award and Springboard (Brighton's festival of performing arts) runs Constance Cox Memorial Classes. Her work is still being produced at theatres internationally, especially her hugely popular stage adaptation of Wilde's *Lord Arthur Savile's Crime*.

1. Elsie Bowerman

2. Dame Dorothy Tutin

3. Maie Ash

4. Phyllis Dare

5. Matilda Betham-Edwards wearing her French and English honours

6. Elizabeth Allan

7. Madeleine Masson

8. Dame Flora Robson

9. Gluck

12. D.K. Broster

13. Vivien Leigh

14. Eva Moore

15. Grace Lane

16. Margaret Leighton CBE

PAULINE CRABBE OBE née Henriques (1914–1998) actress and broadcaster.

Her family moved to London from her birthplace, Jamaica, when she was five. One brother became a Lord Chief Justice; another a university professor. She studied at LAMDA, was a theatre actress and producer, appeared on radio, became one of the first black TV actresses and founded the Negro Theatre Company.

Married three times, she had two children and became a social worker, then secretary of the London Brook Advisory Centre. In 1966 she became the first black woman to serve as a magistrate and in 1969 was appointed OBE. In retirement she ran a playwriting group for the University of the Third Age near her home at 3 Regent's Court, Regency Square, Brighton. She died at the Royal Sussex County Hospital.

ANNA CROUCH née Phillips (1763–1805) singer and actress.

Born in London, she trained in singing and music and as a teenager performed at Drury Lane and other theatres. In 1785 she married a naval officer, but they separated and from 1787 she lived with baritone Michael Kelly and appeared with him in oratorio, concerts and plays. She enjoyed a long and successful stage career, but was chiefly valued for her beauty; when that faded she became a singing tutor. She lived between London and 9 Mulberry Square, North Street, Brighton, died in Brighton and was buried in St Nicholas's churchyard, where her tomb bears a eulogistic epitaph composed by Mr Kelly. [Related image p16.]

MITZI CUNLIFFE née Solomon (1918–2006) sculptor.

A native New Yorker, she studied fine art in the USA, Paris and Sweden. She designed and created jewellery, textiles, ceramics, tiles, bronze door handles, free-standing figures in marble, stone, wood and bronze and the 'Television Jason': the famous BAFTA trophy, a golden, tragic-comic mask that was intended to be used only in 1955, but was retained permanently and is used as BAFTA's corporate image.

In 1949 she married historian Marcus Cunliffe and lived in Manchester and Cheshire, where they raised three children and she created her famous large-scale sculptures, used to decorate the blank outside walls of modern buildings. Her works include two pieces for the Festival of Britain in 1951, one of which ('Root Bodied Forth') was displayed at the entrance; a piece for the School of Civic Design, Liverpool University; a relief panel at Heaton Park Reservoir, Manchester (the only post-war building to be listed for its sculpture); a gigantic, pierced bronze screen for the Red Rose Restaurant at Lewis's department store in Liverpool (the largest of its kind in the world) and four carved stone panels for Scottish Life House in the City of London. These brought widespread public recognition and she was invited to contribute more than fifty articles for magazines and journals on both sides of the Atlantic and to appear on radio and television.

In 1964 she moved to 8 Lewes Crescent, Brighton, becoming a vocal opponent of the proposed marina. From 1967 to 1971 examples of her work toured twenty British and European cities. After divorcing in 1971 she moved to London where, forced to give up sculpting owing to arthritis, she taught at Thames Polytechnic, then in New York, Pennsylvania and Montreal. She was awarded the Widener Gold Medal by the Pennsylvania Academy of Fine Arts, and the Ruskin School of Drawing at Oxford University named a travelling scholarship in her honour. In 1992 BAFTA gave her a special award. She retired to Oxford, where she held her final exhibition in 2001, and where she died. Her daughter Shay is an award-winning theatre costume designer.

KAY DICK pseudonyms Jeremy Scott, Edward Lane (1915–2001) novelist and literary critic.

The child of an unmarried mother who later married a rich Swiss man with the surname Dick, she was educated in Switzerland and London. Her adult life was spent entirely in the literary world, as a bookseller, reviewer, publisher, compiler of literary collections, an editor of books, periodicals and anthologies and the author of nine novels and three works of non-fiction. *By the Lake* (1949), *Young Man* (1951), *Solitaire* (1958) and *Sunday* (1962) were all semi-autobiographical novels and her novella *The Shelf* (1984) was based on the true story of a woman who committed suicide when Miss Dick ended their brief love affair. This may have been Jean Howells who, her daughter claims, committed suicide in 1962 because of her obsession with Miss Dick. From 1940 she shared her life with Kathleen Farrell [131] in Buckinghamshire and London. They moved to Brighton in 1962, parted, but remained in close contact. (Rhys Davies's 1971 novel *Nobody Answered the Bell* was inspired by the women's relationship.)

The leading book reviewer on *The Times* from the 1960s to the 1980s, she interviewed many literary figures, including Daisy Ashford, [231] and Ivy Compton-Burnett [157]. Shena MacKay described her as 'a maverick woman of letters from a more gracious age who cut a dashing figure with her striking good looks, crest of hair, eyeglass, cigarette holder and Jermyn Street shirts'. Michael de-la-Noy claimed that she 'expended far more energy in pursuing personal vendettas and romantic lesbian friendships than in writing books'.

Miss Dick lived in Brighton for nearly forty years (she is listed at Flat 5, 9 Arundel Terrace, Brighton, in the 1960s and 1970s). She died at Dane House Nursing Home, Dyke Road, where she died. She was cremated at The Downs, Bear Road, and in 2003 fifty boxes of her paperwork were sold to the University of Texas archives. Her books are now all out of print.

MAUD DICKINSON (no dates) scientist.

Although born in Somerset she was raised in the USA then returned to England. As a widow she began in 1911 to search for the 'perfect antiseptic'. Visiting the Far East she became interested in vegetable oils, and using cinnabar and silvestre developed an antiseptic perfume which she called 'Dongor' in memory of her late husband, Gordon.

While working on an antiseptic soap in 1913 she noticed a precipitation of tiny, reddish-brown particles on the surface. A knowledgeable journalist, Cayley Calvert,

thought they looked like pitchblende. She experimented with a Bunsen burner, causing an explosion that converted the crystals into sparkling, adamantine ones, reminiscent of radium. This was named radioleum (or organic radium or 'life crystals' or The New Activity). They cleaned dirty wool, stimulated the growth of wallflowers, separated gold from arsenic, made bread without yeast, removed scale from boilers, made better cement, made better coal, produced everlasting crystallised fruit, made hair grow, cured eczema and germinated frog spawn faster than nature. When sealed in a phial the crystals made water effervesce and produced a healthy drink.

She reported her findings in the journal of the Brighton & Hove Natural History and Philosophical Society. Her discovery was recorded in 'A New Activity?' by Frank A. Hotblack, which includes a photograph of her 'in a well-filled pinstripe suit with a wry smile, a couple of medals, a fur stole, a plumed hat and her thumb in her jacket pocket.' She became a member of the Royal Institution in 1916 and founded two companies: the Dongor Hygienic Co. Ltd, New Steine Mansions (listed 1915) and the Brighton Pure Ice Co. Ltd, Russell Street. In the 1920s she lived at 159 Marine Parade, Kemp Town.

Mrs Maud Dickinson and her strange discoveries were featured in articles in the *The New York Times* in July 1922 and the *Journal of Radiological Protection* in September 1996. [Related images p178.]

CHARLOTTE ELLIOTT (1789–1871) hymn-writer.

A distant relation of Virginia Woolf [243], she was born in London and worked as a professional cartoonist, but when severe illness rendered her a permanent invalid she lost the good humour required for such work and turned her literary talent to writing hymns. She moved with her family to Westfield Lodge, Brighton, in 1823.

In 1834 her brother Henry, incumbent of St Mary the Virgin, founded St Mary's Hall at Brighton, 'to give at nominal cost, a high education to the daughters of clergymen'. To raise funds his family organised a bazaar. As Charlotte could not assist physically, her contribution was to write a hymn, *Just as I am*. This was published in the *Invalid's Hymn Book* in 1836 and was included in just about every hymnal in the Christian world for the next fifty years. Her brother admitted: 'In the course of a long ministry I hope I have been permitted to see some fruit for my labours; but I feel far more has been done by a single hymn of my sister's.'

From 1834 to 1859 she edited and contributed to the *Christian Remembrancer Pocket Book*. She wrote a total of 150 hymns, published in five volumes. Her *Hours of Sorrow Cheered and Comforted*, first published in 1836, went into a seventh edition by 1871; her 1842 collection *Morning and Evening Hymns for a Week* 'by a Lady' sold 40,000 copies by 1870.

After the death of her father in 1833 and her mother and two sisters in 1843, she lived abroad with her third sister then spent fourteen years at Torquay before returning to Brighton, where she lived at 10 Norfolk Terrace until her death, cherishing the one thousand letters she had received from those who found succour in her hymns. After a funeral at St Andrew's Church she was buried in the family vault in Hove. In 1930 a tablet in her memory was unveiled at St Mary's Hall School, Eastern Road.

KATHLEEN FARRELL (1912–1999) novelist.

Raised in a large house overlooking the sea at Rottingdean, she attended a nearby convent school. After a spell as secretary to a Labour MP and founding the Gilbert Wright literary agency, in 1942 she wrote *Johnny's Not Home from the Fair*, a memoir about her grandparents, which led to her meeting Kay Dick [129]. For twenty-two years the pair lived together, in Buckinghamshire and London, where they were known for their wild parties, but when they moved to Brighton in 1962 they lived separately. She took a flat next door to her mother's and is listed at 23 North Gardens in the early 1970s. Miss Dick remained in contact, which was not always friendly, and in 1983 Miss Farrell destroyed all the letters she had received from her.

Between 1951 and 1962 she wrote five novels. C.P. Snow described her *Mistletoe Malice* as 'savagely witty and abnormally penetrating'. *The Cost of Living* depicts a woman in Hampstead who spends her time typing someone else's books (as she had for Miss Dick). She knew everyone in literary society and was a long-time friend of Ivy Compton-Burnett [157]. Much of her life was blighted by rheuma-toid arthritis, but she enjoyed driving her specially-adapted car, with which she once knocked a man off his motorbike. She died in Hove.

MARIA FITZHERBERT née Smythe (1756–1837) 'wife' of the Prince of Wales.

Born into a Roman Catholic family in Brambridge, Hampshire, by the age of twenty-four she had twice been married and widowed. The Prince of Wales, six years her junior, proposed without the King's permission and in 1785 they married in secret. Legitimate in the eyes of the church, the marriage was invalid under British law, so they lived apart. He built Marine Pavilion in the fishing village of Brighthelmstone, and his presence made it the most fashionable town in Britain. In 1795 he married his cousin, Caroline of Brunswick, but soon tried to revive his relationship with Mrs Fitzherbert. In 1796 he made a will naming her as sole beneficiary and blackmailed her with threats of suicide. After the Vatican declared the marriage valid, she agreed to meet but not to cohabit with him, and in 1804 moved into Steine House (now the YMCA), near his pavilion.

When they parted in 1809, he gave her a generous allowance that rose by 1830 to £10,000 a year (worth half a million today). He was crowned King George IV in 1820 and after his death in 1830 his successor William IV treated her with great kindness, continuing her large allowance and offering to make her a duchess, which she declined.

She lived in Brighton for the rest of her life, well-respected and treated as royalty. She died at home and was buried in St John the Baptist's Church, where she had worshipped, and where there is a memorial and a plaque. She left £30,000 (worth over £1.74m today) to her adopted daughter. Brighton bus 805 is named for her. [Related image p16.]

CONSTANCE GARNETT née Black (1861–1946) translator.

Like her sister Clementina [123] she was born at 58 Ship Street, Brighton. She attended Brighton & Hove High School, where she befriended Amy Levy [163] and excelled academically, winning a scholarship to Newnham. She read classical languages and philosophy, earning a first-class pass in her exams, but left without a degree as Cambridge University would not give them to women. After a spell as a librarian in the People's Palace in East London she married, settled in Surrey and concentrated on translating Russian literature into English.

A year after her son David was born in Brighton in 1892 she went (alone) to Russia for seven weeks to meet some of the writers she was translating. She translated nearly all the works of Tolstoy and Dostoyevsky and all those of Turgenev, Gogol and Chekov. Critic Oliver Edwards wrote: 'The debt thousands of people in three generations owe her is enormous ... If ever any one person caused a revolution in English reading habits it was Constance Garnett'. Many of her seventy translations are still in print. She retired in 1934 and died at her home in Surrey. Her son married the daughter of Vanessa Bell [214].

Further reading: Garnett, R. (1991) *Constance Garnett: A Heroic Life*.

MOTHER MARY GARSON MBE (1921–2007) founder of the Sisters of Our Lady of Grace and Compassion.

The daughter of a harbourmaster, she gained an MA in psychology from Aberdeen University in her native Scotland. During WWII she was an officer in the WAAF then became an educational psychologist in East Sussex. She converted to Catholicism in 1947 and in 1954, prompted by the squalid living conditions of several elderly ladies, and with a budget of £800 from the church, founded a home for the needy at Preston Park Avenue, Brighton, which accommodated forty residents. She also started the first sheltered accommodation scheme and converted a country club (once the home of Vera Lynn) into a chapel.

In 1959 Bishop Cowderoy advised her to form a pious union of women. She was professed a nun of the Sisters of Our Lady of Grace and Compassion in 1962 and was prioress-general from 1985 until her retirement in 2005. Under her leadership the community adopted the Rule of St Benedict in 1978. She was awarded the Papal Cross, Pro Ecclesia et Pontifice and in 2004 was appointed MBE.

By 2007 the Sisters of Our Lady of Grace and Compassion number over 200, plus there are over 300 paid staff and hundreds of volunteers. They run twenty-seven homes, including seven foundations abroad in India, Sri Lanka, Kenya and Uganda. The congregation continues at St Benedict's, Manor Road, Brighton; St Mary's House, Preston Park Avenue, Brighton; Holy Cross Priory, Cross-in-Hand and St Joseph's, Albert Road, Bognor Regis, where she died. [Related plate 35.]

MURIEL GEORGE (c1883–1965) actress.

Born in London, she was appearing in the West End at sixteen and by 1911 was earning a massive £20 a week at the Lyric Theatre. She was for several years a member of the Follies, produced by Pélissier, the future husband of Fay Compton [156] and in 1922 performed for George V and Queen Mary at the Hippodrome. From the late 1920s she appeared on BBC radio and between 1932 and 1955 played supporting roles in sixty films.

With her second husband, Ernest Butcher, she evolved a technique of singing in folk-dialect. One critic wrote: 'While they are singing "On Ilkley Moor", it is hard not to believe that they have spent all their lives on Ilkley Moor and have arrived at the Coliseum by an altogether inexplicable accident'. They divorced in 1943 and she retired to 5b Harrington Road, Brighton, where she died. [Related plate 56.]

MARIA GIBBS née Logan (1770–1850) actress.

One of three actress sisters, she played London's Haymarket Theatre at thirteen and soon became very popular, drawing a handsome wage of £10 a week by 1804. Fair, plump and merry, her most famous role was 'Jane' in *Wild Oats* by John O'Keeffe [see Adelaide O'Keeffe, 40].

She married twice, firstly to Mr Gibbs and secondly to famous theatre manager and playwright George Coleman, who had been her lover for ten years. Widowed in 1836, she moved to Brighton, where she died fourteen years later at her home, Burlington Cottage, Crescent Place.

MERCEDES GLEITZE (1900–1981) swimmer and philanthropist.

Born at 124 Freshfield Road, Brighton, the daughter of a foreman baker, she was educated in Brighton and Germany then worked as a bilingual secretary in London, where she served her 'apprenticeship' swimming in the Thames. She set a few minor ladies' records, then on 7th October 1927 became the twelfth person, the third female and the first Englishwoman to swim the channel. She left Gris Nez in France at 2.55am, swam twenty miles through fog, narrowly missed being hit by several vessels, arrived at the English shore at 6.10pm, thanked God she was conscious and passed out. Two hours later she was carried out of her rescue boat to the sound of cheering from a large crowd of well-wishers.

She followed this feat in 1928 by becoming the first person to swim the Straits of Gibraltar from Tarifa in southern Spain to Morocco in North Africa. For the next few years she completed many other impressive swims all over the world, and broke the British record for endurance swimming (46 hrs). She combined sport with philanthropy by using all her prize and sponsorship money to found (in Leicester) the Mercedes Gleitze Homes for Destitute Men and Women.

Having married Patrick Carey, she retired in 1933 and had three children. She died in London.

GRACE GOLDIE OBE (1900–1986) television producer.

A graduate of Bristol University and Somerville, she moved to Brighton in the 1920s (and is listed at 46 Selbourn Road in 1925) to teach for three years at Brighton & Hove High School. She had a long and distinguished career at the BBC, where she took over from Hilda Matheson [259] in 1932, and became head of talks and current affairs in 1962.

JULIA GOODMAN née Salaman (1812–1906) portrait painter.

After studying art in her native London, she married at twenty-four and, when her husband became an invalid, supported her family (which eventually included seven children) by painting portraits of nobles and notables. Her career spanned eight decades from her first exhibition in 1836 until her final work in 1904, during which time she produced over 1,000 portraits. A member of the Society of Female Artists, her sitters included Bessie Rayner Parkes [79], Barbara Bodichon [193] and Fanny Corbaux [157]. In retirement she lived with her daughter, Mrs Alice Passingham, and her grandchildren at 56 Clarence Square, Brighton, where she died. She was buried at Golders Green cemetery.

KATHLEEN GUTHRIE née Maltby (1906–1981) painter.

A physician's daughter, she was born in Middlesex but lived from the age of five in Brighton, where she attended St Michael's Hall School. Moving to London in 1921 she studied at the Slade School of Fine Art and won a scholarship to the Royal Academy Schools. She married artist Robin Guthrie, had a son and lived in Hampstead and the USA for a while, before returning to live somewhere in Sussex from 1932. They both made their living painting portraits but her career was eclipsed by his and impeded by childrearing. The marriage ended and she had a nervous breakdown.

After a painful divorce she married artist Cecil Stephenson in 1941 and returned to London, where she painted the war-torn city (her work 'A Bombed Hospital Ward' is held at the Imperial War Museum). In peacetime she depicted local scenes, designed textiles and silk-screen prints, and wrote and illustrated the children's books *The Magic Button* and *The Magic Button to the Moon*.

ALLANAH HARPER (1904–1992) writer.

Born and raised in Brighton, she became a leading society lady in 1920s London and invented the upper-class 'treasure hunt' (the stealing of policemen's helmets etc) lampooned by P.G. Wodehouse. In Paris in

1929 she founded and edited an influential literary review, *Echanges*. This introduced the French to the works of many English writers.

She married Robert Statlender and moved to the USA where, in 1948, she published a book of memories of her childhood, entitled *All Trivial Fond Records* (a quote from *Hamlet*). In 1976 she co-authored an anthology: *Edith Sitwell, Fire of the Mind*. In later life she returned to France but died in England. *All Trivial Fond Records* can still be found secondhand.

EDITH TUDOR HART née Edith Suschitzky (1908–1973) photographer and spy.

An Austrian-born Jew, she came to England in 1925 and trained as a nursery teacher, but later became a photojournalist, concentrating on exposing the harsh conditions of the poor. In 1933 she married a British communist GP and they lived firstly in London, then among the miners in Wales. She photographed scenes that concerned her, wrote two books, and secretly worked for Soviet intelligence (she recommended Kim Philby to the KGB in 1934).

After a divorce in 1945 she struggled to support herself and her autistic son from her erratic earnings as a journalist and author. She opened a photographic studio in Brixton, south London, and in the 1960s moved to Brighton, opened an antiques shop at 19 Bond Street and (probably) lived at 17 Temple Street. She died at Copper Cliff Nursing Home, 74 Redhill Drive, Brighton, and was cremated at The Downs, Bear Road.

(LOUISA) RUTH HERBERT (1831–1921) actress and theatre manager.

A leading West End actress and famous beauty, in the 1850s she sat for Rossetti, who said she had 'the most varied and highest expression I ever saw in a woman's face, besides abundant beauty, golden hair etc'. Like many actresses, she retained her maiden name after marriage to Henry Crabb and was always known as Miss Herbert. She was lessee and manager of St James's Theatre, London, from Christmas Eve 1864 until sometime in 1867. After

retiring she wrote a cookery book in 1894. She died in Brighton and her biography (cited below] was written by her daughter.

Further reading: Surtees, V. (1997) *The Actress and the Brewer's Wife.*

PHOEBE HESSEL née Smith (1713–1821) soldier.

One of Brighton's most famous names, according to her unusually wordy tombstone in St Nicholas's churchyard she was born in London and served all over Europe for many years as a soldier in the 5th Regiment of Foot, receiving a bayonet wound in her arm while fighting at the Battle of Fontenoy in 1745. She is also notable for her extreme longevity. (The veracity of her epitaph is disputed.) She lived at Woburn Place, and Brighton bus 807 is named for her.

DAISY HILTON (1908–1968) and **VIOLET HILTON** (1908–1968) performers.

The Hilton sisters were Siamese twins joined at the hip. They were born at 15 Riley Road, Brighton, to twenty-one-year-old Kate Skinner, a barmaid. A former domestic servant, she had been seduced by the son of her previous employer (thought to be hairdresser Frederick Andress of 5 Brighton Place). She rejected the twins, believing them a punishment from God for giving birth out of wedlock. Their baptism, which was reported in the *Brighton Herald*, took place at the Countess of Huntingdon's Connexion Chapel on North Street [137].

Miss Skinner's midwife and employer, fifty-year-old Mary Hilton, took control of the babies, sold postcards of them (as 'the Brighton United Twins') and charged people tuppence to intimately inspect them at the Queen's Arms, 8 George Street. This generated sufficient income to take a larger pub, the Evening Star in Surrey Street. She exhibited the twins at circuses and fairs, had them trained to perform and controlled them with physical violence.

In 1911 Mrs Hilton, then fifty-three, her (second) husband Henry and her daughter Edith Green exhibited them across Germany and Australia. When Mrs Hilton died in 1919, she 'bequeathed' them to Edith and her husband, Myer Myers, who took them to the USA, where they were trained to sing, dance and play piano, clarinet and saxophone. They were worked mercilessly and 3,500 people came to see each of their four daily Broadway shows.

When the wife of one of the twins' lovers filed for divorce and sued them for damages, their lawyer discovered the full extent of their exploitation: they had generated over a million dollars, but were paid next-to-nothing and in addition were treated as the personal property of Mr Myers. In 1931 a judge awarded them £50,000 and emancipated them.

They went into vaudeville as the Hilton Sisters' Revue, met escapologist Harry Houdini, formed a tap-dancing act, the Dancemedians, with Bob Hope and appeared in a prurient film called *Freaks*. During a UK tour in 1933, booked for four sell-out performances at the Brighton Hippodrome, they sought their mother, only to discover that she had died a penniless spinster in 1912 in Steyning Union Workhouse infirmary, after the birth of her fourth child.

Back in the USA, they were each briefly married, after a long search to find a state that would marry conjoined twins (many officials deemed such a marriage to be bigamous). They squandered the £50,000, worked as strippers and were featured in a film, *Chained For Life*, which was widely banned. They ran a hotdog stand in Miami until rivals objected to 'freaks' stealing their trade, so they went on tour, but the promoter abandoned them, penniless, after a show at Charlotte, North Carolina. They obtained work in a grocery shop and remained there for six years until they died, a few days apart, during an influenza epidemic. The 1997 musical *Side Show* was based on their lives.

Further reading: Jensen, D. (2006) *The Lives and Loves of Daisy and Violet Hilton.* [Related plate 60.]

MARIE HILTON née Case (1821–1896) promoter of child welfare.

Raised by her grandmother in Surrey, she worked in the Sunday school and temperance movements in London and, from 1843, in Brighton, where she lived at 13 Clarence Place. She became a Quaker, married bookseller and stationer John

Hilton in 1853 and lived at 20 Western Place, where she raised a family of five and worked as a children's dressmaker.

In the 1860s they moved to London, where she performed missionary work in the East End slums, opening a crèche to care for the children of working mothers. This expanded to include an infants' home and infirmary, of which she was superintendent; later the infirmary was moved to the country. She edited the yearly *Crèche Annual*, and managed to secure the patronage of Queen Victoria's daughter Princess Helena and the Earl of Shaftesbury. After her death the crèche was transferred to Dr Barnardo's. Her son wrote her biography.

Further reading: Hilton, J.D. (1897) *Marie Hilton, Her Life and Work.* [Related image p181.]

DR GERALDINE HODGSON (1865–1937) senior academic and author.

A physician's daughter, she was born in Brighton, where she grew up at 52 Montpelier Road. After being educated at Newnham she taught at Liverpool, Leamington, Newcastle and Bristol, gaining her doctorate at Dublin and rising through the educational system to be vice-principal of Ripon and Wakefield Diocesan Training College.

As well as many articles for magazines she wrote a large number of books, including novels, fairy tales, collections of Irish poetry, studies of French literature and philosophy, mysticism and biography, among them *A Tragedy of Errors* (1900), *The Teacher's Rabelais* (1904) and *English Mystics* (1922). [Related image p181.]

FRANCES HOGGAN MD née Morgan (1843–1927) physician and social reformer.

The daughter of a vicar, she was born in Wales and well educated in Paris, Germany and Zürich University, where she graduated in medicine in just three years. In 1870 she became the first British woman to earn a European MD degree. She practised privately and at the New Hospital for Women, married George Hoggan in 1874 and with him formed the first wife-and-husband medical practice in Britain. In 1871, with her close friend

Elizabeth Blackwell [224], she co-founded the National Health Society. She published pamphlets and lectured on various aspects of health, and was a vegetarian and anti-vivisectionist. She campaigned for Indian women to be trained as doctors but criticised the militancy of the Edinburgh Seven [237]. With several others in this book she was a signatory to the 1885 women's suffrage petition presented to each member of the House of Lords.

In the 1890s she was working in Monaco. As an elderly widow she lived in Brighton. She died in a nursing home at 13 Clarence Square and was cremated at Woking.

ROSA HOLMES-SIEDLE LDS, RCS (ENG) née Harse (1891–1986) pioneering dentist.

She was born in Wales, where her father owned a decorating company, and studied dentistry at the Royal Free Hospital in London, where she met Bertram Holmes-Siedle, whom she married in 1919. She became the first female qualified dentist to practise in Sussex when, about 1920, the couple set up (and initially lived above] a joint dental practice at 6 St George's Place, Brighton. Much sought-after for her gentleness and skill, she worked in the practice and was also consulting dentist at the New Sussex Hospital for Women, while raising four children.

The family lived at 206 Preston Road from about 1937, then 87 Marine Parade in the 1940s, 3 Bristol Court West, Marine Parade, in the 1950s, then at 19 Crown Street. They had a weekend home, Yew Tree Cottage, Nutley, to which they retired in 1959.

(JANE) ELLICE HOPKINS (1836–1904) social purity campaigner.

Born into a wealthy family in Cambridge, where she founded a mission hall, in 1866 she and her widowed mother moved to Percy House, 10 Norfolk Square, Brighton. A fervent Christian, she worked for the Albion Hill Home for Prostitutes and supported it by writing and selling pamphlets about its rescue work. She also published meditations for the sick, two volumes of poetry, an early sex-education book called *The Story of Life* (1902) and *The Power of Womanhood* (1899),

which was highly praised in the national newspapers. With Sarah Robinson [213] she helped establish a Soldiers' Institute at Portsmouth in 1874.

She toured Britain as a representative of the Ladies' Association for the Care of Friendless Girls, rallying middle-class women to the cause of saving streetwalkers from their lives of immorality and ill-usage. Her campaigning led to the Industrial Schools' Amendment Act of 1880, which sent ex-brothel children to reform schools and was criticised by feminists. She co-founded the White Cross Society to promote sexual chastity in men and published over forty books or booklets on the subject; these were printed in their millions and remained in circulation for decades, making hers a household name.

A lifelong spinster, she was noted for her devotion to her close companion Annie Ridley. In 1881 she was living at 12 College Road, Brighton; by 1901 she had settled at 2 Belle Vue Gardens with her private secretary Phoebe McIsaac — she had previously employed Emily Janes [226] in this capacity. She died at 5 Belle Vue Gardens. [Related image p181.]

ELIZABETH HOWARD née Haryett; the Countess of Beauregard (c1823–1865) benefactor of Napoleon III.

The daughter of a boot-maker, she was born in Brighton and baptised at St Nicholas's Church. In her early teens she went to London to be an actress, had a child at fifteen by a guardsman who showered her with riches, and by seventeen was the wealthiest prostitute in London.

She fell in love with the 'four-and-a-half-foot-high' Prince Louis, nephew of Napoleon Bonaparte and pretender to the French throne. After sheltering him in London she lived in France as his mistress and funded his political machinations, reputedly to the tune of 'five million gold francs'. In return, he promised to raise her to 'the position she deserved'. On becoming Emperor in 1852 he made her Countess of Beauregard, gave her a château and 450 acres near Versailles and an annual income of £20,000 (worth millions today). However, he married someone else. She was furious and repeatedly harassed him and his wife, Empress Eugénie. After a brief marriage to Clarence Trelawny, she devoted the remainder of her short life to charitable works.

Further reading: André Maurois, S. (1957) *Miss Howard and the Emperor.*

COUNTESS OF HUNTINGDON née Lady Selina Shirley; married name Hastings (1707–1791) promoter of Methodism.

The daughter of Earl Ferrers, she married the 9th Earl of Huntingdon, settled in Leicestershire and had seven children in ten years. On her husband's death in 1746 she became a fervent, evangelical Methodist and built a series of Countess of Huntingdon's Connexion chapels, plus a college in Wales to train ministers (it has since moved and is now Cheshunt College). Among her homes was a large estate in central Brighton, in the grounds of which she built her first chapel in 1761. Seating 950, it stood in North Street until 1972 (an office block now covers the site). She cited an ancient ruling that peeresses were allowed to build chapels and appoint ministers, but the bishops opposed her and the Consistory Court ruled that she must register her chapels as dissenting meeting houses. When she built one in London they ordered its closure, but she outwitted them by buying the house next door and claiming it was a private chapel attached to her home — though it seated 2,000.

During her life she gave away £100,000, the equivalent of millions today. She died leaving debts of £3,000 and sixty chapels bearing her name (there was another in Sussex, at West Hoathly); by 2000 only twenty-three remained. She died in London and was buried there.

Further reading: Schlenther, B.S. (1997) *Queen of the Methodists.* [Related image p181.]

JOAN INGPEN née Hamilton Williams (1916–2007) opera manager.

The daughter of a diplomat who was sent on a clandestine British government mission to Russia to rescue the Romanovs and never returned, she was born in London and raised in Ireland and Sussex. She trained at the RAM as a pianist, gaining her LRAM, and during WWII organised forces' entertainments. After co-founding the Philharmonia Orchestra in 1946 she founded an artists' management agency, Ingpen & Williams (her dog's name). She sold it in 1961 to be head of planning at the Royal Opera House, the first of the three venues at which she held important posts. She worked at the Paris Opéra (1971–78) and (at the behest of Placido Domingo) at the Metropolitan Opera, New York, from where she retired in 1987. Described as 'a legendary figure among opera impresarios' she introduced the public to Solti, Pavarotti and Joan Sutherland.

During the forties she married and divorced twice, to Norman Ingpen and Alfred Dietz. From 1950 she lived with actor Sebastian Shaw. In retirement she lived in Brighton, then Hove. She died in hospital in Hove and was cremated. Ingpen & Williams still exists.

ANNA BROWNELL JAMESON née Murphy (1794–1860) writer and art historian.

The child of an artist, she was born in Ireland and raised in Cumberland, Newcastle and London. She was educated by a governess, taught her younger sisters and from sixteen herself worked as a governess until marrying a barrister in 1825. The marriage was never happy: they lived mostly apart from 1829 and in 1838 parted permanently; he allowed her £300 a year. Her only novel, *The Diary of an Ennuyée*, appeared anonymously in 1826, beginning a literary career that spanned thirty years, encompassing prose, travel writing, history, art and literary criticism, reviews and biography. Her work was published in books, magazines and journals. Although she was the first woman to be a professional art critic, *The Times* said she was 'unrivalled'.

She had much to say about her own sex, in biographical works such as *Memoirs of Celebrated Female Sovereigns* (1831), in her writings on Shakespearean women and also in her critiques of society. In her *Commonplace Book* (1854) she bemoaned the trivial education of women, was outraged by the social acceptability of men's violence to wives, called for an end to the double standard of sexual morality and criticised men's legislating for women.

A close friend of Lady Byron [126], with whom she famously fell out, and of Bessie Rayner Parkes [79], in 1856 she was among the feminists Barbara Bodichon [193] drew together and, as an eminent woman, her name headed the petition for a married women's property act. She called for well-trained women to head public institutions and pleaded for more co-operation between the sexes.

Mrs Jameson's income was shared with her two younger sisters and her niece, who never managed to find careers or husbands. By 1851 she was sufficiently impecunious to be granted a civil-list pension of £100. She never owned a fixed residence; her work took her abroad a great deal, mainly to France, Italy and Germany, and while at home she lived either in lodgings or with friends or family. For at least four years (some sources say six) leading up to her death, her main home was with her sisters at 16 Chatham Place, Brighton. She died in the lodgings she used in London while researching at the British Library, and was buried at Kensal Green cemetery. Several likenesses of her are owned by the NPG, including a marble bust. Her civil-list pension devolved to her sisters, who were living at 14 Chatham Place in 1871. In 1878 her niece wrote her biography, which has recently been reprinted.

Further reading: MacPherson, G. (2007) *Memoirs of the Life of Anna Jameson.* [Related image p16.]

CAROL KAYE née Lindsey (1930–2006) singer and actress.

Born in Oldham, she settled with her husband Len Young at Goldstone Crescent, Hove, in 1959. By then she was famous as one-third of the vocal harmony group The Kaye Sisters, who all had blonde, fringe-cut hairdos and identical outfits, but were not in fact related. They recorded singles and albums, and appeared with Judy Garland, Frankie Howerd and Morecambe and Wise, and on Royal Variety Shows.

In the 1970s she turned to acting, appearing in *Coronation Street* and *The Bill.* In 1988 the Kaye Sisters toured the UK then worked with the Glenn and Herb Miller bands, singing Andrews Sisters' numbers until 1999. Well known in

Brighton and Hove, she attended religious services at the Progressive Synagogue and the Methodist Church in Dorset Gardens and supported local charities. In 1997 she moved to Kemp Town. Her final home was Fourways Nursing Home, 3 Bramber Avenue, Peacehaven, where she died. She was buried at the Jewish Cemetery, Old Shoreham Road.

FANNY (FRANCES MARIA) KELLY (1790–1882) actress.

The daughter of a soldier and niece of celebrated baritone Michael Kelly [see Anna Crouch, 129], she was born in Brighton. She made her stage début aged seven at London's Drury Lane Theatre, where she worked for thirty-six years, learning Italian, French, Latin, guitar and harp. She declined many offers of marriage, including one from Charles Lamb, and in 1816 was shot at on stage by a suitor she had declined. Having diligently saved her earnings, she retired aged forty-five with £20,000 (the equivalent of about £1m today), opened a school of drama for women and built a theatre on the back of her house in Soho, though owing to a failure of machinery she lost a considerable sum in this venture. After she died in Middlesex, just two weeks after the Prime Minister granted her a civil-list pension of £150, an obituarist in *The Era* called her 'the mother of the stage'.

Further reading: Francis, B. (1950) *Fanny Kelly of Drury Lane.*

ELIZABETH KENT (1790–1861) botanist.

The daughter of a milliner, she was born in Brighton and, although poorly educated, she applied herself to the study of botany. During the 1820s she made a modest living giving private tuition to women and writing magazine articles, reviews and books, including *Flora Domestica, or, The Portable Flower-Garden* and *Sylvan Sketches* (an encyclopaedia of trees and shrubs). By 1837 she was so poor she was obliged to work as a governess until 1846, when she received a legacy and tried unsuccessfully to open a home for young invalids at St Leonards. She wrote a botanical guide to the south coast, but no one would publish it. After sinking gradually into deep poverty she died penniless in London.

DOROTHY LAWRENCE (1860–1933), **MILLICENT LAWRENCE** (1863–1925) and **PENELOPE LAWRENCE** (1856–1932) founders of Roedean.

The Lawrence sisters were born in London. Dorothy (Dolly) studied at Bedford College; Penelope (Nelly), the only child of their father's first marriage (he had thirteen with his second wife) was a Newnham student; Millicent (Milly), supported by Penelope's earnings as a schoolmistress, studied at the Maria Grey Teacher Training College. Dorothy and Millicent helped their mother open a school in Wimbledon and in 1885 they opened Wimbledon House School at 25–26 Lewes Crescent (moving it later to 35–7 Sussex Square), where they prepared girls for Girton and Newnham.

In 1897 they commissioned a purpose-built school to be built on forty acres of downland overlooking the sea at Roedean. It opened in 1899 and was run along the lines of a boys' public school. The sisters were known colloquially as 'the Firm'. Penelope, the most dominant, took over the academic side; Dorothy, who suffered from poor health, took charge of religion and the chapel; Millicent, who had the best business brain, was responsible for accounts and administration. She also became involved in local issues, the Girl Guides, the New Sussex Hospital, and votes for women (which Penelope was against).

The school became a public company in 1920 and is still thriving; the sisters retired in 1924 and left Sussex forever. Brighton bus 851 is named for them.

MARY ANN LAWRENSON née Molyneux (1850–1943) co-founder of the co-operative movement.

A London printer's daughter and Christian socialist, she was an English teacher until her marriage. In 1883, after having her son, she co-founded with Alice Acland the Women's Co-operative Guild. She became its general secretary, opened its second branch, near her home in Woolwich, and served on its education committee. The guild supported women's rights, equal pay, a minimum wage and maternity benefit. Its activists included trade unionists such as Margaret Bondfield [124]. In its first year the guild attracted 235 members; by 1910 it had 32,000; by 1933, 72,000.

In middle life Mrs Lawrenson moved to Bournemouth, where she worked with the local guild, then as a widow moved to her son's house in Brighton sometime after WWI. She died at Brighton Municipal Hospital, and after a service at St Joseph's Roman Catholic Church was interred in the borough cemetery.

DUCHESS OF LEINSTER née Vivien Felton (1920–1992) social climber.

A poor girl from a Battersea council house, at sixteen (and seven months pregnant) she married salesman George Conner. Twenty years later they were caretakers of a block of flats in Kensington. One resident, Edward FitzGerald, attracted her with his charismatic bearing and aristocratic good looks. When she discovered him to be the 7th Duke of Leinster she resolved to become a duchess, undeterred by the facts that he was a bankrupt twenty-eight years her senior who had three failed marriages. (One of his wives, the mother of his son and heir, former actress May Etheridge, changed her surname to Murray, moved to Bognor, then to Saltdean, where in 1935 she had killed herself by taking a massive overdose.)

Vivien Conner abandoned her husband in 1956 and, once her divorce came through nine years later, married the septuagenarian peer at Brighton Register Office and set about restoring him to his former glory. He had no money, so she started businesses that could capitalise on his title [he was the great-great-great-great-grandson of Emily, the Duchess of Leinster, 50]. Firstly, she leased Ford Manor, Lingfield, on the Bowes-Lyon estate in Surrey, and ran it as a guest house and nursing home for elderly ladies of independent means. When this failed she opened a knitwear company, which went out of business in 1967, by which time they were living at Arundel Lodge, Arundel Terrace, Brighton. For a while they ran a tea-room in Rye, and then she opened a boutique, named after herself (La Duchesse), at 12a Ship Street Gardens, Brighton.

She arranged her husband's discharge from bankruptcy, which enabled him at long last to take his seat in the House of Lords in July 1975. Still poor, she had to borrow a tiara to attend the state opening of parliament and advertised herself in *The Times* as a 'peeress' looking for a job with accommodation. In 1976 the couple visited his son, the Marquess of Kildare, tried to take away a valuable painting and were ejected by the police. Living in a tiny flat in Pimlico, London, a dispute with his son over the Leinster trust fund proved too much and the duke committed suicide in 1978. The new duke provided his stepmother with a home in Chelsea and a small allowance, but she was persona non grata. In 1987 she moved back to Brighton, where, remarkably, she was reunited with George Conner after twenty-seven years apart. She died at the Royal Sussex County Hospital.

EVE LISTER (1913–1997) singer and actress.

Born in Brighton into a theatrical family, her appearance in the chorus line of Noël Coward's London revue *Words and Music* led to a leading part with Muriel George [132] in *Music in the Air* at His Majesty's Theatre. During a long, varied career she was principal boy in pantomimes, appeared in numerous films, toured with musical comedies, starred in many West End shows and on TV, where her final public appearance was in *The Saint* in 1964. She married twice and had a son.

MARIE LÖHR (1890–1975) actress.

An Australian, she was on stage at age four and made her West End début at eleven. She toured Britain, establishing her reputation by playing principal parts in works by Shakespeare, Shaw, Faust and Sheridan. With her husband Anthony Prinsep she had a daughter and managed the Globe Theatre for several years. They divorced and she branched out into light comedy and, from the 1930s, appeared in films. Her final appearance was in 1966, seventy-two years after her first. In later life she lived in Brighton, where she died at her home, 24 Harrington Road. She was buried in London. [Related plate 47.]

EMMA LOMAX (1873–1963) composer.

Her father was curator of Brighton Free Library and Museum from 1879 to 1903; she was born in Brighton and raised at 11 Park Crescent Terrace, 10 Prestonville Terrace, then 4 Cleveland Road. She studied piano at the Brighton School of Music, winning the Goring Thomas Scholarship and earned money performing at the West Pier Pavilion. A graduate of composition and clarinet at the RAM (1904–10), she won the Lucas Silver Medal. She devised the music, libretti, props and lighting for her stage works *The House of Shadows* (1905), *The Wolf* (1906), and *The Brownie and the Piano-Tuner* (1907). The Brighton Municipal Orchestra premièred her instrumental scores, notably the *Toy Overture* (1915). She wrote the text for a recitation to music, *The Prince in Disguise* (1908) and the one-act comic opera *The Demon's Bride* (1909).

Between 1918 and 1938 she was professor of composition at the RAM, an unusual post for a woman. She was active in the Society of Women Musicians and thrice president of the Sussex Women Musicians' Club. She taught until the day she died, in Brighton, aged ninety.

FLORENCE MARRYAT (1838–1899) novelist, singer, actress, journalist and playwright.

The tenth child of novelist Captain Frederick Marryat RN, she was born in Brighton. Her parents separated when she was five and at fifteen she married Colonel Thomas Ross Church in Malaysia and lived in India for seven years. She had eight children with him, divorced in 1879 and married Colonel Francis Lean, editor of *Lean's Royal Navy List*.

She wrote ninety popular novels, which were translated into half a dozen languages. One, *The Nobler Sex* (1892), an account of a woman's misery at the hands of two abusive husbands is thought to be semi-autobiographical. She also wrote an account of her travels in the USA, a description of British Army life in India and *The Life and Letters of Captain Marryat* (1872). After converting to Roman Catholicism she became fascinated by spiritualism, writing several books on the subject. She edited *London Society* magazine; wrote a play (in which she also acted), gave lectures and dramatic readings, sang in operas and ran a school of journalism. She died in London.

HILDA MARTINDALE CBE (1875–1952) pioneering civil servant.

The daughter of Louisa [below] and sister of Dr Louisa [below], she was born in London and lived in Sussex for twenty years, firstly at 212 High Street, Lewes, then at 2 Lancaster Road, Preston. She attended Brighton & Hove High School, Royal Holloway and Bedford colleges, studied sanitation and obtained the Hygiene Certificate. Working for Barnado's, she found foster homes for orphans, and during an around-the-world trip with her mother and sister investigated the care of orphan children in more than a hundred institutions.

In 1900 she was offered a temporary post as a factory inspector for the Home Office and for the next thirty years inspected factories all over England and Ireland, and campaigned to improve the conditions of women and girls in industry. Her high intelligence and dedication to her career led to repeated promotion. She was appointed OBE in 1918 and in 1925 became deputy chief inspector of factory workers of both sexes. Among her many other appointments, from 1933 to 1937 she was director of women's establishment at the Treasury. She pressed for equal pay and the abolition of the marriage bar [8], and was successful in attracting more women into the civil service.

The author of *Women Servants of the State, 1870–1938* (1938), *From One Generation to Another, 1839–1944* (1944) and *Some Victorian Portraits and Others* (1948), she was appointed CBE in 1935 and died in London, leaving her estate to Bedford College.

LOUISA MARTINDALE née Spicer (1839–1914) social activist.

Born in London, she was privately educated and as a young woman founded a Mutual Improvement Association, Sunday schools and the Ray Lodge Mission Station, visited the East End Ragged Schools,

became interested in women's rights and supported the NUWSS. She married in 1871 and in one terrible week in 1874 her husband and her elder daughter died, leaving her with four children from his first marriage, her infant daughter Louisa [below] and pregnant with Hilda [above]. Sending the four eldest to boarding school, she took her two girls abroad then settled at 212 High Street, Lewes, for five years, moving to 2 Lancaster Road, Preston, in 1885 so that her daughters could attend Brighton & Hove High School for Girls.

A close friend of Marie Corbett [202], she became president of Brighton Women's Liberal Association and of the Women's Co-operative Movement. She co-founded, at 4 New Road, a local branch of the Pioneer Club (for women) and a dispensary for women and children, staffed and officered by women, which evolved into the New Sussex Hospital [299]. Her home became a meeting point for governesses and shop assistants such as Margaret Bondfield [124]. By the turn of the century she was living at 13 Tamworth Road, Hove, and about 1903 she moved to Cheeley's, a house at Horsted Keynes, where she built a Congregational church and installed one of Britain's first female pastors, Miss Hatty Baker. As a pacifist she believed that women should promote peace, and near the end of her life frowned upon the law-breaking suffragettes. She died at Cheeley's and was buried nearby in the churchyard of St Giles.

Further reading: Brown, V. (2006) *Women's Hospitals in Brighton & Hove.* [Related plate 20.]

DR LOUISA MARTINDALE CBE, MD, BS, FRCOG, JP (1872–1966) surgeon and pioneer of radium therapy.

The daughter of Louisa [above] and sister of Hilda [above], she was born in London. They moved to Sussex when she was eight, living firstly at 212 High Street, Lewes, then at 2 Lancaster Road, Preston. She studied at Brighton & Hove High School, Royal Holloway College and the LSMW, and qualified MB, BS in 1899.

After five years as an assistant GP in Hull she gained her MD in London in 1906 and moved back to Brighton where she purchased 10 Marlborough Place, set up her surgery, and became the first female GP in town. In addition she was a visiting medical officer to the Dispensary for Women and Children in Islingword Road, physician to Brighton & Hove High School, to Roedean and to the Lawrence sisters [139]. Later she became senior surgeon and physician at the New Sussex Hospital for Women and Children. She was also a feminist and suffragist, and during WWI served for a short time with the SWH in France.

In 1919 she moved her surgery to 11 Adelaide Crescent, Hove, but sold it two years later and moved to London as a consulting gynaecologist and surgeon, continuing to work with the New Sussex. During her long and distinguished career she pioneered the use of radiation to treat women's cancers. As well as writing many learned articles she was the author of three books: *The Woman Doctor and Her Future* (1922), *The Prevention of Venereal Disease* (1945) and her autobiography, *A Woman Surgeon* (1951).

She lived with a woman friend, the Hon. Ismay Fitzgerald, for thirty-five years from 1911. Among their various homes were two in Sussex: Colin Godman's, Perrymans Lane, Furners Green (1920s) and Little Rystwood, Forest Row (1930s). Dr Martindale served as a magistrate in Brighton and East Grinstead and was appointed CBE in 1931. She retired in 1947 and died in London.

Further reading: Brown, V. (2006) *Women's Hospitals in Brighton & Hove.*

HARRIOT MELLON the Duchess of St Albans (1777–1837) actress, banker and philanthropist.

The daughter of an unmarried Irish wardrobe-keeper in a company of strolling players, she first appeared on stage aged ten. According to *The Times* (9th August 1837) she won £10,000 in a lottery about 1805 but chose to continue working. By 1815 she was earning a massive £12 a week. That year she married her wealthy lover Thomas Coutts, within a week of his wife's death. He was seventy-nine; she thirty-seven. His daughters treated her badly, so Mr Coutts left his wife the whole of his fortune and

his share of Coutts Bank. She rose above her step-daughters' hostility and gave each £10,000 a year, but they still hated her and relished the public disdain she received as a working-class woman who had money but no breeding. She proved to be an outstanding businesswoman, insisting on being involved with managing the bank at a time when there were no women in the world of professional finance.

Aged forty-nine she married twenty-six-year-old William Beauclerk, 9th Duke of St Albans, and was again criticised, this time for 'exchanging money for a title'. Among her homes was a ten-bedroomed mansion, St Albans House (now 131 King's Road), on the corner of Regency Square. She delighted the tradesmen and shopkeepers of Brighton with her profuse expenditure.

She died in London and was buried at the St Albans family seat in Lincolnshire. She left £20,000 to one of her step-daughters (with a proviso that her husband was to get none of it) and about £1.8 million to her step-granddaughter Angela Burdett, provided she took the surname Coutts and did not marry a foreigner. Baroness Burdett-Coutts is univerally acknowledged as the greatest philanthropist of the Victorian era, yet Harriot Mellon, who gave her the means, has slipped into obscurity, though Joan Perkin has self-published an enlightening biography. There was a plaque on St Albans House in Brighton but it has been removed. Her memoirs were published by Henry Colborn and a play about her life was broadcast on BBC radio in 1946.

Further reading: Perkin, J. (2002) *The Merry Duchess*. [Related image p181.]

MARY PHILADELPHIA MERRIFIELD née Watkins (1804–1889) art technician, author and natural historian.

The daughter of barrister Sir Charles Watkins, she was born in London, married a barrister and had a daughter and three sons. They lived at 4 Grand Parade, Brighton, where in 1844 she translated (from Italian) *Treatise of Painting*, which led to her being sent to Italy by the Royal Commission on Fine Arts to research the history of painters' materials and techniques. It was extraordinary, and possibly unique, for a woman (particularly a married one) to be chosen for such an assignment. She later wrote the highly influential *The Art of Fresco Painting* (1846, reprinted 1952); *Practical Directions for Portrait-Painting in Watercolours* (1851, reprinted 2001) and *Light and Shade* (1855, reprinted 2005). Her writings appeared in the foremost scientific journals of her day and she was called upon to assist with natural history exhibits at Brighton Museum.

Fascinated by botany, she became a respected authority on seaweed and marine algae and learned Scandinavian languages in order to study scientific literature, to correspond with foreign scientists and to read Ibsen, who had not yet been translated [see Henrietta Lord, 35]. She was one of a small handful of women who managed to establish themselves in the male world of science at a time when women were not admitted to universities. Her only award was an Honorary Associate of the University of Bologna, though a species of marine algae was named for her.

In 1857 she was granted a civil-list pension of £100 a year in recognition of her services to literature and art. That year saw the publication of her book *Brighton Past and Present*, followed in 1864 by *A Sketch of the Natural History of Brighton*. Widowed in 1877 she left 2 Dorset Gardens, Brighton (her family home since at least 1861) to live with her married daughter Emily Daw at Stapleford Rectory near Cambridge, where she died.

Her herbarium went to the British Museum and some of her papers and correspondence are held at Cambridge University's Department of Plant Sciences Library. Her barrister and naturalist son Frederick was revered by Mrs Garrett Fawcett, leader of the women's suffrage movement, because 'in his long life of ninety-three years there is not one branch of the Women's Movement to which he did not give active service and invaluable help'. His two daughters took their mother's maiden name, de Gaudrion, as their middle name. Margaret [151] became a lecturer at Newnham; Flora was secretary of the Brighton Women's Suffrage Society. [Related image p181.]

LADY DOROTHY MILLS FRGS née Walpole (1889–1959) traveller and writer.

The daughter of the 5th Earl of Orford, she was born in London and was married briefly to her cousin, but preferred travel to domesticity. She lived in Paris, the USA, Palestine, Algiers, Haiti and the West Indies, and undertook intrepid, gruelling journeys across parts of Africa and Venezuela, Trinidad, Turkey, Syria, Jordan and Iraq. She travelled alone, off the beaten track, hiring native guides and porters and an assortment of rough-and-ready means of transport, and was the first white woman to travel to Timbuktu by river. Ironically, her only serious travelling mishap occurred in a London taxi, when she sustained head injuries and a permanently scarred face.

She produced novels, magazine articles and at least five travel books about her various journeys and also took the photos to illustrate them. They included *Beyond the Bosphorus* (1926) and *Episodes from The Road to Timbuktu* (1927). A fellow of the Royal Geographical Society and the Society of Authors, she died at Park Royal Private Hotel and Residential Club, 66 Montpelier Road, Brighton.

DECIMA MOORE CBE Lady Moore-Guggisberg (1871–1964) actress.

Born at 21 Regency Square, Brighton, the daughter of the county analytical chemist, she was the youngest of ten children [see Eva and Jessie, 144], of whom five became actresses or singers and five were decorated for their war-work. She sang in the church choir and was educated at Miss Pringle's school and Boswell House College. Leaving Brighton at sixteen, she studied at Blackheath Conservatoire of Music, where she won the Victoria Scholarship for singing and passed the Trinity College, Cambridge Examination in Theory of Music with Honours.

Joining the D'Oyly Carte Opera Company in 1889, she created the role of 'Casilda' in *The Gondoliers*, playing the role for 554 performances. In 1894 she married cast member Cecil Walker-Leigh, had a son and divorced in 1902. In 1905 she married diplomat Major Frederick Guggisberg and moved to Africa, where they co-wrote *We Two in West Africa* (1909). She was vice-chairman of the AFL and a member of the International Women's Franchise Club. While on tour she would leave the theatre between performances to give suffrage speeches. In 1911 she took part in an all-night entertainment as part of the suffragette census resistance [294].

In 1914 she founded the Women's Emergency Corps, the first organisation to replace men with women war workers. Attached to the French Army, she worked as a nurse at Hôpital Militaire 103 in Amiens, was Directrice de Cantine at Depôt des Eclops-Conty, and established the British Navy, Army and Air Force Leave Clubs in Paris and Cologne. She was appointed CBE in 1918.

Her husband became Governor of the Gold Coast, then of British Guiana and was knighted. She was honorary exhibition commissioner and chair of the British Empire Exhibition at Wembley (1923–25). Her husband died at 27 Cantelupe Road, Bexhill, in 1930 and was buried there at St Peter's churchyard, where in 1935 the people of the Gold Coast erected a granite memorial in his honour. In 1936 a burglar stole all her war decorations and souvenirs, as well as her CBE badge. During WWII she reopened her forces' leave clubs and served on the Allies Welcome Committee.

The last surviving creator of an original G & S role, in 1960 she became vice-president of the Gilbert & Sullivan Society. She lived in London then in Lincolnshire, died in a nursing home in London and was buried at Golders Green. [Related plate 46.]

EVA MOORE (1866–1955) actress and suffragist.

The eighth of ten children [see Decima, above and Jessie, below] she was born at 67 Preston Street, Brighton, and educated locally at Miss Pringle's school. She went to Liverpool to study gymnastics and dancing and returned to Brighton as a dance teacher in a private school at 29–30 Brunswick Road, where one of her pupils was the young Winston Churchill, the future Prime Minister. Like her sisters she landed a job with the D'Oyly Carte Opera Company and left Sussex.

One of the best-known actresses of her day, between 1887 and 1923 (when her book of reminiscences, *Exits and Entrances*, was published) she acted in approximately ninety plays, thirteen of them written by her husband, Harry Esmond Jack. Between the wars she appeared in twenty-eight films.

She was also an ardent feminist and suffragist, and co-founded and served as vice-president of the AFL, becoming a familiar figure marching in suffrage processions in London with contingents of other well-known actresses; in addition she was called as a defence witness when Mrs Pankhurst stood trial. She appeared with Muriel Matters [252] in a suffrage gala matinée at London's New Prince's Theatre in 1912, which included scenes from the play *Votes for Women!* by Elizabeth Robins [56]. She resigned from the AFL after members objected to her acting in a comedy sketch in which the heroine preferred kisses to votes. During WWI she helped her sister organise the Women's Emergency Corps.

She had three children, of whom two survived childhood. Her daughter Jill Esmond married Laurence Olivier and later divorced him for adultery with Vivien Leigh [192]. She died in Maidenhead. [Related plate 14.]

JESSIE MOORE (1864–1910) singer and actress.

A Brighton-born soprano, she toured for thirty months with the D'Oyly Carte Opera Company, playing lead roles in Gilbert & Sullivan operas. In Sussex in 1889 she married principal baritone (and later elocution tutor, manager and producer) Lewis 'Jimmy' Cairns James.

Until 1905 she appeared in a variety of comedy and light opera parts in West End theatres, then reliquished her acting career to be 'lady superintendent' of her husband's School of Musical and Dramatic Art. She died at Golders Green aged just forty-six.

HELEN MUSPRATT (1907–2001) photographer.

Born in India, the daughter of an army officer, she opened photographic businesses in Cambridge and Oxford with her colleague Mrs Ramsey. In the 1930s she photographed in the USSR, joined the Communist Party, married railwayman John Dunman and had three children. She was so busy taking photographs to make a living that she had no time to cultivate her artistic side. Only in retirement did she gain renown and recognition; her work was featured in a major exhibition and a book, and she made television appearances.

In the 1990s she moved into a care home in Brighton. She died at Sycamore Court, Bevendean Road, and was cremated.

Further reading: Williams, V. (1986) *Women Photographers: the Other Observers, 1900 to the Present.*

ANNIE FERAY MUTRIE (1826–1893) still-life painter.

Trained at the School of Design in her native Manchester, she became one of Britain's leading oil painters, specialising in studies of flowers. She exhibited at the Royal Academy almost annually between 1851 and 1882. In 1870 she was nominated for associateship of the academy, but could not be elected owing to its ban on female members. In later life she lived in Kent, London, and finally 26 Lower Rock Gardens, Brighton, where she died. Her work can be seen in various galleries and museums, including the V & A.

DAME ANNA NEAGLE DBE real name Florence Robertson (1904–1986) actress and film producer.

The daughter of a sea captain, she was born in Essex. She studied physical training and worked as a dancer and chorus girl in the 1920s. Her regal presence and fine bone structure got her noticed and, changing her name to Anna Neagle in 1930, she became an actress, gaining fame for playing major historical characters including Edith Cavell, Amy Johnson and Queen Victoria, and was Florence Nightingale in *The Lady with a Lamp*. For playing Odette Sansom, an SOE agent, she was appointed an Honorary Ensign of the FANY. She also acted in light-hearted films and musical comedies and was the first actress to appear on the cover of *Life* magazine.

Aged thirty-nine she married well-known director-producer Herbert Wilcox and worked with him on thirty-two productions. In the 1950s she co-produced films with him but lost money on them. A star of the screen for a quarter of a century, she was appointed CBE in 1952 and DBE in 1969. She wrote several books, including her autobiography, and co-wrote one about Elstree studios.

She lived for some years at 18 Lewes Crescent, Brighton, moving later to London and then to Surrey, where she died. She has blue plaques in London and Brighton, where bus 856 is named for her.

Further reading: Neagle, A. (1974) *There's Always Tomorrow.* [Related plate 48.]

JENNIFER NICKS (1932–1980) champion ice-skater.

Her family was related to cricketer John Wisden, founder of the famous almanac, and her parents Jack and Elsie were track athletes who ran Wisden's sports shop at 26 Duke Street, Brighton. Miss Nicks was born in Brighton, and after passing her NSA qualifications (Gold Figures, Gold Pair and Bronze Dance) at the Sports Stadium ice rink in West Street, she taught there.

She and her brother John became well-known amateur skaters, winning many championships. They were British Southern Counties Champions 1952 and British Champions 1947–1950 and in March and December 1952. After being placed fourth at the 1952 Winter Olympics they turned professional in 1953 and that year won Great Britain's first world and European titles in pair skating. They appeared in ice shows all over the world and were instructors in South Africa until 1961, when John Nicks ended their partnership and moved to Los Angeles. Brighton bus 881 is named for them.

DAISY NOAKES (1910–2005) autobiographer and broadcaster.

One of ten children, she was born into a working class family at Prince's Road, Brighton, moving later to Vere Road. She and all her sisters became domestic servants when they reached fourteen. Aged sixty-five she wrote a short, autobiographical work *The Town Beehive: A Young Girl's Lot in Brighton 1910–1934*, which proved so successful that she followed it with two more reminiscences, *The Faded Rainbow* and *Street Noises*. She wrote poetry, became a broadcaster (interviewing fishermen and other tradesmen on BBC Southern Counties Radio) and was featured on TV and in the BBC book *Out of the Doll's House*. Brighton bus 914 is named for her.

HELENA NORMANTON (1882–1957) pioneer barrister and feminist campaigner.

Although born in Essex, she was raised at 4 Clifton Place, Brighton, by her widowed mother, who ran a grocer's and took in boarders. She won a scholarship to York Place Science School (later, Varndean School) in 1896, the year she first thought of becoming a barrister. She left school when her mother died and helped run the boarding-house. In 1901 she was living at 11 Hampton Place, Hove, a boarding house owned by her aunt Eliza Whitehead, while she worked as a pupil-teacher at the local board school.

She gained first-class honours in history at London University and worked as a lecturer. In 1918 she was, as a woman, refused a place as a law student at the Middle Temple. While awaiting her appeal the Sex Disqualification (Removal) Act became law and she immediately reapplied. The first woman admitted, she was called to the bar in 1922, the second female barrister to qualify and the first to practise. By then she had married, and her decision to keep her own name was well-publicised. (In 1925 she went to the USA and conducted a legal case that established American women's right to retain their names.)

A member of the Six Point Group [301] and of the Council of Professional Women, she urged women to break down other male bastions, specifically 'the Church, the Stock Exchange, the House of Lords'. In 1948 she became the first woman to lead the prosecution in a murder trial, and the following year became one of the first two women to be appointed King's Counsel. She was an excellent public speaker, wrote articles for various publications and books on a wide variety of subjects, from Shakespeare to buying a house.

She urged divorce reform, marched against the atom bomb and was the first subscriber to the appeal for funds to build Sussex University. Her death took place in London, where she was cremated, and her ashes were buried at St Wulfran's churchyard, Ovingdean. [Related image p16.]

MOLLIE PANTER-DOWNES (1906–1997) writer.

Born in Ireland, after her father's death in 1914 she and her mother lived impecuniously in a flat at 3 Vernon Terrace, Brighton. They moved later to Rudgwick, where at sixteen she wrote her first novel, *The Shoreless Sea*, and earned her first wage when it was serialised in the *Daily Mirror*. The book version sold well and was reprinted seven times in eighteen months. After writing a second novel she married Aubrey Robinson and moved to London, then in 1931 to Roppeleghs, between Haslemere and Chiddingfold, Surrey, where she raised her daughters and lived for the rest of her life. She built a hut in the woods, where she wrote short stories, two non-fiction works and numerous novels.

Thirty-six of her short stories appeared in the *New Yorker*, which also serialised some of her books and published her 'Letter from London', which started in 1939 as a wartime diary but continued until 1984. She died in a Surrey nursing home and was cremated; her ashes were scattered around her writing hut.

DAME LILLIAN PENSON DBE (1896–1963) historian and senior academic.

A Londoner by birth, she graduated BA in 1917 and PhD in 1921 at the University of London. During WWI she worked for the War Trade Intelligence Department and later lectured at London colleges. She wrote *The Colonial Agents of the British West Indies* and was assistant editor on some of the eleven volumes of *British Documents on the Origins of the War, 1898–1914*.

In 1930 she was appointed to the chair of modern history at Bedford College, where she opposed the introduction of male students. She was later dean of the Faculty of Arts and in 1948 became the first woman to be appointed vice-chancellor of a university. In 1949 she became one of the first two women awarded an honorary LLD by Cambridge University and received eight more, including one from Oxford. Appointed DBE in 1951, she lived in later life in south London and ended her days at Rayland Nursing Home, 54 Marine Parade, Brighton.

DIANA PETRE (1912–2001) writer.

A Londoner, she went to boarding school in Eastbourne and became a writer of short stories, magazine articles, book reviews for the *Daily Telegraph,* and two novels: *Portrait of Mellie* (1952) and *The Cruel Month* (1955). She is best-known for *The Secret Orchard of Roger Ackerley* (1975, reprinted 1985 and 1993), a memoir of her childhood of emotional and physical neglect. Near the end of her life she moved to a nursing home in Brighton, where she died. [Related plate 38.]

HESTER LYNCH THRALE PIOZZI née Salusbury (1741–1821) writer.

As a child in her native Wales, she wrote poetry and translated works from French. Her family arranged her loveless marriage to serial adulterer Henry Thrale, who placed stringent restrictions upon her freedom. She became pregnant thirteen times in twelve years, but only four children lived to maturity. Her husband gave her a set of calf-bound books, each one stamped with the word *Thraliana,* for her to collect anecdotes, thoughts and notes on her family (excerpts were published in 1913). The Thrales had homes in London and (between 1775–85) at 64 West Street, Brighton, where they hosted parties for writers and artists and she became the close confidante of the famous writer Samuel Johnson, who encouraged her literary pursuits and wrote his *Lives of the English Poets* under their roof. She helped her husband to get elected to parliament and assisted in managing his brewery, once saving him from bankruptcy. Widowed at

forty, she sold the business and, in the face of opposition from her family and friends, married singer Gabriel Piozzi.

She wrote several books, including *Observations and Reflections made in the Course of a Journey through France, Italy, and Germany* (1789) and *Anecdotes of the Late Samuel Johnson* (1822), which sold out on its first day. Returning to Wales in 1795 she wrote political pamphlets including 'Address to the females of Great Britain' and a history book, *Retrospection* (1801).

She died at Clifton, was buried in Wales, and is commemorated on the side of Dr Johnson's statue in London. 64 West Street sports a blue plaque commemorating the Thrales, Dr Johnson and writer Fanny Burney, another frequent guest.

Further reading: Clifford, J.L. (1987) *Hester Lynch Piozzi.*

HONORIA PLESCH (1919–1990) artist and designer.

The child of Hungarian parents, she was born in Berlin and grew up in West London, where her father was a physician to the rich and famous. When she took a job as a scenery painter he threw her out because she had disgraced him by working for wages. She became design assistant to Cecil Beaton on the film *Dangerous Moonlight* and was by age twenty established as a film costume designer. During WWII she served with the ATS then with the Army Film Unit as a designer for Ministry of Information films.

In peacetime her career really took off: she was costume designer on fifteen productions including the films *Brighton Rock* (1947), *Stage Fright* (1950) and several in the St Trinian's series. She designed for the London Palladium and the Arts Theatre, and created animated models for Lyons Corner House windows. C.B. Cochran called her 'the most talented designer of her generation'. The 1950s and sixties saw a change of career: she became a scriptwriter, producer and director of revues, films, shows and television and wrote two related books.

In 1963 she bought Patcham Windmill, Mill Road, Brighton, for £8,000. She sold a cottage on the site and restored the mill, cleverly converting it into a luxury home while retaining most of the machinery intact for posterity. She built a brick swimming pool with her own hands (it is now a Koi carp pond) and created a Chinese garden. Although she sold the mill in 1968 she probably still lived locally, because having turned her hand to designing jewellery she opened a shop at the end of the Palace Pier. One day the shop disappeared, swept away in a collision. She began creating jewellery and figurines using precious metals, which she exhibited at the Goldsmith's Hall. She died at Worthing.

ERICA POWELL OBE (1921–2007) civil servant and author.

The daughter of a GP and a nurse, she was born in Brighton and grew up at 4 Old Steine until they moved to Lincolnshire in 1930, when she was nine. During WWII she worked abroad for the British Army and for the International Refugee Organisation. In 1952 she joined the civil service as private secretary to Dr Kwame Nkrumah, Governor of the Gold Coast, then under British rule. During her time there she was appointed MBE in 1958 and OBE in 1960. Her employer became Prime Minister, then President, when the Gold Coast gained independence from Britain. As a member of the overthrown white colonisers, her position as personal assistant to a leading light of black African independence was very difficult, and she left in 1965 after a decade that saw her falsely accused of being a spy and of being his mistress. Months later he was overthrown in a military coup.

In 1970 she took a post as private secretary to Siaka Stevens, Prime Minister and future President of Sierra Leone. Living in the midst of corruption, violence and military coups, once, while she worked alone in the presidential compound, rebels attacked the building with gunfire. She resigned in 1979. During her time as their assistants, she helped both Mr Nkrumah and Mr Stevens to write their autobiographies, and wrote her own.

Further reading: Powell, E. (1984) *Private Secretary (Female)/Gold Coast.*

SYBIL, VISCOUNTESS RHONDDA DBE née Haig; married surname Thomas (1857–1941) suffragist.

Born at 52 Norfolk Square, Brighton, she was raised at 24 Adelaide Crescent, Hove, until 1882, when she married David Thomas MP, with whom she lived between London and Wales. With her only child, Margaret, she joined the NUWSS and later the WSPU. Her sister Lotty (born in Hove in 1859) was also a WSPU member and went to prison, as was her niece Cecilia, who was trampled on Black Friday [294] and later died of her injuries. She raised funds for the cause and in 1913 became treasurer of the East London Federation of Suffragettes. In 1914 she was arrested for holding a public meeting outside parliament and, refusing to pay the fine, served one day in prison. Her daughter, a WSPU member, bombed a post-box, was imprisoned and went on hunger strike.

During WWI Sybil Thomas worked for the National Savings Committee, gave part of her home for use as a hospital and travelled extensively assisting her husband, the Minister of Food Control. She was appointed DBE in 1920. After her death, at her home in Wales, she was buried at Llanwern churchyard.

Some years previously she had persuaded her husband to take their daughter into his business empire and in 1918 he accepted a peerage on the condition that his daughter could inherit it. He died just two weeks later and she, as Viscountess Rhondda, became the leading feminist of her day.

Further reading: Mackworth, M. (1933) *This was My World.*

DAME FLORA ROBSON DBE (1902–1984) actress.

One of seven children of a marine surveyor, she was born in South Shields. She was taught singing and elocution and made her performing début at the age of six. After studying at the Academy of Dramatic Art (later, RADA) she became one of the most famous character actresses of her generation, and proved her considerable versatility by playing roles as diverse as a drunken Scottish prostitute and Queen Elizabeth I. Her first screen credit was in 1931; her last in 1981 and she played Nelly Dean in the Hollywood blockbuster *Wuthering Heights*.

With her two sisters Shela and Darge, she lived at 4 Marine Gardens, Brighton, from 1961 to 1976 (which has a British Film Institute plaque) and at 7 Wykeham Terrace, Dyke Road (Brighton Corporation plaque) until 1984. A third plaque can be found at St Nicholas's Church, where she was a member of the congregation. She became president of the Brighton Little Theatre, chairman of the council of RADA and was appointed CBE in 1952 and DBE in 1960 for services to charity. She died in Brighton, leaving all her plays and theatre books to Brighton & Hove Arts Centre and all her copyrights to the TLGC [see Kitty Carson, 156]. Brighton bus 820 and a theatre in Newcastle were named for her.

Further reading: Barrow, K. (1981) *Flora*. [Related plate 8.]

SUNNY ROGERS (1913–2005) variety artiste and musician.

Having previously worked as a Tiller girl, a choreographer and a producer, and toured internationally as part of a rope-spinning Wild West act, she played stooge, straight-woman and pianist to comedian Frankie Howerd for thirty-five years, during which time millions saw her on stage and TV without ever knowing her name. She rarely spoke; her humour was expressed in music, gestures and facial expressions. When he died in 1992 she retired to a flat in Brighton, where a charcoal drawing of herself and Mr Howerd hung in her hallway. She died at a nursing home in Worthing.

EDITH SAUNDERS (1865–1945) botanist.

Her father owned and ran the Bristol Hotel, 143 Marine Parade, Brighton, where she was born; her mother died before she was six. She left Brighton to study at Handsworth Ladies' College and Newnham, where she gained a pass with first-class honours in natural sciences. As a woman, she was not awarded a degree.

In 1889 she was appointed demonstrator in botany at Newnham and for more than twenty years was lecturer in natural sciences there and at Girton. In 1906 she won the Banksian Medal of the Royal Horticultural Society, was elected president of the botany section of the British Association in 1920 and president of the Genetical Society in 1936. For her pioneering research and her two-volume work *Floral Morphology* (1937–9) she was known as 'the mother of British plant genetics'. She died in Cambridge at the age of eighty when her bicycle collided with a car.

AMY SEDGWICK real name Sarah Gardiner (1835–1897) actress-manager.

Miss Gardiner was born in Bristol, and used the stage name Mortimer before settling on Sedgwick in 1853. After a few acting jobs in the provinces she began her West End career in 1857. A year later, aged twenty-three and having recovered from a serious illness, she married her doctor, forty-eight-year-old William Parkes, at St Michael's Church, Southwick, continuing her career on the London stage. (He died in 1863 and was buried at Southwick.) She had two brief spells in management: in 1866 she ran the Haymarket Theatre during its summer season and in 1868 she opened the Marylebone Theatre as its director. She became well-known in Sussex for her roles at the Theatre Royal, Brighton, where she was known as 'the Queen of Comedy'.

In 1873 she married Charles Pemberton at St Andrew's Church, Hove, styled herself Mrs Sarah Parkes Goostry and retired from the stage. A silk programme on the wall of the stalls foyer at the Theatre Royal declares her farewell appearance. Widowed two years later she returned to work, giving her final London appearance at the Haymarket in 1877. During retirement she took up painting, supported various local charities, taught private pupils and gave dramatic recitals in London and the provinces; indeed, on her sixty-sixth birthday she performed at the Brighton Dome. In 1883 she gave a 'Grand Dramatic Recital' to Queen Victoria and Princess Beatrice [32] at Osborne House, Isle of Wight.

She lived in Brighton for many years, at Clare House, 28 Holland Road and then Bank Lodge, 1 Western Place (now

64 Western Road). In 1893 she moved to Hill View, Lewes Road, Haywards Heath, where she once gave a charity recital. She died there and was buried in the nearby churchyard. [Related images pp16, 178.]

MARY SEWELL née Wright (1797–1884) and **ANNA SEWELL** (1820–1878) writers.

Mary Wright was educated at a dame-school and by a succession of governesses. Her father suffered financial ruin, forcing her to become a governess — she called this 'a great descent in the social scale' — until she was saved by her marriage to Isaac Sewell. With their daughter Anna the couple moved to London, where they had a son and fell into financial hardship. She taught her children at home, buying their textbooks with the royalties from *Walks with Mamma*, the first of her many books, which later included *Homely Ballads* and *Stories in Verse.*

Mr Sewell became a bank manager and the family lived wherever he was posted. They spent twenty-two years in Sussex, at Brighton (1836–1845); Lancing (1845–9); Petlands, New England Road, Haywards Heath (1849–53) and Graylingwell (1853–8). Mrs Sewell carried out charitable and social reform work and became famous for her popular verses (now, alas, forgotten).

At the age of fourteen Anna Sewell sustained an accident that left her a permanent invalid, confined to sick-bed and sofa. She edited and critiqued her mother's work and dictated parts of a story of her own devising to her mother, penning some sections herself. The book took six years to complete and was sold in 1877 to her mother's publishers, Jarrold & Sons, for a one-off payment of £40. Miss Sewell was then fifty-seven and she died five months later. Her book, *Black Beauty: His Grooms and Companions; the Autobiography of a Horse, Translated from the Original Equine by Anna Sewell,* went on to become the sixth best-selling book in the English language and is still in print; in addition it has been adapted for film several times and became a successful TV series. Heyworth School, near her former home in Haywards Heath, bears a blue plaque in her honour.

Further reading: Gavin, A. (2004) *A Dark Horse: The Life of Anna Sewell.*

MARGARET MACNAB TAYLOR (1892–1963) founder of Hamilton Lodge.

Little is known of her life. She was born in Barnet and fifty-three years later founded Hamilton Lodge School, 7 Walpole Road, Brighton, which specialised in the totally deaf, taking children as young as two. By all accounts she was a genius at teaching speech and lip-reading. She also founded the Margaret Taylor Hostel for Deaf Students. She died suddenly at Worthing Juvenile Court and was cremated. Her memorial service was held at St Anne's Church, Eaton Place, Brighton. Her school has expanded considerably and now takes pupils aged five to eighteen.

MINNIE TURNER (c1867–1948) suffragette.

A boarding-house owner, she was secretary of the Brighton Women's Liberal Association (1896–1908), but when the Liberal Party refused to give women the vote she joined the WSPU. She advertised her boarding house, Sea View, at 13 (and later 14) Victoria Road, in all the suffrage newspapers, offering rest-cures, home-made bread and meals in the garden. For several years it was the favourite seaside home, sanctuary and place of convalescence for countless numbers of exhausted or force-fed suffragettes. She later described those years as the happiest of her life and proudly boasted that more suffragette leaders, speakers and prisoners had stayed with her than in any other house in Britain.

She created a library of books related to the women's movement, and collected photographs and autographs of the suffragettes who visited; this priceless collection is now held at the Museum of London. She was arrested twice: once at the Black Friday [294] deputation in 1910 (discharged) and once in 1911 for breaking a window at the Home Office (twenty-one days' imprisonment). Her front bay window was smashed in retaliation, but no one was charged. In 1912, as a member of the TRL she withheld her tax as a political protest and the bailiff took her goods and sold them. Nothing is known about her earlier or later life, though she is still listed at Sea View in 1947. [Related image p175.]

DOREEN EDITH VALIENTE née Dominy, (1922–1999) author and witch.

An architect's daughter, she was born in Surrey, grew up in Dorset, Wales and Hampshire and was educated at a convent. As a child she was fascinated by witchcraft and magic; as a teenager she cast a spell on her mother's work colleague and became a clairvoyant; in adulthood she studied spiritualism and theosophy. Her brief marriage to a Greek seaman ended in widowhood and she wed a Spaniard, Casimiro Valiente. In the 1940s they moved to Bournemouth, where, in 1953, just after the practice of witchcraft ceased to be illegal, she was initiated into the Wiccan religion at a ceremony in Christchurch and became high priestess of a north London coven.

After divorcing, in the late 1950s she moved to Brighton. Here she gave local talks and wrote magazine articles and her first books, *The Charge of the Goddess* (c1960, reprinted 2000) and *Where Witchcraft Lives* (1962), a history of activity in Sussex. From 1964 she was president of the Witchcraft Research Association and wrote several more books: *An ABC of Witchcraft Past and Present* (1973), *Natural Magic* (1975) and *Witchcraft for Tomorrow* (1978). These brought considerable fame and many followers hailed her 'Queen of the Witches' and the Mother of Contemporary Paganism, and credited her with popularising Wicca, but she was too modest to concur. By the nineties she was the best known Wiccan witch in Britain and claimed that Prime Minister Margaret Thatcher was the reincarnation of Elizabeth I.

She lived in a flat, 6 Tyson Place, Grosvenor Street, Brighton, died at Sackville Nursing Home, Sackville Road, Hove, and was cremated at Brighton after a Wiccan funeral service. She left all of her witchcraft-related possessions to the Centre for Pagan Studies, of which she had been patron since 1995.

MARGARET DE GAUDRION VERRALL née Merrifield (1857–1916) classics scholar and parapsychologist.

The granddaughter of Mary Merrifield [142], she was born at 4 Dorset Gardens, Brighton and her family later lived at Belair, St Wilfred's Road, Cuckfield. She studied classics at Newnham from 1875 and was appointed classics lecturer in 1880. Aged twenty-five she married Brighton-born classics scholar Arthur Verrall at St Peter's Church and moved to Cambridge, where she spent the rest of her life. She had two daughters, one of whom died aged two, and worked as a researcher, university lecturer, examiner and writer, serving with Mary Dowson [56] on the committee of the University Club for Ladies.

She joined the Society for Psychical Research in 1889 and served on its committee from 1894, wrote many articles for its journal and reviewed all the papers the society published. Most of her research and writing was concerned with parapsychology, though she also translated academic works with her husband. Renowned not only as one of the best observers of psychic phenomena but as a gifted psychic, she was a sceptical, scientific researcher who carried out experiments in thought transference with her daughter. Between 1901 and 1916 she produced hundreds of scripts of automatic writing and published her own analysis of them, provoking serious academic discussion. She had also been involved in the Palm Sunday Scripts, which concerned psychic messages to Arthur Balfour MP. Sir Oliver Lodge called her 'one of the sanest and acutest of our own investigators', while one obituarist remarked that her death would 'leave a void in her field of research'.

Oppenheim, J. (1985) *The Other World: Spiritualism and Psychical Research in England, 1850–1914.*

LUCY CARRINGTON WERTHEIM née Pearson (1883–1971) gallery founder and author.

Born in Salford, Lancashire, she married the future Netherlands Consul to Manchester in 1906 and had three children. She founded the Twenties Group for artists and opened the Wertheim Gallery in London in 1930, at which she exhibited young, unknown, British artists. It was requisitioned as an air-raid shelter at the commencement of WWII in 1939 and was never reopened. In 1947 she published a book: *Adventure in Art.*

She lived in Brighton for many years, in the 1950s at 19 Middle Street; in the 1960s at 38 Kensington Place and later at Norfolk Square, from where in 1969 a burglar stole fifteen of her treasured paintings. She died in Brighton two years later, leaving many important paintings to the Tate and the National Gallery and to municipal galleries in New Zealand and Australia.

DR OCTAVIA WILBERFORCE (1888–1963) physician.

The great-granddaughter of William Wilberforce, who fought for the abolition of slavery, she was born at Lavington House, Petworth, and moved with her family to Beechwood House, Beechwood Lane, East Lavington, then to Bramlands, a house in Woodmancote.

In 1910, while taking her ailing maid to see Louisa Martindale [141], one of the two per cent of physicians who were female, she was inspired to become a doctor herself. Her parents ridiculed the idea, saying that studying medicine would 'unsex' her and no one would pay to consult her. She declined a proposal of marriage from Charles Buxton, who died suddenly soon afterwards. Lord and Lady Buxton [68] subsequently funded her medical studies when her parents refused to do so. Elizabeth Robins [56] also gave moral and financial support and became her close friend and companion for the next forty years.

Because of her meagre education, she had to engage in private study for several years just to qualify for acceptance to medical school and entered the LSMW in 1913, qualifying LRCS, LRCP in 1920. After working at Graylingwell Mental Hospital, Chichester, and St Mary's Hospital, Paddington, in 1923 she established a general practice at 24 Montpelier Crescent, Brighton, working also at the Marie Curie Hospital in London and the New Sussex Hospital in Brighton, where she was eventually to become chief physician. She became friends with Virginia Woolf [243], to whom she was distantly related.

In 1927 she and Dr Marjorie Hubert leased Miss Robins's fifteenth-century Henfield farmhouse and turned it into a convalescent home for overworked women, naming it Backsettown. Retiring from hospital work in 1954 she continued at Backsettown until her health failed. She died at the New Sussex Hospital and her memorial service was held at All Saints' Church, Hove.

Further reading: Jalland. P. ed. (1989) *Octavia Wilberforce: The Autobiography of a Pioneer Woman Doctor.* [Related images pp176, 300.]

OLIVE WILLIS (1877–1964) founder of Downe House School.

The daughter of a schools' inspector, she was born in London. She spent four of her teenage years at Wimbledon House School, Brighton [see the Lawrence sisters, 139], and after graduating in history at Somerville taught at Roedean for two years from 1902. In 1907 she co-founded, with Alice Carver, a boarding school at Downe, Kent, that quickly became popular and, eventually, famous, producing many distinguished pupils. It moved to Berkshire and by the 1920s was among the top girls' schools in Britain, a position it retains today.

GRACE EYRE WOODHEAD (1864–1936) pioneer of mental health care.

One of eleven children, she was born and raised at 12 Norfolk Terrace (and was still listed there in 1901). She attended Brighton & Hove High School and read history at Lady Margaret Hall. Concerned about the neglect of mentally and physically handicapped children in poor London families and inadequate 'special' schools, she devoted most of her adult life to their welfare. In her thirties she began arranging holidays for them in private homes, mostly in the Heathfield area, though some girls stayed at her residence, 30 Compton Avenue, Brighton. Later she helped to found the Brighton Guardianship Society, with Helen Boyle [155] as medical consultant. From 1926 she worked at an out-patient clinic that opened in the society's offices in Grand Parade. The society managed Tubwell House and Walsh Manor in Crowborough and Dungates Farm in Horam, where boys were trained in farmwork, plus six industrial training centres in the Brighton area, which were the focus of a complaint from the council's housing committee, concerned about the number of what they called 'defectives' being brought into the town.

Miss Woodhead kept close control over the society's work, and its employees and volunteers, well into her later years. She died in a nursing home at 12 Dyke Road, Brighton, and was buried at Woodvale Cemetery. Her memorial service was held at All Saints', Hove. She left £200 to the Brighton Guardianship Society, which was renamed the Grace Eyre Foundation and continues its work at The Avondale Centre, Hove, its home since 1950. A second day care centre was opened in 1998 at Walsingham Road, Hove, for elderly people with learning difficulties. Brighton bus 636 is named for her.

HOVE

ELIZABETH ALLAN (1908–1990) actress.

Born in Lincolnshire to parents who opposed her choice of occupation, she nevertheless appeared in seven films in her first working year, 1931–2, including *The Lodger*, written by Marie Belloc Lowndes [80]. Her twenty-seven-year career in the UK and Hollywood encompassed forty-eight films and twenty-five stage roles. In the 1950s she increased her fame by appearing frequently on the popular TV panel game *What's My Line*. Beautiful and glamorous, she was voted Top Female TV Personality in 1952.

She was married to her agent Wilfred J. O'Bryen from 1932 until his death in 1977. They had two children and lived at Flat 3, 7 Arundel Terrace (late 1950s), 89 Marine Parade (early 1960s), 2 St Catherine's Terrace, Hove (mid-1960s) and in 1969 bought Courtney Tye, Courtney Terrace, Kingsway, Hove. The house now boasts a blue plaque and Brighton bus 655 is named for her. [Related plate 6.]

HONOR APPLETON (1879–1951) artist and book illustrator.

A daughter of the former vicar of St Mark's, Staplefield, she was born at 30 St Michael's Place, Brighton, and lived at 3 Ventnor Villas, Hove, for most of her adult life. She trained at the South Kensington Schools, Frank Calderon's School of Animal Painting and the Royal Academy. Her career began in 1902 when she wrote and illustrated a children's book called *The Bad Mrs Ginger*. Later she illustrated works written by others, using mainly watercolours, sometimes pen and ink and occasionally pen and wash. She painted from a child's viewpoint, often showing adults only from the knees down.

In a career spanning more than forty years, she exhibited at the Royal Academy in London and Brighton Corporation Art Gallery and illustrated over 150 children's books. Her best-known works are probably the illustrations for the 'Josephine' books by Mrs Augusta Craddock, which feature a family of dolls. These were published between 1916 and 1940 and included a sailor-suited duck called Quacky Jack.

She died at Brooklands Nursing Home, Haywards Heath. A year after her death Hove Public Library staged an exhibition of seventy-two of her original paintings for book illustrations, which were later dispersed to galleries around the country. Miss Appleton's artwork continues to be popular and the 'Josephine' books are now highly sought-after by collectors because of the beauty of her illustrations.

LADY BAGOT RRC née Theodosia Leslie (1865–1940) philanthropist and writer.

A baronet's daughter, an earls' niece and a cousin of Clare Sheridan [192], she was born into high society and grew up in a Mayfair townhouse surrounded by servants. Known as 'Dosia', at twenty she married Josceline Bagot, a wealthy career soldier ten years her senior, and bore four children in quick succession. They left his stately home, Levens Hall, Westmorland, in 1888 and lived awhile in Canada.

On their return she became a major force in the founding of a pioneering mobile field hospital during the Boer War, using funds donated by her aristocratic friends. It was named for the Duke of Portland, who insisted that it was 'really Mrs Bagot's', since all he did was donate £5,000 of the £12,000 she raised. The hospital, constructed of tents, was equipped for 104 casualties. In 1899 Mrs Bagot accompanied it by sea to South Africa, where it was erected near Capetown, and lived in the camp as superintendent for four months. She also founded a soldiers' tea hut, supplying snacks and hot beverages to whole regiments of men during the bitterly cold winter. Although she had no nursing qualifications, she travelled with a hospital train to collect the wounded, assisted with nursing and was appointed Nursing Sister in Charge by the War Office for the hospital's journey back to England on the SS *Dilwara*. In 1912 she put together a surgical unit for the Serbian Army during the Balkan War, and the day WWI was declared she organised a hospital to be sent to the front, manned and equipped by the Church Army; it was established at Caen under the French Red Cross. A year later she set up a mobile, voluntary 'Hospital of Friendship' for the Belgian Army, went abroad with it and served as a nursing assistant for most of the war.

A pioneer of country district nursing, she was also a member of the St John's Ambulance, a temperance worker, and a speaker and organiser for her husband during his political campaigns (even though he voted against women's suffrage). She wrote *Shadows of the War* (1900), an account of hospital work during the Boer War, illustrated with her own photographs, and many articles on war which were published in various journals.

She was awarded the Queen's South African Medal, the RRC, the Dame of Grace of the Order of St John of Jerusalem (1901), the Serbian Red Cross, the Médaille de la Reine Elisabeth and 'two British war medals' (unnamed).

Her husband, who served during the Boer War, reached the rank of colonel and was an MP and cabinet minister. He was nominated to be a baronet in 1913 but died before the letters patent had passed the Great Seal. By Royal Warrant she was granted the rank of a baronet's widow and the baronetcy passed to her son, who died in 1920. Six months later she married one of the vicars who had officiated at her husband's funeral in Westmorland, and announced in *The Times* that she would remain 'Lady Bagot'. The Revd Sidney Swann (a famous athlete) became rector of Kingston Buci at Shoreham in the 1920s and by 1933 was incumbent of All Saints', Lindfield, where they occupied Church House (now the Tiger Inn), then The Bowery. She maintained a home in Hove for at least twenty-five years: 7 Fourth Avenue (1910s), 20 Third Avenue (1920s) and 60 The Drive (1930s). She died in Epsom and was buried in Westmorland. Her portrait photo is in the NPG.

KAY BANNERMAN (1919–1991) actress and dramatist.

The daughter of an army captain, she was born in Hove and raised in Scotland and France. After RADA she became one of the most talented young actresses on the London stage, appearing with Phyllis Dare [158] and Flora Robson [148]. From 1945 she wrote comedies and thrillers with Harold Brooke, married him in 1946 and gave up acting in 1948 to join him as a playwright. While raising two daughters they co-wrote nineteen situation-comedy plays; these were produced in the top West End theatres and internationally, while four were filmed. Their greatest success, *Let Sleeping Wives Lie*, was set in a Brighton hotel and ran for 647 performances at the Garrick. They retired to Spain, where she died.

DAME HENRIETTA BARNETT DBE née Rowland (1851–1936) social reformer.

Although she was born into a wealthy London family and need never have worked, she devoted her life to helping the poor and needy. She married likeminded clergyman Samuel Barnett and together they took on the violent and poverty-stricken London parish of St Jude's, Whitechapel, where in 1875 she became Britain's first female parish guardian. Together the Barnetts founded Toynbee Hall, a base for middle-class university students performing social work in the East End slums then terrorised by Jack the Ripper.

Mrs Barnett co-founded the Whitechapel Gallery and the Children's Country Holiday Fund, but is most famous as the visionary who founded Hampstead Garden Suburb. Among her many books on social welfare was *Canon Barnett: his Life, Work, and Friends* (1918). She was among the first women given a CBE when the order was created in 1917 and in 1924 was one of the first to be raised to DBE.

From 1929 she lived between Hampstead Garden Suburb and 45 Wish Road, Hove, serving as vice-president of the Lady Chichester Hospital for Women. She died in London and was buried with her husband's ashes at St Helen's, Hangleton. Brighton bus 656 is named for her, as is Dame Henrietta Barnett School, opened in London in 1911 and still flourishing (and known, appropriately for a girls' school, as 'The Hen Barn'). She has blue plaques in London and Hove.

Further reading: Watkins, M. (2005) *Henrietta Barnett in Whitechapel: Her First Fifty Years.*

EDNA BEST (1900–1974) actress and producer.

Born and raised at Redcliff, Pembroke Crescent, Hove, she enjoyed moderate success on the West End stage and in films before moving with her first husband Herbert Marshall to New York in 1939.

After her divorce in 1940, she began a new career as a radio producer and became famous for creating the popular Basil Rathbone 'Sherlock Holmes' series. She continued to appear in films and in her spare time produced ceramics with Art Deco designs. She died in Switzerland and has a star on the Hollywood Walk of Fame. [Related plate 51.]

(ALICE) HELEN BOYLE MD (1869–1957) physician and psychiatrist.

A native of Ireland, she was educated in Europe, studied medicine at the LSMW in London, qualified via the Faculty of Physicians and Surgeons of Glasgow and Edinburgh and gained her MD in Brussels in 1894. In 1898 she and Dr Jones [162] opened the first all-female medical practice in Hove, at 3 Palmeira Terrace (now 37 Church Road). They were founder members of the Lewes Road Dispensary for Women and Children in Islingword Road, Brighton, and of the Lady Chichester Hospital for Women with Nervous Diseases. Dr Boyle was later honorary consultant at the Royal County Hospital.

During WWI she served in Serbia with a medical mission from the Royal Free Hospital and was awarded a decoration from the Order of St Sava. She was instrumental in setting up the Brighton Guardianship Society with Grace Woodhead [154] and the National Council for Mental Hygiene (now, MIND). In 1939 she became the first female president of the Royal Medico-Psychological Association. In later life she lived with her secretary, Rita Gore-Lindsay, at Rockrose, Pyecombe, where she died. Brighton bus 659 is named for her.

Further reading: Brown, V. (2006) *Women's Hospitals in Brighton & Hove.* [Related images pp174, 300.]

HANNAH BRACKENBURY spelling changed in 1868 to Brakenbury (1795–1873) philanthropist.

A born-and-bred Lancastrian, she lived with her widowed brother James, solicitor to the Lancashire and Yorkshire Railway, in which he invested heavily, making vast profits. Her brother's ill health led them to move to Portslade in 1844, where he promptly died. By the subsequent untimely deaths of his daughter and their brother, by 1864 Miss Brackenbury unexpectedly became sole heir to a stupendous capital sum that gave her an income of £7,000 a year (the equivalent to £400,000 today).

She worshipped at St Andrew's Church, Waterloo Street, where William Rooper, the former rector, helped her choose which charitable causes to support. In seven years she gave away over £100,000 (worth about £6m today), to provide scholarships and professorships at a variety of educational establishments in the north of England. She also funded many public health and medical establishments, including a dispensary in Manchester. In 1867 she donated £20,000 to rebuild the south side of Balliol College, Oxford, creating a beautiful Gothic edifice with a central tower that still bears her name. In 1872, using a piece of land next to her home, she built St Nicholas's School, Locks Hill (now the annex to Portslade County Infants), which bears a plaque in her honour.

She commissioned the construction of the Brakenbury Mortuary Chapel at St Nicholas's Church, which was built over the vault containing the graves of her brothers and her niece. After she joined them a large marble plaque was unveiled, which celebrates her philanthropy.

She left her fortune entirely to public institutions, including the University of Durham (where in 2005 a new hall of residence was named for her); twelve hospitals, seven asylums, four schools and an assortment of other charities including the Lancashire and Yorkshire Railway Benevolent Fund. Locally she left £1,000 to the Sussex County Hospital, £500 to Brighton & Hove Dispensary, £500 to the Lying-in Institution, £500 to the Asylum for Female Orphans and smaller amounts to similar organisations. Altogether in life and death she gave away about £200,000 (the equivalent of about £12m today) which helped untold thousands over several generations to obtain medical treatment and education.

She had several homes locally: 13 Brunswick Terrace (1860s) the modest (considering her wealth) Sellaby House, Old Shoreham Road, Portslade (now a school tuition unit) and 31 Adelaide Crescent, where she died.

KITTY CARSON née Emily Green (c1850s–1919) theatrical philanthropist.

Her life is obscure until 1880, when she married Lionel Courtier-Dutton, a widowed actor who used the professional name Charles L. Carson and had founded the theatrical magazine *The Stage*. After raising his three children she became a comedy actress using the stage name Kitty Claremont, but was more famous for her charity work as founder of the Theatrical Christmas Dinner Fund and co-founder of the Actresses' Orphanage.

Her most enduring creation was the Theatrical Ladies' Guild of Charity, founded in 1891, which existed 'to assist, by the loan of clothes to mother and child, their sisters (whether actresses, actors' wives, choristers, extras, cleaners or dressers, during the period of their maternity'. In addition, 'sewing bees' were held in her house, to create new baby clothes. This remit was later extended to include meal tickets, help with medical and midwifery bills and the supply of costumes for struggling actresses attending auditions.

Described as 'reverenced and beloved by every member of the theatrical profession', she headed the organisation for about twenty years until her death at her home at 45 Norton Road, Hove. In 1965 the TLGC was absorbed by the Combined Theatrical Charities Appeal Council. [Related image p177.]

FRANCES DOROTHY CARTWRIGHT (1780–1863) biographer and translator.

Moving from her native Leicestershire to Worthing in 1824, she set up home with the widow of her uncle, a prominent political reformer, and published a biography of him: *The Life and Correspondence of Major Cartwright* (1826, reprinted 1969), which *The Times* described as an 'ungracious task for a lady' because it dealt with military matters. She also published some of her poetry in 1835 and, most unusually for an Englishwoman of her time, spoke fluent Spanish; in 1844 she published translations of Spanish poetry. She left Sussex for an undetermined period, but returned later to live at 21 Medina Villas, Cliftonville, Hove, where she died.

FAY COMPTON CBE (1894–1978) actress.

The child of thespian parents, at sixteen she made her singing and dancing début on the West End stage. Four weeks later she married the thirty-seven-year-old producer of the Follies, Harry Pélissier, a 'huge, roly-poly of a man'. Within a year a child was born and, just after their second anniversary, her heavy-drinking husband died of cirrhosis of the liver. Within six weeks she was back on stage and over the next five decades played every type of role in all kinds of production, from Shakespeare to pantomime. Her autobiography 'Up To Now' was serialised in 1925 in the *Woman's Pictorial*, which promised that it was 'packed with thrills'. At the age of seventy-three she played her final role, in the TV series *The Forsyte Saga*.

She married four times, was widowed twice and divorced twice. In 1975 she was appointed CBE. She died her home, 10 Eaton Gardens, Hove. Her son Anthony married Ursula Howells [71]. [Related plate 10; image p180.]

DAME IVY COMPTON-BURNETT DBE (1884–1969) novelist.

The seventh of the thirteen children of a homeopath and medical writer, she was the first child of his second marriage. She was born in Middlesex, but when she was seven the family moved to 30 First Avenue, Hove, and six years later to 20 The Drive. They attended various churches including All Saints', and St John's, Palmeira Square, where they paid for a reserved pew. She was educated at home by a governess, and later at Addiscombe College and Howard College, Bedford, then read classics at Royal Holloway, graduating in 1906. After her father died her mother went into excessive mourning for a decade and, using emotional blackmail, tyrannised the children. At the age of twenty-seven Ivy took over the household and became as despotic as her mother.

She wrote her first novel in Hove then, after a series of family tragedies, moved to London in 1914, where she lived for thirty-two years with Margaret Jourdain, a writer and expert on Regency furniture. Her second novel emerged when she was forty-one, and she wrote a further eighteen, all in the form of dialogue and focussing on intense, difficult, tyrannical relationships between people within the closed circles of a dysfunctional family. One reviewer said, 'There is something rather cruel, rather horrible in Miss Burnett's talent.'

She was appointed CBE in 1951 and DBE in 1967 and was elected a Companion of the Royal Society of Literature in 1968. Brighton bus 621 is named for her and she has blue plaques in London and Hove.

Further reading: Spurling, H. (1974) *Ivy When Young: The Early Life of I. Compton-Burnett, 1884–1919* and (1984) *Secrets of a Woman's Heart: The Later Life of I. Compton-Burnett, 1920–1969.* [Related images pp16, 174.]

(MARIE) FANNY CORBAUX (1812–1883) painter and writer.

Although born in France she was raised in England and her family is recorded as living in Winchelsea in 1824. When they fell upon hard times she earned money by painting. She had dabbled in art from an early age but could get no formal education: women were not admitted to the Royal Academy Schools (she later campaigned to change this) and she could not afford private tuition. Despite this, by the age of eighteen she had won five awards from the Royal Society of Arts, including the Large Silver Medal, the Silver and Gold Isis Medals and the Gold Medal for miniatures. At eighteen she was elected to the Society of British Artists and nine years later to the New Society of Painters in Water-Colour. These were extraordinary achievements for a young woman living in a tenement at 5 Hercules Buildings, Lambeth, south London.

Her watercolours feature female subjects, mainly heroines from the works of Shakespeare, Byron and the Bible. Some of her paintings were engraved or lithographed. She created illustrations for a number of books, including Thomas Moore's *Pearls of the East*, and sat for Julia Goodman [135]. She exhibited at the Society of British Artists, the Royal Academy, the British Institution, and in Manchester, Liverpool and Paris. Her exhibitions were mentioned in the top journals, for whom she wrote articles: a series called 'Letters on the physical geography of the Exodus' appeared in *The Athenaeum* and 'The Rephaim' was published in the *Journal of Sacred Literature*. She wrote the introduction to *The Exodus Papyri* (1855) by D.I. Heath.

In 1871 she was awarded a civil-list pension of £50 a year. At that time she was living at 18 Western Cottages, Brighton (now Sillwood Road), while her sister Louisa, also an artist, held the fort at their shared London home at 45 Edwardes Square, Kensington. In the 1870s she retired to 2 Lansdowne Terrace, Hove, where she died a decade later.

ALICE ANN CORNWELL Mrs Whiteman; Mrs Stennard Robinson (1852–1932) goldmining industrialist, newspaper proprietor and club founder.

Born in Essex and raised in New Zealand, she was the daughter of a railway guard who became a gold prospector in Australia. She was married briefly, had a son in 1877 and returned to England, where she reverted to her maiden name. A student at the RAM, she won several gold medals and, while engaged as music tutor at Queen's College, composed popular songs and piano music. However, her father was losing money, so she joined him in Australia and studied geology and mining, even entering mines herself. She struck gold, became spectacularly wealthy and famous, was described as 'one of the most skilful of mining geologists', a 'shrewd businesswoman' and 'one of the most remarkable women of her time', and was dubbed the 'Lady of the Nuggets'. The novel *Madame Midas* (1888), by Fergus Hume, was based on her, and her life story and image appeared in various newspapers and magazines.

She moved to London in 1887 and bought *The Sunday Times*, reorganised the management, increased circulation by 40,000 and installed her fiancé, journalist and war correspondent Frederick ('Phil') Stewart Robinson, as editor until 1890. She sold the newspaper in 1893, married him the following year and returned to Australia, where she was involved in building the harbour at Port Adelaide, and in 1895 speculated £280,000 (the equivalent of £160m today) on 17,000 acres of coalmining land, which did less well than expected.

While her son began a stage career, in 1895 she founded the Ladies' Kennel Association and the *Ladies' Kennel Journal*. Employing only female staff at its central London office and club house, she organised an annual, ladies-only dog show as well as becoming involved with matters such as quarantine laws. Renowned in the dog world, her telegraphic address was 'Bow-wow, London'. She also founded the National Cat Club (1887) and the International Kennel Club (1899). All had royal patronage and are still in existence.

Widowed in 1902, she moved to 19 Palmeira Square, Hove, where she bred pugs. She died at home and was buried at Hove Cemetery. A portrait photograph of her is at the NPG. Her son George Whiteman became Sydney Carroll OBE, edited the *Daily Sketch* and in 1921 was sued by Ethel Irving [190] for libelling her in *The Sunday Times*. Using his inheritance from his mother he co-founded in 1932 the Open Air Theatre in Regent's Park, which continues to flourish.

Further reading: Hobson, H., Knightley, P., and Russell, L. (1972) *The Pearl of Days: An Intimate Memoir of the Sunday Times, 1822–1972.* [Related image p177.]

EDITH CREAK (1855–1919) headmistress.

She was born at 118 Lansdowne Place, Hove, where she lived for many years, later moving to nearby Furze Hill, The Wick. Her siblings were teachers, her mother a headmistress and her father, a nonconformist minister, was proprietor of a local boys' school, at which she was educated, enabling her to take the Cambridge higher local examination (established in 1869 for women intending to teach). By means of the Mill Taylor scholarship she became, at sixteen, one of the first five students at Newnham, passing first-class in divinity, English history, literature, and mathematics at nineteen. As Cambridge would not award degrees to women she was later to spend five years obtaining a BA (Hons) from London University.

After a brief spell at Plymouth High School, and still only twenty, she was appointed head of Brighton & Hove High School, the eleventh establishment opened by the Girls' Public Day School Company. She appointed the staff, organised the premises and planned the entire curriculum, becoming living proof of women's ability to study to a very high level and to take on the management and direction of an important establishment. She was a key figure in the transformation of middle-class girls' education from trivial accomplishments to academic excellence and an inspiration to her girls.

An élitist, she did not support measures to enable the working classes to gain higher education. Her attitude to women's suffrage changed over time: she was a supporter in 1885 but an opponent by 1900. In 1883 she beat thirty-five other candidates for the headship of the newly-opened King Edward VI's High School for Girls, Birmingham. [Related image p176.]

PHYLLIS DARE real name Dones (1890–1975) soprano and actress.

A Londoner, she began her stage career at nine years old and was a star of pantomime and musical comedy by the age of sixteen.

She would sign 300 souvenir postcards a week and was a pin-up girl during WWI. Her elder sister Zena Dare was equally famous and they sometimes delighted audiences by appearing together. At nineteen she embarked on a musical role in *The Arcadians* at the Shaftesbury Theatre that ran for 809 performances.

At just twenty-seven she published her autobiography, *From School to Stage,* and in 1914 wrote a successful children's book called *Kitty in Fairyland.* In 1917 she ceased work for two years after the death of her fiancé (a songwriter from whom she inherited a huge sum of money). On her return to work she recorded songs and also made a successful transition from musical comedy to straight acting roles.

She retired in 1951 and from 1955 until at least 1972 lived at 15 Eaton Gardens, Hove. She later moved to 22 Pembroke Avenue, where she died. [Related plate 4.]

MARGARET MARY DAMER DAWSON OBE

(1873–1920) philanthropist and co-founder of the Women's Police Service.

The daughter of a surgeon, she was born at 1 York Road, Hove. Her family moved to 5 Second Avenue, then 9 Arundel Terrace, Brighton, before settling at 15 Brunswick Square, Hove, in 1899. A handsome private income enabled her to become an accomplished Alpine climber, to rub shoulders with high society and to develop her native musical talent at the London Academy of Music, where she won a Gold Medal. She also campaigned for the humane treatment of animals and was against vivisection.

She co-founded the Women's Volunteer Police Corps in 1914, then the Women's Police Service in 1915, serving as its first commandant. She and her close friend and successor Mary Allen [223] were among the first women in Britain to ride motorcycles. After many years in London she moved in later life to Danehill Lodge, Lympne, Kent. After she died there and was buried at Lympne, her Damer Dawson Memorial Home for Babies carried on its work at Hythe. Mary Allen was a major beneficiary in her will. [Related image p296.]

BARONESS EVELYN DENINGTON DBE née

Bursill (1907–1998) politician.

Educated at Bedford College, she was a journalist, teacher and Labour councillor in London 1945–77. She was the first woman to hold the posts of chair of the GLC housing committee (in charge of 200,000 homes); chair of the transport committee (she tried to introduce a London congestion charge in 1974); chair of the GLC 1975–76 (she gave free bus passes to pensioners) and chair of Stevenage Development Corporation 1966–80. A small yet intimidating woman, known as the 'Empress of the South Bank', she was appointed CBE in 1966, DBE in 1974 and raised to the peerage in 1978.

With her husband Cecil she moved from Stevenage to Brunswick Square, Hove, commuting to the House of Lords by train. She moved into a nursing home in 1997 and died the following year at the Royal Sussex County Hospital, Brighton.

CARMEN DILLON (1908–2000) theatrical

set designer and **UNA DILLON CBE** (1903–1993) founder of Dillon's bookshop.

One of the four Dillon sisters, Carmen qualified as an architect and was recruited by Wembley studios in the 1930s. Her first assignment was to build a prison cell set for £19. When she spent £21, the director cited this as conclusive proof that women cannot manage money. So began her thirty-five year career, for twenty-five of which she was the only woman in the trade. Although she rose to chief art director, she was not permitted to issue orders to male staff, nor to wear trousers, and she faced ongoing harassment from male co-workers, who accused her of depriving a man of a job. She moved to Pinewood Studios and worked as art director on dozens of films, winning an Academy Award for her sets for *Hamlet* in 1949. Her later credits included *Doctor in the House, The Omen* and two 'Carry On' films.

Una worked as an organiser of bookstalls for a mental health charity until she borrowed £800 to buy a run-down bookshop she had spotted in Gower Street, Bloomsbury, London, which she transformed into Dillon's. She built it up into a flourishing business with a worldwide reputation and an annual turnover of £1m. When she was fifty-three the shop was taken over by London University as a limited company, using her stock and goodwill. She retained shares and insisted that the shop continue to bear her name. The recipient of an honorary MA in 1965, she remained on the board of directors until 1977. Eventually Dillon's merged with Waterstone's and her name was obliterated from shops, though it lives on in the Waterstone's Una Dillon Memorial Bursary, University of London. She was appointed CBE in 1968 for services to bookselling.

After sharing a huge mansion flat in Kensington with another sister (a university lecturer) for forty-four years, in 1985 Una and Carmen bought a Victorian villa in Hove. They both died at Victoria Nursing Home, 96 The Drive.

MURIEL DOWDING née Albino; first married name Whiting; Lady Dowding (1908–1993) animal rights campaigner.

Born in London, she was educated in Kent and at the Convent of the Holy Child in St Leonards [see Cornelia Connelly, 248]. Later she became a theosophist and vegetarian and studied the works of Anna Kingsford [250]. She married, had a son and was widowed, then wed the elderly Air Chief Marshal Lord Dowding, the man universally attributed with winning the Battle of Britain during WWII.

In 1959 she launched the 'Beauty Without Cruelty' campaign against cosmetics tested on animals and the wearing of fur coats. She published a magazine, *Compassion*, and opened a shop selling her Beauty Without Cruelty cosmetics and a boutique to sell fake furs, and organised alternative fashion shows in London, New York and Amsterdam. She became vice-president of the RSPCA and, as president of the National Anti-Vivisection Society, led demonstrations, presented petitions to parliament and spoke at international conferences. She habitually took stray animals into her home and in 1977 (while living at Tunbridge Wells) founded the Lychgate Animal Sanctuary in Coldwaltham. For outstanding service to the RSPCA, in 1979 she received the Richard Martin

Award, and in 1980 published her book, *Beauty not the Beast.*

At The Pines Nursing Home, Furze Hill, Hove, where she had lived for two years, Lady Dowding died penniless, having given all her money to charity.

FLORA FREEMAN (c1869–1960) philanthropist and writer.

As a wealthy surgeon's daughter, she enjoyed a substantial private income. She founded clubs for 'rough girls' in the slums of her native London and one for impoverished laundresses in Brighton in 1901, to provide somewhere for girls to go after their day's work other than public houses, where they might easily fall into alcoholism or prostitution. She questioned the girls about their working conditions and gave them helpful advice, and also imparted, *most coyly*, sufficient information about sexual matters to keep the girls chaste. Miss Freeman maintained links with similar enterprises such as the Factory Girls' Country Holiday Fund and the National Vigilance Association. She founded the non-denominational Brighton Girls' Club Union, which was by 1917 affiliated to the Federation of Working Girls' Clubs. She ran the union and published its journal for at least eleven years, during which time she converted from high-church Anglicanism to Roman Catholicism. Later she became a member of the third order of St Francis, a Roman Catholic lay order.

Her many books included *Our Working Girls, How to Help Them* (1908), an instructional manual teaching well-off women how to set up, fund and run clubs for poor girls; *The Patience of Perla* (1906), the story of a highly moral, working-class girl who lives in a seaside town, with a preface written by local Anglo-Catholic clergymen and *On the Right Trail: Friendly Counsel for Catholic Girl Guides* (1921). In 1916 had she founded the Roman Catholic Girl Guides and was captain of the 6th Hove company until 1923. In 1919 she revived the girls' club that she had founded in 1909. Its activities included first aid, gardening, dancing and the production of plays. The club was not only self-supporting, it donated money to the Catholic Women's League.

A resident of Sussex for sixty years, in 1901 and 1911 she was living at 10 Cromwell Road, Hove, and in 1917 and 1946 at 3 Ranelagh Villas. She died at Lee House, 61 Dyke Road, Brighton. After a requiem mass at Sacred Heart, Norton Road, Hove, she was buried at Hove cemetery.

RENÉE GADD (1906–2003) dancer and actress.

A native of Brazil, when her parents separated in 1914 she came to England. At the age of fourteen she worked as a chorus girl in Brighton to pay for her sisters to attend private schools. By sixteen she was on the West End stage and soon appeared in productions alongside famous dancer Fred Astaire, who became her lover. She turned to straight acting in 1929 and was a leading lady in films during the early 'talkie' era. Her busiest period was from 1932 until 1950, when she appeared in supporting roles in twenty-seven films, ending with *The Blue Lamp*.

She married three times, to Guy Tooth, Harry Hardman and Joe Wilson. After the latter's death about 1981 she bought a mansion flat in Hove, where she lived for two decades until her death.

OLIVE GILBERT (1898–1981) contralto.

A schoolmaster's daughter, she came from Wales to train with the Carl Rosa Opera Company in London and sang at Covent Garden and the Lyceum and Strand theatres from 1919. From 1935 until 1951 she was closely associated with Ivor Novello, who wrote many parts for her in his Drury Lane musicals. She had a powerful but melodious voice and a gift for comedy, made some recordings and appeared in one film (in 1949).

Her career spanned six decades, and in her mid-sixties she played Sister Margaretta in over 2,000 performances of *The Sound of Music* (1961–7). In 1973 she unveiled Novello's blue plaque on the building in Aldwych where they each had a flat. She retired to Hove, where she died. Her memorial service, at St Paul's, Covent Garden, was attended by Dame Anna Neagle [145].

HARRIETTE EDITH GRACE (1860–1932) figure, landscape and still life painter.

Born and raised at 26 York Road, Hove, she was one of five daughters, four of whom were gifted: Ellen was a musician; Frances, Anna and Harriette were artists. According to the *Brighton Herald*, 'At one time it was almost a fashion to be painted by one of the talented three sisters', but Harriette, a painter in oils and watercolours, was the most successful.

She began her training with evening classes at the Brighton School of Art, and later attended the Royal Academy Schools, the South Kensington Life Schools and Heatherley's. A member of Sussex Women's Art Club and the Art Circle, she won a Gold Medal and the Princess of Wales Scholarship at a national drawing exhibition held at Exhibition Buildings, South Kensington; the Royal Academy (architectural) Silver Medal for perspective drawing; the Hill Silver Medal at Brighton and the Bronze Medal of the Brighton Horticultural Society. For thirty years her life was an endless round of teaching, sketching, painting and exhibiting all over the UK and abroad. She also undertook about eighty commissions for portraits and signed all her work 'H.E. Grace'.

By 1901 she was living at 54 York Road with her two artist sisters. The three held a joint exhibition in the Lady Wolseley Room at Hove Public Library in 1931. Weeks later she moved into a local nursing home, where she died. She was buried in Hove Municipal Cemetery. Two of her paintings are in Hove Museum & Art Gallery.

CORNELIA JAMES née Katz (1917–1999) glove-maker to royalty.

She learned glove-making at art college in her native Vienna and at twenty-one escaped from Austria (then overrun by Nazis) with a large quantity of leather. She visited England en route to the USA but after meeting Jack James decided to stay here. Their marriage was a long and happy one, and produced two children. They settled at Hawkers Buildings, Davigdor Road, Hove, and she worked as an occupational therapist for wounded soldiers. After the war she set up a glovemaking company, Cornelia James Ltd, at 123 Havelock Road, Brighton, and before long her work was drawing fulsome praise from top society couturiers Norman Hartnell and Hardy Amies. In 1947 she was asked to make gloves for Princess Elizabeth to wear on her wedding day; the following year she launched her most famous range: 'leather gloves in one hundred colours' and was soon employing 500 staff to keep up with the huge demand from private clients and department stores worldwide.

She was an enthusiastic member of the Worshipful Company of Glovers and the National Association of Glove Manufacturers, whose first Glove Fair was held in Brighton (she entertained the exhibitors at her home afterwards). She continually sought ways to improve glove-making and promote glove-wearing, but their popularity declined and she began to manufacture silk scarves and ties while continuing to produce gloves for the theatrical world. Adding the Queen Mother and Princess Anne to her list of devoted clients, in 1979 she was granted a Royal Warrant. In 1989 she received the Freedom of the City of London. She supported several local charities, favouring the heart unit at the Sussex County Hospital and Martlets Hospice, Wayfield Avenue, where she died.

(LILLIE) MABEL JONES MB, BS, MD (c1870–1923) pioneering physician.

Probably born in Canada, she studied medicine at the LSMW, qualifying in 1893. She came to Hove in 1898 with Helen Boyle [155] and they set up the first all-female GP surgery in Hove, at 3 Palmeira Terrace (now 37 Church Road). She left Hove about 1908 and moved to Glasgow, where she lived and worked for the rest of her life. During WWI she worked with Belgian refugees and was awarded the Médaille de la Reine Elisabeth. She died in mysterious circumstances: she jumped, fell, or was pushed out of a train while en route from Scotland to Bexhill.

Further reading: Brown, V. (2006) *Women's Hospitals in Brighton & Hove.*

EDITH LANCHESTER (1871–1966) feminist incarcerated for her beliefs.

The daughter of a prosperous architect, she was born and raised at 1 St John's Terrace, Hove. In the 1880s her family moved to London, where she studied botany and zoology at Birkbeck Institution,

winning the Apothecaries' Company prize, and attended Maria Grey Teacher Training College. She worked as a teacher and then as a secretary, was employed by Eleanor Marx to type Karl Marx's notes, became a clerk at a gold mining company and stood for election to the London School Board.

By twenty-four she had embraced feminism, atheism, vegetarianism and socialism. She told her family that, owing to the anti-woman marriage laws [8], she intended to live out of wedlock with James Sullivan. Her outraged father had her examined by Dr Blandford, a leading mental specialist and eminent author of *Insanity and its Treatment*. He immediately signed emergency commitment papers under the Lunacy Act of 1890, explaining that as he would certify a person for threatening suicide, he was therefore certifying her, because cohabitation amounted to 'social suicide' for a woman. While she struggled and screamed, her father and brothers (one of whom was reported to be 'of Herculean proportions') forced her into a brougham carriage, where they bound her arms and legs with rope (though she fought so violently that she smashed a window) and locked her up in The Priory Institution, a private lunatic asylum in Roehampton, Surrey.

Deeply shocked, Mr Sullivan sought the advice of magistrates and contacted national newspapers, who publicised the 'Lanchester Abduction Case' (it even made *The New York Times*). His MP appealed to the Commissioners of Lunacy, who pronounced her foolish but perfectly sane and released her after just four days, leaving Dr Blandford publicly disgraced. She engaged (future Prime Minister) Herbert Asquith QC, MP to investigate whether she could take legal action against those concerned (the result of this is unknown). In the aftermath the case was universally discussed, verbally and in print, with strong views for and against. Even socialists were split: most of the SDF supported Miss Lanchester and condemned the kidnapping, but even they worried about being tainted with her 'immorality'. Keir Hardie, leader of the Independent Labour Party, thought she had discredited socialism, but feminists and radicals hailed her a heroine.

Miss Lanchester was disowned by her father (though her mother later bequeathed her £400). She cohabited with Mr Sullivan for fifty years until his death in 1945. They had two children, and after one reacted badly to a vaccine they repeatedly moved lodgings to avoid the other being vaccinated. They also objected to the poor education meted out to girls, and sent their daughter to be educated with her brother at Mr Kettle's progressive boys' school at Clapham Common.

A pacifist during WWI, afterwards she joined the Communist Party and worked with her son as a puppet-maker and weaver. As a widow she moved to Brighton, where she lived for twenty-one years, displaying communist posters outside her flat and attending political meetings. She died at her home, 18 Highcroft Villas, where she had lived since at least 1959. Her daughter Elsa became a famous actress and married the actor Charles Laughton.

Further reading: Lanchester, E. (1983) *Elsa Lanchester Herself.* [Related image p16.]

(MABEL) GRACE LANE (1876–1956) actress and producer.

The daughter of a journalist, she was born in Surrey and started her acting career in amateur Savoy operas and in comedies with Willie Edouin [brother of Rose Bryer, 125]. She soon became a celebrated leading lady on the West End stage, described as being 'endowed with graces of face and figure which leave nothing to be desired'.

She married Sussex-born Kenneth Douglas Savory in 1903, had two sons, and was widowed in 1923. In her sixties she toured Canada and Australia, producing as well as acting, and in her seventies played Gertrude in *Hamlet*. She lived in Berkshire and died at a nursing home in Hove. Her son Gerald became head of plays at the BBC. [Related plate 15.]

AMY LEVY (1861–1889) writer and poet.

A Londoner, she lived in lodgings for three years from 1876 at 27 St Michael's Place, Hove, while attending Brighton & Hove High School, where she was well known for developing a crush on Edith Creak [158]. The first Jewish woman to attend Newnham, her best-known work was the controversial *Reuben Sachs* (1888, reprinted 2001). At twenty-seven she committed suicide and was the first Jewish woman to be cremated in England.

Further reading: Beckman, L. H. (2000) *Amy Levy: Her Life and Letters.*

VICTORIA LIDIARD née Simmons (1889–1992) social campaigner.

One of twelve children, she was born in Berkshire. Her father treated his daughters less favourably than his sons, and so she, her three sisters and their mother became campaigners for women's rights and joined the WSPU in 1907, chalking pavements and addressing meetings at Bristol Docks. In 1912 she took part in a mass glass-smashing raid from Marble Arch to Tottenham Court Road, shattering all the windows in Oxford Street, then lobbed a stone at the War Office in Whitehall, breaking a window. She and two hundred others were sentenced to two months' hard labour in Holloway but, like most suffragette prisoners, served only a short time. She had been a vegetarian since the age of ten, which bewildered the prison cook, who once gave her a meal comprising 'almost half a pound of butter beans'.

She worked in photographic studios in Kent and, while selling *Votes For Women* at Herne Bay met a member of a male suffragette support group, Alexander Lidiard, with whom she was later to enjoy fifty-four years of wedded bliss. During WWI she ran a guest-house in Kensington for professional women and worked weekends in a munitions factory making anti-aircraft shells. She married Major Lidiard in 1918 and they trained as ophthalmic optometrists, then an unusual profession for a woman. From 1927 they worked as consultants at the London Refraction Hospital and opened practices at Maidenhead and High Wycombe.

They retired to Hove, living at 3 Derek Avenue then, by 1963, at Flat 1, 14 Palmeira Avenue. Here she worshipped at St John's Church, campaigned for women to be ordained to the priesthood and wrote letters to female MPs on various issues. Aged ninety-nine she published two books: *Christianity, Faith, Love and Healing* and *Animals and All Churches.*

In 1989 she celebrated her hundredth birthday and died two years later at the Royal County Hospital, Brighton, leaving a bequest to the World Society for the Protection of Animals. A plaque erected on her house in 1996 was unveiled by the Speaker of the House, Betty Boothroyd MP. Brighton bus 643 is named for her. [Related plate 45.]

BLANCHE LITTLER OBE née Richeux; Lady Robey (1899–1981) theatrical producer.

She was born in Kent to parents who managed both the Royal Artillery Theatre in Woolwich and Ramsgate's Victoria Pavilion. Her widowed mother married Frank Littler in 1914 and her children took his surname. From the age of sixteen Blanche co-managed the Royal Artillery Theatre and during the 1930s and 1940s she and her younger brothers Prince and Emile [see Cora Goffin, 204] were the most powerful figures in the theatrical world, with a monopoly on pantomimes and musicals and in control of half the theatres and touring companies in Britain. She formed a company, Blanche Littler Productions Ltd, based in London's Regent Street, and was managing director of Prince Littler Theatres and Tours. The Littlers' theatrical production and management empire kept 28,000 people in employment.

She met famous music hall star George Robey, ('the Prime Minister of Mirth') when he starred in one of her productions in 1934 and she became his manager. Though thirty years his junior, she married him in 1938. They lived at Grand Avenue Mansions, Hove, then in Saltdean, where he died in 1954, shortly after receiving a knighthood. She gave his trademark stage costume to the Livesey Museum, London, and moved to a flat in King's Gardens, Hove, to be near her brother Sir Emile, with whom she was still producing West End musicals. Lady Robey was well-known for her charity work and was appointed OBE in 1975 for 'public service, particularly in Sussex'. She died in Hove, leaving a large collection of valuable furs, which were auctioned after her death.

IDA LUPINO (1918–1995) actress, director and producer.

Her father Stanley, a famous music hall star, was one of the famous Lupinos, known as 'The Royal Family of Greasepaint'. Her mother, Connie O'Shea, was one of ten children, all of whom went on the stage. Ida was born in south London and, when she was seven, her parents went to the USA, leaving her at Clarence House boarding school, 4 Norman Road, Hove, which now bears a plaque in her honour. She appeared in local shows at the Brighton Hippodrome and Hove Town Hall, and wrote and produced a play in which she took a leading role.

About 1930 she moved to the USA and appeared in sixty-four films by 1978. In 1949 she became one of the few female director-producers; her credits include five films and some TV programmes including *Alfred Hitchcock Presents* and *Bewitched*. She won an acting award in 1943, was the second woman to be admitted to the Director's Guild and has two stars on the Hollywood Walk of Fame. She married and divorced three times (to two actors and a producer) and died in Los Angeles. Brighton bus 632 is named for her.

Further reading: Donati, W. (1996) *Ida Lupino: A Biography.* [Related plate 58.]

SUSAN MACFARLANE (1938–2002) artist.

Born in Hove, she moved in childhood to Hampshire, studied at Winchester School of Art and enjoyed painting nature, landscapes, archaeology, people at work and health-related subjects. She lived in Sri Lanka, Hong Kong, Greece and also in France, where she created thirty-five square metres of stained glass for Holy Trinity Church, Cannes.

In the nineties her exhibitions 'The Woollen Mills of Stroud', 'A Picture of Health' and 'Living with Leukaemia' became famous after being featured on radio and TV and on a 26p stamp. Married to Ronald Mackay, she was the mother of two sons. While working on the paintings for a new medical exhibition called 'Blindness and Sight', she was killed in an accident outside her studio in Petersfield, Hampshire.

ANNIE PARLANE MACPHERSON (1825–1904) philanthropist.

She left her native Scotland to perform unpaid mission work for the poor of London's East End, about some of whom she wrote *The Little Matchbox-Makers* (1866). After founding a series of children's homes and, in 1869, a Home of Industry in Spitalfields, she was convinced that emigration was the only permanent answer to poverty. She took fifty families to Canada, a year later accompanied a hundred children there. In 1870 she wrote *Canadian Homes for London Wanderers* and *The Little London Arabs*. By 1893, 5,730 vagabond children had been rescued from the city streets, slums, workhouses and impoverished parents and sent to receiving homes in Canada to be placed with prosperous families or apprenticed to a trade. She personally made the sea voyage over 120 times, making her unique among women of her era.

The Macpherson homes also acted as distributing centres for other charities, including Dr Barnardo's, which eventually took them over. She was involved in many other missions and established the Bridge of Hope refuge for women. She retired in 1902 to Hove, where she died at her home, 9 Sackville Road. She was buried at the City of London cemetery, Essex. Her organisation continued to send children to Canada until 1920 and the Gap Project in Bethnal Green in east London continues her charity work today.

KATE MENGES née Whitcher (1867–1955) and **ISOLDE MENGES** (1893–1976) violinists.

Katherine Whitcher was born in the East End, grew up at 6 Heene Road, Worthing, and studied violin in Germany, where she met John Menges. They married in East Preston in 1892 and lived at 27 Clarendon Villas, Hove, where they both became eminent violin tutors as well as teaching all four of their children. In 1925 Madame Menges founded the Brighton Symphonic Players, installing her son Herbert as conductor. (He went on to develop it into the Brighton Philharmonic Orchestra and was its musical director for the rest of his life.) Widowed before 1938, she moved to Barnes, London.

Her daughter Isolde was born and raised in Hove and educated in Brighton and Russia. For thirty years from 1913 she was in worldwide demand as a virtuoso soloist and recording artiste. In 1920 she married Tod Boyd and two years later became the first violinist to make a complete recording of a Beethoven concerto with orchestra. She was awarded a professorship at the RCM in 1931 and that year formed the Menges Quartet, which gained success and renown all over Europe. In her fifties she retired from performing and taught at the RCM, which later established its Isolde Menges Prize in her honour.

FLORENCE FENWICK MILLER pseudonym Filomena (1854–1935) pioneering journalist and feminist activist.

A close friend of Anna Kingsford [250], she was born into a poor London family. Aged seventeen she began to study for a degree in medicine at Edinburgh University [see Dr Jex-Blake, 236] but partway through her group's progress was blocked by the authorities. She returned to London and trained as a midwife, delivering the babies of poor East Enders. She was elected to the London School Board aged twenty-two and befriended Anna Kingsford [251]. After marrying clerk Fred Ford in 1877, she made history by publicly announcing her intention to retain her maiden name both professionally and privately, though prefixed with the title 'Mrs'. After consulting solicitors the authorities had to accept her decision. She further scandalised them by supporting Annie Besant [246] and Charles Bradlaugh [see Hypatia Bonner, 42] during their obscenity trial and ignored calls for her resignation. Her two daughters, Irene and Helen, born in 1880 and 1881, both took her surname.

Her career as an influential and respected public speaker and journalist soon overtook midwifery as her main source of income and the pursuit of women's suffrage became a very important part of her life. In 1889 she co-founded the Women's Franchise League and joined Jane Cobden Unwin [58] as part of a delegation to Chicago in 1893. Five years later she represented Britain in

Washington DC at the founding conference of the International Woman Suffrage Alliance. She was a member of the WSPU but took no part in militancy; her daughter Irene was imprisoned as a suffragette and was present at the tax-resistance siege of Dora Montefiore[226].

In 1890 she was elected to the Institute of Journalists and for thirty-two years wrote the 'Ladies' Notes' in the *Illustrated London News*, for which she produced an impressive 1,500 columns. She bought and edited the feminist weekly the *Woman's Signal* (1895–99) and, most unusually for a woman, was a staff journalist on the *London Daily News* (1902–4) and a columnist until 1918. Among her published books was a biography of Harriet Martineau in 1884.

Some sources state that her husband left her for a musical hall actress about 1894. She lived in London until later in life when she moved to Reigate, Surrey, moving to 23 Brunswick Road, Hove, by the 1930s. She ended her days at Hertford House Nursing Home, 45 Cromwell Road, Hove, and was cremated. The proceeds of the sale of her house in Hove was divided between her daughters.

Further reading: Van Arsdel, R. (2001) *Florence Fenwick Miller*. [Related images pp177, 179.]

DR SHEILA PATTERSON née Caffyn; later Pridmore (1918–1998) pioneering social anthropologist.

Miss Caffyn was born in Kent and educated at Roedean, Oxford University and the LSE. During WWII she was a civil servant at Polish House, London, and was briefly married to Captain Gadomski.

She studied black South Africans and wrote *Colour and Culture in South Africa* (1953) and *The Last Trek* (1957). After a brief marriage to Captain Patterson, by whom she had a daughter, she spent two years researching the Polish community in Canada and on her return married Tadeusz Horko in 1955, with whom she set up home at Flat 3, 8 Adelaide Crescent, Hove, living there for at least nine years, probably longer. During that time she undertook research among West Indians in Brixton, which resulted in her best-known book, *Dark Strangers* (1959). This was followed by *Immigrants in Industry* (1968), which

earned her a PhD. From 1958 she worked for the Institute of Race Relations, edited its newsletter and wrote *Immigration and Race Relations in Britain 1960–1967* (1969). She researched in Barbados and St Vincent, then for sixteen years edited *New Community*, the journal of what is now the Commission for Racial Equality.

In later life she lived between Hove and Spain until she entered Victoria Highgrove Nursing Home, 59 Dyke Road Avenue, Hove, where she died.

MARY PHILLIPS (1880–1969) suffragette and newspaper editor.

A leading suffragette, she worked for the WSPU all over Britain and for the East London Federation of Suffragettes. She served several terms of imprisonment and holds the record for the longest suffragette 'stretch': eleven weeks and three days. Like many others, she went on hunger strike. When the vote was won she became a newspaper editor and member of the Six Point Group [301]. She lived at 29 Shelley Road, Worthing, in the 1940s and Hovedene Hotel, 15–17 The Drive, Hove, in the 1960s. She died there and was cremated.

Further reading: Phillips, M. (1956) *The Militant Suffrage Campaign in Perspective*.

MARGARET POWELL née Langley (1908–1984) author.

A working-class girl, she was obliged to go into domestic service at fifteen, working in Brighton and London, eventually rising to the position of cook. She married a milkman and took evening classes at Hove, where a tape recording of her reminiscences led to an offer to publish her memoirs. *Below Stairs* (1968) was a surprise success; it sold 14,000 copies in a year and was followed by several more books on the same theme. At the age of sixty-two she was able, for the first time, to buy a home of her own.

She went on the speaking circuit and produced a cookery book, another autobiographical work, *My Mother and I* and a biography of Prince Albert. She then turned her attention to writing fiction and her final novel, *The Butler's Revenge*, appeared just before her death. She died in Hove, where her home, 222 Old Shoreham Road, has a blue plaque. Brighton bus 837 is named for her.

BRIGADIER DAME JEAN RIVETT-DRAKE DBE, DL, JP (1909–1999) director of the WRAC.

Born into a prosperous Lancastrian family, she moved to Sussex in the late 1930s and volunteered to drive motor vehicles for the FANY. She transferred to the ATS and was commissioned in 1942, commanding military transport services for the supply of ammunition and fuel. She was mentioned in dispatches and was appointed MBE in 1947.

In 1949 she joined the WRAC and was placed in command of a thousand servicewomen in Singapore. Her intellect and leadership qualities led to her repeated promotion, reaching the top post of director by 1961. She broadened the variety of servicewomen's trades and skills and founded a WRAC museum at Guildford. She retired in 1964 aged fifty-five and was appointed DBE.

She created an extremely busy life for herself in Hove, where she lived at 87 Hove Park Road. She was a deputy lieutenant for East Sussex and served on its county council, was a magistrate, a member of Hove Borough Council (and mayor 1977–8), a lay member of the Press Council and president of the Brighton Youth Orchestra. She died a millionairess, leaving a major bequest to Brighton Philharmonic Orchestra and a smaller sum to Hamilton Lodge School [see Margaret Taylor, 150].

JOAN HODGSON RIVIÈRE née Verrall (1883–1962) translator and psychoanalyst.

A vicar's daughter, she was born at 52 Brunswick Square and raised at 20 Buckingham Place, Hove. She was taught at home by her mother (a former governess) then at St Michael's Hall, Brighton, before boarding at Wycombe Abbey. After spending a year in Germany, becoming fluent in the language, she worked as a dressmaker, married a barrister and had a daughter.

She co-founded the British Psycho-Analytical Society in 1919, met Freud, was analysed by him in Vienna in 1922, and translated a considerable body of his work for British publication. From 1930 she worked as a training and supervising psychoanalyst and was among the pioneer women in the profession. Among her many learned papers was the ground-breaking 'Femininity as a masquerade'. She lived and died in London.

Further reading: Hughes, A. (ed) (1991) *The Inner World and Joan Rivière: Collected Papers, 1920–1956.*

PATSY ROWLANDS (1934–2005) actress.

Born in London, she was educated at convent schools and won a scholarship to the Guildhall School of Speech and Drama in London, where she gained the highest exam marks of any pupil in England. She had a long and varied acting career for over half a century, performing on the West End stage, on TV and in films, becoming nationally famous for playing 'Betty', Sid James's neighbour in the TV series *Bless This House* (1971–76) and for appearing in nine 'Carry On' films.

She married Malcolm Sircom and had one son. After living in Hove for many years she died there, at Martlets Hospice, Wayfield Avenue.

WILHELMINA STITCH née Jacobs; real name Ruth Collie (1888–1936) writer.

The granddaughter of an eminent rabbi, she was born in Cambridgeshire to an English father and Polish mother. At twenty she married lawyer Elisha Cohen, had a son and went to live in Canada in 1914, where she amused herself by writing verse for newspapers as 'Sheila Rand'. After the sudden death of her young husband left her penniless she scraped a living by contributing articles, verse and columns to Winnipeg newspapers. Returning to England she married surgeon Frank Collie and, using the pseudonym Wilhelmina Stitch contributed a rhyme a day under the title 'The Fragrant Minute' to the *Daily Sketch* as well as writing for other top publications including *Punch*, the *Sunday Graphic* and the *Daily Herald*, where her readership exceeded two million. She also gave talks, was a member of the Magicians' Club, served on the Council of Women Journalists and published a couple of dozen books, mainly anthologies of poems. By the thirties she was one of the most syndicated writers in the British Empire, was parodied by comedians and described in the *Guardian* as 'the hearts-and-flowers laureate'. She lived at 26 Brunswick Square,

Hove, then 23 Vallance Road and later at 114 Church Road. She died at her pied à terre in London's Mayfair, and her ashes were buried at Golders Green, where the gateway clock and a large plaque were erected in her honour.

MENTIA TAYLOR née Clementia Doughty (1810–1908) social campaigner.

Leaving her native Norfolk, she worked as a governess at Hove House, Hove Terrace, until in 1842 she married (in Lewes) the fabulously wealthy P.A. Taylor (a cousin of her employer, the Revd J.P. Malleson, who conducted the ceremony). He became an MP and the owner of perhaps the most expensive private home in England, Aubrey House, Kensington (which now bears a blue plaque for the Taylors, among others).

As philanthropists and social reformers, their home was a centre for all kinds of radical movements. They were both active in welfare work connected with the American Civil War, but when Mrs Taylor applied to join the London Anti-Slavery Society she was informed that women were not admitted. Forming a similar organisation, for women only, she realised that her sex also needed emancipation from slavery and she spent the rest of her life trying to achieve that aim.

She became closely associated with Barbara Bodichon [193], Bessie Rayner Parkes [79] and Florence Fenwick Miller [165] in various campaigns for women's rights, including the Society for Promoting the Employment of Women, and in 1859 became a shareholder of their *English Woman's Journal* (ironically, her shares were registered to her husband, since English law did not allow a married woman to hold them). In 1867 she invited a group of women into her house to discuss women's suffrage and they founded the LSWS; she was elected treasurer and donated the first £50. Her home was the venue for the collation of various sheets of paper that bore the 1,499 signatures on the first-ever women's suffrage petition that John Stuart Mill presented to parliament in 1867.

In 1869 she co-founded the Ladies' Educational Association, which campaigned for women to be admitted to University College. She served on the committee of the New Hospital and the executive of the Married Women's Property Committee, established a Home for Young Women Servants and was treasurer of the Vigilance Association for the Defence of Personal Rights. Widowed in 1891, in her nineties she joined the Emancipation Union.

Mrs Taylor lived in Sussex for thirty-five years. In 1873 her husband sold Aubrey House and they moved firstly to 22 Marine Parade, Brighton, then in 1884 to 16–18 Eaton Place, Hove, where she died, two years short of her century.

VESTA TILLEY née Matilda Powles; Lady de Freece (1864–1952) actress.

Born in Worcester, she appeared at the age of four as 'The Great Little Tilley' and at six was dressing as a boy to delight music hall audiences. Making her London début aged eleven, she soon became one of the highest-paid and most famous music hall artistes, singing and dancing in a wide range of 'breeches roles' as sailors, soldiers and gentlemen and appearing frequently at the Hippodrome Music Hall in Middle Street, Brighton.

She married lyricist (later, Sir) Walter de Freece, honeymooned at the Grand Hotel, Brighton, and continued with her career until her final appearance in 1920 completed fifty-two years on the stage. In 1947 she bought a home at 8 St Aubyn's Mansions, King's Esplanade, Hove, and died five years later. [Related plate 54.]

LYDIA YAVORSKA née Lidia Borisovna von Hübbenet; Princess Bariatinsky; Lady Pollock (1869–1921) actress.

The daughter of a Russian policeman, she was born in Kiev. She studied in Paris and became a well-known actress. When she married Prince Vladimir Bariatinsky in 1896, his family haughtily refused to receive her, a mere 'showgirl'. The couple moved to London in 1909, where she appeared in the West End, Liverpool and Manchester in her own productions of plays written by her husband, Ibsen, Zola, Strindberg, Gorky and her future husband. During the Coronation Suffrage Pageant of 1911, the largest and most spectacular demonstration of the campaign, by invitation of Elizabeth Robins [56] she led the AFL contingent on horseback, in the character of Ibsen's 'Hedda Gabler'.

She lived in Russia for most of WWI and during the Revolution, and was reputed to have suffered terrible privations, which were later blamed for her early death. She founded and was chairman of the Great Britain to Poland Fund to help Polish refugees left starving and homeless by the German invasion. After WWI she helped the Russian people, organising charity matinées to raise funds.

She divorced in 1916 and in 1920 married playwright John Pollock Bt. She died a year later at her home in Carlisle Road, Hove, and was buried at St Nicholas's Church, Shoreham. Her memorial service was held in the Russian church, London.

After her death an auction was held to sell seven hundred valuable items, including numerous furs, extravagant theatrical costumes and exquisite jewellery. Portrait photographs of her are held at the V & A and the NPG.

OVINGDEAN

BRIGADIER DAME MARGOT TURNER DBE, RRC (1910–1993) chief military nurse and prisoner of war.

A London-born QAIMNS nurse, during WWII she served in India, Malaya and Singapore, from where she was being evacuated when her ship was sunk by Japanese warships and the survivors machine-gunned from aircraft. Somehow, she and the other survivors managed to swim to a desert island. They were rescued three days later by a ship that was also sunk by the Japanese. This time, she and another nurse swam to a raft, using which they saved eight other adults and six children from drowning. For four days she endured the horror of seeing all fifteen of them die, mainly from sunstroke and dehydration. Somehow she alone survived, living on seaweed, and rainwater collected in the lid of her powder compact or sucked from the fabric of her dress. She was found by the Japanese, roasted brown and almost dead. They locked her in a prison cell for six months with an ever-changing assortment of thieves and murderers on death row, then put in a women's prison camp for three years and made to dig graves for fellow inmates as they died of starvation or

dysentery. Half-starved and with her front teeth missing, in 1945 she was repatriated to England and returned to her family's home in Hove, where she convalesced.

Incredibly, just six weeks later she reported for nursing duties. She was posted to various trouble-spots across the world, including Cyprus, Libya and Eritrea, serving, in all, thirty-one years. She rose to colonel commandant of QARANC and matron-in-chief and director of Army Nursing Services. She was awarded the RRC in 1956 and appointed MBE in 1946 and DBE in 1965. After initially refusing, she agreed to appear on the biographical TV programme *This is Your Life*. Her war story inspired the TV series *Tenko*, about women interned in Japanese prisoner-of-war camps. In later life her eyesight failed and she moved into St Dunstan's Home for blind ex-service people at Ovingdean, where she died.

Further reading: Smyth, J. (1983) *The Will to Live: The Story of Dame Margot Turner.*

PORTSLADE

LIZZIE BAXTER née Foster (1837–1926) evangelist.

Born in Worcestershire, in 1866 she became superintendent of the Mildmay Deaconesses' Training Home in Islington, designing their distinguishing bonnet and dress. After marrying the Revd Michael Paget Baxter, an evangelist deacon and editor of the *Christian Herald*, she became with him a travelling religious crusader, distributing thousands of gospels and tracts in Britain and Europe. Most unusually for a woman at that time, she even preached, but only in Germany, where it was more socially acceptable for women. In Islington in 1883 she founded Bethshan, a home of holiness and divine healing, and in 1886 opened a college where she and her husband trained hundreds of missionaries, sending them to Ceylon and India. In 1894 they left for a world tour, speaking on divine healing and the call of Christ.

Widowed in 1910 she settled at 4 Western Esplanade, Portslade, a terrace built in 1908 by her son Michael, Lord of Lancing Manor and editor of the *Christian*

Herald, who lived at no. 1 with his daughter Betty [below]. Mrs Baxter died there and was buried in London. The terrace is now known as Millionaire's Row and astrologer June Penn, the last member of the Baxter family to live there, was still in residence in 2007.

(VIOLET ELIZABETH) BETTY BAXTER (1901–1972) founder of the Silver Lady Fund.

The granddaughter of Lizzie Baxter [above], she was born in London where, driving her car one cold night in 1922 she saw some poor old tramps. She stopped and gave each one the price of a cup of tea and a silver-sixpence. She repeated her kindness a few more times and was soon dubbed the 'silver lady'. Accepting the nickname, she set up the Silver Lady All Night Travelling Café, which plied the streets giving out hot drinks, bread and dripping, saveloys, milk, biscuits, cigarettes, boots and clothing to all who were in need. In 1930 she founded the Elizabeth Baxter Hostel for Distressed Women and Girls at 52 Lambeth Road, London, and produced a film, *The Night Patrol,* showing how London's homeless survived. One scene that showed how easy it was for girls to be tricked into prostitution was cut by the film censor, prompting George Bernard Shaw to publicly protest, because vulnerable girls ought to be warned about such matters.

By the 1930s Miss Baxter was placing twice-weekly appeals in *The Times* for donations to her fund. Money and bequests flowed in (one woman left £10,000 in 1941, worth half a million today). Every Christmas she hired the basement of Central Hall, Westminster, where she gave a banquet followed by variety entertainments to 600 homeless people.

On the death of her father in 1947, she became MD and life chairman of the *Christian Herald.* She lived for sixty-five years between her family's homes in London and 1 Western Esplanade, Portslade, where she died.

Eighty-five years since she founded it, the Silver Lady Fund still hands out free food at 6.30am daily from a white van, though the bread and dripping have been replaced by pasties, pies and sausage rolls. Since 1970 the fund has been administered from Bexhill. It recently provided five MiPods (sleeping capsules) to Brighton's homeless. The hostel she founded has moved to Peckham and the Lambeth Road premises now houses the Elizabeth Baxter Centre, a walk-in medical centre for the homeless. [Related image p179.]

(MARY) ANNESLEY KENEALY (1861–1926) lecturer and novelist.

Born and raised at 8–9 Wellington Road, Portslade, she was the sister of Arabella [171] and daughter of Edward Kenealy MP, a disgraced QC who was barrister for the infamous Tichborne Claimant. Their parents moved to Lancing in the 1870s, where they provided their daughters with an excellent home education in Latin, Greek, science and mathematics.

After training as nurses at St Bartholomew's Hospital, London, she and her sister Henrietta went to Hamburg as volunteers during a cholera epidemic in 1892; her description of their work was published in the *Daily Graphic.* She later visited the USA and Europe to study their hospital systems, was appointed by a Royal Commission to judge the Hygienic and Sanitary section of the World's Fair in Chicago in 1893, and was invited to prepare the official report of the department for presentation to the U.S. Congress. Back in the UK she became well known as a freelance lecturer to the National Health Society and various county councils, and contributed to many periodicals, including the BMJ. She also wrote several novels including *The Poodle Woman* and *The Thing We Have Prayed For* ('a racy, vivacious story').

Despite being a woman of science she was evidently given to emotional outbursts and dramatic gestures. In 1910 she sued Lord Northcliffe for wrongful dismissal and when she lost pretended to kill herself by taking (fake) poison in the *Daily Mail* offices. In 1915 she sued W.H. Smith & Son for slander, claiming they caused her to have no income. During the case she ostentatiously drank a (non-lethal) phial of poison in court and was later summonsed for attempting suicide. In 1918, while living in Lancing, a court ordered her to pay £500 damages for libelling, William Chorley, the highly-respected founder of the Southern Homes of Rest in Lancing, two doors from the home she shared with her mother:

Terrace House, 2 The Terrace, Brighton Road. She was also sued for libel by her brother Edward in 1921 but the case was withdrawn after she apologised.

She died in a hotel in London, leaving instructions and funds to endow a single-bedded ward at the Royal Free Hospital in her mother's memory, and a fund for the Annesley Kenealy Bequest, which she founded in order to give grants and pensions for 'necessitous women writers only'. The balance of her estate of £12,000 went to her sister Henrietta.

DR ARABELLA KENEALY (1859–1938) writer and sociologist.

The sister of Annesley [above], she was born and raised at 8–9 Wellington Road, Portslade, moving later to Terrace House, 2 The Terrace, Brighton Road, Lancing. She studied medicine at the LSMW, gained her LRCP and LKQCPI and practised as a doctor in London and Watford for six years until she contracted diphtheria.

A friend of Anna Kingsford [251], she studied eugenics and human evolution and wrote twenty-nine novels and sociological books, including *Dr Janet of Harley Street* (1893), which had a lesbian theme, and *A Semi-Detached Marriage* (1898), as well as her late father's memoirs. In *Feminism and Sex-Extinction* (1920) she argued that feminism made women wish to remain single, which was unnatural and would lead to 'sex-extinction'. For most of her life she lived between London and the family home at Lancing. She was buried at Hangleton Church, Portslade, near her late brother, who had been editor of the *Daily Mirror*. [Related images pp 177, 180.]

PRESTON

DR ANNIE PORTER FZS (1880–1963) parasitologist.

A poulterer's daughter, she was born at 8 Lewes Road, Preston and her family moved to 10 Preston Street, Brighton, by 1901. She studied botany at University College, London, and her PhD thesis was on animal parasites. After marrying Harold Fantham she retained her own name and lived in South Africa, then Canada, where they had long and distinguished careers. Between

1914 and 1938 she wrote and illustrated several books, some with her husband, who was a professor of biology at Cambridge, including *Some Minute Animal Parasites; or, Unseen Foes in the Animal World* (1914).

As a widow she moved to London and was honorary parasitologist to the Zoological Society at Regent's Park. She left her considerable wealth to various universities, including £10,000 to Christ's College, Cambridge.

ROTTINGDEAN

ENID BAGNOLD CBE, FRSL Lady Jones (1889–1981) novelist and dramatist.

Leaving her native Kent to attend finishing school in Paris, she later rented a flat in Chelsea, studied art and took a notorious, fifty-six-year-old rake as a lover. During WWI she was a nurse, about which she wrote *A Diary Without Dates* (1918). The book criticised hospital administration and within a half-hour of publication the military authorities had dismissed her. Determined to help the war effort, she went to France as a volunteer motor-driver.

When she married Sir Roderick Jones of Reuters News Agency, the Archbishop of Cape Town performed the ceremony and the reception was attended by hundreds of aristocrats and diplomats. The couple made a pact: in return for being his perfect society hostess, she was to have three hours' uninterrupted writing time each day. In 1923 they bought North End House, Rottingdean (which Sir Roderick extended by purchasing the neighbouring building, Gothic House); Rudyard Kipling's former home, The Elms, on the village green and a racing stable. Lady Jones took part in Rottingdean Fair and other local events. They had three sons and a daughter, Laurian, whose governess was a graduate of Girton. The family employed a cook, butler, housemaids, a lady's maid, two nursery nurses, a chauffeur (there were three cars, including a Rolls Royce) and a groom (they had four horses). Nursery nurse Kay Roetman recalled: 'There was a round tower room at the top of the house where Lady Jones would hide herself to write in peace ... She was a flamboyant, emotional woman, sometimes irrational, but totally without snobbery ... I remember taking Richard to Newhaven, driven by the chauffeur, of course, to see his mother off to France, and she walked the whole length of the quay arm-in-arm with me'.

After writing two novels she embarked upon books for children. *Alice and Thomas and Jane* (1930), about three children who live in a large house in Rottingdean, was illustrated by the author and Laurian, then nine. *National Velvet* tells of a fourteen-year-old girl who wins a horse and (disguised as a boy) rides it to victory in the Grand National. The heroine's family was inspired by that of a Rottingdean butcher, Mr Hilder. The book was also illustrated by Laurian, then fourteen, and is still in print. Nine years after publication, a screenplay based on *National Velvet* was made into the film that launched twelve-year-old Elizabeth Taylor into mega-stardom. Owing to Lady Jones, surprised locals got the chance to meet Miss Taylor when she visited her in Rottingdean in 1939, 1955 and 1970.

Lady Jones wrote seven novels, nine plays, books for children, volumes of poetry and an autobiography. She was elected a Fellow of the Royal Society of Literature and appointed CBE in 1976. Prescribed morphine after a hip operation, she became addicted and for twelve years injected up to 350mg a day. She sold the family's London home in 1969 but in 1977 placed an appeal in *The Times* seeking a basement flat in Hamilton Terrace, Maida Vale, London. She was evidently successful, for her address when she died was 17a Hamilton Terrace. She was cremated at Golders Green and her ashes were buried at Rottingdean. Brighton bus 602 is named for her, and she has plaques in London and Rottingdean. [Related image p175.]

BRENDA DE BANZIE (1909–1981) actress.

The daughter of an orchestral musician who had played for Queen Victoria, she was born in Manchester. After voice training and dancing school she sang in a choir, toured with repertory companies in the UK and USA and made her West End début in 1942. She won the Clarence Dewent Award for Best Acting Performance of the Year for her 1952 role in the thriller *Murder Mistaken*. By her own volition, she did not work in films until she was forty-two. Her greatest screen success was in *Hobson's Choice* (1954), which was followed by her acclaimed role opposite Laurence Olivier in both the 1957 stage production and the 1960 film version of *The Entertainer*, which won her a nomination for Broadway's 1958 Tony Award. Altogether she appeared in thirty-three TV and stage productions, including *Doctor at Sea* (1955), *The 39 Steps* (1959) and *The Pink Panther* (1963).

She married actor Rupert Marsh, with whom she lived during the 1960s at the Penthouse Flat, Old Norton House, The Green, Rottingdean. She died during surgery in hospital at Haywards Heath. Her son, Antony, and her niece, Lois de Banzie, also became actors. [Related plate 57.]

EDNA DEANE real name Edna Morton Sewell (1905–1995) champion ballroom dancer and author.

Of English parentage, she was born in South Africa and brought to England as a toddler. After making her dancing début at twelve she had professional tuition and became a ballroom dancer. In the 1920s she danced nine times with Prince Edward (later Edward VIII), inspiring the famous song *I danced with a man who danced with a girl who danced with the Prince of Wales*. She and her partner won the British foxtrot championship in 1929 and in 1933 became both the British and the world professional ballroom champions. This led to a leading part in a show at the London Palladium in 1929 as 'Edna Deane, The Queen of Dance', and to her becoming the first ballroom dancer to be treated as a celebrity. Fred Astaire called her 'authentic poetry in motion.'

She married twice: in 1935 to James Kendal and in 1950 to restaurateur John Fuelling. By 1951 she was living at St John's, Vicarage Lane, Rottingdean. She wrote a book, *Ballet to Remember* (1947) and a play, *The Shepherd's Tale*, which won the Sussex Drama Festival Award at Glyndebourne in 1957. She ran the Deane School of Dance and Drama, and from 1967 until 1979 owned a boutique, 'Tallboys' at 66 High Street, Rottingdean. On her ninetieth birthday she received fan mail from admirers who still remembered 'the divine Edna'.

SALTDEAN

ETHEL FROUD (1880–1941) feminist and trade unionist.

The daughter of a butcher, she was born in a village in Kent, where she became a schoolmistress. Moving to London she became involved with the National Union of Teachers, the Women Teachers' Franchise Union and the National Federation of Women Teachers, of which she became the first full-time, salaried general secretary. In this role she helped to transform it into the autonomous NUWT and travelled to Paris and the USSR as a conference delegate. She joined the WSPU, served it well as a gifted speaker, an efficient organiser and a member of its drum and fife band, and was once sheltered from an angry mob by railwaymen who locked her in a waiting room. She was an active member of the Six Point Group [301] and led the final suffrage deputation to the prime minister in 1927.

She retired at the age of sixty to a house in Tye Close, Saltdean, which she named Rhondhurst in honour of Viscountess Rhondda, daughter of Sybil [148], and Emmeline Pankhurst [294], who were the founders, respectively, of the Six Point Group and the WSPU. She died at the house just a year later and was cremated at Brighton.

ELINOR GLYN née Sutherland (1864–1943) novelist, screenwriter and director.

Born in Jersey, and raised there and in Canada, she came from a family with high society connections. She married at twenty-eight and on honeymoon in Brighton her wealthy husband hired Brill's Baths in Pool Valley to watch her swim naked. He later drank and gambled away his fortune while she raised two daughters and supported the family by writing, firstly, magazine articles, then racy novels which sold in their millions to a lascivious public, after being lambasted by highbrow critics as 'immoral' and banned from libraries.

In 1915, when she sued the Western Film Company for infringement of copyright, the judge refused to protect her interests because, he said, her 1907 novel *Three Weeks* was 'grossly immoral' and the film 'indescribably vulgar'. In it the heroine committed adultery on a tiger-skin rug, prompting this ditty:

> Would you like to sin
> With Elinor Glyn
> On a tiger skin?
> Or would you prefer
> To err with her
> On some other fur?

A parody of *Three Weeks*, called *Too Weak*, was published anonymously by someone using the humorous pseudonym 'Ellova Gryn', but the original went into many editions, the latest in 1996.

Mrs Glyn lived variously in London, New York, Paris, Russia and Brighton, and had plenty of affairs with aristocratic men of the type featured in her books. George, Marquess Curzon of Kedleston, was her lover from 1906 to 1916. In addition to writing twenty-two novels and fourteen non-fiction works, in the 1920s she wrote or co-wrote several screenplays and was their production supervisor in Hollywood, where she was considered an expert on style, fashion and upper-class English manners. Her romantic comedy film *It* gave famous actress Clara Bow her nickname as 'The It Girl' ('it' being sex-appeal). In 1927 Lorenz Hart wrote Mrs Glyn into his song, *My Heart Stood Still*:

> I read my Plato
> Love, I thought a sin
> But since your kiss
> I'm reading Missus Glyn

Later she directed her own films in England, where she lived for many years at 17a Curzon House, Chichester Drive West, Saltdean, moving to Chelsea during WWII, where she died. Her grandson, Sir Geoffrey Davson Bt., changed his name by deed poll to Anthony Glyn in her honour and wrote (among many other books) her biography.

Further reading: Glyn, E. (1936) *Romantic Adventure, Being the Autobiography of Elinor Glyn;* Glyn, A. (1955) *Elinor Glyn;* Hardwick, J. (1994) *Addicted to Romance.* [Related plate 39.]

20 The Drive, Hove, where Dame
Ivy Compton-Burnett spent her
teenage years (photo: Val Brown).

Rockrose, Clayton Hill,
Pyecombe, once the country
retreat of Dr Helen Boyle
(from an old photograph).

13–14 Victoria Road, Brighton, formerly Minnie Turner's Sea View Guest House

North End House, Rottingdean (right) and its diminutive neighbour, Gothic House, now Aubrey House, which bears a plaque to Enid Bagnold and the writer Angela Thirkell (a writer who visited as a child).

24 Montpelier Crescent, Brighton, once the home and surgery of Dr Octavia Wilberforce, and the home of her friend Elizabeth Robins. Fittingly, it is today a medical centre (photo: Val Brown).

Brighton & Hove High School, The Temple, Montpelier Road, Brighton, alma mater of seven of our notable women and workplace of Edith Creak. It has been considerably altered since its construction in the 1820s.

Images of (left to right) Alice Cornwell, Arabella Kenealy and Florence Fenwick Miller, the *Women's Penny Paper*, 1889. Cartoon of Kitty Carson as 'The Queen of the Sewing Bees', *Call Boy* magazine, 1895.

SHOW WORK DONE BY 'LIFE CRYSTALS'

Mrs. Dickinson's Discovery Represented as Reviving Soil, Cleaning Boilers, Curing Disease.

COMPANY TO EXPLOIT IT

But Users of Scarab-Born Rays Are Divided as to the Extent of Their Powers.

By Wireless to THE NEW YORK TIMES.

LONDON, July 12.—Opinions as to the value of the alleged discovery of a substance of strange radioactive powers, made by Mrs. Maud Dickinson of Brighton, differ greatly. Her neighbors show little interest in it and the local press makes no reference to the marvels which have been revealed by The Daily Express.

Mrs. Dickinson's discovery was explained as beginning with a self-created scarab or beetle of old Egypt to which the ancients attributed marvelous properties. This scarab, she said, formed crystals outside and away from the bottle in which it was kept and when these crystals were dipped in water, the water acquired remarkable radioactive powers.

The discovery was made by accident, according to the account. Following a test of some small crystals there was an explosion.

"When this was over," said Mrs. Dickinson, "I found a fine white crystal like a diamond and also a particle of matter which I have since found to be a scarab."

The scarab was placed in a bottle and continued to throw off minute crystals which are those now used. The scarab, Mrs. Dickinson believes, is not an insect but a vegetable form of life.

"Perhaps," she said, "it is the source of all life."

When THE NEW YORK TIMES correspondent visited Mrs. Dickinson's house on the Marine Parade, Kemptown, yesterday, he was informed that she was away for a few days, but he could probably see her assistant, Mr. Lloyd, today. On calling at the hour given he found Mr. Lloyd would not be interviewed, as Mrs. Dickinson had given strict instructions that no one should give any information except herself. He also learned that she was in London and might be reached at the office of the company she is forming to put her preparations on the market, the Actifum Development Company, Limited. A friend of Mrs. Dickinson's, Walter by name, thought he could let her know THE NEW YORK TIMES correspondent would be back in town in a few hours and was anxious to see her, and the correspondent had a messenger sent to the company's office to ask for an appointment. This messenger was told that no further information concerning Mrs. Dickinson could be given and that The Express articles should not have been published.

Miss Amy Sedgwick brought with her from Manchester an excellent reputation, stamped not only by provincial applause—which is in itself but a poor criterion of dramatic ability—but by the approbation of metropolitan critics and actors who in the course of their summer wanderings have singled out this young lady from the herd of aspirants pressed upon their notice. The *Lady of Lyons* was the play, and Miss Sedgwick is admirably adapted for the heroine: her figure is tall and graceful, her features handsome and mobile, her elocution very clear and well modulated. All her movements are those of the best class of actress, thoroughly at home upon the stage, and well-trained in the arcana of her profession: a little over-trained, perhaps, as the only defect to be observed last night was that throughout she was a little too artificial, and lacking in natural impulse. There is, however, not the least doubt that Miss Sedgwick's has been the most promising and satisfactory *début* that we have had for some time.

DISCREDITS 'LIFE CRYSTALS'

Dr. Whitlock Says Mrs. Dickinson's Proof Is Unscientific.

Dr. H. P. Whitlock, curator and head of the Department of Mineralogy of the Museum of Natural History, said yesterday that he did not take seriously the reports of the discoveries made by Mrs. Maud Dickinson of Brighton, England, who is said to have come upon a substance of strange radioactive powers.

"There does not seem to me to be anything in the supposed discoveries of Mrs. Dickinson," said Dr. Whitlock. "The question of the spontaneous generation of life was threshed out sixty or seventy years ago, and since then nobody has laid claim to discovering evidence of spontaneous generation per se. The workings of the radioactive substance do not seem credible to me.

"I do not think Mrs. Dickinson's results have been sufficiently established. The cleaning of pipes and boilers by her crystals is of doubtful validity. It is said the water is radioactive, but she does not say how she found out it is radioactive. No test is given to prove its radioactivity. The method of proof is wholly unscientific."

Hot Tea
Bread and Dripping at Midnight

is given free to hundreds of homeless and hungry men and women from THE SILVER LADY'S ALL-NIGHT TRAVELLING CAFÉ which has never failed them yet.

A typical scene at the All-night Travelling Cafe.

Please help us this Christmas by sending a gift of money to :

Some thousands of Bed and Breakfast tickets are also given.

MISS BETTY BAXTER
THE SILVER LADY FUND, 6, Tudor Street, London, E.C.4

THE WOMAN'S SIGNAL

A Weekly Record and Review devoted to the interests of Women in the Home and in the Wider World.

Edited by MRS. FENWICK MILLER.

Appeal by Betty Baxter for donations to the Silver Lady Fund, *The Times*, 1936; the nameplate of Florence Fenwick Miller's weekly feminist newspaper, 1897.

Facing page: report and rebuttal of Mrs Maud Dickinson's scientific discoveries, *The New York Times*, July 1922; Amy Sedgwick, *Daily News*, 1857; Mary Braddon, *The Era*, 1898.

FAY COMPTON

Commences Her Life Story

"Up To Now"

The charming "Barrie Heroine" describes some of the people she has met, and many of her adventures on the road to fame. The life of an actress is packed with thrills, interesting meetings, and exciting moments. Miss Compton has had her full share of these and she tells her story in a most delightful and intimate manner. You will thoroughly enjoy these reminiscences.

Begin them TO-DAY in this week's
WOMAN'S PICTORIAL

MRS. CONSTANCE GARNETT

To Constance Garnett, whose death at the age of 85 was announced on Wednesday, innumerable readers on both shores of the Atlantic are grateful for the world she revealed to them. Thanks to her we can read most of the Russian classics in translations as spirited and idiomatic as they are accurate—all of Turgeniev, Dostoievsky, Gogol, and Chekov, with "War and Peace" and "Anna Karenina." Into this immense achievement she put more than a sensitive literary conscience and a scientific respect for both the languages in which she worked; she felt for the Russia of the last century an affection that made her, in the act of translation, its sympathetic interpreter.

Advert for Fay Compton's article in the *Woman's Pictorial*, 1925; Dr Kenealy, 1915; Pearl Binder, 1961 and 1964; Isolde Menges, 1913; Constance Garnett, 1946; all from *The Times*.

"A notable work of art"
ARABELLA KENEALY'S
Great Success

THE THING WE HAVE PRAYED FOR

A 3rd large edition at once called for

The DAILY CHRONICLE says:

"Miss Arabella Kenealy has achieved in her new novel a notable work of art. Like all remarkable works of imagination, her story contains something new and memorable. Miss Kenealy's aristocratic cads and bounders and her fast women deserve that Gillray should return to earth to draw them. Her artistic energy makes them alive."

The DAILY MAIL says:

"A racy, vivacious story, telling of the ambitions, heartburnings, and disappointments of a social climber. Here is drama enough with sprightly dialogue and lively and shrewd commentary. Miss Kenealy ensures a never-flagging interest. A book which is entertaining up to the last page."

A WOMAN'S JOB?

Sir,—Even in this desperate nuclear age men politicians are still thinking in terms of personal and national prestige. Women, practical realists, are thinking of the future of the children of the world.

Before the statesmen succeed in settling their future by blowing the world up, might it not be a sensible idea to appoint a woman as the new Secretary-General of the United Nations?

Yours, &c.,
PEARL BINDER.

BRIGHTON PROJECT

Sir,—Those who live in Brighton, and all who love this unique resort, will welcome Sir William Holford's letter (September 17).

However, the proposed £9,500,000 Marina raises graver problems than its siting. There are grounds for fearing that it is a mere sprat to catch a whale, the whale being the miles of open beaches.

Once private development is permitted on part of the foreshore the gadarene scramble for the rest of the beaches will be on. I understand that up to now development on the foreshore has been refused in the West Pier area. But public opinion is slow to mobilize and developers work fast. There is a real danger that Brighton may suffer the fate of some continental and American seafronts in which the beaches are completely sealed off from the public.

The sea at Brighton should remain free to us all and so should the Brighton beaches.

Yours, &c.,
PEARL BINDER.
2 St. Margaret's Place, Brighton, Sussex.
Sept. 19.

Adverts in *The Times:* Mrs Merrifield, 1857;
Miss Braddon, 1889; Arabella Kenealy, 1893;
Arabella Buckley, 1880; Geraldine Hodgson,
1901; Louisa Costello, 1844; Ellice Hopkins,
1901. Etchings: Countess of Huntingdon
(top), Harriot Mellon and Marie Hilton.

East Sussex

Annie Besant

ALCISTON

PROFESSOR CAROLINE SPURGEON (1869–1942) literary scholar, and **PROFESSOR VIRGINIA GILDERSLEEVE** (1877–1965) academic.

The daughter of an army captain, Caroline Spurgeon was born in India and educated at Cheltenham Ladies' College, King's College and University College, and achieved first-class honours in English at Oxford University, which at that time did not award degrees to women. An expert on Chaucer and Shakespeare, her doctoral thesis, submitted to the University of Paris, *Chaucer Devant la Critique en Angleterre et en France* was published in 1911 as two books (one in French; one in English). In 1913 she became the first female professor employed by any British university, when appointed at Bedford College (since 1900 a part of the University of London). During her distinguished academic career she received many awards, gave learned papers in various countries and wrote several scholarly books, including her pioneering *Shakespeare's Imagery and What it Tells Us* (1935) which was reprinted sixteen times by 2001 and was described by George Rylands as 'a monumental work without a single dull page'.

In the late 1890s she met her lifelong love Lilian Clapham MBE (1871–1935), captain of the England women's hockey team and a civil servant at the Ministry of Labour. In 1918 she met New Yorker Virginia Gildersleeve, the USA's most eminent female academic and the only woman involved in writing and signing the UN Charter, who was for thirty-six years the Dean of Barnard College (where she had studied). With Hertha Ayrton [63] they were involved in founding the International Federation of University Women in 1919, of which Professor Gildersleeve was twice president.

In 1925 the two professors bought the eighteenth-century Old Postman's Cottage, Alciston, living between there and the USA for ten years. Miss Clapham retired there and was involved with the local village community. A frequent guest was Dame Margaret Tuke, for twenty-two years

principal of Bedford College (it became part of the University of London under her direction). No stranger to Sussex, she had boarded at St John's, Withdean.

After Miss Clapham died and was cremated, Professor Spurgeon placed a memorial stone in her honour in Alciston churchyard. The professors sold the cottage and from 1936 lived permanently in Arizona, USA. Professor Spurgeon died and was cremated there and, at her request, her friend brought her ashes to Alciston after the war and had them interred alongside those of Miss Clapham. By then Professor Gildesleeve had set up home with Elizabeth Reynard, an English professor twenty years her junior. Professor Spurgeon left part of her estate to endow a scholarship or fellowship at Bedford College. The Professor Gildersleeve International Fund, founded by IFUW members in New York in 1969, currently campaigns to help women and children in developing countries.

Further reading: Gildersleeve, V. (1954) *Many a Good Crusade.* [Related images pp16, 265.]

DAME (CICELY) VERONICA WEDGWOOD OM, DBE (1910–1997) historian.

The daughter of a baronet, a descendant of famous potter Josiah Wedgwood and a cousin of composer Ralph Vaughan Williams, she was born in Northumberland. She was an exceptionally gifted child, and by the age of twelve had written a play, three novels and a history of England (all unpublished). She learned French, German, Dutch, Italian, Spanish and Swedish and studied classics and modern history at Lady Margaret Hall.

Her career spanned fifty years, during which time she wrote (as C.V. Wedgwood) more than twenty authoritative works of history on subjects such as Charles I, the Civil War and Cromwell. She was literary adviser to the publisher Jonathan Cape and deputy editor of the feminist journal *Time and Tide.* A reviewer for the *Daily Telegraph,* she also judged literary prizes, tutored at Somerville and lectured all over the UK and USA. She was the first woman trustee of the NPG and president of both the English Association and of the Society of Authors. She received many honorary degrees, was appointed CBE in 1956 and DBE in 1968 and in 1969 became the third woman ever to receive the Order of Merit.

In her first year at Oxford she had met her lifelong companion Jacqueline Hope-Wallace, later a senior civil servant and CBE. The couple shared a London home with Jacqueline's brother, Philip, but when he died in 1979 they moved to Whitegate, Alciston, where Dame Veronica did most of her writing and where they entertained many famous writers, artists and politicians. She died a millionairess and was buried in Alciston churchyard under a modest headstone.

ALFRISTON

DOROTHY CLEWES née Parkin (1907–2003) children's novelist.

A native of Nottingham, at eighteen she received a £100 advance for her first novel *The Rivals of Maidenhurst* (1925) but didn't write another until the 1940s. Nevertheless, over the next thirty years she wrote over seventy books for beginner-readers, children and teenagers, which were popular on both sides of the Atlantic. Her last work was *Nothing to Declare* (1976) but she lived to see her earlier 'Willie' series reprinted in 1991.

In 1932 she married a fellow author and settled in Kent. As a widow she moved to Soleig, King's Ride, Alfriston, her home for thirty-five years. She died in Seaford.

ALICE GREGORY CBE (1867–1946) hospital founder.

A clergyman's daughter, she was born in south London, though her mother hailed from Midhurst. She was educated by a governess and in her late twenties studied at Dr McCall's Clapham School of Midwifery; she was later to serve with Dr McCall [75] on the LCC health committee.

In 1899, while working as a midwife in Somerset, she met hospital matron Lelia Parnell and nurse Maud Mabel Cashmore (1875–1949). Their mission was to raise the status of midwives, which were seen as the lowest form of nurse, and to reduce the number of maternal deaths, then over 3,000

a year. The government had passed a law in 1902 preventing unqualified women from attending the birth of their poor neighbours but had supplied no alternative.

In 1905 the trio founded the Home for Mothers and Babies in Woolwich as a maternity hospital that would also train midwives. In 1909 it received official recognition from the Central Midwives' Board and Florence Nightingale sent a letter of congratulation and a donation to the rebuilding fund. By 1915 the home had amalgamated with the Lying-in Hospital for Married Women and expanded to accommodate a national midwives' training school. The hospital was so popular that, by the 1920s, there was a seven-month waiting list. By the 1930s 800 women were admitted each year and 1,000 turned away. By then the hospital was training women from all parts of the world and Miss Gregory had been appointed CBE (in 1929).

Her father, the Very Revd Robert Gregory DD, was from 1891 the Dean of St Paul's Cathedral, and she lived for some years at the deanery. He gave his whole-hearted support and some large donations to her endeavours, but worried that she was overworking. He had a house built for her on the South Downs overlooking Alfriston, naming it The Sanctuary; she and Miss Cashmore spent all their weekends and holidays there for three decades. She retired at the age of seventy-eight and died at The Sanctuary a year later. Miss Cashmore died on holiday in Bavaria and was cremated in Munich. The hospital to which they had given their lives closed in 1984.

Further reading: Morland, E.C. (1951) *Alice & the Stork, or the Rise in the Status of the Midwife as Exemplified in the Life of Alice Gregory, 1867–1944*. [Related images p267.]

BARCOMBE

DOROTHY CRISP (1906–?) writer and head of the British Housewives' League.

Born in Leeds, she became a public speaker and writer on nationalism, contributing to the *National Review* in the 1920s. By the mid-1940s she was famous as the 'belligerent and outspoken champion' of the right-wing British Housewives' League, whose meetings frequently descended into boos, catcalls and physical tussling for control of microphones. Hecklers once got so out of hand at the Royal Albert Hall that the police were called, though she was later cheered for threatening to throw Aneurin Bevan over Westminster Bridge if he brought in the National Health Act. The police were summoned twice to maintain order at an uproarious meeting in which she expelled several executive members amid shouted accusations of 'dictatorship'.

Among her books were *The Rebirth of Conservatism* (1931) and *Why We Lost Singapore* (1944), described as 'so unmitigatingly racist that it's painful to read'. She also wrote a novel, *Aprons of Fig Leaves* (1943) and founded a small publishing company, Dorothy Crisp & Co Ltd. She stood (unsuccessfully) as an independent candidate in the Acton by-election of 1943, the year an edition of the *Sunday Despatch* was banned in Eire because it contained her criticisms of de Valera's government.

She married John Becker in 1945, retaining her name. Moving to Kent she had a daughter, to whom Ida Copeland [257] was godmother. In 1947 she won substantial damages for libel against the *New Statesman* and the following year was halfway through a similar case against the *Daily Herald* and expecting her son, when her husband was shot dead in his office in Singapore (a special constable, he was helping the police to arrest a crazed man). Because he was off duty the government denied her a pension, but after a three-year struggle she finally got £500 a year. By then she was bankrupt, her publishing company had folded, and her libel case was abandoned (she tried unsuccessfully to revive it in 1959).

She lived in Sussex for about fifteen years. In 1958, 1965 and again in 1969 she was convicted of fraud for obtaining credit while an undischarged bankrupt and served three terms in Holloway. During this period, when not a guest of Her Majesty, she lived at Overs Farmhouse, Barcombe; Jigg's Cottage, Jevington, Polegate; somewhere in Hartfield and Woodland Drive, Hove, by 1969. She moved to Oxford by 1975, after which no more is known.

HON. SYLVIA FLETCHER-MOULTON CBE, JP (1902–1989) barrister and political organiser.

The daughter of the future Lord Moulton of Bank, Lord Justice of Appeal, she was born in London and spent her childhood between the USA, Naples, London, and Bank, Hampshire. On her father's death in 1921 she inherited £81,000 (the equivalent of about £3m today). She read history and law at Girton and was called to the Bar in 1929, working in the Chancery Division until 1937. In 1935 she purchased the Court House estate, Barcombe, which she owned until her death. From at least 1953 until the 1970s this was also the address of the vice-chair of the Conservative Party Organisation, Marjorie Maxse [187].

During WWII she was West Midlands regional administrator of the WVS. After the war she created a beautiful garden at Court House and a small business growing flowers for sale at Covent Garden market. In 1945 she joined the Lewes Conservative Association and was women's chairman for the Southeast Area, national women's chairman, then Southeast Area chairman.

She was a member of the Royal Commission on Penal Reform, the Department of Inquiry into the Sunday Observance Acts, the Council of Tribunals, the Council of Southampton University, and was chair of Westfield College, University of London, and Chailey Heritage Hospital [see Grace Kimmins, 197]. From 1947 until 1973 she was a magistrate in Lewes and was appointed CBE in 1961 for political and public service. She was also a governor of Girton, and her papers are held in its archives.

DAME MARJORIE MAXSE DBE (1891–1975) political organiser.

The daughter of the British vice-consul, she was born in Algiers and spent WWI as an auxiliary in a military hospital in France, was appointed MBE in 1918 and came to England. From 1921 she worked for the Conservative Party's Women's Unionist Organisation, serving as chief officer (1931–39), the highest position held by a woman in any party. She had no feminist agenda and was more interested in what women could do for the party than vice versa.

During WWII she was vice-chair of the WVS for Civil Defence, adding a CBE to her honours before leaving to become vice-chair of the Conservative Party Organisation. In 1948 she joined Evelyn Emmet [29] on a Conservative committee on women. Its charter — *A True Balance*, published in 1949 — denounced sex discrimination and proposed equal pay (in some circumstances) but was rejected at the party conference. In 1952 she was appointed DBE and in retirement performed voluntary work for the Diocese of Chichester.

Her home from 1953 to 1972 (perhaps longer) was Court House, Barcombe, the home also of Sylvia Fletcher-Moulton [187]. In the 1960s she also had a London home at 17 Onslow Square. She died at St George's Retreat, Ditchling.

Further reading: Maguire, G.E. (1998) *Conservative Women: A History of Women and the Conservative Party, 1874–1997.* [Related image p275.]

BATTLE

ELIZA ACTON (1799–1859) writer.

Her family came from Suffolk whence, soon after her birth in Battle, they returned. Miss Acton ran a school for girls near Ipswich, lived in France for a while, and composed and published poetry. By 1837 she was living at Tonbridge, Kent, where she wrote *Modern Cookery for Private Families* (1849), which was into its fourteenth edition by 1855 and was for fifty years the most popular cookery book in England, making hers a household name. She invented the format, since followed by every cookery writer, of listing the exact ingredients and the time needed separately from the recipe. In later life she moved to Hampstead. Elizabeth David [241] wrote the introduction to *The Best of Eliza Acton* (1968) and *Modern Cookery* was reprinted in 1993.

BINNIE HALE (1899–1984) singer and actress.

Beatrice Hale-Monro was born into a theatrical family in Liverpool. Defying her father she left her convent school to go on the stage in 1917 and by the 1920s the stick-thin platinum blonde was one of the highest paid musical comedy stars. She was very versatile: as a soprano, comedian and mimic she was equally at home in light opera, pantomime, musical theatre, film sets and recording studios. From the late 1940s until her retirement in 1959, she acted in straight roles. In 1924 she married actor Jack Raine, with whom she had a daughter, but they divorced in 1935. In retirement she lived in Battle and died in hospital in Hastings. Her rendition of her most famous song, *Spread a Little Happiness*, which she sang 529 times during the run of the 1929 musical *Mr Cinders*, can be heard on Youtube.com. [Related plate 41.]

JEAN STONE (1854–1908) historian.

Born in Brighton and educated in France and Germany, she converted to Roman Catholicism. She wrote magazine articles, entries for *The Catholic Encyclopaedia* and a number of books, of which her best known was *The History of Mary I, Queen of England* (1901). She lived in London and retired to Sussex, living firstly in Storrington then at 77 High Street, Battle, where she died. Her *Studies from Court and Cloister* was reprinted in 2006.

BEAUPORT

CAROLINE BURGES (d1863) inventor.

The daughter of Sir James Bland Burges Bt., the owner of Beauport estate, she was one of the 'Local Heroes' featured in the BBC2 programme of that name in May 2000, because she invented and patented a 'drawing, sketching and delineating machine', a model of which was demonstrated by Adam Hart-Davis.

Nothing else is known about her, though her family is well-documented. Her brother Charles changed his surname to Lamb in 1821, inherited the Beauport estate and was the grandfather of Mary Currie [189].

MARY CURRIE née Montgomerie Lamb; pseudonym Violet Fane; Lady Currie; Baroness Currie (1843–1905) poet, writer and translator.

The great-niece of Caroline Burges [188], she was born at Littlehampton nine years after her parents' elopement and left with her grandparents Sir Charles and Lady Mary Lamb at Beauport while her parents travelled. When her father died in 1856, she was sent to Scotland to be raised by Lady Eglinton (her grandfather's step-grandson's wife), who introduced her to London literary society. Against the wishes of her family she began an artistic career by etching the illustrations for a reprint of Tennyson's *Mariana* (1863). In 1864 she married Henry Singleton of Hazely Heath, Winchfield, Hampshire, and while raising four children wrote for periodicals under the pseudonyms 'V', 'Pamela', 'Kajin' or 'Vera' and published books as 'Violet Fane'. Her popular volume of love poems, *From Dawn to Noon* (1872), gained her considerable renown amongst London society, though a critic in *The Graphic* commented, 'we must own to disliking the idea of woman pouring out her soul to man'. Her collections of poetry were admired as much by titled ladies of leisure as by shop-girls and her lyric *For Ever and For Ever* was sung by all and sundry. *Denzil Place, A Story in Verse*, the tale of an adulterous wife who marries her lover after her husband's death, was criticised in the *Pall Mall Gazette* as 'ignoble, insidious' and 'hardly intended for decent people'.

A great beauty and a witty conversationalist, her circle of friends included Oscar Wilde, Robert Browning and Algernon Swinburne. Her blatant adultery caused tongues to wag and filled the columns of the gutter press; her many lovers included Wilfrid Scawen Blunt [see Lady Anne Blunt, 92]. Widowed in 1893, after an interval so short it was barely decent she married her long-term lover, Sir Philip Currie, a senior civil servant in the Foreign Office and from 1899 Baron Currie of Hawley. They lived in Turkey and Italy, where he was British ambassador, and she wrote articles for English magazines and two more volumes of poetry, using her real name. They retired to Hawley, Hamphire, in 1903. Lady Currie died at the Grand Hotel, Harrogate, and was buried at Mattingley Church, ten miles from Hawley. Her book *Denzil Place: A Story in Verse* (1875) was reprinted in 1996.

BEDDINGHAM

JASMINE ROSE-INNES FRSL née Gordon-Forbes (1915–1998) designer, painter, photographer and writer.

Born in Somerset and raised in Rhodesia, she came to England in 1938 and worked as an art editor and typographical designer for *Geographic Magazine*. From 1947 she lived in Africa, returning in 1962 with a husband and two children. She taught typography and photography and wrote a memoir of her childhood, *Writing in the Dust* (1968) which was awarded the Heinemann Prize and led to her being elected a Fellow of the Royal Society of Literature. The book can still be bought second-hand.

As a painter she held numerous exhibitions in Sussex and London and in later life took up etching. She lived in London, Surrey and, by 1972, at The Lay Cottage, Newhaven Road, Beddingham, where she died.

BEXHILL

MARY GRANT BRUCE née Bruce (1878–1958) children's writer.

Her literary career began in her native Australia, where she wrote short stories for newspapers and magazines. Between 1910 and 1942 she wrote thirty-seven books, including fourteen known as the 'Billabong' series, which became best sellers. Some were broadcast on British radio in the 1930s and one was made into a TV series in 1991. She moved to England in 1913 and after marrying George Bruce had two children and lived variously in Australia, Ireland and England, where she wrote much of her work and where she retired, as a widow, in 1949. She died in a nursing home in Bexhill and was cremated at Hastings.

CONSTANCE MARY COLTMAN BD née Todd (1889–1969) first female minister.

She was born in London into a Presbyterian family, but when that church would not entertain the idea of her studying for the ministry she read history at Somerville then obtained special permission to study theology at the all-male Mansfield College. She took her bachelor of divinity degree at London University and in 1917 became Britain's first female minister when she was ordained into the Congregational church at Mayfair. Her fiancé was ordained alongside her and they married the next day. While working together in Essex, Suffolk, Buckinghamshire and Oxford they raised three children. She held feminist views and in 1918 officiated at a service of thanksgiving for women's suffrage held at City Temple. She retired in 1949 and after her husband died in 1957 moved to 1 Maytree Gardens, Bexhill, where she ended her days.

FLORENCE HAYDON real name Hepworth (1838–1918) actress.

A barrister's daughter, she was born in Holborn and raised in Chelsea, London. Using the stage surname Haydon she specialised in the portrayal of 'comfortable, kindly, stupid' characters. In 1858 she appeared in pantomime at the Theatre Royal, Brighton, directed by Henry Nye Chart, husband of Ellen [126] and played her first West End role at another Theatre Royal, in London's Haymarket, in 1860.

In 1866 she married barrister John Waugh, had three daughters and was widowed in 1878 when her eldest child was nine. In 1887 she returned to the stage, appearing at St James's Theatre with Winifred Emery [235]. While never among the top-name stars (though she did once top the bill in 1912) she was a well-known, well-loved, stalwart supporting actress who devoted thirty-six years of her life to the theatrical profession. Her final role, at age seventy-seven, was in 1915, after which she retired to an apartment at 5 Linden Road, Bexhill, where she died three years later.

DAME WENDY HILLER DBE (1912–2003) actress.

Born in Cheshire, she spent six years as a boarder at Winceby House School for Girls, South Cliff, Bexhill. Here she turned her northern accent into an upper-class southern one, developed a passion to act and won a voice competition in Hastings in 1928. From 1930 her stage, film and TV career spanned nearly sixty years. Among her final roles were Princess Dragomiroff in *Murder on the Orient Express* (1974) and Lady Bracknell in *The Importance of Being Earnest* (1985).

She married Ronald Gow, had two children, and lived in Buckinghamshire until her death. Appointed OBE in 1971 and DBE in 1975, she was nominated for several awards, winning an Oscar in 1959. She joked that money was more important than honours, and when she died her estate was worth £1.9 million.

MONA INGLESBY real name Vredenburg (1918–2006) founder, director and leading ballerina of the International Ballet.

The daughter of a Dutch businessman, she was born in London. She started to train at the age of four and made her stage début within a year. From twelve she trained with Marie Rambert and performed in ballets. At twenty-one she made her choreographic début and at twenty-three founded the International Ballet in Glasgow. She was its first ballet master, its director and its prima ballerina. She married Major E.G. Derrington in 1946 and had a son. The company closed in 1953, when she retired. Near the end of her life she moved to a nursing home in Bexhill, where she died.

ETHEL IRVING real name Frances Irving (1869–1963) actress-manager.

At sixteen she was a chorus girl at the Gaiety Theatre and she played her first leading role in 1898. She became a star of London music halls and West End musical comedies, acquiring the nickname 'Birdie' along the way. Thousands of photo-postcards spread her fame far and wide, a waltz was named in her honour and in the 1890s she worked for six years in the

USA. For short periods she managed two London theatres: the Criterion in 1905 and the Globe in 1913. She took her own theatre company to Australia in 1911 and to South Africa in 1916 and 1926. From 1922 to 1933 she made a handful of films: her best known was *Call Me Mame,* in which she played the title role.

Married to actor Gilbert Porteous, she was widowed in 1928. From about 1934 she lived with her niece at Narkunda, Hartfield Road, Cooden, Bexhill, where she died. [Related plate 52.]

ADA NUGENT JACKSON née Ada Louise Martin; pseudonym Jim's Wife (1859–1935) balladeer.

The Gordon League provided 'happy evenings' at which middle-class do-gooders entertained the poor with songs, dances, lantern-lectures and theatricals and produced three series of books containing 'ballads for working men and women', purportedly written by 'Jim's Wife'. She was, in fact, the wife of Clement, a tutor at Oxford University.

Mrs Jackson's ballads were rhymed life-stories, morality tales and lay sermons, with a heavy emphasis on teetotalism. Series one, published in 1903, went into at least a dozen editions, prompting two more series. She also gave lectures to women on social and religious topics. In 1901 the Jacksons were renting 21 Oriental Place, Brighton, but later moved to Bexhill. Widowed in 1924, she died at her home, Green Harbour, 9 Warwick Road.

DAME KATHLEEN LONSDALE DBE, FRS née Yardley (1903–1971) crystallographer.

A postmaster's daughter, she was born in Ireland and raised in poverty in Essex, where she won a scholarship to a high school for girls; however, as the only pupil taking physics, chemistry and higher maths she had to attend classes at a boys' school. At sixteen she entered Bedford College and at nineteen graduated top of her year and joined a university research team. After marrying in 1927 she had three children and became a lecturer at Leeds University and the Royal Institution. She won the Davy Medal, was one of the first two women to be elected a Fellow

of the Royal Society, the first female president of the British Association for the Advancement of Science, vice-president of the Atomic Scientists' Association and vice-president of the International Union of Crystallography.

A Quaker and pacifist, she was president of the British section of the Women's International League for Peace and Freedom. In 1943 she served a month in Holloway for choosing not to pay the £2 fine imposed for refusing to register for war work. In prison she worked on the classification scheme for crystals which became the International Tables of Crystallography. She later served as a prison visitor. In 1946 she became the first female professor at University College, where she was head of the department of crystallography. Appointed DBE in 1956, she moved to 125a Dorset Road, Bexhill, in 1961 and lived there for nine years. She died in hospital in London. The Lonsdale Building of University College is named for her and the Institute of Physicists has proposed a blue plaque in her honour.

CLARA EVELYN MORDAN (1844–1915) suffragist and benefactor.

Born into considerable wealth in a Kensington mansion, she spurned marriage because of the legal disabilities of wives [8]. In 1866 she heard the MP John Stuart Mill's speech on women's suffrage and joined various women's rights societies, supported them financially and served on their committees for forty-four years. In 1910 she joined the WSPU, which she supported most generously. She gave a splendid silk banner for use at a mass rally in Hyde Park and presented a valuable amethyst, pearl and emerald necklace to Mrs Pankhurst [294]. A major benefactor of St Hugh's, she endowed a scholarship with £1,000, specifying that the recipients must be unconnected with animal experiments.

In later life she was described as 'a queer bird-like little lady who might have stepped out of one of Dickens' books' (*DNB*). Tuberculosis caused her to move with her close companion Mary Gray Allen to Bexhill, where she spent the rest of her life at Capel-ne-Ferne lodging house, 18 Marine Mansions. She campaigned for women's suffrage for half a century, dying just three years before women won the vote. She left £10,000 to St Hugh's, which funded the Mordan Library, named for her (now Mordan Hall). Miss Allen, who died in 1925, left £36,000 to St Hugh's. [Related images p269.]

JOAN TEMPLE (1887–1965) actress and dramatist.

Trained at RADA, she appeared on the West End stage in 1909 and toured the provinces for twenty years, except during WWI when she was engaged in war work at the British Naval Mission in Rome. After the war she turned increasingly to writing plays, which became very popular by the 1930s; the best known was *No Room at the Inn*, which was adapted into a film. In the 1950s she lived at Myrtle Cottage, Hollier's Hill, Bexhill, moving in the 1960s to Flat 1, Brassey Court, Cantelupe Road, where she died.

BLACKBOYS

ANNE FREMANTLE née Huth Jackson (1909–2002) writer.

The granddaughter of Sir Mountstuart Elphinstone Grant Duff, she was born in France but her family home until 1922 was Possingworth Manor, a 2,000-acre estate near Blackboys. For a lark she and her sister would dress as paupers, wait at the gate and beg arriving guests for pennies, then appear as themselves at dinner, to the bewilderment of the visitors. She studied modern languages at Cheltenham Ladies' College, at Oxford and at the LSE, then married the Hon. Christopher Fremantle.

In the 1930s she discovered a collection of letters between Captain Fremantle (an ancestor of her husband) and a Miss Wynne and edited them into her best-selling, three-volume work, *The Wynne Diaries*. She wrote over thirty other books, contributed articles and reviews to prestigious papers and magazines in London and New York, and once stood (unsuccessfully) for parliament. During WWII she broadcast on BBC radio, then lived for many years in the USA and China.

VIVIEN LEIGH née Vivian Hartley; Lady Olivier (1913–1967) actress.

Of English parentage, she was born in India and studied at RADA in London. She married barrister Herbert Leigh Holman and became a Shakespearean stage actress, using his middle name. Clare Sheridan [below] was a close friend and Miss Leigh stayed with her at Brede Place in 1934. Her film role as Scarlett O'Hara in *Gone with the Wind* in 1939 launched her into international stardom and during her high-profile acting career she won a clutch of major awards, including two Academy Awards (Oscars) and the French Knight's Cross of the Légion d' Honneur.

Having divorced in 1940 (her husband assuming custody of their seven-year-old daughter), she married heart-throb actor Laurence Olivier, with whom she had been living for three years, while he was married to the daughter of Eva Moore [146]. She was prone to phases of mania and depression brought on by stress, they both had affairs, and in 1960 he divorced her. He became Lord Olivier, married the actress (later, Dame) Joan Plowright and moved to 4 Royal Crescent, Brighton.

Miss Leigh bought Tickerage Mill, Tickerage Lane, Blackboys, in 1961, where she enjoyed creating the garden, watching the swans, moorhens and ducks and entertaining many famous guests including Winston Churchill, Rex Harrison and Noël Coward. She described the house as 'an absolute dream', adding, 'I am miserable at the thought of having to leave it'. She died in London where, for several evenings, the exterior lights of every West End theatre were dimmed for an hour. Her ashes were scattered over Tickerage pond and a blue plaque was placed on her Belgravia flat.

Further reading: Capua, M. (2003) *Vivien Leigh*. [Related plate 13.]

BREDE

CLARE SHERIDAN née Frewen (1885–1970) sculptor and writer.

A cousin of Florence Aylward [245], she was born in London. Her Frewen ancestors owned Brickwall, a mansion at Northiam, for three hundred years. Her parents bought the fourteenth-century manor house Brede Place when she was a child, and she was educated between Brede, Ireland, a Paris convent and a finishing school in Germany. She eschewed her position as a high society débutante, preferring the company of writers and artists.

In 1910 she married Wilf, who was the great-great-grandson of the playwright Richard Brinsley Sheridan. After her daughter died in 1914 she discovered a talent for sculpture while modelling an angel for her grave and was later formally trained. She lost her husband in WWI and raised two children alone, making a living as a sculptor, working in bronze, wood, alabaster and terracotta. A convert to Roman Catholicism, she created a large number of religious carvings which can still be seen in churches at home and abroad.

As a sculptor her sitters included her cousin Sir Winston Churchill, H.G. Wells, Lord Asquith, Marconi and Mahatma Gandhi. After travelling to the Soviet Union in 1920 to sculpt Lenin and Trotsky she was ostracised in Britain and went to live in the USA, befriending Charlie Chaplin, whom she modelled in bronze. She became European correspondent for an American newspaper, covering the Irish Civil War and the Greek–Turkish War, and wrote eighteen books, including novels, travel-books and an autobiography. An adventurous traveller, she went with her brother to Russia by motorcycle and sidecar, lived with her children in Turkey and on the edge of the Sahara in Algeria (where her son died) and stayed for six months on a reservation with the Blackfoot Indians.

For half a century Brede Place was the home to which she returned from her travels, where she spent the war years and where she entertained her friends, including Vivien Leigh [above]. In 1956 she moved to Belmont House, overlooking Hastings Old Town, where she set up a studio and converted the turret room into her private chapel. She enjoyed fundraising for the Stables Theatre and sculpted the head of the model fisherman who today stands at the helm of the Enterprise inside the Fishermen's Museum.

She died in a nursing home in Dorset and was buried beside St George's Church, Brede, which houses a memorial she carved in honour of her late son. Her collection of North American artefacts is exhibited in Hastings Museum & Art Gallery and there is a blue plaque on Belmont House.

Further reading: Leslie, A. (1976) *Cousin Clare.* Taylor, B. (2007) *Clare Sheridan.* [Related plate 50.]

BRIGHTLING

BARBARA LEIGH SMITH BODICHON (1827–1891) artist, and founder of the organised women's rights movement.

The daughter of Ben Smith MP and Annie Longden, a teenage milliner, she was born in Whatlington. Her parents moved to Pelham Place, Hastings, in 1833, by then with five children and still not married. Her mother died on the Isle of Wight a year later and the family moved to 9 Pelham Crescent, Hastings, their home for seventeen years (it bears a blue plaque). In 1846, Bessie Rayner Parkes's family moved into no. 6 and they soon became close friends and were firm allies for two decades [79]. Both had famous cousins who were pioneers for women in the medical professions: Miss Smith's was Florence Nightingale and Miss Parkes's was Dr Elizabeth Blackwell [224].

Barbara's father gave her a large private income, making her independent for life. In 1854 she began her feminist work by collecting all the laws specifically relating to women into a booklet which, although short, proved to be very influential. She attended Bedford College, studying politics and art, which became her parallel careers, neither of which was affected by her 1857 marriage to Frenchman Eugène Bodichon. She founded a progressive school in London, and gained renown both as a painter of landscapes and for her deep involvement in four major women's campaigns: for property rights, career opportunities, the vote, and higher education. She wrote on these subjects in newspapers, magazines, pamphlets and books and began Britain's first organised feminist action when, in 1856, she drafted a petition calling for married women to retain their property (an idea that was initially ridiculed, but led to changes in the law in 1870 and 1882). She founded the first feminist discussion group, co-founded an employment bureau for women and co-owned *The English Woman's Journal,* using it to spread news of the activities of the women's rights movement.

During the mid-1860s she inaugurated Britain's first petition for votes for women, thus co-founding the organised suffrage movement. Of all her activities, she is best known for co-founding Hitchin College with Emily Davies [39]. This was later moved to, and was renamed, Girton and eventually became part of Cambridge University.

Since her marriage she spent half of each year in Algiers and half in London. Her family owned considerable rural land around the Glottenham and Brightling areas, and in 1863 she built a house, to her own design and specification, at Scalands Gate, Brightling Road, covering the internal walls with her own paintings. Here she entertained the most eminent literary, artistic and political figures of the day, while an extension to the house served as a night-school for underprivileged farm labourers. The Bodichons had made a pioneering legal contract that their offspring would take the surname Bodichon-Leigh, but died childless. In her will, Madame Bodichon left £10,000 to Girton College, ensuring its survival. She had no children, but treated young Hertha Ayrton [63] like a daughter and left her a bequest. She died at Scalands and was buried at St Thomas à Becket Church, Brightling, where her epitaph is almost indecipherable. A fund currently exists to renovate her grave.

Further reading: Hirsch, P. (1998) *Barbara Leigh Smith Bodichon: Feminist, Artist and Rebel.* [Related images pp263, 291.]

FLORENCE ANNIE YELDHAM (1877–1945) historian of arithmetic.

A schoolmaster's daughter, she was born in the School House at Brightling. Her family moved in 1884 to London, where she studied at Bedford College, graduating with a BSc in pure mathematics, experimental physics and zoology.

She became a schoolteacher and in 1913 published the one-sheet *Percentage Tables* and later wrote a related article in the *Mathematical Gazette.* The inadequacy of mathematics textbooks prompted her to take a PhD in the history of science and she published two pioneering books: *The Story of Reckoning in the Middle Ages* (1926) and *The Teaching of Arithmetic through Four Hundred Years, 1535–1935* (1936). She retired to Surrey, where she died.

BURWASH

WINNIE TURNER (1903–1983) sculptor.

Educated at a convent, at the Central School of Arts and Crafts (where her father taught) and at the Royal Academy Schools, where she won a scholarship and many prizes, she specialised in sculpting bronzes of the female form, often using herself as a model. She became a Fellow of the Royal Society of British Sculptors, exhibited widely and over many decades, and taught at the Central School until she married sculptor Humphrey Paget.

In 1940 she moved to Broom Cottage, Westdown Lane, Burwash, where she lived for forty-three years. Her works can be seen at the Tate Gallery, the Ashmolean Museum in Oxford and Hove Museum and Art Gallery.

BUXTED

BRENDA PYE née Capron; first married name Landon (1907–2005) artist.

Her father was a barrister; her mother was distantly related to Anna Whistler [229]. She was born in Somerset and lived between London and Sussex for eighty-seven years. Educated at Eastbourne Ladies' College, she won a scholarship to study at Eastbourne College of Art, where she won a Gold Medal, a scholarship to Chelsea School of Art and a travelling scholarship to Paris. After a brief first marriage, during WWII she lived in Lewes, where she helped run the art gallery at Miller's [233]. After the war she was art mistress at Fairdene School, where she set up a pottery, opening another at Glynde Place, Glynde.

In 1961 she married Cecil Pye (nephew of the founder of Pye radio and television). He built a studio for her in the grounds of Britts, his Jacobean farmhouse in Buxted, and she entered her most productive period, painting portraits, flower studies, views of Ashdown Forest and landscapes in Scotland, Wales, France, Portugal, Italy and South Africa. Her work was exhibited at the Royal Society of Portrait Painters, the Paris Salon in France, the Royal Society of British Artists, the Royal Academy and the Association of Women Artists. A member of the Association of Sussex Artists, she also held one-woman exhibitions in Sussex. She died in London.

CATSFIELD

ANNIE, LADY BRASSEY née Allnutt; Baroness Brassey (1839–1887) traveller, collector and writer.

The daughter of a prosperous wine merchant, she was born in London. At twenty-one she married the wealthy Thomas Brassey; they had a son and four daughters, one of whom was Muriel, later Sackville [260]. Her husband became Lord of the Admiralty and MP for Hastings and built a mansion, Normanhurst Court, Catsfield, in 1870. Their London home was 24 Park Lane (later the Lady Brassey Museum) and their town house in Claremont is now Hastings Library. Her husband was knighted in 1881 and given a baronetcy in 1886.

As a member of Hastings' upper-class society, she performed charity work and was appointed a Dame Chevalière of the Order of St John of Jerusalem in 1881, but is chiefly famous for circumnavigating the globe on the family yacht, *Sunbeam*; for returning with hundreds of artefacts from different cultures, some of which are in Hastings Museum; and for her journals that record details of the family's epic sea voyages, which were published as books, including: *A Voyage on the Sunbeam, Our Home on the Ocean for Eleven Months* (1881); *In the Trades, the Tropics and the Roaring Forties* (1885) and *The Last Voyage* (posthumous, 1889). On the first voyage there were forty-three on board, including 'two dogs, three birds and a charming Persian

kitten ... The kitten soon disappeared, and it was feared she must have gone overboard down the hawse pipe'.

Baroness Brassey died (of malarial fever) on board the *Sunbeam* and was buried at sea. Her husband erected a beautiful memorial to her in Catsfield Church.

Further reading: Micklewright, N. (2003) *A Victorian Traveller in the Middle East: The Photography and Travel Writing of Annie, Lady Brassey*.

COUNTESS BRASSEY née the Hon. Sybil de Vere Capel (1858–1934) suffragist and philanthropist.

The granddaughter of the Earl of Essex and daughter of Viscount Malden, she was born in London. Aged thirty-one she married fifty-four-year-old Baron Brassey, widower of Annie [above] and father of Muriel, aged eighteen [262]. They lived between his luxurious homes in London and Catsfield and were the most celebrated figures in Hastings' society. As the MP's wife, in a grand ceremony in 1891 she opened the new pier at St Leonards. After having a daughter, they spent five years in Australia, where her husband was Governor of Victoria and she founded the Children's Protection Society in 1896. On their return to Hastings in 1900 the town laid on a festival and magnificent banquet dinner. The 1901 census shows the Brasseys at Normanhurst, looked after by seventeen resident servants.

Baroness Brassey was committed to women's emancipation. She joined the NUWSS and was president of the Hastings branch. In May 1911, the year her husband was raised to the peerage as Earl Brassey, he announced that he could no longer differ from his 'dear wife', converted to feminism and became a prominent figure in the local suffrage movement. He also supported the cause of women's higher education by donating the modern-day equivalent of a quarter of a million pounds to Girton. Their only child, Lady Helen de Vere Brassey, was also a feminist campaigner and in May 1916 she joined Marie Löhr [140] and Lady Diana Manners [29] outside Harrods, shaking collection tins to raise money for women's war service.

Countess Brassey's philanthropy centred on health: she was a patron of the Middlesex Hospital, London, and according to her obituary during WWI had 'her own hospital in Sussex' and also one in Egypt. During that war she gave over part of her London house to the YWCA, and served as chairman of the London units of the SWH.

The earl was hit by a taxi while crossing a road in London in 1918, died some days later and was buried at Catsfield. The Dowager Countess Brassey spent the rest of her life between Kensington and Surrey, visiting Hastings in 1927 to lay the foundation stone of the the orthopaedic block of the Royal East Sussex Hospital, of which she was president. She died in London and was buried at Golders Green.

D.K. BROSTER (1877–1950) novelist.

Liverpudlian Dorothy Kathleen Broster attended Cheltenham Ladies' College and earned two degrees in modern history at St Hilda's, but had to wait twenty-two years to receive her BA and MA. She worked at Oxford for thirteen years as secretary to a professor, published some poems and short stories and co-authored two novels with Gertrude Taylor. During WWI she worked for the Red Cross in Britain and France, nursing wounded Belgian and French soldiers. On 14th October 1920 she helped make history: she was among the first fifty women to be awarded degrees at Oxford university.

She wrote fifteen romantic, historical novels and some short stories with supernatural themes. Styling herself 'D.K. Broster', she was assumed to be a man, something she was happy to go along with. Described in *The Times* as 'an accomplished, lively and picturesque storyteller who provided graceful reading', her masterpiece was a trilogy set during the 1745 Jacobite rising, comprising *Flight of the Heron* (1925), *The Gleam in the North* (1927) and *The Dark Mile* (1929). *Flight of the Heron* was dramatised on radio in 1957 and adapted into a TV series in 1968.

In the 1930s she bought Broomhill, a four-bedroom, three-reception, detached country house in Farthings Lane, Catsfield, where she lived with her lifelong companion Gertrude Schlich. She died in Bexhill Hospital and was cremated at Charing, Kent. Her house was auctioned a few weeks later 'by order of her executrix' — presumably, Miss Schlich, who moved to a cottage in Surrey and published a posthumous collection of her friend's poetry.

For eighteen years Miss Schlich placed 'In Memoriam' notices 'to the dear memory of' Miss Broster in *The Times* on the anniversary of her death, dying four weeks before she was due to insert the 1969 notice. The works of D.K. Broster continue to be read more than half a century after her death; indeed her collection of short stories, *Couching at the Door*, was reprinted in 2007. [Related plate 12; image p281.]

CHAILEY

MARJORIE LOUISE DAVIES née Clements (1906–2007) artist.

Born in London, by the age of ten she had won several school prizes for her artwork and at seventeen enrolled in St Martin's School of Art. She began her career as a portraitist working in oils when she received a commission to paint the American ambassador's children. In her twenties was she engaged by the Link Studio to illustrate *My Magazine*. Her first colour illustrations appeared in *Blackie's Annual* in 1931 and three years later she was hired by the publishers Hutchinson to produce colour plates and line drawings for their new editions of Lewis Carroll's *Alice in Wonderland* and *Through the Looking Glass*. She worked in the design studios of wallpaper manufacturers Shand-Kydd, for whom she created a highly popular children's design depicting the Pied Piper of Hamelin. She continued with her career after marrying John Davies in 1935, but when WWII began he joined the army and the studio closed, so she volunteered for the WLA and was posted to various farms in Sussex.

In 1950 she contacted Enid Blyton to offer her services, and was told not to send samples 'unless they were first-class'. She sent some, and became for the next ten years one of the author's favourite artists, producing over a hundred drawings and pictures for her many children's magazines and books, most notably the 'Bedside', 'Holiday' and 'Flower' annuals as well as the *Enid Blyton* and *Sunny Stories* magazines and numerous book and magazine covers, however, she turned down a commission to illustrate the 'Famous Five' series.

During this time she and her husband lived in Hertfordshire until, in 1953, they bought a pretty, half-timbered, sixteenth-century cottage at Coppard's Bridge, Chailey, that was their home for half a century. She ceased illustrating during the 1960s and created a classic cottage garden. Widowed in 1967, within a few years she had become an award-winning landscape painter. During her eighties her watercolours were exhibited annually by the Society of Women Artists. A decade later she designed Chailey's village sign and sketched local buildings for the cover of the monthly parish magazine. She retired on her 101st birthday and lived alone until a few weeks before her death, at Nightingale's Nursing Home, 38 Western Road, Newick.

DAME GRACE KIMMINS DBE née Hannam (1870–1954) disability reformer.

The daughter of a tailor-draper, she was born at Lewes and as a Wesleyan sister in London she ran a group for disabled people, known as 'the Guild of the Brave, Poor Things', that she developed into a national network. In 1896 she established a Guild of Play in Rotherhithe, London, and wrote her one novel, *Polly of Parker's Rents*, about life in the slums. She later wrote a few books about national and peasant dances and songs; all are now out of print. She married LCC educational psychologist Charles Kimmins and had a son.

In those days cripples, as they were called, were treated as useless but Mrs Kimmins wanted to teach them pride and self-sufficiency. Despite having no educational qualifications or medical knowledge, in 1903 she and Alice Rennie rented a former workhouse at North Common, Chailey and, calling it the Heritage Craft Schools for Crippled Boys and Girls, installed seven boys from the London slums. A disused industrial school was taken over and more disabled children arrived from London. Eventually the LCC subsidised Chailey Heritage from its rates. She and the children slept outside all year round, being covered by tarpaulin in bad weather. Each child made a wooden ladder, symbolising the rungs of life he or she could ascend, and some were buried with their ladders. Chailey was dubbed 'the public school of crippledom': royalty and aristocracy were escorted through its workshops; Bishops and archdeacons gave sermons in its chapel. The children sang and formed a guard of honour for any well-heeled visitor, who always left a sizeable donation. Casualties of WWI were rehabilitated at Chailey, increasing its fame. The Duke of Norfolk was president, the Queen Mother and Princess Louise became patrons and Lady Denman [32] gave a series of benefit concerts at her London residence.

The site expanded many times and an old windmill was restored, its sails ceremonially restarted by Princess Alice. In 1928 an annexe was opened at Tidemills, Bishopstone [see Muriel Powell, 68], paid for by Colonel and Mrs Warren of Horsham, and St Margaret's Chapel was opened at the girl's section at Chailey Clump. The main chapel was paid for by Mrs Rose of Newick and dedicated by the Bishop of London. It was said that the chapel clock tower had only three faces; that facing North Chailey was blank, because Dame Grace refused to 'give the time of day' to villagers, who objected to having such a school in their midst.

After WWII Chailey was taken under the wing of the NHS. Mrs Kimmins described herself as 'heartbroken to lose it'. For her marvellous achievements she was appointed Dame (later, Lady) of Grace of the Order of St John of Jerusalem in 1926, CBE in 1927 and DBE in 1950. She lived at Chailey Heritage the rest of her life and died at the King Edward VII Memorial Hospital, Haywards Heath. There is a Grace Kimmins Gardens in Southwark and a Grace Kimmins House at Chailey Heritage School.

Further reading: Kimmins, G.T. (1948) *Heritage Craft School and Hospital*.

CHELWOOD GATE

MARGARET VYNER (1914–1992) actress and playwright.

Leaving her native Australia for Paris, she became a chorus girl then a model. By 1935 she was so famous that Cole Porter wrote a new line for his song *You're the Top*: 'You're the top, you're an ocean liner; You're the top, You're Margaret Vyner'.

She married Bexhill-born heart-throb actor Hugh Williams. In the 1950s and early 1960s they were one of the most fashionable double-acts on the West End stage. Together they wrote some half-dozen light comedies, including *Plaintiff in a Pretty Hat* (1956), *The Grass is Greener* (1958), the book for the musical *Charlie Girl* (1965) and *Let's All Go Down the Strand* (1967). From 1954 until 1961 they lived at Gosses, on Harold MacMillan's Birch Grove Estate, Chelwood Gate. They moved to Portugal for tax reasons, where she opened a boutique, was widowed, married again, returned to England and died in Reading. She had three children. Michael is an actor, Hugo a poet, and Sussex-born Polly (1950–2004) was a model and actress who was married to actor Nigel Havers.

CHIDDINGLY

DAME ANGELA OLIVIA PERY CH, GBE, DL née Trotter; Countess of Limerick (1897–1981) head of the International Red Cross.

The daughter of a diplomat, she was born in Kent and grew up in Romania, where the future King Carol (then a child) once bit her on the arm, leaving her with a permanent scar. She falsified her age to serve as a VAD nurse in France during WWI, and after studying social science at the LSE joined the Red Cross. In 1926 she married Major the Hon. Edmund Colquhoun Pery (later, 5ᵗʰ Earl of Limerick). They honeymooned at Stanmer Park near Brighton and in 1934 bought Chiddinglyly Place, where they raised three children and ran a dairy farm.

Early in her marriage she served as a poor law guardian, borough councillor and chair of the public health committee in Kensington (where they had a second home), becoming involved with the LCC, a women's health centre and a society for promoting female employment. She also championed the highly controversial family planning movement, for which she was once pelted with stones by an angry mob of Glaswegians and nicknamed 'the Countess of Contraception'.

Serving the Red Cross for sixty years, she was head of the London branch during the Blitz, then vice-president of the British Red Cross in charge of international operations. She travelled to conferences worldwide and carried out many field inspections: between 1945 and 1958, for example, she visited sixteen countries, including Iraq, Russia, China and several in central Africa, where she met tribesmen and visited native reserves and mountain villages in a white jeep. She was appointed chairman of the International Red Cross in 1965, received over twenty medals and awards, including the highest distinction of the IRC, the Henri Dunant Medal, in 1975. She was appointed GBE and Companion of Honour for a lifetime of public service.

Her fifty-one years of happy marriage to Lord Limerick, also a GBE and CH, was ended in 1967 by his suicide (he shot himself). Retiring in 1973 she served as a deputy lieutenant for West Sussex from 1977. Like her husband, she died at Chiddingly Place and was cremated after a service at St Margaret's Church, West Hoathly. Her son Patrick (who had inherited the earldom and the estate) married Sylvia Lush, who became chairman of the British Red Cross.

Further reading: Lindsay, D. (1992) *A Form of Gratitude: The Life of Angela Limerick.*

COLEMAN'S HATCH

OLIVE DEHN (1914–2007) writer.

Of German extraction, she was born in Lancashire and went to boarding school at Seaford. As a teenager, while staying with relatives in Germany she was arrested and deported for satirising the Nazis. She married David Markham in 1937 and in the 1940s bought Lear Cottage, between Coleman's Hatch and Chuck Hatch, a five-acre smallholding without electricity or mains water. Here she grew organic vegetables and kept ducks, hens, geese, prize-winning pigs and a cow.

She and her husband became involved in the peace movement, and during the Campaign Against the Abuse of Psychiatry they were arrested, stripped, searched and detained at Moscow Airport. Among their house-guests were a Russian dissident and the famous writer Bertrand Russell. She wrote stories for BBC radio's *Childrens' Hour* and won a radio drama competition with *There Must I Be*, an account of her childhood. Her poems appeared in numerous magazines and she produced eleven novels and two volumes of poetry. Her final book, *Out of My Mind: Poems 1929–1995* (2006) was published when she was ninety-one.

Her brother Paul wrote the screenplay for *Goldfinger*. Of her four daughters, Kika and Petra are actresses, Jehane is a poet and Sonia an artist: she illustrated her mother's book *The Pike Dream* (1958). Her husband died at Lear Cottage in 1983; she died at Wych Cross.

CROWBOROUGH

FLORENCE CARLYLE (1864–1923) figure and portrait painter.

A descendant of philosopher Thomas Carlyle, she was born in Canada. Her mother encouraged her artistic talents by engaging a private tutor from New York, and in 1890 she went (without a chaperone) to Paris, where she studied, and first exhibited in 1893. Her work was later shown at the Royal Academy in London and at many galleries on both sides of the Atlantic.

Returning to Canada in 1896, she was elected a member of the Ontario Society of Artists and was one of the first women elected an Associate of the Royal Canadian Academy. By 1899 she had studios in New York and London, and a steady demand for her work. Art historian Joan Murray said, 'Her often large and imposing narrative treatments are viewed as part of the missing

history of the representation of women created by a woman who loved women.'

In 1913 she and her life companion Julie Hastings bought The Cottage at Sweethaws, Crowborough, either renaming it or moving to Yew Tree Cottage, where some of her best work was produced. She remained for twenty years and died there. Recognised as one of the outstanding portrait and genre painters of her generation, her works can be found in a number of collections in Canada and London.

VALERIE FINNIS Lady Scott (1924–2006) horticulturalist and flower photographer.

The daughter of Constance Finnis, who created the Iceland poppies that bear her name, she was born in Crowborough and moved to Kent as a child. She studied at Waterperry Horticultural School for Women, Oxfordshire, and taught there for twenty-eight years. She married Sir David Scott and their home in Kettering became a place of pilgrimage for gardeners. A specialist in alpines, a lecturer and broadcaster, she was among the first women to be a botanical photographer. In 1975 she was awarded the Victoria Medal of Honour by the Royal Horticultural Society, and several plants were named for her. In 1990 she founded the Merlin Trust to help young horticulturalists.

MARY GORDON (1861–1941) physician and pioneer prison inspector.

Born in Lancashire, she defied her parents (who believed, as many did, that studying anatomy degraded women) to study medicine at the LSMW and at medical schools in Glasgow and Edinburgh, graduating LRCP, LRCS, LFP&S. In 1891 she opened a London practice and seventeen years later, still with the disapproval of her family, became the first woman to be appointed an inspector of Prisons and State Inebriate Reformatories, responsible for about forty jails, an alcoholics' home and a borstal.

At the time many suffragettes were being imprisoned, and when police raided the WSPU offices [see Rachel Barrett, 47] they discovered that Dr Gordon had been secretly corresponding with one of its leaders, Emmeline Pethick-Lawrence, a close friend of Mary Neal [63]. The Home Office demanded that she publicly dissociate herself from the WSPU; her refusal rendered her persona non grata until her retirement. In 1914 she took a sabbatical in order to serve with the SWH in Macedonia and Serbia for the duration of the war.

She retired in 1921 and boarded at the Crest Hotel in Crowborough. Soon afterwards she bought a house in that town called Hawk Wood, which was to be her home for the rest of her life. An advert in *The Times* in 1933 indicates the presence of another woman: she sought a married couple to work as cook-general and house parlour-man to 'two ladies'. Three years later she sought a 'superior working housekeeper' for one lady.

She wrote one novel, *A Jury of the Virtuous* (1907) and *Penal Discipline* (1922) a book about female prisoners. When she was seventy-five Leonard and Virginia Woolf [243] published her book *The Chase of the Wild Goose: The Story of Lady Eleanor Butler and Miss Sarah Ponsonby, Known as the Ladies of Llangollen*, a fictionalised biography of two aristocratic Irish women who fell in love, eloped, and lived together for fifty years, and with whom Dr Gordon claimed to have psychic contact. The income from the book helped to pay for a memorial to the ladies that Dr Gordon had placed in the church of St Collen in Llangollen, Wales, in 1937. The marble relief sculpture was executed by Warnham-born Violet Labouchère (Mrs Matthews) and, intriguingly, the faces of the ladies of Llangollen were in fact those of herself and Mary Gordon. [Related image p282.]

WILLA MUIR OBE née Anderson; pseudonym Agnes Neill Scott (1890–1970) translator and writer.

A Scotswoman and classics graduate of St Andrew's University, between 1930 and 1962 she translated, in collaboration with her husband, more than forty novels, including the works of Franz Kafka. She also wrote two novels (*Imagined Corners* and *Mrs Ritchie*), an autobiography (*Belonging: A Memoir*) and a study of

poetry (*Living with Ballads*). She narrated her short stories on BBC radio and a documentary about her life was broadcast on Radio Four in 1985. She lived in many places across Europe, including three years at Crowborough from March 1929.

DAME JEAN DOYLE DBE, AE, WRAF, ADC Lady Bromet (1912–1997) director of the WRAF.

The only daughter of the famous writer Sir Arthur Conan Doyle, she was born and raised at Windlesham, Crowborough. When she was a child her father criticised the suffragettes and in response they poured acid into the Royal Mail pillar box outside their house with the intention of damaging his correspondence. As a child Jean Doyle was a tomboy who equalled males at cricket and boxing. She attended Granville School, Eastbourne, then spent several years caring for her widowed mother. Aged twenty-six she joined No. 46 (County of Sussex) RAF company, attached to the ATS as an aircraftwoman and served throughout WWII with the WAAF, becoming air commandant in 1948, the year she was appointed OBE. Concerned at the loss of her staff upon marriage, she introduced measures to make it possible for wives to remain in WRAF service. During the 1950s she held various senior posts in the WRAF, becoming director in 1963. That year she was appointed DBE and became aide-de-camp to Queen Elizabeth. For serving ten years in the auxiliary air force she was given the Air Efficiency Award.

When Windlesham was sold in 1955 (it is now a residential care home) she arranged for her parents' remains to be re-interred at Minstead, Hampshire. She fought (and won) a legal battle with publishers over the copyright of her father's works, of which she became executor. At fifty-three she married seventy-four-year-old Sir Geoffrey Bromet, retaining her name. She retired the following year, 1966, and worked in an honorary capacity for various service charities. She died a millionairess in London, leaving some of her father's rare manuscripts to be auctioned at Christie's in aid of RAF groups and other forces' charities. [Related image p266.]

DAME LOUISA WILKINSON DBE, RRC née Lumsden (1889–1968) head of QAIMNS and QARANC.

Born in Sunderland, she had just completed her nurse's training when WWI began and she joined QAIMNS, serving in England and Malta. In 1917 she married Robert Wilkinson, who died on active service six months later. In 1926 she was one of the pioneer nurses posted to India, returning during WWII to be principal matron at the War Office, setting up the army's nursing services, then returned to India as chief principal matron, with the colossal task of organising all the Indian military nursing services and auxiliary nursing centres. She founded a nurses' training scheme for Indian women, and established a school of nursing administration.

She served QAIMNS as its matron-in-chief and controller-commandant 1944–50. After retirement she was president of the Royal College of Nursing and helped to establish QARANC, becoming its first controller-commandant. Among her many honours were a BEM and ARRC in 1919; the RRC, First-Class, in 1941; an OBE in 1943 and CBE in 1946, Commander of the Order of St John of Jerusalem in 1947 and a military DBE in 1948.

For fourteen years from 1954 she lived at Oakhurst, Innhams Wood, Crowborough. She died en route to the War Memorial Hospital and, after a funeral at All Saints' Church and cremation, her remains were interred in the town's garden of remembrance in Herne Road.

ENID WILSON (1910–1996) golfer and writer.

As a child in Derbyshire she was mad about golf, and her expulsion from Harrogate Ladies' College (for being 'a damned nuisance') left her free to play it all day. At fourteen she reached the semi-final in the girls' championship and won it the following year. At eighteen she won the ladies' championship, became one of only three women ever to win it three times in succession and later played for England and in the Curtis Cup. At twenty-four she retired from competitive

play, designed a range of equipment, wrote a column for *Golf Illustrated* and became golf correspondent on the *Daily Telegraph*. During WWII she served in the WAAF.

In the 1960s she wrote *A Gallery of Women Golfers* (modestly omitting herself) and *Golf for Women*. She retired in the 1970s, playing golf as a hobby into her eighties and becoming vice-president of the Ladies' Golf Union in 1978. She died at her home, Redbridge Oast, Redbridge Lane, Crowborough.

DANEHILL

DAME MARGERY CORBETT ASHBY DBE, LLD née Corbett (1882–1981) social justice campaigner.

The daughter of Marie Corbett [202] she was born in London and raised at Danehill. As teenagers she and her sister Cicely [203] co-founded the Younger Suffragists, while studying at Newnham she joined the NUWSS and by nineteen she was secretary of the Constitutional Suffrage Movement. After training as a teacher she turned to politics, giving persuasive speeches on behalf of her father, who became MP for East Grinstead in 1906. When the Liberal Party failed to support women's suffrage she resigned from its Women's Federation and co-founded the Liberal Suffrage Group. She became secretary of the NUWSS, edited its journal and served on its national committee. In 1910 she married a barrister, Arthur Ashby, and had a son during WWI while he was in the trenches. She worked in hospitals and on the land, and ran a children's canteen at Woodgate.

After both the war and the vote were won in 1918, she stood for parliament, the first of her seven unsuccessful attempts to get elected. The War Office recruited her to work with Mary Allen [223] in establishing female police in Germany. She attended the 1919 Versailles Peace Conference as a member of the International Alliance of Women and was British delegate to the Geneva Disarmament Conference in 1932, but resigned three years later in protest at government policies. She was a member of the WFL and the National Union of

Societies for Equal Citizenship, president of the International Woman Suffrage Alliance 1923–1946 and editor of the *International Women's News* 1952–1961. She co-founded the Townswomen's Guild and was its president until 1935. Her other areas of concern included Indian child-brides, female doctors, family allowances and peeresses' right to be admitted to the House of Lords. She served on countless committees, wrote hundreds of articles, appeared on TV and radio debates and lectured in thirty-seven countries. She received honorary LLDs from Mount Holyoke College, USA, and the University of St Andrew's, and was appointed DBE in 1967.

Her active involvement with the feminist cause spanned eight decades, from 1904 until at least 1980 when, at the age of ninety-eight, she participated in a Women's Day of Action in London, at which she was acknowledged as the (unofficial) leader of the British liberal-feminist movement. She had moved to Horsted Keynes in 1936 and ended her days there at her house, Wickens. Her memorial service was held at Westminster Abbey. The TG inaugurated a Dame Margery Corbett-Ashby Lecture series, the first of which was given by the Prime Minister, Margaret Thatcher, in 1982.

Further reading: Ashby, M. (1997) *Memoirs*. [Related images pp16, 277.]

MARIE CORBETT née Gray (1860–1932) social activist.

Born in Kent to parents who were Liberal reformists, by 1871 her family was living at 102 King's Road, Brighton. At twenty-two she married radical barrister Charles Corbett, who two years later inherited the 840-acre Woodgate estate, Danehill, with its mansion house, several farms and two dozen cottages. The estate was to be their home for the rest of their lives.

Within forty-two months of marriage they had three children [see Margery, above and Cicely, below], whom they educated at home in classics, history, mathematics, scripture and piano, while a local woman was engaged to teach them French and German. Margery Corbett recalled: 'My parents were Liberals ... at

that period as much hated and distrusted by the gentry as Communists are today, and regarded as traitors to their class.' Nevertheless, they were deeply involved in the community and, after the passage of the Municipal Franchise Act, Mrs Corbett joined the Uckfield Board of Guardians and later became the first woman to serve on Uckfield District Council. Mr Corbett was a JP and, from 1906, the Liberal member for East Grinstead, a seat later held by Lady Emmet [29].

Marie Corbett was an ardent feminist who shocked her upper-class neighbours and acquaintances by riding a bicycle and worse, by wearing *breeches*. A close friend of Mrs Martindale [141], she co-founded the Liberal Women's Suffrage Society, but when the Liberal government refused to give women the vote she switched allegiance to the NUWSS. In 1911 she and Muriel Sackville [260] founded the East Grinstead Suffrage Society, and with Mrs Corbett's daughters gave weekly public speeches in the High Street, where they found little support. Eighty per cent of local women didn't care about getting the vote and anti-suffragist men were vocal and occasionally rowdy [277]. Mr Corbett was a firm supporter of women's rights; he co-founded a local branch of the Men's League for Women's Suffrage in 1913 and was treasurer of the New Sussex Hospital for Women, a position later held by his son.

After WWI Marie Corbett became a poor law guardian. Visiting Uckfield Workhouse she was shocked to see orphaned and abandoned children sharing wards with the elderly and mentally afflicted. She placed them instead with local families, then did the same at Eastbourne Workhouse and at one in London. She is assumed to have died at Woodgate, which was sold in 1937 and is now Cumnor House Preparatory School.

Further reading: Ashby, M. (1997) *Memoirs*. [Related plate 61; image p279.]

CICELY CORBETT FISHER (1885–1959) social activist.

The daughter of Marie Corbett [above] and sister of Margery [201], she was born and raised at Woodgate, Danehill. She studied at Somerville then worked with Clementina Black [123] on the Women's Industrial

Council. An activist in the Anti-Sweating League, in the years leading up to WWI she organised conferences and demonstrations and gave many public speeches. After WWI she was active in the Labour Party and the Women's International League.

In 1913 she married radical journalist Chalmers Fisher, both taking the surname Corbett Fisher. They shared a love of motor-racing and owned a supercharged M.G. that Mrs Fisher raced at Brooklands. She died at Danehill. [Related image p279.]

URSULA POWYS-LYBBE (1910–1997) photographic interpreter and portraitist.

Born in Berkshire, she was educated at Sacred Heart School, Brighton. During WWI she joined the WAAF and was engaged in photographic interpretation at Mednemham in Buckinghamshire, identifying ninety-six (almost all) of the enemy's V-1 flying-bomb launching sites, an experience she wrote about in her book *The Eye of Intelligence* (1983).

In the 1930s she was a photographic portraitist for London's high society. She married Australian Druce Buckland in 1946 and worked in the outback, returning to England in the 1950s, where she continued her photographic career. She died at St Raphael's Nursing Home, Danehill.

ANTONIA WHITE real name Eirene Botting (1899–1980) novelist.

The daughter of a governess and a schoolmaster, she was born in London, and from the age of sixteen worked successively as a governess, clerk, actress and advertising copywriter. She wrote short stories for newspapers and several novels, including *Frost in May* (1933) and *Beyond the Glass* (1954), which both went into many editions, most recently in 2006. Married three times before she was thirty, she spent nine months in Bethlem psychiatric asylum, where she suffered hallucinations and was forcibly fed, and had a lesbian affair with novelist Djuna Barnes. She died at St Raphael's Nursing Home, Danehill, a year before her novels were dramatised on BBC TV, and was buried in the Catholic cemetery at West Grinstead, close to where her father's family had lived for generations.

DITCHLING

VICTORIA DRUMMOND MBE (1894–1980) marine engineer.

A god-daughter of Queen Victoria, she was born into high society at Megginch Castle, Perthshire, and was destined for a life of upper-class idleness and luxury. However, she was fascinated by machinery and amused everyone by saying she wanted to be a ship's engineer, an absurd ambition for a refined young lady débutante. Her chance came during the wartime labour shortage: in 1916 she managed to persuade a local garage to take her on trial mending lorries, and subsequently won an apprenticeship. After studying with an engineering tutor she landed a job at Dundee's Caledon Shipworks, the sole woman among 3,000 men.

In 1920 she passed her apprenticeship exams top of her group and after two years of unsuccessfully applying for jobs was engaged as tenth engineer by the prestigious Blue Funnel Line. The first woman ever to wear its gilt-buttoned, epauletted uniform, she set off on the first of her forty-nine voyages below decks in a greasy, noisy, steam-filled engine room. Prejudice hampered her entire career. Examiners were deeply reluctant to give a woman responsibility, but by sheer persistence she eventually rose to fifth engineer; however, they stubbornly failed her for chief engineer thirty-seven times, despite her qualifications and aptitude, simply because they could not allow a woman in that important role. During the 1930s she could get no work and during WWII was told the sea was 'too dangerous' for women, so she dodged bombs on dry land instead as an ARP warden in London.

Eventually, a foreign ship engaged her. When the SS Bonita was attacked by enemy aircraft, in the chaos, with debris flying across the engine room, she sent her stokers to safety and, although injured, coaxed the engine to record speed and saved the ship and its crew from bombing and machine-gun fire. Her next ship was also attacked, killing one crew member and injuring two. She was appointed MBE in 1941 and was the first woman awarded the Lloyd's War Medal for Bravery at Sea.

She was a member of the Institute of Marine Engineers, who named the Victoria Drummond Room for her. During the war a restaurant in Lambeth was named for her, as was the Victoria Drummond Award for outstanding service in the Merchant Marine. When she was sixty-five the authorities finally relented and passed her as chief engineer, in which capacity she embarked upon her final trip, to Hong Kong, three years later. In 1974 she moved to St George's Retreat, Ditchling Common, where she spent the final six years of her life. Her unfinished memoirs were turned into a book by her niece, Jean Cherry Drummond (Baroness Strange).

Further reading: Drummond, C. (1994) *The Remarkable Life of Victoria Drummond, Marine Engineer.* [Related image p275.]

CORA GOFFIN Lady Littler (1902–2004) musical comedy actress.

Born in London, at the age of ten she appeared at the London Palladium as a dancer with the Russian ballet then she toured and played the West End in various breeches roles, notably Little Lord Fauntleroy. In her twenties she appeared in films, musical comedies and pantomimes, and spent her thirties playing a seemingly endless succession of principal boys. (Noted for her exuberant thigh-slapping, she insured her legs for £20,000.) Hers was a household name and her image adorned chocolate boxes, cigarette cards and magazine covers. After she appeared on radio she was so inundated with fan mail that the BBC hired a secretary especially to deal with it. Her income supported her mother, grandmother and three maiden aunts, and enabled her to commission theatrical costumes from leading designers.

Aged thirty-five she married theatrical impresario (later, Sir) Emile Littler, brother of Blanche [164] and ceased work in 1940. In 1946 they purchased the Downmere estate at Poynings, where her name lives on in Cora's Walk. Unable to have children of her own, she adopted two baby girls, Judy and Merrilee. They lived for a while at King's Gardens, Hove, and about 1972 moved to Lime Dykes, Lewes Road, Ditchling, where she died three decades later, having outlived Sir Emile by nineteen years. [Related plate 25.]

CHRISTIANA, LADY HERRINGHAM née Powell (1852–1929) artist and benefactor.

One of nine children, she was born into wealth in Kent, was raised in Surrey and in 1880 married Sir Wilmot Herringham. Her father gave her £43,000 (worth about a quarter of a million today) and she became well known as a woman learned in the arts after she travelled to India and copied the Buddhistic paintings on the walls of the Ajanta Caves and translated the *Book of the Art of Cennino Cennini.* She was a painter in watercolours and also in tempera, the use of which she is credited with reviving, and art correspondent for *Burlington Magazine.* In 1903 she gave £200 to found the National Art Collections Fund (later called the Art Fund) which over a century helped museums acquire 850,000 works of art.

She ended her days at St George's Retreat, Ditchling. Her belief in equal rights for women led to her husband's bequeathing their daughter £45,000, much of which she used in the service of art and literature.

Further reading: Lago, M. (1995) *Christiana Herringham and the Edwardian Art Scene.* [Related image p275.]

ETHEL MAIRET née Partridge (1872–1952) hand-weaving revivalist and author.

A Devonshire chemist's daughter, she studied piano at the RAM then worked as a governess. Her 1902 marriage to Ananda Coomaraswamy led her to visit Ceylon, where she admired the local embroidery and other textiles, arts and crafts. The couple wrote a book on the subject and went to India, again collecting examples of local crafts. She divorced and, alone in her isolated Devon bungalow, experimented with hand-weaving and dyeing.

After marrying Philippe Mairet she carried on her textile work at Shottery, near Stratford-upon-Avon, wrote *A Book on Vegetable Dyes* (1916) and displayed her work at London craft exhibitions. In 1916 they visited the Guild of St Joseph and St Dominica, a community of artists at Ditchling Common, and decided to move there, having a house (Gospels) built on Beacon Road to accommodate her weaving workshop and dye house. Using hand-spun British wools and imported cotton and silk yarns she produced furnishings, rugs, blankets, scarves and neckties in plain woven cloths, some coloured with vegetable dyes. She exhibited her work throughout the country, and sales were brisk. With Philippe she ran the New Handworkers' Gallery in London, which closed in 1931. After they separated she co-founded the Red Rose Guild of Craftsmen, researched handweaving across Europe and published *Handweaving Today, Traditions and Changes* in 1939, the year she became the first woman to win the coveted Royal Society of Arts RDI (Royal Designer for Industry) award.

During her thirty-two years at Gospels she trained over 130 handweavers from all over the world and inspired thousands more. She was active to the very end, carrying on her weaving shop single-handedly and with much energy and zest for life. In the 1950s the Mairet Hand Loom Weaving shop opened at 68a East Street, Brighton. She died at home and was buried at Dyke Road Cemetery, Brighton.

Further reading: Coatts, M. (1995) *A Weaver's Life: Ethel Mairet.* [Related image p264.]

ESTHER HALLAM MEYNELL née Moorhouse (1878–1955) novelist and biographer.

Her family came to Sussex from her birthplace, Leeds, when she was ten. Their first home was 6 Highcroft Villas, Brighton, then they moved to Redholm, London Road, Patcham, by 1901, remaining there until her marriage. She was educated at home and became fascinated with naval history; her first book was *Nelson's Lady Hamilton* (1906). In 1909 she married master printer and typographer Gerard Meynell, cousin of Viola [53]. They had two daughters and enjoyed homes in London and Sussex. According to one source they lived near Pulborough, possibly Humphrey's Homestead, Greatham, country estate of his Meynell cousins.

She wrote a book a year, encompassing fiction and biography, including the life of Anna Magdalena Bach. In the 1930s she moved to Ditchling, where she lived in, built or converted various properties, including Broadmeadows, Beacon Rd; Laine End, North End; Lime Dykes,

Lewes Road [see Cora Goffin, 204] and Conds Cottage, High Street, which she wrote about in *Cottage Tale* (1946). In 1947 she converted Beulah Baptist Chapel into a house, 9 East End Lane. She produced several other related books including *Sussex Cottage* (1936), *Building a Cottage* (1937), *Country Ways* (1942) and more books on Sussex. Widowed in 1942, she died at Conds Cottage. [Related image p281.]

EASTBOURNE

JEAN ANDERSON (1907–2001) TV actress.

Born in Eastbourne, which she left as a child, her most famous roles were as Mary Hammond in *The Brothers* and Joss Holbrook in *Tenko* [see Margot Turner, 170]. She worked into her nineties, appearing in a stage production of *Endgame* in 2000.

MABEL LUCIE ATTWELL (1879–1964) illustrator.

The daughter of an East End butcher, her career began in her mid-twenties when she created colour illustrations for ten books. She married painter and illustrator Harold Earnshaw and began designing postcards and greeting cards using her three children as models for her idealised, red-cheeked, chubby-legged toddlers. These formulaic illustrations of 'kiddiwinks' brought huge commercial success: they appeared on thousands of artefacts all over the world, including fifty books, a thousand designs for postcards, advertisements, posters, biscuit tins, figurines, trinket boxes, handkerchiefs, calendars, china, wall plaques and dolls. The nurseries of the Princesses Elizabeth and Margaret contained twenty-four complete place settings of Mabel Lucie Attwell china, used later by Prince Charles. In the 1930s she was commissioned to illustrate Princess Margaret's personal Christmas card. At the other end of the socio-economic scale, even the humblest household could afford a postcard and during WWI thousands were sent to cheer up British troops. Her husband lost his right arm on active service in the war, learned to draw with his left hand and became her assistant.

She contributed to several periodicals and annuals, drew a comic strip called 'Wot a Life' in the *London Opinion,* painted posters for London Underground and illustrated advertisements for top brands. The name of one of her most famous drawings, 'Diddums', even entered the English language. She illustrated *Peeping Pansy* and *The Lost Princess* by Marie, the Queen of Romania, and *Peter Pan and Wendy* by Sir J.M. Barrie, who had requested her personally. She provided the paintings for many popular texts including *Mother Goose, Alice in Wonderland, The Water Babies, Grimms' Fairy Tales* and *The Steadfast Gabriel* by Mary Howitt [226].

In the 1920s and 1930s the Earnshaws had a series of homes in Sussex; in Mermaid Street, Rye; at Church Farm, Litlington, near Alfriston, and at a farmhouse at West Dean (now the Manor House), where they lived for two years. Their final Sussex home was Ocklynge Manor, Eastbourne, where she experienced two severe losses: her son died in 1935, followed by her husband two years later. They were buried at East Dean. She moved first to London then in 1945 to Cornwall, remaining active as an artist to the end of her life. *The Mabel Lucie Attwell Annual,* which began in 1922, continued for ten years after her death. A centenary exhibition was held in her honour at Brighton Museum in 1979.

Today, anything with an original Attwell illustration is highly collectable, and lately her work has appeared on fridge magnets, trays, wipe-clean boards and jigsaws. Her daughter Marjorie (Mrs Wickham) also became an artist and in the 1970s illustrated jars of Robinson's baby foods.

Further reading: Henty, J. (1999) *The Collectable World of Mabel Lucie Attwell.*

ADA ELLEN BAYLY pseudonym Edna Lyall (1857–1903) novelist.

The daughter of a barrister, she was born at 5 Montpelier Villas, Brighton, and educated by her uncle in Surrey and at private schools at Brighton. Devising her pen-name 'Edna Lyall' by transposing nine letters of her three names, she wrote eighteen novels.

She befriended Charles Bradlaugh MP and his daughter Hypatia Bonner [42] and helped pay his electoral expenses. After his death she founded a memorial fund in his honour. The hero of her third novel *We Two* (1884) was based on him. By then she had only received £50 in royalties, but her next work, *In the Golden Days* (1885), the first one written in Eastbourne, was a big money-spinner and *Hope the Hermit* was the last book read to John Ruskin on his deathbed. She revealed her true identity in 1886, after an impostor in Ceylon claimed to be 'Edna Lyall', and to quash a rumour that she was incarcerated in a lunatic asylum. Prompted by this episode, she wrote her very successful *Autobiography of a Slander* (1887), which was translated into several languages. Three years later the semi-autobiographical *Derrick Vaughan: Novelist* appeared, followed in 1894 by *Doreen,* a story based on the Irish troubles and dedicated 'in gratitude and reverence to the Right Honourable W.E. Gladstone'. Her next work, *The Autobiography of a Truth* (1896) dealt with the Armenian cause and her royalties were donated to the Armenian Relief Fund. She also dealt with the second South African war in *The Hinderers* in 1902 and later that year her autobiography *The Burges Letters* was published.

From age twenty-seven until her death twenty-eight years later she lived at 6 College Road, Eastbourne [see Mrs Bentley, below] with her sister Amy and brother-in-law the Revd Jameson, where she lived a life 'of greater quietude and seclusion than any other English novelist of equal celebrity' (*The Woman's Signal,* 1896). Despite being a lifelong semi-invalid owing to rheumatic fever, she managed not only to write but to perform religious, charitable and political work. In 1887 she gave St Saviour's a peal of three bells, named for the leading characters in three of her books: Donovan, Erica and Hugo. She was also a member of the congregation of St Peter's, to which she presented new seating. A suffragist, she served as honorary secretary of her local branch of the Women's Liberal Association.

She died at home, leaving specific instructions for her funeral and requesting that no one go into mourning 'unless they very particularly wished and then very slightly'. Her ashes were placed at the foot of the old cross in Bosbury churchyard, Herefordshire, where her brother was vicar. In 1906 a memorial window by Kempe was placed in her honour in St Peter's Church, which was demolished in 1971. [Related images pp268, 281.]

HENDRINA BENTLEY née Kloekers (1855–1938) missionary and translator.

Born in China to Dutch parents working as missionaries, she wanted to become one herself, but was prevented because she was a single woman. However, after she married English Baptist missionary William Bentley DD in 1885, she accompanied him to the Congo, where they worked together. She was the first Western woman to learn the Kikongo language, and with her husband produced a dictionary, a grammar and a translation of the New Testament (he alone is credited with these works). They had two children and Mrs Bentley founded and ran a school at Wathen Baptist Missionary Station in Tumba, south Congo.

In 1904 they settled in Bristol, where he died the following year. In later life she lived with her daughter at 6 College Road, Eastbourne [see Miss Bayly, 206], where she died. After a service at Ceylon Place Chapel she was buried with her husband in Bristol. [Related image p268.]

JESSY BLACKBURN née Tryphena Thompson (1894–1995) aviator.

The child of wealthy parents, she was born in Worcestershire and orphaned in childhood. In 1914 she met Robert Blackburn, who was fanatical about the new craze of flying machines and within a year, using her inheritance and his father's money, they set up Blackburn Aircraft. The firm began by supplying planes to the Admiralty for use in WWI, flourished after the war and until the 1950s was among the world's leading aviation companies. Until 1936 she took a full share in everything connected with the exciting new technology and was among the first women to fly in a monoplane and to act as co-pilot, which she did in 1915. She also competed in the 1922 and 1928 King's Cup Air Races.

She lived for some years in Greece, where Blackburn Aircraft built planes and an aerodrome for the Greek government, and in Switzerland, where her son was receiving lengthy treatment for TB. Her second son was killed in a road accident. Married and divorced three times, from the late 1950s she reverted to her first married surname, Blackburn. At some point she moved to Eastbourne, where her 100th birthday was celebrated by a function at the Grand Hotel. She died in Eastbourne a year later.

ANGELA CARTER née Stalker (1940–1992) writer.

The daughter of a journalist, she was born at 12 Hyde Gardens, Eastbourne, and grew up in Yorkshire and London. After a brief spell as a reporter she married Paul Carter and read English literature at Bristol University while writing short stories and essays, and also novels: her third won the Somerset Maugham Award. She left her husband and lived in Tokyo, Bath, then London, where she remarried and had a son.

In her twenty-five-year career she wrote novels, short stories, radio plays, poetry, children's books, fairy tales, essays, screenplays, newspaper articles and a libretto for an opera, and taught creative writing at four universities in three countries. Her book *Nights at the Circus* won the 1984 James Tait Black Memorial Prize for literature. Her novels have been described as fantasy, macabre, Gothic, grotesque, baroque, parody, allegory, symbolic, science fiction and 'postmodernist, intertextual webs'.

Her work is widely studied at universities and she was hailed by critics as 'one of the most vivacious and compelling voices on the English literary scene', and 'the funniest novelist of her generation, as well as the most subversive and anarchic'. She died in London and was cremated at Putney.

DAME MARY CHESHIRE DBE née Lloyd (1902–1972) director, WRNS.

The daughter of a draper, she was born at 15 Sussex Gardens, Eastbourne. She joined the WRNS at the late age of thirty-seven and just eleven years later became its director. Appointed OBE in 1946 while superintendent of the Portsmouth Command, and DBE in 1952, she retired in 1954 and married in 1963. Her requiem mass, at Westminster Cathedral, was attended by Queen Elizabeth.

(SUSAN) ADA FLATMAN (1871–1952) suffragette.

Born in Cambridgeshire, she broke with convention by travelling alone to explore Australia and Ceylon. Returning in 1907 she became an organiser for the militant WSPU, working all over Britain. During WWI she campaigned for women's suffrage in the USA and for Russian refugees in Poland; in peacetime she suspected she was on a blacklist, because all her attempts to get employment in the USA and Canada met with refusal.

She settled in Eastbourne in 1936, where she was visited by former suffragette leader Christabel Pankhurst, a long-term correspondent and was for forty years a close friend of Minnie Turner [150]. She became known to a younger audience when BBC radio broadcast her reminiscences of her suffrage days. She died at 11 Upperton Road, Eastbourne. [Related image p16.]

AGNES GIBERNE (1845–1939) writer.

The daughter of an army major, she was born in India and lived in London and Somerset. By 1881 her family had settled in Eastbourne, firstly at 25 Lushington Road, then 5 Hyde Gardens by 1891, where they still lived a decade later. She wrote over a hundred books, encompassing evangelistic and moralising children's fiction, scientific textbooks and a biography of author and missionary Charlotte Tucker. A keen amateur astronomer, she helped establish the British Astronomical Association and was a pioneer of popular science. Her most famous book, *Sun, Moon and Stars: Astronomy for Beginners* (1879) went into several editions on both sides of the Atlantic, selling over 24,000 copies. She died at a nursing home, 16 Motcombe Road, Eastbourne, and her funeral was at St Mary's Church.

MARY ANN GILBERT (c1782–1845) pioneer of allotments.

Known as 'the heiress of Eastbourne Park', at Northiam in 1808 she married Davies Giddy (later an MP and president of the Board of Agriculture). In 1817 he adopted her family surname in honour of her uncle, whose massive wealth and extensive lands he inherited through his marriage to her. The couple lived at Eastbourne Place, a 'substantial brick edifice' to the south of St Mary's Church, and raised eight children.

At the time, thousands of unemployed Sussex labourers were living on parish relief paid for by a poor rate. Mrs Gilbert, a member of the Labourers' Friend Society, believed that people should not be given handouts but the means to be independent. About 1830 she employed paupers to convert shingle on the seashore to the east of Beachy Head into productive land by covering it with a layer of clay soil, to enable barleycorn and potatoes to be grown. Her scheme was a resounding success: soon 174 former paupers were supporting their families from selling the produce of this land and 117 had paid the next year's rent.

Next, she pioneered a method of letting portions of land to the poor to cultivate crops. Her Eastbourne, Willingdon and East Dean allotments initially comprised four acres divided amongst fifty tenants and were a huge success, saving many from the workhouse. By 1835 she had 213 tenants; by 1844, over 400. Her scheme reduced the poor rate by more than half, despite an increase in the poor population.

She trained her allotment holders in spade husbandry, commerce and thrift, lent them money to buy livestock and equipment, supplied tanks to collect rainwater and introduced a water filtering system. After conducting experiments and investigations into everything related to allotments, she circulated her findings to every interested person and organisation, constantly updating and improving the instructions given to her tenants and encouraging them to compete for prizes at Battle Horticultural Show. To teach the methods she had devised, in the early 1840s she founded agricultural schools at Willingdon and East Dean. Her reports and articles were circulated across Britain and her experiments attracted international attention. Before long, wealthy landowners and aristocrats began to write from the USA and Ireland asking for information, advice and guidance. She also appraised them of the moral aspects of her scheme: having an allotment was 'an inducing motive for [tenants] not to do anything wrong, whereby they forfeit their land'. In the course of thirteen years only one of her 443 tenants had been convicted of any crime and not one had failed to pay the rent; having an allotment also kept them too busy to spend time in beer shops.

She died at her home and was buried in the churchyard of St Mary's, where there is a memorial to her husband. Having inherited from his mother's family, her son John Davies Gilbert (1811–1854) played a significant role, as landowner, in the development of Eastbourne.

LOUISA, LADY GOLDSMID née Goldsmid
(1819–1908) feminist campaigner and benefactor.

Born in Brighton into a wealthy, dynastic, Jewish family, she spent the whole of her adult life helping the poor and needy and — most especially — every campaign and organisation to improve the lives of women of all classes, including the Governesses' Benevolent Institution, women's hospitals the Society for Promoting the Employment of Women, as well as individuals pursuing higher education or vocational training. She sponsored Hertha Ayrton [63] to study at Girton (towards the founding of which she gave £100) and endowed three scholarships for female pianists at the RCM. On behalf of the working classes she campaigned for fair wages for factory women and was so incensed by the exclusion of women from the chain manufacturing industry that she personally led a protest deputation to the Home Office. To help all mothers, she financially supported the campaign that culminated in the Guardianship of Infants Act 1886.

A member of the Langham Place circle, a feminist discussion group of the 1860s which included Barbara Bodichon [193] and Bessie Rayner Parkes [79], she signed the 1866 women's suffrage petition; co-founded the LSWS, with Emily Davies [95] and Mentia Taylor [167]; became an executive committee member of the NSWS; was involved, alongside Clara Mordan [191] and Agnes Garrett [75], with the Central National Committee for Women's Suffrage in the 1880s and joined a suffrage deputation in 1891.

She was president and treasurer of a committee of a hundred women that in 1886 commissioned Britain's leading architect Basil Champneys to create an ornamental drinking fountain as a memorial to the late Henry Fawcett, MP for Brighton, to honour his contribution to women's emancipation. A female sculptor, Mary Grant, was commissioned to create a bronze medallion, the centrepiece of which is a relief of his face. The memorial cost over £600 (worth over £60,000 today), which was raised by donations and fifty women attended the unveiling on the Thames Embankment, where it still stands today.

She married her cousin Sir Francis Goldsmid MP, the first Jewish QC, who inherited a baronetcy in 1859. After he was killed falling from a moving train at Waterloo Station in 1878 she lived for eighteen years with concert pianist Agnes Zimmermann [212], between her smart central London house and Red Lodge, 6 Devonshire Place, Eastbourne. The 1901 census shows the pair being amply looked after by eleven resident domestic servants. She died in London, leaving a major bequest to the Princess Alice Memorial Hospital, Eastbourne, a colossal sum to the LSMW and the equivalent of millions to Girton. The rest of her money was divided among dozens of charities and hospitals, almost all benefiting the Jewish community or women. [Related image p270.]

HILDA GREGG pseudonym Sydney C. Grier
(1868–1933) novelist.

A vicar's daughter, she was born in Gloucestershire and raised in Greenwich. She was taught by a governess until she was fourteen, then her father died and she and her mother moved to Enys Road in Eastbourne (by 1891 they were living at Kirkley, 27 St Anne's Road). After attending Eversley High School she took her BA at London University and became a teacher. From 1886 she earned money writing short stories for magazines, but from 1895 to 1925, having landed a publishing contract with Blackwood's, she wrote a novel a year under her pseudonym. Judging by the reviews, 'Sydney' was for many years believed to be a man; however, a critic in the *Pall Mall Gazette* published his doubts when he read that the heroine in *Peace with Honour* (1897) refused to give up her career upon marriage.

In 1926 she moved to Avonmore, 48 St Leonards Road, where she died seven years later. Secondhand copies of her book *An Uncrowned King* (1896) are available today, but at a high price.

DR MARJORIE GRICE-HUTCHINSON MBE

Baroness von Schlippenbach (1909–2003) expert on Iberian economics.

She was born at The Lodge, 4 Silverdale Road, Eastbourne, where she lived until 1924, when her family moved to Spain. During WWII she performed intelligence work for the Foreign Office in London and later taught Spanish at various universities, including the LSE, where she studied economics, becoming an authority on commerce in the Iberian peninsula, about which she wrote many books and articles for learned journals. Owing to her work, historians now refer to the 'Mediterranean tradition' in economic thought.

She married a Spanish nobleman in 1951 and returned to Spain, where she founded a school for the poor. She inherited a farm on her husband's death and gave it to Malaga University in 1984; it is now a centre for scientific research and a botanical garden. The recipient of one American and many Spanish honours, she was appointed MBE in 1975. She died in Malaga.

BESSIE HUTCHINS (1858–1935) feminist social investigator.

Born into a wealthy family, she was educated at King's College for Women (London) and the LSE. She spent much of her life in the service of working women, publishing a great number of reports and giving university lectures on their conditions of work, their wages and the history of laws that affected them. Among her published works were the co-written *A History of Factory Legislation* (1903) and *Women in Industry after the War* (1917). She established a scholarship at the LSE and died at her home, 6 Granville Court, Granville Road, Eastbourne.

ANNIE MARIA KEARY (1825–1879) writer.

A Yorkshirewoman and author of children's books and grown-ups' novels, she lived most of her life in the north, but died at 9 Lismore Road, Eastbourne. Some of her works, notably the 1857 work *Heroes of Asgard* (tales from Scandinavian mythology, co-written with her sister Eliza) were reprinted over a century after her death. Her sister published *Annie Keary: A Memoir*, in 1882. [Related image p280.]

ROSEMARY FAITH MCCALL OBE (1919–2004) audiologist and founder of Link.

She and her mother left her native Surrey and moved to Eastbourne in the 1920s, where she devoted herself to the study of cello and ballet. During WWII she worked with elderly and ex-service personnel at Blenheim Palace, which drew her attention to the scarcity of help for the deaf. She trained as an audiologist and lipreading tutor, worked at Eastbourne and District General Hospital and taught nurses all over Britain how to communicate with deaf patients.

By 1951 she founded the Eastbourne and District Hard of Hearing Association and in 1972 began the Link Centre for Deafened People, initially at her home, 1 East Dean Road, Eastbourne (where she lived for at least fifteen years); eventually it secured its present premises at 19 Hartfield Road. This grew into a national body, the UK's only such organisation. She was involved with many similar charities, as patron, president, life or honorary member and wrote several books, the best-known was *Hearing Loss? A Guide to Self-help* (1991). Having dedicated almost fifty years to helping the deaf, aged seventy-three she flew to Australia to be keynote speaker at a 'Better Hearing' conference. The recipient of many awards, she was appointed OBE in 1998.

DAME ELLEN MUSSON DBE, RRC, LLD (1867–1960) promoter of nursing.

One of twelve children, she was born in Lancashire and worked as a governess before deciding at the age of twenty-seven to devote her life to promoting nursing as a profession for women. She campaigned to improve conditions and salaries, instigated training courses and clubs and held many distinguished offices, including chairman of the General Nursing Council, president of the National Council of Nurses, vice-president of the College of Nursing and treasurer of the International Council of Nurses. During WWI she was responsible for the recruitment of nurses for Britain and overseas and ran a military hospital. She was awarded the RRC, First Class, and later received an honorary LLD degree, the International Florence Nightingale Medal, the CBE and DBE.

In later life she moved to Pevensey Bay and then to Eastbourne, where she spent the rest of her life with her brother and sister at Badlesmere, 10 Trinity Trees, where she died. Her portrait is in the NPG.

WINIFRED, LADY PECK née Knox (1882–1962) novelist.

One of six children, her grandfather was the Bishop of Lahore, India, and her father was a rector. She was born in Oxford, but when she was ten her mother died (in Brighton) and she was sent to be raised by her evangelical aunt in Eastbourne, where for four years she attended 'an old-fashioned school' which she described in her books *A Little Learning* (1952) and *Home for the Holidays* (1955).

She was among the first forty pupils at Wycombe Abbey, where she excelled and, returning to Oxford, she gained a first-class degree in modern history at Lady Margaret Hall. In 1903 her father became the Bishop of Manchester where, in 1911, she married schools' inspector (later, Sir) James Peck. She raised three sons and wrote a long series of very popular novels, including *Tranquillity* (1944) and *Winding Ways* (1951) as well as short stories for several literary magazines. She died in Scotland, where her husband had been minister of food.

EMILY PHIPPS (1865–1943) feminist trades unionist.

A native of Devon and graduate of London University, she was head of Swansea Secondary School for thirty-one years. She was among the first women to be elected to the executive of the NUT, was on the central council of the National Federation of Women Teachers (1913–1937) and its president for two years. The leader of several deputations and protests she later wrote pamphlets about equal pay for female teachers [see Ethel Froud, 173]. With her life partner, teacher Clare Neal, she was an activist in the WFL from 1908. They evaded the 1911 census by spending the night with three other feminists in a cave on the Gower peninsular in Wales. [294] She became president of the NUWT, and in 1918 stood for parliament as an independent. Despite torchlit publicity parades by thousands of London teachers she failed to get elected, though she did regain her deposit.

In 1919 she founded *The Woman Teacher*, a feminist newspaper that she edited for eleven years, during which time she began a new career. After studying at the Middle Temple she was called to the bar in 1925 at the age of sixty, then worked as honorary legal adviser to the NUWT and wrote the *History of the National Union of Women Teachers* (1928). She lived with Miss Neal for over forty years, and after her death moved in the 1920s to 26 Arundel Road, Eastbourne, where she lived for many years with NUWT treasurer Adelaide Jones. She died in Berkshire and a building at the University of Swansea is named for her.

GEORGIANA SOLOMON née Thomson (1844–1933) suffragette.

Londoner Mrs Solomon lived a genteel, quiet and uneventful life until the age of sixty-four, when she became a militant suffragette, and over the next few years was roughed up by the police, arrested and imprisoned. She is best known for smashing nine small windows in the office of Black Rod at the House of Lords, and 'cherished with pride the great memory' of the month she spent in Holloway with fourteen other WSPU members in 1910.

Upon their release they were greeted by a brass band and three hundred sympathisers (headed by Mrs Pankhurst) and treated to a slap-up lunch at the Criterion Restaurant. She died at Espérance private hospital, Hartington Road, Eastbourne, and was buried in Ocklynge Cemetery.

(MARY) NOËL STREATFEILD OBE (1895–1986) writer.

A descendant of the prison reformer Elizabeth Fry, her grandfather was the rector of Frant (where she was born) and her father was his curate. When she was a toddler the family moved to Amberley vicarage, where her father was incumbent, and when she was six they moved again, to St Peter's in St Leonards (where the former vicarage bears a blue plaque in her honour). She attended Hastings and St Leonards Ladies' College, where she was a disruptive pupil, began an unauthorised magazine and was expelled. From 1911 her family lived at St Mary the Virgin rectory, Eastbourne, until 1928, when her father became Bishop of Lewes. She attended Laleham School, where she began to write plays, then enrolled in Eastbourne School of Domestic Economy. During WWI she worked in a military kitchen and wrote and produced children's plays at Eastbourne's Winter Gardens Theatre to raise funds for the war.

After training at RADA she was an actress for ten years, performing in repertory, revues and pantomime, and touring South Africa, New Zealand and Australia. After her father's death in 1929 she decided to become a writer. She produced fairy stories for magazines and sixty-four books, of which forty-nine were for children. Many were adapted for TV and radio, and the best-known is *Ballet Shoes* (1936), from which she made a comfortable living. She never thought herself too lofty to meet her readers; she replied to every fan letter and gave talks in public libraries. In her sixties she published details of her early life in *A Vicarage Family* (1963).

During WWII she was an ARP warden and WVS volunteer in London, where she lost almost all her possessions when her flat was bombed. A lifelong spinster, she enjoyed close relationships with Daphne Ionides (1920s–40s), Margot Grey (1950s–60s) and Theodora Newbold. She was appointed OBE in 1983 and died in a nursing home in London three years later. She was buried at Westerham, Kent. [Related image p269.]

PROFESSOR BEATRICE WHITE (1902–1986) literary scholar.

Born in Cambridgeshire, she took her BA and MA at King's College, London, becoming a specialist in the field of early Renaissance literature. She wrote several books including *Mary Tudor* (1935), *Cast of Ravens, the Strange Case of Sir Thomas Overbury* (1965) and an introduction to an academic book on witchcraft. She lectured at Westfield College, London, from 1936 until her retirement in 1969, when she settled in Eastbourne, continuing to write academic essays into her eighties.

She died at her home, 4 Abbotsrood, 1 Milnthorpe Road, Eastbourne, and was buried in Hailsham. The English Association offers an annual Beatrice White Prize for outstanding scholarly work in the field of English Literature before 1590.

AGNES ZIMMERMANN (1847–1925) concert pianist, composer and founder of a church.

Leaving her native Germany, from age nine she studied at the RAM. Her fifty-year performance career began at age sixteen when she played Beethoven at the Crystal Palace, then in central London. She composed suites and sonatas for chamber orchestra and pieces for piano solo and voice. For eighteen years she lived between London and Sussex with Louisa, Lady Goldsmid [209], to whom she was famously devoted. She became involved in her friend's feminist activities and attended suffrage meetings. In 1907, while living at Red Lodge, 6 Devonshire Place, Eastbourne, she founded the Roman Catholic church of St Agnes in Whitley Road. Her portrait photograph now hangs in the church hall, which was opened in 2003.

After Lady Goldsmid died in 1908 Miss Zimmermann returned to London, where she died, leaving her fortune to the Catholic church, charities and hospitals (including £1,200 for a bed to be named for her at the New Hospital for Women) and various sums to her servants. Her valuable collection of Edward Lear watercolours was bequeathed to the NPG, while her library of sheet music, including her own compositions, was left to the RAM. [Related plate 18; images pp270, 280.]

EAST HOATHLY

SARAH ROBINSON (1834–1921) evangelist and army temperance activist.

One of six children, she was born in south London. Her mother was from Lewes and little Sarah grew up at Prospect House, also known as Heasmond's, on her family's estate at East Hoathly, where her father farmed 120 acres. She played with toy soldiers with her younger brothers and eagerly read about Christian military heroes, until the age of ten when she was sent to an academy for young ladies in Brighton for four years. Raised as a Calvinist, she converted to Anglicanism at Chiddingly church in 1851 (some fifteen years later she would become a Presbyterian).

She left Sussex aged twenty-four and settled at Boxhill in Surrey. Her fervent religious feeling combined with a firm belief in temperance led her to become involved with the Aldershot Mission Institute, which provided off-duty soldiers with an alcohol-free place for socialising, relaxation, education, entertainment and prayer meetings. Working with the National Temperance League, between 1865 and 1873 she visited military garrisons all over England. Soon people were calling her 'the Soldier's Friend' and news of her good works spread the length and breadth of Britain. In 1874 she and her like-minded friend Ellice Hopkins [136] converted a pub to create the Portsmouth Soldiers' Institute in the High Street, which assisted, accommodated, educated and entertained wounded soldiers and sailors, their wives and families. Within two years it was nationally famous and was honoured with a visit from the Duke of Cambridge, commander-in-chief of the British Army. She also established a 'Sailors' Welcome' in Queen Street, near Portsea dockyard gates and two coffee taverns for servicemen.

Partially disabled by a spinal complaint, in 1889 and 1891 she travelled 3,000 miles in a specially adapted coach, delivering 165 speeches across England and Scotland to raise money for the institute. Her physical problems forced her into semi-retirement at fifty-eight and she moved to The Hut, Burley, Hampshire, which she shared with Alice Walker, who had been superintendent of the Soldiers' Institute for thirteen years. She contributed to a collection of essays entitled *Woman's Work in the Temperance Reformation* (1868) and wrote *A Life Record* (1898), *The Soldier's Friend, A Pioneer's Record* (1913) and *My Book: A Personal Narrative* (1914). She died at home and was cremated at Woking. A block of flats in Southsea is named for her.

EWHURST

LILY LAMBERT MCCARTHY CBE née Lambert; first married name Fleming (1914–2006) collector and benefactor of Nelsonia.

New Yorker Mrs McCarthy was a Listerine mouthwash heiress who became involved in charity work for the Royal Navy while in the USA. In 1971 she bought Court Lodge, a Tudor house on Dagg Lane, Ewhurst, where she expanded her collection of Nelson artefacts until it filled the former dairy, later called the Nelson Room.

In 1972 she became the Royal Naval Museum's most important benefactor when she donated her entire collection, which included six oil paintings, 300 prints, 200 books and newspapers, porcelain, ceramics, cameos and a full-length bronze. She also gave a 1,000-volume book collection to Portsmouth Central Library. She was appointed an honorary CBE in 1972 and returned to the USA in the 1980s. Her collection is still displayed in the Lambert McCarthy Gallery at Portsmouth alongside Nelson's flagship *Victory*.

FAIRLIGHT

ETHEL RICHARDSON pseudonym Henry Handel Richardson (1870–1946) writer.

Of Irish heritage, she was born in Australia and studied piano in Leipzig in 1888. After marrying John Robinson, a professor of literature, in 1894 she settled in London in 1903, where with her sister she supported the suffragette movement.

In 1919 she befriended Olga Roncoroni, a eurhythmics teacher twenty-three years her junior, who in 1921 moved in as companion and secretary. 'Henry' wrote seven novels and four short stories, always under a male pseudonym because: 'many people thought women wrote only romantic nonsense'. Her books dealt with taboo topics such as homosexuality, suicide and syphilis and two were adapted into films.

After John Robinson's death the two women moved to Green Ridges, Tilekiln Lane, Fairlight, in 1934 and *The Young Cosima* (1939) was written there. Although she left Australia aged eighteen, all of her books were set there and she has been called the most remarkable novelist Australia ever produced. She was part-way through her autobiography when she died, at her home. Her ashes were scattered out to sea. *Myself When Young* was finished by Olga Roncoroni and Edna Purdie and published in 1948. (Miss Roncoroni moved to St Leonards, firstly to 46 Kenilworth Road, then 15 Dane Road, moving to Flat 3, 33 Warrior Square by 1968.)

In 1957 Miss Richardson's house in London acquired a blue plaque, but the building has since been demolished, as has Green Ridges. The National Trust of Australia runs her childhood home in Chiltern, Victoria as a museum in her honour. Some of her books were reprinted in 2007.

Further reading: Ackland, M. (2005) *Henry Handel Richardson: A Life.*

FAIRWARP

JOAN TETZEL (1921–1977) actress.

Born in New York, her career spanned thirty-five years, encompassing Broadway and the West End, Hollywood and TV. She is best known for playing Judy Flaquer in Hitchcock's *The Paradine Case.*

She married twice, firstly to John Mosman, then (as his fourth wife) to actor Oscar Homolka in 1949. She worked in England and New York in the 1950s and 1960s, and played in a long West End run of Alan Ayckbourn's *How the Other Half Loves* in 1970. Her final appearance was in a TV film with her husband in 1975.

The couple lived permanently in England from 1962 and in the early 1970s settled at a house called Beri-Be-Dahn (now Tibbs House) on what is now Lampool Road, where she ended her days. Her husband died in hospital just three months later and they were buried under a single headstone outside Christ Church, Fairwarp.

FALMER

(MARY ANN) BUZZ GOODBODY (1947–1975) theatre director.

A London barrister's daughter, she lived mainly in Sussex from 1955 to 1967, being educated at Roedean then at Sussex University, where she won a prize for her adaptation and direction of Dostoyevsky's *Notes from the Underground*. In 1967 she was married briefly to Edward Buscombe and began her career with the RSC, first as a personal assistant, then as an assistant director. A Marxist-feminist, in 1971 she co-founded the Women's Street Theatre Group. By this time she was in charge of Theatregoround, the RSC's touring section, and in 1974 became its youngest — and its first female — artistic director, at the Other Place Theatre at Stratford, where she directed many famous stars including Dorothy Tutin [49].

She gained acclaim for her productions of *King Lear* and *Hamlet*, the second season of which opened in April 1975. That month she committed suicide in her Islington flat. The RSC planted a memorial tree in her honour and the National Student Drama Festival founded an annual Buzz Goodbody Award for Directing.

FIRLE

VANESSA BELL (1879–1961) post-impressionist and abstract painter and designer.

She trained in art in her native London, where she lived with her sister Virginia Woolf [243], her two brothers and others at 46 Gordon Square. The artists, writers and intellectuals who gathered there became known as the Bloomsbury Set and have been described by some as glittering artistic and literary geniuses and by a book reviewer in the *Guardian* as 'a precious coterie of back-stabbing creeps'.

In 1907 she married poet, painter and art critic Clive Bell. She openly took as lovers the artists Roger Fry and Duncan Grant, an upper-class Scottish bisexual who had previously enjoyed affairs with John Maynard Keynes, his own cousin Lytton Strachey, and Vanessa Bell's brother. Mr Fry exhibited Mrs Bell's works, and at his Omega Workshops introduced her to using art for ornament and decoration on tapestries, carpets, embroideries, pottery, furniture and book jackets. Duncan Grant encouraged her to produce larger decorative works and in the 1940s they created murals at Berwick church and at Charleston. She also illustrated many of her sister's books.

While they were living at Asheham House, Southease, her sister discovered an eighteenth-century farmhouse called Charleston, set close to the foot of the South Downs at Firle. Mrs Bell wrote: 'It's most lovely, very solid and simple, with ... perfectly flat windows and wonderful tiled roofs.' Mrs Bell, her two small sons Julian and Quentin, her lover Duncan Grant, his male lover and an assortment of animals moved in during WWI (the men evaded military service by claiming to be conscientious objectors who were performing farm work). Initially, Mrs Bell lived in primitive conditions: the house was without gas or electricity and the water was pumped daily by hand. Virginia Woolf wrote: 'Nessa is four miles on the other side of the down, living like an old hen wife among ducks, chickens and children'. She and her friends decorated the walls with murals, painted the furniture and filled the house with their own artwork. Eventually her husband moved in and the Bells, Mr Grant and their children lived at Charleston until their deaths. The house became a second home for the Bloomsbury Set, including Lydia Lopokova [below].

Clive Bell did not object to his wife's cohabiting with Duncan Grant on and off for forty years: he had numerous affairs himself, often bringing his girlfriends to Charleston to live for long periods. He accepted Angelica, his wife's child by Mr Grant, and until she was nineteen she believed him to be her father (she called her autobiography *Deceived with Kindness*). Mr Grant's lover, David Garnett, son of Constance [132] was present at Angelica's birth and, twenty years later, married her.

Mrs Bell suffered much unhappiness. Roger Fry died in 1934, her son Julian (lover of the spy Anthony Blunt) was killed in 1937, her sister committed suicide in 1941 and Duncan Grant fell in love with (yet) another man in 1946. She died at Charleston and was buried, without a service, in St Peter's churchyard in Firle. Later that year sixty of her paintings were displayed in a memorial exhibition in London. Mr Grant, who moved one of his former lovers into Charleston, lived there until his death in 1978 and was buried alongside Mrs Bell.

The Charleston Trust was formed in 1980 to buy the house (for £50,000) and restore it to its former glory. Now one of England's art treasures, Charleston contains a huge collection of artwork by Grant, Bell, Fry, Picasso, Derain, Sickert, Hamnett and Baynes.

Further reading: Spalding, F. (1983) *Vanessa Bell*. [Related image p271.]

LYDIA LOPOKOVA Lady Keynes (1892– 1981) prima ballerina.

Trained at the Imperial School of Ballet in St Petersburg, her London début as première danseuse with Diaghilev's Ballets Russes in 1918 enchanted audiences and critics (one called her 'a ravishing little lady') and stole the heart of bisexual economist John Maynard Keynes (later Baron Keynes of Tilton). She remained in England to be near him and they wed in 1925 on the day her previous marriage was annulled (her first husband had married her bigamously). The partnership prompted this ditty:

What a marriage
of beauty and brains
The fair Lopokova
and John Maynard Keynes.

Mr Keynes's former lover Duncan Grant was a witness to the ceremony and the couple moved into Tilton Farmhouse, close to Charleston, where Mr Grant cohabited with Mrs Bell [above].

Lydia Lopokova was at the top of her profession and in 1929 performed at the Royal Albert Hall for George V and Queen Mary. She retired from dancing aged forty-one and tried acting, but her strong Russian accent limited her roles and about 1938 she retired from professional life to care for her husband, who died at Tilton in 1946. Lady Keynes was a widow for thirty-five years and died at Threeways Nursing Home, Beacon Road, Seaford.

Further reading: Keynes, M. (1983) *Lydia Lopokova*. [Related plate 26.]

FOREST ROW

(AMY) VIOLET NEEDHAM (1876–1967) children's writer.

The granddaughter of an earl and daughter of an army captain, she was born in London into a household full of servants. She was educated by a residential governess and lived in Rome for six years, then in 1902 her mother (Hendrika Amelie Charlotte Vincentia de Tuyll de Serooskerken) bought Tylehurst in Forest Row, the family home for thirty-five years. The first story Violet sent to a publisher met with rejection but was published twenty years later (*The Black Riders*, 1939) when she was sixty-three. This sold well, and by the time she was eighty, eighteen more of her children's novels had been published, including *The House of the Paladin* (1945). Her books encompassed romance, suspense and the supernatural; some were broadcast on BBC radio, and two were set in Sussex. In *The Bell of the Four Evangelists*, 'Marvel's Folly' is based on Brambletye House and 'Lavender Platt' is named after a real cottage; both are in Forest Row, as is 'Merlyns' in *The Horn of Merlyns*.

After her parents' deaths in the 1930s she moved firstly to London and, in the 1950s, to Horton Hall, Gloucestershire. She was famed for driving dangerously (she had a car smash at the age of eighty) and for smoking Turkish cigarettes through an oval, shagreen holder. Eighteen years after her death (at Horton Hall) the Violet Needham Society was formed.

Further reading: www.violetneedham society.org.uk [Related image p283.]

FRAMFIELD

GEORGINA WELDON née Thomas; later Treherne (1837–1914) musician and litigant.

One of seven children, she was born in London and raised in Florence. In 1852 her mother, Louisa Dalrymple, inherited the 1,600-acre Gate House estate, between Cross-in-Hand and Framfield. It comprised a twenty-three bedroomed mock-Elizabethan mansion, three farms, numerous cottages and the manors of Isenhurst, Downash, Bowly and Possingworth. By law it passed immediately to her husband, Morgan Thomas MP, JP, DL. The family settled on the estate and in 1856 changed their surname to Treherne. At a ball in Brighton Georgina met Lieutenant Weldon from Preston Park barracks, but her father forbade their marriage because he had no money. After she was caught in *flagrante delicto* with another man her father imprisoned her at home. Once free she married Harry Weldon in 1860 and her father disowned and disinherited her.

In 1863 Mr Weldon secretly took a teenaged mistress, who bore him a daughter and was his partner for life. His grandmother's death placed £10,000 a year at his disposal and in 1870 he leased Tavistock House, London, which included a small theatre added by Dickens, a former occupant. Mrs Weldon was by then a spiritualist and vegetarian and an adherent of rational dress for women as well as a singer, composer and teacher. As a vocalist she had 'few equals and very few superiors' and she sang at prestigious venues in London and Paris. She published *Hints for Pronunciation in Singing* (1872) as well as songs and memoirs, and turned Tavistock House into a residential school of music for young orphans. The French composer Charles Gounod was a house-guest for three years.

In 1875, by mutual agreement, Mr Weldon left, giving her the house lease and £1,000 a year. Three years later he offered eminent psychiatrist Dr Forbes Winslow £400 a year to incarcerate her in his private lunatic asylum. Using false names he and his colleagues visited, engaged her in a few minutes' chat about spiritualism, and left.

They signed a lunacy order, forced their way back in and tried to take her away to the asylum. She barricaded herself in a room until they left then went into hiding for a week until the lunacy order expired. As a married woman she could not sue anyone [7] so she published *The History of my Orphanage, or The Outpourings of an Alleged Lunatic* and *How I Escaped the Mad Doctors* (1882) and spoke publicly to expose the scandal that owners of private, profit-making asylums could certify anyone as a lunatic for personal gain.

In 1882 she made a legal application for her husband to return, but he ignored the magistrate's order, which normally led to a prison sentence for contempt of court, but to keep him from prison the law was changed in 1884 (it was even nicknamed 'the Weldon Relief Act'). During the two years that case made its way though the course, the law changed in 1882, allowing wives to sue. Mrs Weldon was unshackled: in her first year she initiated twenty-five legal actions and founded a newsletter, *Social Salvation*. One of the first women to represent herself in court, she met her costs by appearing in music halls, earning a massive £70 week. She successfully sued all the participants in the plot to certify her a lunatic. Her first case against Dr Forbes Winslow failed, but cost him his professional reputation; her second resulted in her winning £1,000 damages. Later she won £1,000 from her husband and substantial sums from the other three doctors and was awarded a record £10,000 damages for being libelled by Mr Gounod. By 1900 she had brought over a hundred cases to court. She was herself sued for libel and served a month in Newgate in 1880 and six months in Holloway in 1885. On each release she was cheered by thousands of well-wishers. She retained her prison clothes and wore them while delivering public speeches on judicial and prison reform.

Georgina Weldon's name and image became ubiquitous: she was reputed to have filled as many newspaper columns as a cabinet minister, was featured in magazines, poems and cartoons and her face — fifty times larger than life — appeared in adverts on London buses. Despite being severely criticised, mercilessly lampooned and deeply insulted by the popular press, she was nevertheless much in demand as a speaker, became vice-president of the Magna-Chartists and was invited to debates in the House of Lords.

Her musical career was not entirely abandoned; she continued to perform until 1884, singing at promenade concerts with a women's choir that she trained and directed, composing children's songs using her own translations of French texts and, as 'Grannie Weldon', publishing *Cradle Song, Pussie's Christmas Song* and *The Song of the Sparrow* (1908).

She moved to Brighton when she was seventy and lodged with Mrs Gunn at Sillwood House, where she died. Her body was taken by train to Mayfield, where she was interred in the Dalrymple family vault in St Dunstan's Church. A painting of her, dated 1845, is in the Watts Gallery. (Her husband, by then Sir Henry, married his mistress in 1915 and died four years later.)

Further reading: Grierson, E. (1959) *Storm Bird: The Strange Life of Georgina Weldon.* Thompson, B. (2001) *A Monkey Among Crocodiles.* [Related image p280.]

(ROSE) MARJORIE WESTBURY (1905–1989) soprano and radio actress.

A native of West Bromwich, she studied at the RCM and became a well-known soprano, appearing frequently on radio as a singer and an actress in musical plays. She played the voice of Churchill in childhood in the film *The Young Winston* and won two awards as Radio Actress of the Year. Her biggest break came in 1938 when she was chosen for the part of Steve, the wife and assistant of detective Paul Temple, a role she played on radio in nearly 100 episodes during the 1940s and 1950s. She was inundated with fan-mail from listeners and in 1957 received a bequest of £15,000 from Olivia Parker, who had committed suicide.

In 1982 she celebrated fifty years with the BBC Drama Repertory Company and the following year played her final role, at the age of seventy-eight. From the 1960s she lived at The Hundred House, Pound Lane, Framfield, moving later to a farmhouse in Maresfield, where she died. The Paul Temple series has recently been broadcast in its entirety on BBC Radio Seven, reviving her fame.

FRANT

FREDA HOWITT GWILLIAM CBE (1907–1987) educationist.

Her birthplace is unknown, but after graduating in history at Girton she became a schoolteacher, then a lecturer at Bishop Otter College, Chichester, before being appointed principal of Brighton Training College. Aged nearly forty she became the first female educational adviser at the Colonial Office, in which role she travelled the world to inspect the quality of the education of girls across the British Empire. She held the post for twenty-three years, and was appointed OBE in 1954, CBE in 1966, and honorary DLitt in 1973. In retirement she lived with her late brother's family at One Ash, The Green, Frant, where she died.

FRISTON

EDITH NESBIT (1858–1924) writer.

Nicknamed Daisy, she was born in London and grew up at Western Road, Brighton. In adulthood she held very advanced feminist and socialist views, joined the Fabian Society, left off her corsets, cropped her hair, took up smoking and mixed with social reformers including Clementina Black [123] and Annie Besant [246]. She married Hubert Bland in 1880 and had three children by 1885. Theirs was an open marriage, and his child by his mother's servant and two more by their own housemaid were raised by Mrs Bland as her own. Under the genderless name E. Nesbit she wrote forty children's novels and twenty works with other writers. Her most famous story was *The Railway Children* (1906), which became a popular film.

She lived variously in London, Kent and Sussex, where she rented Crowlink House, near Friston, from 1911 to 1915, in which she wrote *The Incredible Honeymoon*. After Mr Bland's death she married Thomas Tucker in 1917 and moved to Dymchurch, Kent, where she died and was buried. Her books are still in print.

Further reading: Moore, D.L. (1933) *E. Nesbit*.

FURNERS GREEN

DOROTHY LAYTON née Osmaston; Lady Layton (1887–1959) suffragist and politician.

The daughter of a barrister, she was born in London, attended boarding-schools at Bexhill and Surrey then went up to Newnham in 1906 to read history and economics. Like her mother she became a suffragist, joined the NUWSS, gave public speeches, sold copies of *The Common Cause* on street corners and joined suffrage marches.

Moving to Surrey, she became involved in Liberal politics and the National Union of Societies for Equal Citizenship, campaigning for family allowances. Later, while living in Wimbledon, she was elected to the executive of the League of Nations Union and became a fervent advocate of birth control in Britain and also in India, which she visited in 1929. She was a member of the British Committee for Indian Women's Franchise and chairman of the British Women's Advisory Council on Indian Affairs, and was involved in rescuing refugee children from the Spanish Civil War, helping Chinese refugees from the Sino–Japanese War, and saving European refugees from totalitarianism. In 1937 she toured Yugoslavia, Romania and Czechoslovakia to promote solidarity against the Nazis.

From 1941 to 1949 she lived at Twitten House, Furners Green, during which time she was president of the Women's Liberal Federation (1947–9), chairing a committee of inquiry into women's status which culminated in a report called *The Great Partnership*. She was involved in many other good causes too numerous to mention, and was also noted as a great lover of art and music. She had married in 1910 and had seven children (and eventually twenty-three grandchildren). After her death her husband Walter, editor of *The Economist* and founder of the *News Chronicle*, who had been raised to the peerage in 1947, wrote her biography, *Dorothy* (1961), in which he praised her for combining motherhood with a busy career of public service.

GLYNDE

PEGGY ANGUS (1904–1993) artist.

One of thirteen children of a railway engineer, she was born in Chile. Her family settled in London and she attended North London Collegiate School and, from 1922, the Royal College of Art. A painter, designer, handworker and teacher of folk art, she trained as a teacher and from 1931 taught at Eastbourne School of Art. She inspired many, preaching that art was for everyone and those who could not practise it should become patrons and collectors.

In 1933, while lodging at Tile Barn, a cowman's cottage near Alfriston, she discovered Furlongs, an isolated pair of Victorian flint cottages between Firle and Glynde. She lived in a tent nearby until the owner, a sheep-farmer, allowed her to rent it. Furlongs was her country home for more than half a century. Like Vanessa Bell's house [214] it had outside privies, one cold tap and no electricity, yet she created a wonderfully decorative interior, covering the walls with patterned papers printed in emulsion paint from lino blocks, and filled the house with paintings of the Sussex countryside. Furlongs became a Mecca for the artistic community of Sussex and a hive of activity, packed with objets d'art created by her many visitors. The luckiest slept on straw palliasses; the overflow was accommodated in two old, covered, Boer War fever wagons, discovered in a ditch near a cement works on the other side of the Downs by painter Eric Ravilious and his wife Tirzah (a designer of marbled wallpapers). Among her other visitors were an architect who commissioned her to design tiles for public buildings, kitchens and fireplaces, and a journalist, Jim Richards, to whom she was married for twelve years.

An active member of the Artists' International Association, she became head of art at North London Collegiate School from 1947 until 1970, where she caused a stir by insisting on being called 'Miss Angus' when she was a divorcee with two children. She stayed in London during the week and at Furlongs at weekends, and occasionally at her Hebridean home-cum-studio on the Isle of Barra.

Her work was used commercially in the 1950s, especially in school and college buildings. One of her most famous tiled murals, at Susan Lawrence Primary School, London, which she designed as part of the Festival of Britain in 1951, is still in place today. She invented a form of marblised decoration, silk-screened onto glass, which was sold under the trade-name Anguside and used at Gatwick Airport (it was removed during the rebuilding in the 1960s). In 1958 she created a fifty-foot mural for the British Pavilion at the Brussels World Fair. Two years later she won the Sanderson Centenary Competition for her 'Velvet' wallpaper design, and built up a successful wallpaper business that offered a bespoke service to clients; her handblocked designs came in a range of patterns, including abstract, pastoral and heraldic.

She exhibited at the Towner Art Gallery, Eastbourne, in 1987 and three times in London, where a posthumous exhibition took place in 2005. Two of her paintings can be found at the NPG. Her granddaughter Emma Gibson continues the wallpaper business and is currently charging £75 a roll.

Further reading: Trant, C. (2005) *Art for Life: The Story of Peggy Angus.*

KATHLEEN PICKARD-SMITH née Pickard (1902–1998) gardener and writer.

The daughter of the land agent for Glynde estate, she was born there and raised at Home Farm, moving later to Harveys, a fifteenth-century cottage on the other side of the road, where she remained for most of her life. She studied at Brighton School of Music, 5 Marlborough Place, and became its principal after gaining her LRAM. However, it is for her knowledge of gardening and reptiles that she is best known. A member of the Wild Flower Society and the Alpine Garden Society, she enjoyed field trips locally and nationally and wrote for *Sussex County Magazine.*

In 1945 she married Frank Smith, a Canadian soldier billeted in Lewes. During the 1950s she wrote a book about the creation of her extraordinary garden at Harveys, which she filled with rare and unusual plants that even experienced gardeners could not identify. Publishers rejected it, but accepted her other work,

Living with Reptiles (1961), based on her personal experience of the small lizards, terrapins and tortoises that thrived on her premises. First-time visitors assumed the iguana on top of the piano was stuffed — until its head turned to stare at them! She once took a litter of baby terrapins to London in her bra and was caught exercising them in a hand-basin at the Alpine Garden Society. She explained that, as they were newborns, she could hardly leave them alone all day. She died in Brighton, and her papers are held in the National Archives.

VISCOUNTESS WOLSELEY (1872–1936) horticultural college owner and writer.

The only child of a field marshal in the British army who became a baron when she was ten and a viscount three years later, Frances Garnet Wolseley was born in Ireland. Her family lived wherever her father's career took them, and during a stay in Cyprus she developed a deep and abiding interest in horticulture. After her father's retirement in 1899 the family lived at Home Farm, Glynde Place (where in 1901 they had nine resident servants) then rented Old Farm House (now Trevor House).

At a time when gardening was strictly a man's trade and women were not admitted to the Royal Horticultural Society's degree course, she engaged an amateur female gardener, took in two female students and rented some glebe land to accommodate a market garden. In 1906 she rented five-and-a-half hilly acres on the edge of Glynde village, an area known as Ragged Lands, where she founded the College for Lady Gardeners. She built a five-bedroom house on the site, where the first students lived, but later reserved it for herself and her house-servants, sending students out to lodgings. She extended it in 1910 to include a lecture room with bedrooms over. The college was exclusively for educated ladies of refinement, with fees set high to exclude the working classes (in 1915 they were £20 a year, lodgings £1 a week and lectures £6 a week). Students wore a uniform comprising boots and leggings under a short skirt, a shirt and tie, and a felt hat. The work was arduous, the discipline military and medals were awarded. They had a half-day off a week and a month's leave each year. Flowers and produce were sold, the students earning commission. One group of students created a garden for the King Edward VII Sanatorium at Midhurst.

Although dedicated to promoting gardening as a career for ladies and to supporting the new Women's Institutes, she took no interest in the suffrage movement, then at its height. In 1913 she inherited her father's title by special remainder and that year was elected to the Worshipful Company of Gardeners of the City of London. She wrote several books, including *Gardening for Women* (1915). During WWI she helped the Board of Agriculture obtain jobs for women on farms. In 1918 she moved in with widow Mrs Mollie (Mary Isabel) Musgrave at Massetts Place, Scaynes Hill, near Lindfield, where they ran a school to instruct local women in the management of smallholdings and the production of food. She moved to Ardingly in 1925, where she built Culpeper's, lived alone and wrote local history articles and several books, including *Some Byways in Sussex* (1930). She died there and her ashes were buried at St Andrew's Church, Beddingham.

After Lady Wolseley left, Ragged Lands was run by 'Captain' Elsa More, who made the students salute her. Much later, the house was inhabited by Janet Lane-Claypon [254]. There is a Wolseley Room at Hove Library and in 1939 a memorial in her honour was erected at Ardingly.

Further reading: Crook, D. *Ragged Lands* (2008). [Related plate 28; image p104.]

GLYNDEBOURNE

AUDREY MILDMAY (1900–1953) soprano and co-founder of Glyndebourne Opera.

The daughter of a clergyman, she was born at Herstmonceux and taken as a baby to Canada, where she later trained as a singer. In her twenties she studied in London, then toured Canada and the USA in 1927–8. A light, lyric soprano, she performed with the Carl Rosa company and was engaged by John Christie to sing in one of the operas he staged in the Organ Room of his manor house on the Glyndebourne estate, inherited from his father. They married in 1931. One day he suggested building a tiny theatre but persuaded him to 'do the thing properly,' so they built a 300-seat auditorium with an orchestra pit and the most up-to-date equipment. At the first Glyndebourne Festival in 1934 she sang the lead in *Le Nozze di Figaro* (later issued on record). The productions drew international interest and Glyndebourne became one of the most famous musical events in the world.

During the 1930s she performed and recorded in the UK and Europe until WWII, when she took her two small children to Canada for safety. Her final operatic appearances were in Montreal in 1943. The following year she returned to Glyndebourne and is credited with first suggesting that Edinburgh have a festival. Her health declined rapidly and she died young; indeed, her father, who lived nearby at Little Manor, Ringmer, outlived her. Her son Sir George Christie CH was chairman of Glyndebourne Festival from 1958 until 1999, when his son Gus took over.

GROOMBRIDGE

JULIE TULLIS née Palau (1939–1986) mountaineer.

Of Spanish and German ancestry, she was born in Croydon and evacuated during the war to a farm in Norfolk; as a teenager she took up rock-climbing. Aged twenty she married Terry Tullis and while raising two children ran the village shop and climbing café in Groombridge, and also worked as climbing instructors.

When their children were teenagers the couple embarked on an expedition to Peru, where she climbed two Andean peaks. She joined forces with film-maker Kurt Diemberger, veteran of five Himalayan expeditions, becoming his sound recordist. Already in her forties, she embarked on six major expeditions with him to the highest mountains in the world. The first was to Nanga Parbat, where the expedition leader would not allow her to climb above first camp. Nevertheless, their film won awards. In 1983 they climbed the north side of K2, the second highest mountain in the world. They returned less than a year later to climb the Abruzzi Ridge in Pakistan, then Broad Peak, where they had difficulties on the descent and survived an avalanche.

In 1985 they undertook expeditions to Everest and Nanga Parbat, filming both. They made a documentary about a remote Tibetan Village, which won a first prize at the Trento Mountain Film Festival.

A year later they again climbed K2. This took enormous courage, because that year's eleven K2 expeditions had resulted in the deaths of eight climbers. They (and others) reached the summit on 4th August, claiming a record: it was the highest peak any British woman had ever climbed. On the descent they were caught up for ten days in ferocious weather. Mr Diemberger was one of the two survivors; Mrs Tullis and four others died. She was buried in a crevasse at Camp 4 and a memorial was later placed on Gilkey Cairn. During the climb she had recorded a diary and, astonishingly, the tape was found on a glacier in 2005.

Further reading: Tullis, J. (posthumous, 1987) *Clouds from Both Sides.*

HADLOW DOWN

DIANA ROWDEN (1915–1944) SOE agent.

An army major's daughter, she was born in London and spent part of her childhood in France until being brought to live at Hadlow Lodge, Wilderness Lane, Hadlow Down, in 1927. After attending boarding school in Surrey she left for Paris, studied at the Sorbonne and became a journalist.

During WWII she was an ambulance woman for the Red Cross, then joined the WAAF in 1941, whence she was recruited to the SOE in 1943. She went to France undercover and worked as a courier in the Resistance. In 1944, betrayed by a double agent, she was imprisoned at Fresnes, interrogated for two weeks by the Nazis in Paris then, along with three other female SOE agents, was injected with phenol (a deadly poison) and cremated in the Natzweiler-Struthof concentration camp furnace in the Vosges mountains. She was twenty-nine. Awarded the Croix de Guerre and a posthumous MBE that was later withdrawn, she is commemorated on a plaque at the former concentration camp and on a tablet on the side wall of St Paul's Church, Knightsbridge.

Further reading: Nicolas, E. (1958) *Death Not Be Proud.*

HAILSHAM

FANNY CRADOCK née Phyllis Pechey (1909–1994) pioneer TV chef and author.

Born in the East End, she worked in a series of menial jobs until 1949 when, despite having no formal training, she published *The Practical Cook*. This proved very popular and led to her performing public cookery demonstrations; first in clubs and halls, then in theatres where, flamboyantly attired in a ballgown and tiara, she henpecked her monocled, top-hatted public-schoolboy sidekick and stooge, Major Johnnie Cradock, assumed to be her husband. They wrote a food column in the *Daily Telegraph* (1950–55) and in 1955 she became Britain's first TV celebrity chef. She had her own series for fifteen years and wrote ten booklets to accompany it, as well as twelve best-selling cookbooks. In addition she wrote five novels, some under the name Frances Dale, among them *The Lormes of Castle Rising*.

By the late 1960s she drove a Rolls-Royce and lived in a mansion. Her millions of viewers and readers would have been shocked if they knew her secrets: she had been expelled from school for holding a séance, believed she could communicate with Louis XIV, had abandoned both her sons in infancy, was a bigamist, and was not even married to Johnnie, who had walked out on his wife and four small children to live with her. She married four times, to Sidney Evans in 1926, Arthur Chapman in 1928, Greg Holden-Dye (bigamously) in 1939 and Johnnie Cradock (again bigamously) in 1977.

By the 1970s her style of cooking was outmoded, her pancake make-up and chiffon gowns farcical, and she had become a figure of fun, mercilessly parodied by comedians. In 1971 millions watched her wipe her nose on the back of her hand while cooking; in 1976 she was so rude to a member of the public on live TV that the BBC immediately terminated her contract. She appeared on chat shows and game shows until she stormed off set after discovering that fellow guest Danny La Rue was a man in drag.

In the 1980s the Cradocks lived quietly at 29 Cooden Drive, Bexhill. After Johnnie's death in 1987 she moved to Chichester, where in 1991 a journalist friend found her living in squalor and moved her to a nursing home, Ersham House, Ersham Road, Hailsham, where she died. Like Johnnie she was cremated at Langney, Eastbourne, where there is a memorial plaque. She has a blue plaque in London and her life has been dramatised twice, as *Doughnuts like Fanny's* (renamed *Fanny Cradock: The Life and Loves of a Kitchen Devil*) and *Fear of Fanny*.

Further reading: Ellis, C. (2007) *Fabulous Fanny Cradock: TV's Outrageous Queen of Cuisine.* [Related plate 62.]

HARTFIELD

THE HON. AGNES ETHEL HORSFIELD MBE née Conway (1885–1950) historian and archaeologist.

The daughter of Lord and Lady Conway, she studied at Newnham and from 1905 assisted her parents in restoring the ruined Allington Castle, Kent, transforming it into one of the finest medieval buildings in England. In 1918 she organised an important and ground-breaking exhibition on 'Women and War' at Whitechapel Art Gallery, which honoured women's great contribution to the war effort.

During her career as an archaeologist she discovered the sanctuary of Petra in Jordan in 1929 and married the expedition leader George Horsfield in 1932, the year her co-written book *Henry VII's Relations with Scotland and Ireland 1485–1498* was published. They worked for twelve years as archaeologists in Transjordan, and wrote many articles for academic journals.

Towards the end of her life she entered a nursing home, Hartwell House, Hartfield, where she ended her days. She had inherited Allington Castle on her mother's death in 1933; after her own death it was sold and became a nunnery.

KITTY MARION real name Katherina Schafer (1871–1944) actress and suffragette.

A native of Germany, she became a successful music hall artiste (working a season at the Empire, Hastings, now, alas, the De Luxe amusement arcade). From about 1908 she lived in Hartfield, joined the WSPU in Brighton and, with Elizabeth Robins [56] co-founded the Actresses' Franchise League. She was first sent to Holloway in 1908, for throwing stones at a post office in Newcastle. As a protest against suffragettes being treated as common criminals rather than political prisoners, she gnawed a hole in her mattress, made a heap of the stuffing, twisted pages torn from her Bible into tapers, smashed her cell window, reached out to a gas light for the flame and set her bed ablaze. In 1913 she set fire to a mansion, Levetleigh at St Leonards; to the grandstand at Hurst Park racecourse and to several houses in Liverpool and Manchester. She was never prosecuted for these acts, but for other offences was imprisoned seven times, went on hunger strike, was force-fed 232 times in a fourteen-week period and convalesced at Backsettown [299].

When WWI began she returned to the West End stage and formed a choir to raise money for East End children; however, her German nationality gave the government a perfect excuse to deport her. She went to the USA, where she was arrested nine times and served a month in prison for publishing information on contraception. In 1921 she co-founded the first birth-control clinic, but it was swiftly closed down by the police. She died in New York and her typed autobiography is in the Museum of London. [Related plate 40; image p276.]

HASTINGS

MARY ALLEN OBE (1878–1964) suffragette and pioneer police officer.

After living a quiet, middle-class domestic life until her thirties, she joined the WSPU suffragettes, served three terms of imprisonment, went on hunger-strike and was force-fed. From 1912 she was organiser for the Eastbourne, Bexhill, St Leonards and Hastings branches, she became a close friend of Isabel Sieveking [228] and shared a speaking platform with Mrs Pankhurst [294] at a rally at the Public Hall (now Yates's) in Hastings.

During WWI she was commandant of the WPS, founded by her friend Margaret Damer Dawson [159]. Wearing a military-style uniform, she rode a motorcycle and sidecar and served in Grantham, London

and Hull; her OBE was for this work. After the war the WPS was dissolved, but for twenty years Miss Allen, wearing a peaked cap, riding breeches, jack-boots and a military overcoat, travelled the world giving lectures to promote and advise on the employment of female police officers. She wrote *Pioneer Policewoman* (1925) *Woman at the Crossroads* (1934) and *Lady in Blue* (1936). After meeting Hitler and Göring she became a Nazi sympathiser and chief women's officer of the British Union of Fascists. In 1953 she became a Roman Catholic. She died in Croydon. [Related image p296.]

GILLIAN BARGE real name Bargh (1940–2003) actress.

She left her birthplace, Hastings, in childhood, trained at Birmingham Theatre School and appeared on stage and screen for four decades. She played all the major London theatres and internationally, and in 2001 was nominated for a Laurence Olivier Theatre Award as Best Supporting Actress. Her TV credits included *Softly, Softly*, *All Creatures Great and Small* and *One Foot in the Grave*. Her final appearance was in the film *Love, Actually* in 2003. She married twice, the second time to the actor Clive Merrison.

MATILDA BETHAM-EDWARDS (1836–1919) novelist and travel-writer.

A farmer's daughter, born in Suffolk, her first novel, *Kitty*, published when she was twenty-one and still being reprinted in her seventies, was followed by a succession of novels and short stories which ranged widely over subjects of contemporary interest. She was of Huguenot descent on her mother's side and a year-long visit to France in 1874 aroused her enthusiasm for what she called her 'second native land.' Thenceforth, while continuing to write popular novels, she devoted herself to the cause of improving Franco–British relations by books which explored both the land of France and the life and temperament of its inhabitants. She was awarded a civil-list pension in England and a prize at the Anglo-French Exhibition of 1908. The French Government made her an Officier de l'Instruction Publique de France.

She was acquainted with many of the major figures of the day and her autobiographical books include vivid reminiscences of, among others, George Eliot and Henry James, Franz Liszt and Lord Kitchener. She was a close friend and travelling companion of Barbara Bodichon [193] and a friend of Mentia Taylor [167].

When ill health cut short her travels she retired to Villa Julia, 1 High Wickham, Hastings, in 1884 and embarked on a series of six novels based on the Suffolk farm life she had known as a girl. As popular novelist, travel writer and propagandist for entente cordiale she was a vigorous and admired contributor to the Victorian scene. She died at Villa Julia, which now bears a plaque in her honour. [Entry by Professor Joan Rees.]

Further reading: Rees, J. (2006) *Matilda Betham-Edwards*. [Related plate 5; image p281; biography p303.]

ELIZABETH BLACKWELL MD (1821–1910) pioneer physician and author.

Born near Bristol and raised in the USA, in 1845 she decided to study medicine, although it was considered ridiculous, indecent and even dangerous for women. After a succession of sixteen medical schools refused to admit her, she was eventually accepted by Geneva College, New York, where she was greeted with blatant hostility, barred from classroom demonstrations and ostracised. Despite everything, in 1849, ranking first in her class above the 150 men who had opposed and taunted her, she became the first woman in the world to qualify as a doctor.

Working in a midwifery school in Paris she lost the sight in one eye through infection, preventing her chosen career of surgery. She moved to London in 1850, but no practice would employ a female doctor, so she opened an infirmary and a dispensary for poor women and a private practice, and worked as a professor of gynaecology at the LSMW. In 1858 she became the first woman on the newly-founded British Medical Register. This was deeply distressing to many male doctors and foreign qualifications were immediately deemed no longer acceptable for registration. It was eight years before Elizabeth Garrett Anderson was accepted onto the register, and nineteen before a third female name appeared.

In 1879 she leased Rock House, Hastings, a ten-roomed, square residence perched above the sea on the West Hill, where she lived with her adopted daughter Kitty Barry (who was secretary, housekeeper and companion) and two servants. Two years later she co-founded the Moral Reform Union and opened a branch in Hastings. She wrote several books, including *The Human Element of Sex* (1884) and *Pioneer Work in Opening the Medical Profession to Women* (1895) and sent articles and letters to the local press about conservation, the environment, the East Hill funicular railway and the tramways. She attended public meetings about local issues including poverty, stood (unsuccessfully) for the Board of Guardians and fought (again unsuccessfully) against Hastings Grammar School's policy of excluding girls from scholarships.

In 1883 she purchased Rock House, and about 1889 her sisters Anna and Marian bought two adjoining semi-detached houses in Dudley Road. After Anna died in 1890 Marian lived in rented rooms at 1 Gloucester Place, closer to her sister Elizabeth, until her own death in 1897. Dr Blackwell died at Rock House, her memorial service was held at St Clement's Church, she was buried in Scotland and has a blue plaque in London. In 1914, when Hastings held a Pageant of Heroes, a long procession of girls and women marched to Rock House, where suffragist leader Millicent Garrett Fawcett unveiled a memorial plaque.

Further reading: Baker, R. (1995) *The First Woman Doctor*. [Related images pp16, 273.]

DOLLY COLLINS (1933–1995) folk musician, composer and arranger.

She was born at Hastings & St Leonards District Maternity Home, Fern Bank, 90 Old London Road, Hastings. Her father was a milkman; her uncle, Fred Ball, discovered the original manuscript of *The Ragged Trousered Philanthropists* and wrote a biography of Robert Tressell. She grew up at 54 Emmanuel Road until her family was bombed out during WWII. For a while they lived with an aunt at 27 Canute Road then moved to 117 Athelstan Road until about

1960. She learned piano and sang in choirs and at socialist meetings.

As an adult she became well known as a composer, arranger and keyboardist in the world of traditional English music. She revived the use of medieval instruments such as flute organ, crumhorn, sackbut, shawm, rackett and rebec, and was commissioned to write and arrange for groups, notably The Incredible String Band, and had her own: the Dolly Collins Harmonious Band.

With her sister Shirley she led the English folk revival and made fifty-nine recordings. From 1966 the sisters performed at festivals and concerts, and their recording of 'The Sweet Primeroses' was reviewed in *The Times*. Their best-known work was a thirty-minute song suite entitled 'Anthems in Eden', commissioned by and broadcast on BBC Radio One in 1968 and later recorded. In 1973 they played the Royal Festival Hall.

Her musical work was not lucrative and she had a series of jobs in shops and factories, as a bus conductress and as a postal sorter. In the 1960s she worked as a telex operator in Hastings while living for two years in an ex-Maidstone & District double-decker bus parked in a nearby field, until her boyfriend bought her a home at 2 Stonestile Lane, Westfield. In 1968 she married David Busby and had a son (who became a musician under the name Buz Collins). She divorced and married Stuart Hollyer in 1989 and from 1992 lived at Hooked Mead Cottage, Crawley Lane, Balcombe, where she died. She was cremated in Brighton.

A boxed set of the recordings she made with her sister was released as 'Within Sound' in 2002. All their major albums have been re-issued: *For As Many As Will* in 1993, *Love, Death and the Lady* in 2003 and *The Holly Bears the Crown* in 2005.

Further reading: Collins, S. (2003) *America over the Water* (autobiography). [Related plate 24.]

DAME CATHERINE COOKSON DBE née McMullen (1906–1997) novelist.

Katie McMullen was born in South Shields to an unmarried, alcoholic barmaid and was raised by her grandmother. From fourteen she was a domestic servant then a laundress at two workhouses before ending up, by 1929, as laundry manageress at Hastings Workhouse in Frederick Road. Earning £3 a week, a good wage for a woman, she had an assistant, ten outdoor staff and twenty-five mentally-ill inmates as helpers. The workhouse soon became Hastings Municipal Hospital and she worked there for ten years. From 1931 she rented rooms at West Hill House, Exmouth Place. By managing insurance policies and working a fourteen-hour day she saved enough to buy The Hurst, 124 Hoadswood Road, a fifteen-roomed property that she ran as a boarding house for deprived people suffering from tuberculosis, epilepsy and other disorders.

In 1940 she married, at St Mary Star of the Sea Church, Thomas Cookson, a maths teacher at Hastings Grammar School. In 1954 they moved to Loreto, 81 St Helen's Park Road, where they lived until 1976. A stillborn child was followed by three miscarriages. She became depressed, had a nervous breakdown and was given electric shock treatment.

She found solace in writing and co-founded the Hastings Writers' Group. Aged forty-four, she published the first of her stories, many of them about hardship, poverty, tragedy and working class people struggling to better themselves. Eventually she produced ninety-six novels, which sold over 125 million copies, some of which have been translated into twenty or so languages and adapted for stage, film and radio. The eighteen dramatised for TV were watched by ten million viewers. She was for twenty years the author most borrowed from libraries (some books were written under the names Catherine Marchant and Katie McMullen) and by 1995 was the thirteenth richest woman in the UK.

Appointed OBE in 1985 and DBE in 1993, she died in Newcastle. She left £8.5 million, much of it to good causes, but nothing to any association in Sussex, her home for forty-seven years. In contrast, Hastings has been loyal to her: she has two blue plaques and when in 2006 her extensive gardens and magnificent oak tree alongside Loreto were under threat of being obliterated for new housing development, Hastings councillors blocked the plan.

Further reading: Cookson, C. (1993) *Our Kate.* [Related image p271.]

ISABELLA NEIL HARWOOD pseudonym Ross Neil (1837–1888) novelist and playwright.

A journalist's daughter, she was born in Dorset and, after working as a book reviewer, she wrote several successful novels, which were published anonymously, including *Abbot's Cleve* (1864) and *The Heir Expectant* (1870). Under her male pseudonym she also wrote a number of dramas, including *Lady Jane Grey* (1871) and *Andrea the Painter* (1883); reviewers always referred to her as a man. She lived with her father in London until 1883, when they moved to South Bank, 55 Baldslow Road, Hastings. She outlived him by only one year, both dying at home. [Related image p281.]

MARY BOTHAM HOWITT née Botham (1799–1888) social reformer and writer.

Born in Gloucestershire, she married William Howitt in 1821. They had four children and became Unitarians in the 1840s. She was editor of *Howitt's Journal,* and *The People's Journal,* and translated Hans Christian Andersen's fairy tales from Swedish. Between them, the Howitts wrote 180 books. Bessie Rayner Parkes [79] once commented that few who recited the line 'Will you walk into my parlour, said the Spider to the Fly' realised that it came from Mrs Howitt's *Sketches from Natural History.*

Mary Howitt helped to organise the petition for married women's property rights and supported the Anti-Corn Law League and anti-slavery movements. She and her husband lived all over Britain, but were residing at Clive Vale Farm, Hastings, in the late 1850s and their address in the spring of 1865 was West Hill Lodge, St Leonards. After 1870 the Howitts lived abroad, and became Roman Catholics.

EMILY JANES (1846–1928) women's welfare activist.

A wealthy Hertfordshire lady who had no need to make a living, she undertook a lifetime of hard, tiring, unpaid work for the benefit of women less fortunate than herself. Working for the church led to her involvement with the Girls' Friendly Society, and she was for ten years honorary secretary of the Ladies' Associations for the Care of Friendless Girls, and a member of the National Vigilance Association (formed 'to repress criminal vice and public immorality'). Her workload was exhausting: in 1891 for example, she travelled hundreds of miles over the railway network and by horse-drawn carriage to speak at 170 meetings; she also attended numerous committees and spent three hours a day on correspondence.

She then became organising secretary, lecturer and journal editor for the NUWW. Again her workload was extraordinary: in 1895 there were ten branches; by 1918, 130. In 1898 she took on another large task: editorship of the *Englishwoman's Yearbook and Directory,* founded by Louisa Hubbard [66]. Infirmity forced her retirement at the age of seventy-one and she moved to Dunclutha, St Helen's Park Road, Hastings, her home for about a decade. She ended her days in a nursing home in Hampstead, London, and her memorial service was held at Christ Church, Westminster.

DORA BARROW MONTEFIORE née Fuller (1851–1934) suffragist and socialist.

Her father came from Hove, but she was born in London and raised in Surrey, where she was educated by governesses before being sent to Mrs Creswell's school in Brighton. She moved to Australia, where she married and had two children. In 1889 her husband was lost at sea, leaving her wealthy, but she discovered that widows had no right to guardianship of their own offspring. This awakened her to women's poor legal status and led her to join the women's movement in 1891.

Returning to England she became an activist within the NUWSS, WFL and WSPU as well as several socialist organisations and was once arrested during a protest in the lobby of the House of Commons. In 1906 she became a tax resister and was barricaded in her London home for six weeks, addressing the visiting crowds from her upper windows [294]. Back in Australia she edited a socialist magazine and during WWI joined the Communist Party of Great Britain, served on its council, and later represented the Communist Party of Australia in Moscow.

She wrote many pamphlets and books, including *Singings Through the Dark* (1898), *The Woman's Calendar* (1906), *The*

Position of Women in the Socialist Movement (1909), *The People's Calendar* (1919), *Race Motherhood: Is Woman the Race?* (1920) and her autobiography *From a Victorian to a Modern* (1927). She had a series of homes in Sussex, including Araluen, Beacon Gardens, Crowborough, and Melbourne, 11 Edwin Road, Hastings, where she died.

MARIANNE NORTH (1830–1890) painter.

Her family was the richest, best-connected and most prestigious in Hastings, where she was born. Her father Frederick was MP for Hastings, a magistrate and the town's mayor, and she was presented to Queen Victoria when she was twenty-one. She was privately educated and travelled abroad a great deal with her family.

When her parents' death and her sister's marriage left her rich, free and alone, aged forty-one she let the family mansion, Hastings Lodge, Old London Road, and spent the next thirteen years travelling to six continents, painting flowers and plants in unusual and exotic locations which had rarely been visited by British women, such as Brazil, Japan, Borneo, Java, Ceylon, the Himalayas, Sarawak, Hawaii, Honolulu and Africa.

After lengthy steam-ship voyages she travelled in horse-drawn carriages, ox- and bullock-carts, in canoes, on horseback, and by foot along dirt-track roads and jungle paths. As a wealthy MP's daughter she was sometimes invited to stay at colonial mansions or booked into hotels, but often stayed with the locals, bedding down by campfires, in jungle huts and tents, on verandas or in dilapidated barns. Travelling across the world alone was daring, but she also threw aside the restrictions of Victorian middle-class femininity, tramping through jungles, shortening her petticoats, sewing bank-notes into her dresses, wearing workaday clothes and sturdy boots, and developing hefty biceps from carrying her easel and paints. While in the Seychelles in 1883 her nerves 'broke down from insufficient food and overwork'. Despite that, she travelled to Chile and planned a trip to Mexico, but was too tired and ill to travel. She completed an impressive 848 botanical oil paintings in thirteen years and funded a special building at the Royal Botanical Gardens at Kew to house them.

One obituary, in the *Pall Mall Gazette*, said that she 'put into fifteen years of travel work that might have filled out at least three lives'; another, in the *Manchester Times*, stated that her paintings 'represented the most remarkable work of the kind ever executed by a single hand'.

The most famous female artist of her era, she had one genus and four species named for her. In 1884 a letter from Queen Victoria's private secretary revealed that, had Miss North been a man, she would have been knighted. But there was no honour available for the monarch to give to women [15] so Miss North received merely a signed photograph of Her Majesty. From 1885 she rented Mount House, Alderley, Gloucestershire, where she died at the age of just fifty-nine. The North Gallery is today still one of Kew's main attractions.

Further reading: North, M. (1980) *A Vision of Eden: The Life and Work of Marianne North.* [Related image p16.]

MARY RALEIGH RICHARDSON (c1882–1961) suffragette.

Born in England, she was raised in Canada and returned at age sixteen. She worked as an artist and freelance journalist, but after seeing the suffragettes attacked by the police on Black Friday [294] she joined the WSPU, becoming drum major in its marching band and one of its most militant activists, using the nickname Polly Dick. In just two years she was arrested nine times. She smashed windows at the Home Office in Whitehall and in Holloway Prison, set fire to a country house and bombed at least one railway station. In Holloway she went on hunger strike and was force-fed. She persuaded the Bishop of London to support votes for women and presented a petition to the reigning monarch, George V by leaping onto the running board of his carriage. An officer reared on his horse and felled her with the flat of his sword, then the enraged crowd fell upon her. The police rescued her, but not before her collarbone was fractured. She was with Emily Wilding Davison [95] when the latter ran in front of the King's horse at the 1913 Epsom Derby. Miss Richardson was beaten about the face and then chased by an angry mob to Epsom Downs station, where a sympathetic railway porter gave her sanctuary.

Her most infamous deed occurred on 10th March 1914, when she slashed with a meat cleaver Velázquez's 'Rokeby Venus' — a painting that had cost the National Gallery a whopping £45,000 — to draw public attention to the plight of WSPU leader Mrs Pankhurst, then on hunger strike. She received eighteen months with hard labour and a new nickname: 'Slasher'. From then, many museums banned all unaccompanied women. During and after WWI she wrote a novel and three volumes of poetry, joined the Labour Party and stood unsuccessfully for parliament several times. In the 1930s she was organising secretary of the women's section of the British Union of Fascists, then gave up politics in 1935 to devote herself to raising her adopted son, Roger. Although on her first visit to Hastings in 1913 pepper was thrown in her face, she retired there, living in a flat at 46 St James's Road. She died there and was cremated; her ashes were taken by Roger Richardson to his home in south London. Her suffragette prison medal was auctioned in 2003 and sold for £22,874.

Further reading: Richardson, M. (1953) *Laugh a Defiance*. [Related images p278.]

ISABEL DE GIBERNE SIEVEKING née Giberne (1857–1936) writer and suffragette.

A cousin of the poet Gerard Manley Hopkins, and daughter of the Chief Justice of Bombay, she was born and raised in Surrey, where she learned French, German and Greek and studied the great writers. After her marriage in 1891 she lived at Harrow and raised four children. She became secretary of the local PNEU, for whose journal *The Parents' Review* she wrote 'The British Parent and the Game Fetish' and 'Dietary in English Public Schools'.

By 1909 she was a widow living at 1 Exmouth Place, Hastings. She joined the local WSPU, although health concerns limited her activities to writing and public speaking. A close friend of Mary Allen [223], she took a keen interest in the WPS. She was a devout Anglo-Catholic and was fascinated by psychic phenomena. Between 1909 and 1912, under the name I.G. Sieveking, she wrote a novel and several important works of biography and history, including *The Memoirs of Sir Horace Mann*, *Autumn Impressions in the Gironde*, *A*

Turning-Point in the Indian Mutiny and her best-known book, *Memoirs and Letters of Francis Newman* (1909, reprinted 2007).

During WWI she founded The Hastings Herb Depot at 9 King's Road, St Leonards, working in the shop daily for several years. Her mission was to teach people the medicinal use of herbs and how to use free food, such as edible fungi. After the war, then in her sixties, she founded the Fellowship of Women, to ameliorate the loneliness of elderly widows and spinsters. Her diaries and notes, and a biography of her mother and other female relatives, are held at the University of Indiana. Her son Lancelot, whose godfather was G.K. Chesterton, became a TV writer and producer.[Related image p262.]

ANNA WHISTLER née McNeill (1804–1881) icon.

A native of New York, Mrs Whistler is the figure in the famous portrait 'Arrangement in Grey and Black No 1', colloquially known as 'Whistler's Mother', painted in 1872 in Chelsea. She was a devout Christian, and her artist son James so admired her that he adopted her maiden name as his middle name. From 1875 she lived at Talbot House, 43 St Mary's Terrace, Hastings, where she died. The house bears a plaque to her son.

HEATHFIELD

RUTH GIPPS MBE (1921–1999) pianist, conductor and composer.

Her Swiss mother was a piano teacher who ran a music school at their home, 14 Parkhurst Road, Bexhill, where Ruth was born. She was educated locally at Brickwall School, The Gables, and Bexhill County School, and gave her first piano performance at the age of four at the Grotrian Hall, London. Aged eight she performed her own composition, *The Fairy Shoemaker*, at the Brighton Festival, at ten was the soloist in Haydn's keyboard concerto in D major at the Colonnade, Bexhill, and at fourteen performed Beethoven's piano concerto No. 5 at the Hastings Festival. After failing the performer's licentiate of the RAM three times, she gained the Diploma of Associate of the RCM, and her BMus and DMus degrees, becoming (at twenty-seven) the youngest doctor of music in the UK.

Though her tone poem *Knight in Armour* was performed at the last night of the Proms, she barely scraped a living as a freelance performer and after marrying Robert Baker, clarinettist with the City of Birmingham Symphony Orchestra, joined it herself, playing piano, oboe and cor anglais as well as conducting and composing. During WWII she gave recitals at the National Gallery and raised a son.

In 1955 Dr Gipps founded the London Repertoire Orchestra and in 1957, despite opposition, became the first woman to conduct the all-male London Symphony Orchestra and the first woman to conduct at the Royal Festival Hall (the programme included her own cantata, 'The Cat'). She won the Cobbett Prize of the Society of Women Musicians, founded the Chanticleer Orchestra and in 1969 was the first woman to conduct a symphony of her own on BBC radio. Her seventy compositions, which included concertos, tone poems, string quartets, symphonies and a ballet, made her one of Britain's most prolific female composers.

She taught at Kingston Polytechnic, Cambridge University, at Trinity and the Royal colleges of music, became chairman of the Composers' Guild and was appointed MBE in 1981, the year she joined a small group of successful career women who wanted to abolish the Equal Opportunities Commission. Moving to Heathfield in her sixties, she was organist and musical director of its choral society. In 1988 she conducted a London concert that comprised works written entirely by female composers of the past 300 years. She died in Eastbourne District General Hospital.

Further reading: Halstead, J. (2006) *Ruth Gipps: Anti-Modernism, Nationalism and Difference in English Music.*

DOROTHY EVELYN THOMPSON (1888–1961) mountaineer.

The daughter of avid hill-walkers, she was born in Kensington, London, and made her living as an academic secretary. She joined the Fell and Rock Climbing Club in 1919 and by 1920 had climbed in Corsica, the Pyrenees and the Alps. She was among the first women to earn acceptance as an equal climbing partner with men and in 1929 became the first woman to ascend Mont Blanc by Brouillard Ridge. In 1934 she climbed it again, via the Aiguille de Bionassay, returning via Peuteret Ridge, the first such descent. She also took up ski-mountaineering. In the 1940s she settled at Donnithorne, Station Road, Heathfield, where she wrote her reminiscences, *Climbing with Joseph Georges* (posthumous, 1962). She died at home and was cremated at Eastbourne.

MONICA YOUNG (1929–2004) potter.

French by birth, she attended Ealing Art School, intending to learn sculpture, but when informed that it was 'unsuitable' for women she studied painting instead. After a long career as a portrait painter and illustrator, in 1969 she became a potter. She worked for five years in a studio in a former milk shed in Heathfield, making ceramic pots larger than herself, and in 1974 moved to Yorkshire. She won the Gold Medal at the International Craft Exhibition in Munich and her giant pots became so popular that she could barely keep up with demand. They are now collectors' items that change hands for thousands of pounds and are on display in the foyers of embassies across the world.

HURST GREEN

ELIZABETH LONGFORD CBE née Harman; Countess of Longford (1906–2002) biographer and historian.

A second cousin of Neville Chamberlain and the daughter of a Harley Street surgeon, she was born in London. She studied at Lady Margaret Hall then spent six years lecturing in English, politics and economics for the Workers' Educational Association. Receiving five proposals of marriage, she accepted Frank Pakenham, the future Lord Longford, to whom she was married for sixty-nine years. He was Conservative and Catholic; she was Labour and Anglican. He converted to socialism and she converted to Roman Catholicism. She stood unsuccessfully for parliament three times; he became leader of the House of Lords.

After raising eight children she was in her fifties before the first of her many books was published. Among them were biographies of Caesar, Victoria, Wellington, Elizabeth II and Wilfred Blunt [see Lady Anne Blunt, 92]. Winner of the James Tait Black Memorial Prize and the *Yorkshire Post* Prize, she received an honorary doctorate from Sussex University in 1970 and was appointed CBE in 1974. She was a trustee of the NPG and a member of the advisory committee of the V & A.

Her offspring included the historians Antonia Fraser and Thomas Pakenham, the novelist Rachel Billington and the poet Judith Kazantzis; her niece is Harriet Harman MP. She died at Bernhurst, Station Road, Hurst Green, where she had lived for nearly five decades.

HURSTPIERPOINT

ELIZA FLOWER (1803–1846) organist and composer.

Born in Essex, raised in London and largely self-taught, she became an organist and composer, producing more than sixty hymns and pieces including *Fourteen Musical Illustrations of the Waverley Novels* (1831) and *Songs of the Seasons* in 1834. As assistant musical director at South Place Chapel she adapted and arranged harmonic pieces for services, trained choirs and gave organ concerts, sometimes accompanied by her sister Sarah Adams, whose famous verse *Nearer, my God, to Thee* Eliza (and others) set to music. She performed the same service for a political reform anthem by Harriet Martineau. Her musical career was exceedingly unusual for a woman of her era and many acclaimed her the greatest female composer of all time. Poor health obliged her to live for long periods in the Sussex countryside. She died at Hurstpierpoint and was buried in Essex.

ETHEL ROSALIE SYKES (1864–1945) author and philanthropist.

Wealthy and well-educated, she co-founded the Royal Central Asian Society in 1905. From 1910 to 1912 she taught at Queen Mary's College, Lahore, and in 1915 published, in two volumes, *Readings from Indian History for Boys and Girls*. In the

1920s and 1930s she was the Lady Margaret Hall representative on the committee of the University Women's Club and performed charity work for the Pilgrims of Hope at St Mary Abbot's Hospital, Kensington.

In later life she moved to Sussex, and died at Bankey Field Nursing Home, Hurstpierpoint, leaving £500 to the Oxford Mission Sisterhood.

LAUGHTON

ELEANOR FARJEON (1881–1965) writer.

The daughter of an author, she was born in London, where she wrote her first two novels, *Pan Worship* (1908) and *Nursery Rhymes of London Town* (1916). In 1917 she rented a cottage somewhere near Amberley and lived alone there for two years, writing *Martin Pippin in the Apple-Orchard*, and *Elsie Piddock Skips in Her Sleep*, which she dedicated to 'the children of Sussex' who skipped in the lane outside her cottage. These books established her as a children's writer, but she also wrote an operetta, verses, songs, stories, plays and novels, including *Ladybrook,* a rustic, Sussex tale. Her best-known work is perhaps the hymn *Morning Has Broken* sung by millions of schoolchildren over decades and recorded by Cat Stevens in 1971. The recipient of several professional awards, she declined the offer of a DBE.

A friend of Esmé Wynne-Tyson [75], in the 1930s and 1940s she lived between The Hammonds, Laughton, and her home in London, where she died. Some of her works are still in print, and the Children's Book Circle bestows an annual Eleanor Farjeon Award for distinguished contribution to children's books.

Further reading: Hamilton, H. (1966) *The Eleanor Farjeon Book: A Tribute to her Life and Work.*

DAME EVELYN FOX DBE (1874–1955) mental health reformer.

Leaving her native Ireland, she studied modern history at Somerville then decided to devote her life to the welfare of mentally handicapped people. She trained at the Women's University Settlement in Southwark and in 1913 became honorary secretary of what is now the National

Association for Mental Health (MIND). From its austere beginnings (a borrowed typewriter and a promise of £10) under Miss Fox's direction it grew to be a national society with an annual income of £100,000. She travelled nationally for the society, served on various committees, gave evidence to royal commissions, was honorary secretary of the Child Guidance Council and the driving force behind the creation of British Epilepsy Association. For this work she was appointed CBE in 1937 and DBE in 1947.

By 1945 she and her sister moved to Laughton, living successively at houses called Annette, Wealdworth and finally The Nook, where she died. A special needs school in Blackburn is named for her.

LEWES

DAISY ASHFORD (1881–1972) child writer.

She was born in Surrey, but when she was eight her family moved to Southdown House, 44 St Anne's Crescent, Lewes, thence to Redholme, Prince Edward's Road, by 1901. Throughout her childhood she invented stories, and until she learned to write would dictate them to her father. Aged seventeen she went as a boarder to the Priory of Our Lady of Good Counsel at Haywards Heath. This spelled the end of her literary endeavours: she never wrote another story. In 1904 her family moved to Bexhill, where she worked at the Catholic Soldiers' Club before marrying James Devlin and moving to London, later running various businesses in Norfolk.

In 1917 she was sorting through some old paperwork when she stumbled across her childhood writings. She sent one story, *The Young Visiters, or, Mr Salteena's Plan*, handwritten in Lewes in 1890 in a small, purple, twopenny notebook, to a friend who showed it to a publisher's reader. To her astonishment it was published in 1919 with a preface by Sir J.M. Barrie [see Cynthia Asquith, 85]. It was a runaway success, being reprinted eighteen times that year, and was adapted into a play, a musical and a film, and is still in print. Because of the success of *The Young Visiters*, some of her other work ended up in print and she

also wrote her autobiography, which she burned before it could be published.

Further reading: Malcolmson, R.N. (1984) *Daisy Ashford: Her Life.* [Related image p16.]

DAME BERYL PASTON BROWN DBE (1909–1997) educationist.

Educated at a high school in her native Streatham Hill in London and at Newnham, she trained as a teacher and held increasingly important posts at Portsmouth Training College, Goldsmiths' College, London, and Newnham, becoming principal of Leicester City Training College and later of Homerton College, Cambridge. Here she introduced the pioneering, four-year bachelor of education course, which laid the foundations for a Cambridge degree in education. She believed passionately in change and modernisation, transforming the college's authoritarian culture into one of consultation and delegation, and she created an academic board. She was chairman of the Association of Teachers in Colleges and Departments of Education and edited its journal, was chairman of the principals' panel and a member of the Newsom committee. In 1967 she received a damehood for outstanding services to education.

In 1971 she retired with her Siamese cat to an eighteenth-century cottage at 21 Keere Street, Lewes, worked for Age Concern and as a tutor for the Open University, which awarded her an honorary degree in 1978. She died at home and was cremated at Brighton.

JOAN DAVIES COOPER CB (1914–1999) child care reformer.

Her birthplace was the Moravian religious settlement in Manchester, where she attended university. An atheist, she started her social work in the local slums, devoting herself to the needs of vulnerable and deprived youngsters. During WWII she worked with evacuee children in Derbyshire, rising to assistant director of education by the age of twenty-seven and setting up the first child guidance clinics.

In 1948 she became the first children's officer for East Sussex. She spearheaded innovations borrowed from other parts of the world and transformed the way children in care were treated by retraining staff, closing all the large children's homes and replacing them with foster care and small homes. She was elected president of the Association of Children's Officers in 1954 and served on the National Advisory Council on Child Care at the Home Office, played a major role in setting up the National Children's Bureau in 1955 and became president of the Association of Children's Officers in 1965, the year she became chief inspector of the Children's Department at the Home Office, which over six years she transformed beyond recognition. She was a major influence on the 1969 Children's Act and served as director of the new social work service at the Department of Health and Social Security. The driving force behind most of the major developments in her chosen field over a period of nearly thirty years, the Queen appointed her a Companion of the Most Noble Order of the Bath (CB) in 1972. After retiring in 1976 she worked for voluntary organisations and was an honorary research fellow at the University of Sussex (1979–99).

She wrote three books, including *The Creation of the British Personal Social Services* (1983) and countless learned articles for professional journals, was chairman of the Central Council for Education and Training in Social Work (1984–86) and Parents for Children (1979–87), and vice-president of the National Children's Bureau (1964–99). From 1951 she lived in Lewes, firstly at 39 Gundreda Road, then Garden House, Painstwitten, then 2a Abinger Place. She died at Brighton General Hospital and was cremated. Her obituary in *The Independent* was written by Barbara Kahan [61].

ALICE DUDENEY née Whiffin (1864–1945) novelist.

The daughter of a customs officer, she was born in London. Her parents moved to Brighton in 1876 and she was educated at Hurstpierpoint. In her late teens she was apprentice to a music seller at 3 Castle Square, Brighton, then worked as visiting secretary to the head of the publishers Cassell until her marriage in 1884 to Mayfield-born civil servant and mathematical puzzle expert Henry Dudeney.

In 1897 they built a house in Surrey, and while raising a daughter she produced at least seven novels, of which the first was *A Man with a Maid* (1898). She also wrote dozens of short stories for *Harpers Magazine* and *Windsor Magazine* and kept detailed diaries of her everyday life, which have lately been edited and published. In total she wrote about forty novels of which some — including *The Day I Forgot* and *Folly Corner* — were adapted for the West End stage. They were all set in Sussex and she was compared to Thomas Hardy for her descriptions of rural life. Her stories were usually romantic, although one, *The Maternity of Harriott Wicken*, was described as 'a vigorous and outspoken work that shocked'.

The Dudeneys became well-known in literary and journalistic circles and famous with the public, but in private Henry was a difficult and volatile man. She left him, lived at Littlewick Meadow, then Pigeon House, both in Angmering, and conducted a love-affair with another man. After a reconciliation they lived at 138 High Street, Lewes, from 1914. In 1921 they bought Castle Precincts House (now called Brack Mount House) as their residence, and acquired a number of other properties, which they let, including Castle Banks, The Lean-To, The Old Poor House, and Mount Cottages (two of them). Her husband, who was organist at St Michael's Church and president of the Lewes Chess Club, died in 1930. In 1937 she bought Brack Mount (the second motte of Lewes Castle), a piece of land that adjoined her house, and immediately sold it on to the Sussex Archaeological Society at cost price, to prevent its falling into the wrong hands (it had previously been used as a tea garden by the Lewes Arms). It is now a Scheduled Ancient Monument. Mrs Henry Dudeney (as she is styled on all her books) died at her home and was buried, as was her husband, in Lewes Cemetery.

Further reading: Crook, D. (1998) *A Lewes Diary: 1916–1944*. [Related plate 29; image p281.]

EUNICE FROST OBE (1914–1998) publisher.

One of the few women in the masculine world of publishing in the 1930s and 1940s, she has been dubbed 'the personification of Penguin Books'. She joined the company as a secretary in 1935 but was soon dealing so effectively with authors, editors, agents, illustrators, printers, accountants and banks that she became the company's chief acquiring and co-ordinating editor. During WWII she directed the publication of 700 titles and set up the firm's New York branch. In 1961 she became the first woman in her field to be appointed OBE and soon afterwards became the first woman on Penguin's board of directors.

Nicknamed 'Frostie', she was lofty and irascible to her underlings at work and cantankerous in private life. Her marriage to poet and mathematician Harry Kemp was short-lived. She retired early and in the 1950s lived at The Lodge, Southern Heights, Stone Cross, Crowborough, then Linden Cottage, Stone Cross. From the 1960s she lived at 5 Priory Crescent, Lewes, a handsome Regency townhouse. She died in a local hospital, leaving all her money to charity and her body to medical research. Her papers are held at the University of Bristol.

EVE GARNETT (1900–1991) author and illustrator.

Born in Worcester into a wealthy family, she studied at Chelsea School of Art and the Royal Academy Schools. Her first important commission was to illustrate Evelyn Sharp's 1927 book *The London Child*. This opened her eyes to the plight of the poor and she later painted a forty-foot mural at the Children's House in Bow and published an illustrated book, *Is it Well with the Child?* (1938).

Her first novel, *The Family from One End Street*, about a Sussex washerwoman married to a dustman, was rejected by a dozen publishers before Frederick Muller took a gamble on it in 1937. The following year it won the Carnegie Medal for the best children's book, beating J.R.R. Tolkien's *The Hobbit*! It has remained in print ever since and has been serialised on radio and translated into many languages. It was followed by *Further Adventures of the Family from One End Street* (1956) and several others, the last being her autobiography, *First Affections* (1982). She illustrated several books by other authors and exhibited her artwork at the Tate Gallery, the LeFevre Gallery and the New English Art Club. She loved to travel and crossed the Arctic Circle sixteen times. She wrote a radio play, *The Doll's House in the Arctic*, and a related book, *To Greenland's Icy Mountains* (1968).

Eve Garnett lived in Lewes for at least fifty years (her mother lived and died in Chiddingly). In the 1940s she resided at 116 High Street, moving later to 12 Keere Street, and then to 43a St Anne's Crescent. She died in a local nursing home.

JENNY HENGLER (1849– ?) circus star.

The daughter of a riding master and circus proprietor, she was born at his travelling circus during a short stay in Lewes. She was performing by the age of seven and by her twenties was the most famous equestrian act of her era.

She married a fellow rider, Waldemar Kamienski, in 1874 and worked in his circus before moving to the USA, where she retired from performing and had three children.

CAROLINE BYNG LUCAS (1886–1967) **and FRANCES BYNG-STAMPER** née Lucas (1882– 1968) artists and gallery owners.

Caroline was born in Brighton and Frances in Kensington; their father was the first recipient of the Victoria Cross. They were both rather snobbish and incorporated the surname Byng into theirs just to claim a connection to the noble family from which they were descended (their great-grandfather was the 6th Viscount Torrington).

Caroline studied art in Paris, Rome and London, becoming a potter, sculptor, painter and printmaker; Frances married Welshman Edwin Stamper in 1909 and had a son, Douglas, in 1911 (his godmother was Princess Louise). In the mid-1920s, using an inheritance from their mother, they bought the Northease estate at Rodmell, comprising a manor house, a sheep and dairy farm, twenty cottages and 1,000 acres. In 1927 Douglas fell out of a train during a prank and died. The three were in mourning for some time. In 1932 they sold the Northease estate and lived between Wales and a pied-à-terre in London, where Miss Lucas painted, exhibited, and learned sculpture. The sisters produced a short documentary film in 1939 called the *Caves of Perigord*, showing Paleolithic paintings and carvings with a background of music and narration. Mrs Stamper became a patron and collector of art and co-founded the Contemporary Arts Society. She was widowed in 1939.

The sisters bought Miller's, St Anne's Hill, Lewes, converted the stables into an exhibition area and gallery and opened an arts' centre, staging over fifty exhibitions, concerts, dance performances, film shows, plays and lectures in four years. Participants included Lydia Lopokova [215], Ethel Mairet [204], Brenda Pye [194] and Vanessa Bell [214]. They bought other properties in Lewes (including Westgate House) and used one as an art school. In 1945 the sisters founded the Miller's Press, creating hand-pulled lithographs by a variety of artists; Miss Lucas herself produced six lithographs of scenes of Lewes and Brighton. They published *Twelfth Century Paintings at Hardham and Clayton* (1947), inaugurated the Byng-Stamper Prize for Landscape Painting, founded the Society of London Painter-Printers and began an appeal to restore the ruins of Lewes Priory.

The gallery and press closed in the mid-1950s and in the 1960s the sisters became permanent residents of nearby Shelley's Hotel, where they died. They were buried at Rodmell. Miss Lucas's painting of Adelaide Crescent is in Brighton and Hove Art Gallery. The stables were demolished in 1972 and Miller's is currently a guest house.

Further reading: Crook, D. (1996) *The Ladies of Miller's*.

MARY ANN MANTELL née Woodhouse (1796–1869) fossil-finder.

As a child in her native London she became fascinated by fossils and found a fellow enthusiast in her father's physician, Gideon Mantell, whom she married. He bought a practice in Lewes and was military surgeon to the Royal Artillery Hospital in Ringmer. In 1818 he bought two houses at Castle Place, where they raised four children. The couple enjoyed fossil hunting together, and one day in 1822 while he was attending a patient at Whiteman's Green, near Cuckfield, she killed time by exploring a pile of quarry rocks, among which she discovered the first known tooth of a giant, herbivorous dinosaur called the Iguanodon. Her husband publicised the find to all interested parties.

They moved to Brighton in 1833 and he became obsessed with fossils, neglected his medical career and ran into financial difficulties. He turned the family home into a fossil museum and Mrs Mantell moved out, taking the children. They had a trial reconciliation, then she left him permanently in 1839 and later lived with her daughter Ellen in Hampshire.

A monument has been placed at Whiteman's Green to commemorate her discovery, but a large plaque on their house in Lewes claims that Gideon Mantell found the Iguanadon bones; his wife is not mentioned.

Further Reading: Cadbury, D. (2000) *The Dinosaur Hunters*. [Related image p262.]

JOAN MAUDE (1908–1998) actress.

The daughter of Nancy Price [59] and cousin of the actor-manager Cyril Maude [see Winifred Emery, 235], she began her career in the West End at the age of thirteen and was cast in over fifty productions on stage and screen. She was the first actress to play the saucy role of Salome when the censors' ban was lifted in 1931 (though her performance was slated by the critics).

She had a long and successful career and two blissfully happy marriages, the first to reporter Frank Waters, who died in 1954 and by whom she had a daughter; the second to Oliver Woods, chief assistant to the editor of *The Times*. In the early sixties they lived at 22 Marine Square, then at 8 Rifle Butt Road, Brighton, moving to 6 High Street, Southover, in 1971. He died the following year and Mrs Woods spent her second widowhood alone, taking her Bichon Frise dog, Perrier, for a daily walk on the South Downs. She died at home.

ISABEL THORNE née Pryer (1834–1910) medical pioneer.

Born in London, she was educated there at Queen's College and the Female Medical College (opened in 1864 to train midwives). She married and moved to Shanghai, where after the death of her infant son she became convinced of the need for female doctors and decided to study medicine. She joined Sophia Jex-Blake [236] to become one of the Edinburgh Seven and was subsequently among the fourteen original pupils at the LSMW in 1874. However she abandoned her medical career in 1877 by taking up the post of LSMW honorary secretary, which she held for thirty years.

From 1879 she lived at Southover Grange, Lewes, with her husband, who served a year as mayor until his death in 1885. In the 1880s she was secretary of the Association for the Promotion of Food Culture by Women. She let the Grange from 1897 while she lived in London, then sold it in 1901 to Violet Gordon Woodhouse [242]. She died in London but her ashes were buried in the churchyard of St John's, Southover.

In 1914 an LSMW scholarship was named for her. Her daughter Isabel married Frank Verrall, whose father owned Southover Brewery; her daughter May and son Attwood became doctors. [Related image p266.]

MARGARET WOLPE née Leslie Smith (1919–2006) artist.

Her mother was a dog breeder and Cruft's judge, her father a farmer-butcher in Lewes. Born in Plumpton, after her mother died she was raised by her grandmother and attended school in Bexhill. She became interested in monumental masonry, took lessons in lettercutting and produced her first big stone carving, of St Christopher, at seventeen, then studied at Westminster School of Arts, winning a medal for memorial stonework.

She married art teacher Berthold Wolpe in 1941. During WWII they lived in London, where she worked as a firewatcher, designed field patterns for the RAF to camouflage runways, welded aircraft parts and took dressmaking commissions. After the war she studied at the Central and the Chelsea schools of art, received tuition from Henry Moore then taught and practised art in a variety of forms including sculpting in wood and stone, carving,

making jewellery, silverwork, painting, illustrating and enamelling. She worked for the National Trust, restoring mouldings and arranging swags and drapes, designed bookjackets for the publisher Faber, and painted portraits.

She raised her four children between London and a cottage somewhere in Lewes, where they mixed with local artists and searched the Downs for interesting flints and the beach for driftwood. Widowed in 1989, she spent her final years in London.

LITTLE COMMON

(MAUD) WINIFRED EMERY (1861–1924) actress.

A Mancunian, she came from a theatrical family and appeared on stage at age eight. From her West End début in 1874 she enjoyed a brilliant, fifty-year career as a versatile and popular actress. A specialist in Shakespeare, Shaw and Wilde, she could make an audience laugh or reduce them to tears with her skills in comedy and pathos.

In 1888 she married actor-manager Cyril Maude, cousin of Joan Maude [234] and lived in a large, posh house in Kensington looked after by five resident servants. During a seven-year maternity break she had three children and adopted her brother's daughter Winifred after he abandoned his family in 1895. (In 1911 the librettist Sir W.S. Gilbert died while swimming with her other niece, Isabel.)

From 1903 they lived at The Corner, Barnhorn Road, Little Common, an eight-bedroomed house in an acre of beautiful gardens. She died there, and was buried at St Mark's Church, Bexhill, as Winifred Emery, having never taken her husband's surname. Such was her eminence that George V and Queen Mary sent Mr Maude a telegram of condolence. He put The Corner on the market within four weeks. A complex of flats called Greyhorses now covers the site, though the boundary of their garden is still clearly defined and an outbuilding remains (Chevrons Cottage). Mr Maude remarried and appeared in the 1938 fundraising matinée for the Downland Trust [see Nancy Price, 59]. [Related plate 63; image p283.]

MARESFIELD

MARY ELIZA FULLERTON (1868–1946) writer.

An activist in various social reform organisations including the women's suffrage movement in her native Australia, she was later hailed as one of that country's finest writers and was the recipient of many literary prizes. She produced stories, articles and verse for various magazines, sometimes using the pseudonym 'Alpenstock', wrote two collections of verse, her reminiscences of childhood (*Bark House Days*) and several novels. Her collections of verse *Moles do so Little with their Privacy* (1942) and *The Wonder and the Apple* (1946) were published under the initial 'E', though her identity was revealed after her death.

In 1909 she became romantically attached to Mrs Mabel Singleton, a young mother. Having previously spent a year together in England they returned in 1922 and cohabited for seventeen years at Letchworth and Kensington. According to Miss Fullerton's diaries the women shared a bedroom. In 1939 and in poor health, she moved to Sussex, staying briefly with her niece Sophie in a farm near Worthing before becoming a paying guest of musician Beatrice Williams at Sandbank, Budletts, near Maresfield. She died there six years later and was buried at St Bartholomew's Church, Maresfield, her cousin officiating at the funeral.

Further reading: Martin, S. (2001) *Passionate Friends: Mary Fullerton, Mabel Singleton and Miles Franklin.*

MARK CROSS

SOPHIA JEX-BLAKE MD (1840–1912) pioneer of medical women.

The daughter of an attorney and aunt of Katherine Jex-Blake [53], she was born at 16 Croft Road, Hastings. At age eight she attended boarding school but, frustrated with the curriculum of superficial accomplishments, changed schools six times in eight years. In 1851 her family moved to 13 Sussex Square, Brighton. Denied the education given to her brother, she went 'into hysterics' to force her father to allow her a mere year's study at Queen's College. She later taught maths there, though her father forbade her to accept a salary.

On a trip to the USA to study teaching methods she met a female doctor and resolved to open the medical profession to women in Britain. At that time there were two women on the medical register [see Elizabeth Blackwell, 224] but new rules had made it impossible for any woman to become the third unless she qualified at a British medical school, none of which would admit women. After many refusals Edinburgh Medical School grudgingly accepted her and six others, They became, in 1869, the first group of women students at any British university and were known as the 'Edinburgh Seven'. The progress of the Seven was widely publicised because they suffered four years of harassment, insult and hindrance from male students, lecturers and university authorities determined to prevent women from getting trained. Miss Jex-Blake and others, including Isabel Thorne [234], hired premises and lecturers and founded the London School of Medicine for Women. In 1877 she travelled to Berne in Switzerland to gain her MD and, later the same year, after the change in the law, was able to qualify as a doctor by gaining the Licentiate of the King's and Queen's College of Physicians of Ireland.

She became the fifth woman on the British Medical Register and Scotland's first female GP when she set up in Edinburgh. She opened a dispensary for poor women, which later expanded to become the Edinburgh Hospital for Women, and founded the Edinburgh School of Medicine for Women in 1887.

Retiring in 1899 she bought Windydene, Mark Cross, a fifty-year-old house with eight acres, which she shared with her former pupil Dr Margaret Todd [below]. She kept a herd of cows and managed a dairy, a kitchen-garden and an orchard, in which her gardeners grew peaches, figs and grapes. She supported the Edwardian suffrage movement and waged a campaign against 'the reign of terror' of speeding motor-cars, having discovered while being taken for a daily drive in her carriage that they filled the village with dust, noise and danger. She died at Windydene and was buried at St Deny's Church, Rotherfield.

Further reading: Roberts, S. (1993) *Sophia Jex-Blake. A Woman Pioneer in Nineteenth Century Medical Reform.* [Related images pp16, 264.]

MARGARET TODD MD pseudonym Graham Travers (1859–1918) physician and author.

After working as a schoolteacher, Scottish-born Miss Todd became in 1886 one of the first students at the Edinburgh School of Medicine for Women. The four year course took her eight years because during her studies she wrote *Mona Maclean, Medical Student,* described in *Punch* as 'a novel with a purpose' and was one of the earliest members of the Women Writers' Suffrage League. She won the Silver Medal for Practical Anatomy and after graduating in 1894 took her MD in Brussels and was appointed assistant medical officer at Edinburgh Hospital and Dispensary for Women and Children.

In her spare time she wrote short stories for magazines and several novels, including *Kirsty O' The Mill Toun* (1896) and *Windyhaugh* (1898), under her pseudonym, although reviewers were not fooled and called her 'Miss' Travers; by 1913 even her publishers added 'Margaret Todd MD' in parentheses in their advertisements. In 1913 she suggested the word 'isotope' to her distant relation Frederick Soddy of Eastbourne. Greek for 'at the same place', it suited his purpose perfectly and using it he went on to win the Nobel Prize for Chemistry in 1921.

She was for over twenty years the companion of Dr Jex-Blake [236], upon whose retirement in 1899 they moved to Windydene, Mark Cross, where Dr Todd became a full-time author, writing *The Way of Escape* in 1902 and *Growth* in 1906. After her friend's death she wrote, under her own name, *The Life of Dr Sophia Jex-Blake,* a book described by a reviewer in *The Globe* as having reached 'the level of the rarest masterpieces of biography'. She died aged fifty-eight, just three months after the book was published. At that time she was living in Highgate, London. According to one source, she committed suicide; her obituary in *The Times* states only that she died 'in a nursing home'.

She left £3,000 to Lady Beilby and Dr Mary McDougall to help women studying medicine, and this was used to create a scholarship in her name at the LSMW. Her novels are still available secondhand, though at a high cost. [Related image p264.]

MAYFIELD

JOYCE HICKS OBE née Edkins (1900–1995) wartime fire officer.

A graduate in physiology at Bedford College in her native London, she was forced to resign from her teaching job when she married in 1924, so she took up golf and played for Surrey. In 1939 she joined the Women's Auxiliary Fire Service as a part-time appliance driver, and during the war was chauffeuse to London's fire chief during the heavy bombing. One night in 1940, with no thought for her own safety, she drove her boss to London's docks to superintend the fight to extinguish the worst blaze of the Blitz and demonstrated considerable personal bravery on the scene as the firemen worked throughout the night. She became famous around the world, though not by name, when her boss's report of the night's dramatic events was published internationally.

In 1941 she became one of the first three female 'brass hats' of the National Fire Service, when she was placed in charge of recruitment. In 1943 she was promoted to deputy chief woman fire officer, and by 1945 was regional woman fire chief for the Eastern Region, based at Cambridge, and the recipient of an OBE. In peacetime she played golf at national level and was president of the Ladies' Golfing Association in 1977. She lived at Rose Meadow, Meres Lane, Five Ashes, Mayfield, moving in 1963 (the year she was widowed) to Irving's Ghyll Cottage, Fletching Street. [Related image p268.]

BELLE RENNIE (1875–1966) founder of educational establishments.

She was born Isabel Moorhouse in County Durham and became Rennie when her widowed mother married the family GP. They lived at Harrogate, Torquay then Sway, Hampshire, where her stepfather built Quarr House and she set up the first fully-equipped nursery in 1913, having studied under Maria Montessori in Rome.

She played a key part in the foundation of the Conference of the New Ideals in Education in 1912, and in 1917 founded the Gipsy Hill Training College for Nursery and Infant Schools, which she set up with her own money, purchasing two houses in Dulwich Wood Avenue, south London, and leasing others nearby for use as classrooms and hostels. She ran it for nearly thirty years using the Montessori methods, supporting it financially when it hit hard times and winning official approval from the Board of Education.

After it was taken over by Surrey County Council in 1945 and relocated to Kingston, she remained a governor for some years. As honorary secretary of the Dalton Association, in 1932 she co-authored with Dr Charles Kimmins, husband of Grace [197], *The Triumph of the Dalton Plan* and, having assisted with the foundation of Gordonstoun, Bryanston and Stowe schools, founded Abinger Hill Public School near Dorking (with Dr Kimmins as chairman), a preparatory school where boys could be taught on the Dalton plan. From 1946 she lived at Knowle Hill, Newick Lane, Mayfield, moving in 1954 to Tunbridge Wells, where she stayed permanently in bed, because she had always hated getting up. She died at Tunbridge Wells. In 1975 her college became part of Kingston Polytechnic, now Kingston University.

MUDDLES GREEN

LEE MILLER Mrs Bey; Lady Penrose (1907–1977) photojournalist.

Born in the USA, she was a model who during the late 1920s and early 1930s established photographic studios of her own, firstly in Paris, then in New York, working on portraiture, fashion and surreal images. In the mid-1930s she married an Egyptian and lived in his native country, but left him in 1937 for surrealist artist (later, Sir) Roland Penrose, with whom she moved to England. As a staff photographer for *Vogue* magazine, she worked in Greece, Romania, Austria and Hungary, creating portraits of many famous persons.

During WWII she became an accredited photographer and correspondent with the US Army, and was probably the only female military photojournalist in the world. For eighteen months she endured extreme hardship, danger and emotional anguish. She photographed the WRNS, the siege of St Malo, the fighting in the Vosges Mountains and the devastating damage inflicted on London during the Blitz. She was present at, and took many photographs of, the liberation of four Nazi concentration camps, presenting deeply harrowing images to a stunned world.

After marrying Roland Penrose in 1947 she had a son, and in 1949 they bought the eighteenth-century Farley Farm, Muddles Green, where they amassed a huge collection of art, and where Mr Penrose's first wife, poet Valentine Boué, lived with them for a while. Lee Miller's war work had left her traumatised; she became depressed and sought solace in drink, but by the 1960s she had recovered and was featured in magazines as a gourmet cook.

She died at home, where her ashes were scattered in the garden. After Sir Roland's death in 1987, their son turned the house into a gallery, museum and archive of his parents' work, including 40,000 of his mother's negatives. Lee Miller has a blue plaque in London and one at Farley Farm.

Further reading: Burke, C. (2006) *Lee Miller: On Both Sides of the Camera*. [Related image p272.]

NETHERFIELD

DAME RUTH BUCKLEY DBE, JP (1899–1986) pioneering barrister and local politician.

The daughter of Judge Henry Buckley, who became Lord Wrenbury when she was six, she was born in Kensington and raised at Old Castle, Dallington (which remained her family's home throughout her life). One of the first two female student barristers to take part in the Lincoln's Inn moots in 1926, she was called to the bar later that year. She became a magistrate in 1935 and during the 1950s and 1960s was one of the most influential figures in local affairs in Sussex.

She was the first female chairman of East Sussex County Council, an active member of the South East Metropolitan Hospital Board and the only woman on the Local Government Boundary Commission, which she joined in 1958. Her sound knowledge of local government and the hospital board made her the perfect guide when Chailey Heritage Craft Schools and Hospital [197] made the difficult transition from a private to a state-owned hospital. From 1934 until at least 1981 (possibly until her death) she lived at Tollwood, Netherfield Road, Netherfield.

NEWICK

MARY IMPEY née Reade; Lady Impey (1749–1818) natural historian.

The daughter of Sir John Reade, she was born in Oxfordshire. In 1768 she married Elijah Impey and had four children in five years. Leaving them behind she went to live in India in 1774, because her newly-knighted husband had been appointed chief justice of Bengal. The Impeys immersed themselves in the ancient culture and were patrons of the arts. Lady Impey made a special study of birds and wild animals, which she kept in the gardens of their mansion. Between 1777 and 1782 she commissioned three Indian artists to create a series of nearly 200 large drawings (mostly of birds) of her collection. They were carefully numbered and the captions were inscribed by clerks as being 'in the collection of Lady Impey'. These beautiful drawings, often life-sized, proved to be of great importance to ornithologists and were later referred to in academic works. While in India she bore a further four children, and the family was painted by the German artist Zoffany.

Returning to England in 1784 she had a ninth child. Sir Elijah leased Newick Park from 1794 and after his death in 1809 she moved to London, where she died. Both were buried in the family vault at Hammersmith. The impeyan pheasant was named in her honour after she attempted to domesticate it in India and naturalise it in England. The paintings she commissioned were acquired by the Linnean Society in 1855 and in 1963 sixty-three of them fetched £6,000 (worth nearly £90,000 today) at auction. Newick Park is now a luxury hotel.

NORTHIAM

SHEILA KAYE-SMITH (1887–1956) novelist.

A doctor's daughter and a distant relation of M.M. Kaye [241], she was born at Battle Lodge, Dane Road, St Leonards and attended Hastings & St Leonards Ladies' College. Nearly all of her stories and novels are set in the Sussex countryside, where she had spent much of her childhood, staying at farms. Her first novel *The Tramping Methodist* was published when she was twenty-one, but it was *Sussex Gorse*, which appeared eight years later, that made hers a famous name.

One night in 1913 the house opposite theirs was burned down by suffragettes. She slept throughout the drama, but awoke to find that, although she took no part in the women's rights movement, the town was buzzing with rumours that she was responsible [see Kitty Marion, the real culprit, 222]. In 1924 she married curate Theodore Fry and moved to London, where she supported a scheme to provide lodging houses for homeless women. In 1929 they bought Little Douce Grove, near Northiam, an estate that had appeared in three of her novels. The house had double oasts, three cottages, four acres of gardens, sixteen acres of grassland and twenty acres of woodland. They both converted to Roman Catholicism and built the chapel of St Thérèse of Lisieux, one of four Roman Catholic heroines of whom she wrote in her 1953 book *Quartet in Heaven*, which also features Cornelia Connelly [248].

Although her most meritorious book was probably *Joanna Godden* (1921, reprinted 2007) her most commercially successful was *The End of the House of Alard* (1923), which was based on a real family in Winchelsea. Her fiction works included *Weald of Kent and Sussex* (1953) and the autobiographical *Three Ways Home* (1937). In the late 1920s she broadcast her works on the radio, worked as a book reviewer and judged literary prizes. She died at home and was buried at her chapel. A commemorative plaque was placed on her former home in Dane Road. [Related images pp276, 282, 283.]

NUTLEY

DOROTHEA BROOKING née Wright (1916–1999) TV producer and director.

Initially an actress, she married John Brooking and had a son. During WWII she was posted to Shanghai, where she started writing and producing radio programmes. Back home she worked for BBC radio then TV, gaining wide renown for adapting, producing and directing *The Railway Children*, *Great Expectations* and *Tom Sawyer*, which were watched and loved by millions, and three different productions of *The Secret Garden* spanning twenty-five years. A friend of Rumer Godden [244], she adapted her novel *The Diddakoi* for TV. After working in schools' programming, later in her career she acted in repertory and wrote radio plays using the stage name Daryl Wilde.

She divorced in 1951 and, in the early sixties, settled at Pilbeams, Forest Bank, Nutley, with archaeologist Wilfred Synge. While they waited for his divorce she called herself Mrs Synge to avoid scandal, but he died in 1971, two weeks before their wedding. With her son, Tim, she was active in Nutley Drama Group, serving as president until her death. In 1980 she won the Pye Colour Television Award for Distinguished Services to Children's Television. Mrs Brooking was described in *The Times* as 'one of a generation of forceful, independent women who helped to shape the BBC', while Anna Home called her 'one of the most influential makers of drama'. She died at Haywards Heath.

BARBARA WILLARD (1909–1994) novelist and scriptwriter.

The daughter of an actress, she was born in Hove and became a writer of novels, short stories and film scripts. She lived with a woman friend, the writer Frances Howell, firstly at Quince Cottage, The Street, Kingston, Lewes (1946–51) then at Forest Edge, an eighteenth-century cottage in Clockhouse Lane, Nutley. The pair occasionally collaborated professionally and during WWII worked as script editors for 20th Century Fox.

Her magnum opus was a series of seven books known as the Mantlemass Novels, about several intertwining Sussex families

living in the Ashdown Forest area. Some of her later novels are also set there. *The Times* described her work as 'an amusing flow of feminine wit', and she won the *Guardian* Award for Children's fiction (worth a hundred guineas) for *The Iron Lily* (1973), and the Whitbread Children's Book Award for *The Queen of the Pharisees' Children* (1983).

In later life she enjoyed visiting schools and libraries to talk to her readers, and loved the countryside, the forest and gardening. She fought to preserve Ashdown Forest, was a member of the Board of Forest Conservators and wrote books celebrating the countryside, including *Sussex* (1965).

PEASMARSH

LINDA MCCARTNEY née Eastman; Lady McCartney (1941–1998) photographer, campaigner and musician.

A native New Yorker, she was born into a wealthy family. She studied fine art at the University of Arizona, married a fellow student, had a daughter, Heather, and divorced. After teaching herself photography she began taking portrait photos that were snapped up by magazines across the USA and were eventually to appear in fifty galleries worldwide. While working as a rock music photographer for *Rolling Stone* magazine she was sent to capture images of The Beatles. She married Paul McCartney and became keyboard player, backing vocalist and photographer with their successful band 'Wings' from 1971 to 1979, taking their three children on many tours.

The couple had a very happy marriage. They bought a 933-acre estate off the west side of Tanhouse Lane, a mile south-west of Peasmarsh, where their children attended local schools. The estate included Woodlands Farm, Beanacres, Blossom Farm, an estate lodge, numerous cottages, barns, a pond and a pavilion. They established an organic farm and recruited a fleet of staff. In 1975 they turned vegetarian and she became an outspoken campaigner for animal welfare, co-founded Animal Line and published *Home Cooking* (1989), which became, transatlantically, the best selling vegetarian cook-book of all time, and in 1993 launched a range of meat-free convenience foods that made her a millionairess.

She drew up her will at Hog Hill Mill, Workhouse Lane, Icklesham, a smock windmill whose renovation her husband funded and which served as his recording studio. When her husband was knighted in 1997 she became Lady McCartney, but neither of them used their titles. A year later she died in California, having tried to cure herself of cancer at her Sussex home. In accordance with her wishes, her ashes were scattered at the farm in Peasmarsh, which her husband still owns.

Further reading: Fields, D. (2001) *Linda McCartney.*

PETT

FAY GODWIN née Simmonds (1931–2005) landscape and portrait photographer.

Of English and American parentage, she was born in Berlin. She moved to London, married the editor-in-chief of Penguin books and had two children. Her hobby was taking family photographs and she toyed with the idea of becoming a professional, but when her husband walked out in 1969 he told her to get a secretarial job as she'd never survive in the male world of photography. Rising to this challenge, she bought a big, expensive camera on borrowed money. Her first commissions were for book jackets and authors' publicity shots, but she was later to gain high acclaim for her beautiful landscape work and her portraits of Poet Laureate Ted Hughes and novelist Doris Lessing. She collaborated with several writers to produce books of poems or prose and photographs. The Arts Council gave her one of its first major awards for photography and she was an honorary fellow of the Royal Photographic Society. Her work was exhibited all over the world, from small venues such as Rye Art Gallery to the NPG and the V & A.

Her strong belief in the right to roam the countryside led to her becoming president of the Ramblers' Association (1987–1990) and her related book *Our Forbidden Land* (1990) won the first Green Book of the Year Award. She lived at Pett Level and died in Hastings.

PEVENSEY

M.M. KAYE (1908–2004) novelist.

The daughter of a British civil servant posted to India, Mary Margaret Kaye was born in Simla. She loved her native country and soaked up every detail of its culture. When her family moved to England, she made her living painting and selling Indian pictures, then wrote children's books (as Mollie Kaye). When she had earned sufficient money, she returned to India, where she had a child with, and subsequently married, army officer G.J. Hamilton, with whom she had a second daughter. When he retired in 1967 they moved to England, eventually settling in Pevensey.

She wrote more children's books, seven detective novels and several works of history. Her internationally-acclaimed book *The Far Pavilions* (1978) sold over fifteen million copies, was translated into sixteen languages and adapted into a TV series and a West End musical. Widowed in 1985, she wrote three volumes of autobiography, the last appearing in 1999. She moved to Hampshire, then to Suffolk, where she died.

POLEGATE

ELIZABETH DAVID CBE, FRSL née Gwynne (1913–1992) cookery writer.

Her grandfather was a viscount; her father, Rupert Sackville Gwynne, was MP for Eastbourne; her aunt was Violet Gordon Woodhouse [242]. She was born at Wootton Manor, a redbrick Jacobean farmhouse, educated at home until age eleven, then went to boarding-school, studied at the Sorbonne and lived with a French family. She almost became an actress, but instead travelled with her lover by yacht to Italy, Greece, Crete and Egypt, where she married an army officer. They lived in India for five years, then she left him, settled in London in 1946 and began a series of passionate love-affairs. She greatly admired the works of Hilda Leyel [78], and began to contribute cookery columns to newspapers and magazines and in 1950 wrote *A Book of Mediterranean Food*. This went into many editions, most recently in 2005; similarly, her 1951 book *French Country Cooking* has been constantly in print for half a century.

Credited with introducing French and Italian food into homes, restaurants and grocery shops across the UK, she advised top chefs and opened a cookery shop. She won the Glenfiddich Writer of the Year award, was given honorary doctorates by the universities of Essex and Bristol, was awarded the Chevalier de l'Ordre du Mérite Agricole, elected a Fellow of the Royal Society of Literature in 1982, and appointed OBE in 1976 and CBE in 1986. She recovered from a drink and drugs dependency to co-found the successful Elizabeth David chain of kitchenware shops. She died in London and was buried at the family church of St Peter's, Folkington. Her life story was dramatised on TV in 2006.

Further reading: Cooper, C. (1999) *Writing at the Kitchen Table: The Authorised Biography of Elizabeth David*.

VIOLET GORDON WOODHOUSE née Gwynne (1872–1951) musician.

Her mother was a talented vocalist; her brother Roland became mayor of Eastbourne; her brother Rupert became MP for Eastbourne; his daughter was Elizabeth David [above]. She was born at Harley Street, London, and grew up at Folkington Manor from 1876 to 1895, where her wealthy family employed twelve resident servants. Taught by a governess, she had private piano lessons from age seven, from seventeen was taught by leading piano teacher Oscar Beringer, and studied at the RAM.

In 1891 she was presented to the Princess of Wales. Briefly engaged to Lord Gage, owner of Firle Place estate, in 1895 she married John Gordon Woodhouse. Her father had forbidden her to perform in public, but once married she gave amateur piano recitals; however, she was not well known until she revived the use of the harpsichord and clavichord, virginals and spinet, early-music instruments that had fallen into disuse over the years (hers were copies made by Dolmetsch). She also revived the keyboard works of Scarlatti and Byrd, and was noted for her 'scrupulous fidelity' to the music as written. Her recording career lasted only from 1920 to 1928, but she was the first person whose harpsichord playing was recorded onto disc and broadcast on radio.

She was a professional for only a few years; after 1926, when her husband inherited a fortune (because his two aunts were murdered by their butler) she performed solely in her own salon to an invited audience of eminent musicians, artists and literary figures who fawned on her, some almost grovelling at her exquisitely-shod feet, hailing her the greatest virtuoso clavichordist of her day and a rival to the great Wanda Landowska on the harpsichord. Said to 'cast a captivating spell' over members of both sexes, several women fell in love with her including Miss Radclyffe Hall [245], who dedicated a book of erotic poems to her.

She became equally famous for her living arrangements, usually described as her 'Ménage-à-Cinq'. The Woodhouses initially lived between a Georgian town house in London and Wootton Manor, Folkington, which they leased from her father. In 1901 they lived for three months at Cobbe Place, Firle, then bought Southover Grange, Lewes, from Isabel Thorne [234] for £7,000, living there until 1907, when they moved to Stratford-upon-Avon. Having married platonically, in 1899 she invited her lover William (from 1933, Viscount) Barrington (1873–1960) into the marital home at Wootton Manor. Four years later witty barrister Max Labouchère (1871–1918) joined them at Lewes, followed by cavalry officer and musician the Hon. Denis Tollemache (1884–1942), who moved in permanently in 1904. Despite being called the 'Woodhouse Circus' by society critics, the five lived together in perfect contentment until war came in 1914: three of the men enlisted and one was killed. The remaining four moved to Nether Lypiatt, Gloucestershire in 1923, where they lived together for the rest of their lives.

She died in London and at her funeral at Folkington Viscount Barrington was chief mourner; he organised her headstone and her memorial tablet inside the church. He and Mr Woodhouse continued to live happily under the same roof until the latter's death in 1951. (Nether Lypiatt later became the home of Prince and Princess Michael of Kent.) In 1996 a collection of thirty-three of Violet Woodhouse's existing recordings was issued on CD (which is more hiss than music). Her great-niece wrote her biography in 1997, and an opera, *Violet*, based on her life, premiered in 2005.

Further reading: Douglas-Home, J. (1997) *Violet: The Life and Loves of Violet Gordon Woodhouse*. [Related image p266.]

RODMELL

(ADELINE) VIRGINIA WOOLF née Stephen (1882–1941) novelist and essayist.

The sister of Vanessa Bell [214], she was born into a wealthy, intellectual but unconventional London family and was educated at home. The house she shared with her siblings became the focal point of writers, artists and critics known as the Bloomsbury Set. She married Leonard Woolf in 1912 and, like most of the Set, who were said to 'live in squares and love in triangles', had at least one love-affair with a member of her own sex; her relationship with Vita Sackville-West (who had afffairs with two other women in this book) is well documented.

In 1915 she and Leonard founded the Hogarth Press, at their home in Richmond, Surrey. They kept a house in the capital until 1940, and is associated with several addresses in Sussex. She stayed at 9 St Aubyn's, Hove, in 1899 and 1900; with friends at Forest Row and with her brother Adrian at his house The Steps, Playden, in 1905. In 1910 she lodged at the Pelham Arms, St Anne's Hill, Lewes, while house-hunting. She found a new semi in Firle and renamed it Little Talland, taking possession in 1911, but it did not suit and she and her sister rented Asheham House, Southease, the following year (it was demolished in the 1990s). In 1913, after a suicide attempt, she recuperated for two months at Dalingridge Place near East Grinstead, the home of her step-brother George Duckworth. In 1919 the Woolfs bought The Round House, Pipe Passage, Lewes, the base of a former windmill, but they never moved in, having found the seventeenth-century, weatherboarded Monk's House in Rodmell, her home for the rest of her life. She joined the local Labour Party and served as treasurer of the WI.

She wrote nine novels, about 400 essays and two feminist treatises, nearly 4,000 letters and thirty volumes of diaries, much of which has been published. Lauded by critics as one of the greatest writers of her era, highly praised for her erudition in literary circles worldwide, and claimed by many to be a genius, she refused her appointment as Companion of Honour in 1935 as well as offers of honorary degrees from Manchester and Liverpool universities.

A lifelong sufferer of depression, she had two nervous breakdowns. The day after being examined at 24 Montpelier Crescent, Brighton by her friend and physician Octavia Wilberforce [152], Mrs Woolf drowned herself in the River Ouse near Monk's House. Her ashes were buried in her garden under an elm tree, now long gone and replaced by a portrait bust of her by Stephen Tomlin. There is a Virginia Woolf Society of Great Britain, and Monk's House is owned by the National Trust and open to the public every summer. Brighton bus 887 is named for her, and she has a blue plaque in London.

Further reading: Lee, H. (1997) *Virginia Woolf*. [Related plate 36; images pp269, 271, 281.]

ROTHERFIELD

(ELAINE) THÉRÈSE LESSORE (1884–1945) painter.

The granddaughter of Wedgwood's pottery designer and daughter of an artist, she was born in Southwick and raised at The Manor House, High Street, Rotherfield, though the 1891 census shows her and her sister at 14 Cornfield Road, Eastbourne (probably a boarding school).

She moved to London and married, firstly, artist Bernard Audeney then, in 1926, artist Walter Sickert; all three were members of the Bloomsbury Set. With Mr Sickert she led a peripatetic existence, although a good deal of her work can be found in the Brighton area. Famous for her paintings of parks, children, hop-pickers, circuses, fairs, Sussex fishermen, and 'Brighton to Ovingdean: The Interior of the Bus', she also painted textiles and ceramics. She died in Kent.

VIOLET HONNOR MORTEN (1861–1913) health writer.

Born in Surrey, she studied at Bedford College and the London Hospital and qualified as a certificated nurse and midwife. For many years she worked among the East End poor at Hoxton Social Settlement, which she had founded, and lectured widely on health issues for the Technical Education Board and the Home Office (including inside Wormwood Scrubs Prison) and was a lecturer on sick nursing at Borough Polytechnic (now South Bank University).

In 1891 she wrote *The Nurse's Dictionary* (which was into its 29th edition by 1980), the first and most successful of her many related books. She also edited and annotated an edition of the letters of Abelard and Heloise in 1901, and wrote *The Life of an Enclosed Nun, St Clare and her Order,* and *Questions for Women (and Men)*. She founded the Women Writers' Dinner, which was held annually from 1889, and co-founded the Nurses' Co-operation and the Association of Asylum Workers. She served several terms on the London School Board, to which she had been elected as a 'Progressive' candidate in 1897.

As well as taking a special interest in the medical welfare of children, she put forward a proposal to run evening classes in prisons. She was also involved in the women's suffrage movement and prison reform. For over ten years she boarded what were then described as 'helpless and defective' children at her home, Oakdene, Town Row, Rotherfield, where she died.

RYE

MARY AIKEN née Hoover (1905–1992) painter.

Educated at art schools in her native USA, in France and in Germany, after painting large frescos in Madrid she spent a year in Ibiza, painting the islanders and their landscape. Back in New York she won several fresco commissions, gave fourteen group and solo exhibitions in two years, and sold two of her paintings to the prestigious Metropolitan Museum.

When in 1937 she married, as his third wife, poet Conrad Aiken, her career was completely eclipsed by his. They moved to Jeake's House, Mermaid Street, Rye, where he had lived with his previous wives [see Joan Aiken, 70], created a painting gallery in the house, stayed there until 1940 then returned in 1945 until 1947, when they left Sussex, never to return. [Related image p263.]

MONICA EDWARDS née le Doux Newton (1912–1998) author.

A clergyman's daughter, she was born in Derbyshire and moved with her family to Rye, where her father was incumbent of the Church of the Holy Spirit. She made friends with local fishermen and at twenty-one married Bill Edwards, who owned a fishing hut on Camber Sands and shared her interest in performing acrobatics (the couple later sold postcards of themselves practising in costume).

She wrote articles and verse for various publications and edited a magazine. After having two children they moved to Punch Bowl Farm in Surrey in 1947, where she wrote over fifty books in thirty years, starting with *Wish for a Pony* (1947) and ending with *Badger Valley* (1976). Her children's story books were of the middle-class genre and are divided into the Romney Marsh series and the Punchbowl series. The fifteen set in Sussex drew on her childhood and featured local landmarks, although she changed the town names. *Storm Ahead* (1953) was based on the maritime disaster of 1928, when the Rye harbour lifeboat Mary Stanford capsized and seventeen local men were drowned (her father was one of the two vicars who conducted the funerals). She also wrote five autobiographical works, a filmscript and five works of non-fiction. A lover of the countryside, in her will she left land to the Downland Trust.

RUMER GODDEN OBE (1907–1998) writer.

Christened Margaret Godden, she was born at Meads, 30 Milnthorpe Road, Eastbourne. Her childhood was divided between Bengal in south Asia, and Moira House School in Eastbourne.

A prolific writer, among her seventy works were biographies, children's books, anthologies, collections of poetry and twenty-four novels. Her first big hit, *Black Narcissus*, appeared in 1939 and has never been out of print; it became a best-seller and was adapted into a film (as were six others). From 1945 she lived in England and in the 1960s her address was Little Douce Grove, Northiam, once the home of Sheila Kaye-Smith [239]. She later moved to Rye, the setting of one of her children's books (*A Kindle of Kittens*). She occupied Henry James's former home, Lamb House, for seven years until 1973, writing *In This House of Brede* there, and moved to Mermaid Street by 1976. When appointed OBE in 1993 she was living in Scotland, where she died. Her ashes were buried with her husband's in Rye, where a memorial service was held. Her books remain popular and some were reprinted in 2006.

Further reading: Chisholm, A. (1999) *Rumer Godden.* [Related image p283.]

MARGUERITE RADCLYFFE HALL (1880–1943) poet, songwriter and novelist.

Dorset-born and a graduate of King's College, London, she wrote verse, music, songs, short stories and eight novels. *The Well of Loneliness* (1928) gained fame when it was banned for obscenity because of its lesbian theme. It has never been out of print and the latest edition appeared in 2006.

Miss Hall lived in luxury, firstly with society beauty Mabel Batten, twenty-four years her senior, who died in 1916; then with Miss Batten's cousin, Una Troubridge [below] for twenty-eight years, in various locations, including two in Rye: The Forecastle, Hucksteps Row, and Blackboys, High Street (which bears a plaque) in the 1930s. Miss Hall, with cropped hair, gentlemen's tailored suits, spats and monocle, acted as Mrs Troubridge's husband, calling herself 'John'. The sexual nature of their relationship became public knowledge during the trial of her novel. By all accounts she was a demanding, autocratic and ruthlessly unfaithful lover. She conducted séances to contact the late Miss Batten and brought her mistress (Evgenia Souline) to live with them. A convert to Roman Catholicism, she died and was buried in London, where she is honoured with an English Heritage blue plaque.

Further reading: Souhami, D. (1998) *The Trials of Radclyffe Hall*; Baker, M. (1985) *Our Three Selves: A Life of Radclyffe Hall.* [Related plate 21; images pp263, 280.]

UNA VINCENZO TROUBRIDGE née Taylor; Lady Troubridge (1887–1963) sculptor and writer.

A student of the Royal College of Art in her native London, she set up a sculpture studio, where she produced her most famous work 'Nijinsky as The Fawn'. Obliged to marry for financial support, she chose naval captain (later, Admiral) Ernest Troubridge, a widower twenty-five years her senior, by whom she had a daughter. In 1917 she left him for Marguerite Radclyffe Hall [above] and gained a legal separation in 1919, some months before he received a knighthood. She lived with Miss Hall for twenty-eight years in various locations, including two in Rye.

Between 1930 and 1961 she wrote several books, including *This Man and This Woman*; and *The Life and Death of Radclyffe Hall*, and translated books from French, including *The Little World of Don Camillo*, *Under the Bolshevik Uniform* and works by Colette. She was noted for wearing a monocle and immaculate male dress suits in the 1920s dressing as an elegant lady in the 1930s and for wearing her late girlfriend's exquisitely-tailored suits (altered to fit) in the 1940s.

In later life she bred pedigree dogs and was a member of the Ladies' Kennel Club. A convert to Roman Catholicism, after Miss Hall's death she moved to Florence and died in Rome. [Related image p263.]

ST LEONARDS ON SEA

FLORENCE AYLWARD (1862–1950) composer.

A cousin of Clare Sheridan [192], she was born and raised at Brede, where her father was rector. She was educated at home, soon becoming known as an infant prodigy, and by the age of twelve her compositions were being used in village concerts. She later attended the Guildhall School of Music, where she learned piano, organ and orchestration. In her lifetime she wrote the music to over 150 published songs, usually ballads on romantic or patriotic themes, including *Song of Sussex* (1927) and *My Sussex* (1931). Some pieces were recorded and broadcast on radio, and her most famous was *Beloved, it is Morn*. Married to Harold Kinder, she bore a son in 1885 and lived at Byways, Hillside Road, St Leonards, from at least 1931. She died at home and her ashes were interred at Brede; her son Harold lived in the house until 1958. All of her sheet music is long out of print, but is available on the second-hand market.

FANNY BECKETT née Bousfield; first married name Thomas (1821–1902) philanthropist.

After marrying a naval captain, she left her native Surrey when he was posted to Harris in the Outer Hebrides in 1857. To help impoverished locals she built a Free Church and manse at Tarbert in 1860, helped over 800 people to emigrate to Australia and Canada, built a cottage at Manish to accommodate a village nurse and set up a fund to pay her salary. She gave considerable help to the Scottish Home Industries, opening agencies in Edinburgh and (later) in London to enable Harris women to sell their home-produced hosiery nationally. By the early 1880s the women's textiles were more remunerative than the farming and fishing industries run by their menfolk. Their stockings won First Prize at the Edinburgh Exhibition of 1886 and their tweeds gained a Medal for Excellence. She became a director when the Scottish Home Industries was turned into a limited company in 1896.

As a widow she married another naval man, Commander James Beckett RN, and in 1890 they settled at his house, Avondel, Hollington Park, St Leonards, looked after by five servants. She lived there until 1902, shortly before her death in Edinburgh.

ISA BENZIE (1902–1988) broadcaster.

A Glaswegian, she read German at Lady Margaret Hall and joined the BBC in 1927 as a secretary. She worked in the foreign department and in just six years rose to become a department director, only the second woman to win such promotion. She was largely responsible for founding Radio Four's pioneering morning news programme, *Today*, and was its first editor and senior producer.

At thirty-five she married twenty-six-year-old TV producer John Morley, and was forced to leave her job owing to BBC rules. After having a daughter she divorced, and returned to the BBC during WWII as producer of talks, a post she held for twenty years until her retirement in 1964. She lived in St Leonards for many years and died at St Helen's Hospital, Hastings.

ANNIE BESANT née Wood (1847–1933) social reformer and theosophist.

Born in London, she was educated in Devon by Ellen Marryat, aunt of Florence [140]. While living with her mother at Warrior Square, St Leonards, she married the Revd Frank Besant at St Mary Magdalen Church in 1867. She had two children, and left her husband in 1873, taking her daughter. Her life was spent in the service of a dozen great causes, about which she wrote many related pamphlets, articles and books, including socialism and Indian home rule. Inspired by Clementina Black [123], she led the Bryant & May factory workers out on strike. After being prosecuted with Charles Bradlaugh [see Hypatia Bonner, 42] for obscenity for publishing Charles Knowlton's *The Fruits of Philosophy* (which advocated birth control) she was labelled an 'unfit mother' and lost custody of her daughter. She was a close friend of Florence Fenwick Miller [165], Muriel Sackville [260] and of Mary Dodge [256], who settled a life income on her. She died in India and has a blue plaque in London.

Further reading: Taylor, A. (1992) *Annie Besant: a biography.* [Related images pp16, 184.]

LADY BOOTHBY née Louisa Cranstoun Macnamara; stage names Louisa Mordaunt; Louisa Cranstoun Nisbett (1812–1858) actress, theatre manager and novelist.

The daughter of an army officer-turned-actor, she was born in London. By the age of ten she was on the West End stage and touring the provinces (her sister Jane was also an actress). At nineteen she married Alexander Nisbett and left the stage, but was widowed months later when he fell from his horse. With her inheritance she bought a villa and kept a carriage-and-pair.

She returned to work in 1832, gaining popularity for her comedy roles at the Drury Lane and Haymarket theatres. In 1834 she was engaged as manager of the Queen's Theatre, earning a handsome £20 a week and for about a year from 1835 managed the Theatre Royal, Adelphi (now the Adelphi Theatre) in the Strand. At thirty-two she married, against his family's wishes, seventy-year-old Sir William Boothby Bt., who died eighteen months later. She wrote a novel, *Leonora*, and returned to acting in 1847. Described as 'the most radiant and enchanting of the old stage beauties', her portrayal of Lady Teazle, her final role in 1851, was 'bewitching and brilliant'.

After visiting friends at Quarry Castle, St Leonards, for years, in 1846 she purchased a nearby villa, Rosemount, on Quarry Hill, had it altered to accommodate a private theatre, and moved there permanently when she retired. A keen toxophilite, she was a member of the Queen's St Leonards Archers. She died at Rosemount, which has since been demolished. Worthing Museum has an oil painting of her, while the NPG has three lithographs. [Related image p280.]

ELSIE BOWERMAN (1889–1973) suffragette and pioneer barrister.

Her mother Edith was born in Suffolk and grew up at Sinnock Cottage, Hastings Old Town. Her father was a prosperous draper who died when she was five. Elsie was born in Kent and raised at Thorncliffe, 145 London Road, St Leonards, she boarded at Wycombe Abbey and read modern languages at Girton, where she joined the WSPU. In the holidays she was an activist in the Hastings branch, where her mother ran the suffragette shop at 5 Grand Parade, St Leonards (one of Elsie's numerous inherited properties). Her mother (from 1907 Mrs Chibnall) took part in the Black Friday [294] deputation, was injured on another soon afterwards, was an activist in the local TRL, and was a close friend of Isabella Harrison [249]. In 1912 mother and daughter sailed first class on the *RMS Titanic* and when it sunk they were rescued in lifeboat 6.

During WWI Elsie Bowerman served as an orderly with the SWH in Russia, receiving the Certificate of the Russian Medal for Meritorious Service. Later she went on a nation-wide speaking tour with the Pankhursts [294] in an attempt to prevent post-war industrial unrest and in 1918 acted as Christabel Pankhurst's election agent. In the early 1920s she co-

founded the Women's Guild of Empire with former suffragette Flora Drummond and served it for almost ten years.

Having bought Northwood farmhouse, East Lavington, in 1924 she became one of the first female barristers — and the first to address the Old Bailey — practising until 1938. That year she co-founded the WVS. During WWII she worked for the Ministry of Information then joined the BBC Overseas Division, becoming chief of General Services, responsible for conferences, at a handsome salary that reached £840 a year. In 1946 she sailed to New York to work for the United Nations as acting chief of the Division for the Advancement of Women.

She returned to England and lived between her London flat and one at 25 Silchester Road, one of her many St Leonards rental properties, and in 1961 she bought Batchelors, a seventeenth-century house on Cowbeech Hill, near Hailsham.

She wrote two short books: *The Law of Child Protection* (1933) and *Stands There a School* (1965). The latter was about Dame Frances Dove, founder of Wycombe Abbey School, where both names live on in the Dove–Bowerman Trust, to which she bequeathed the bulk of her estate. In her unpublished autobiography, *Reflections of a Square*, she expressed disappointment that after her generation of feminists had worked hard to free women from being sex objects for men's use, the 1960s sexual liberation movement had to a great extent returned them to that role.

She died at the Princess Alice Hospital, Eastbourne and, after a funeral service at St Mary the Virgin, Warbleton, was buried alongside her parents at Hastings cemetery. [Related plate 1; images pp268, 298.]

MABEL CAPPER (1886–1966) suffragette and socialist.

Joining the WSPU in Manchester in 1907 she worked full-time as (in her words) 'a voluntary soldier' for the cause. With her mother and aunt she was a member of the Church League for Women's Suffrage, while her father was a branch secretary in the Men's League for Women's Suffrage. She served six terms of imprisonment between 1908 and 1912, went on hunger strike and was force-fed. She arrived for one court appearance in a costume entirely composed of the colours of the WSPU, with a hat-band, sash and belt each bearing the legend 'Votes For Women', and proceeded to assert that it was not she who had obstructed the police, but vice versa.

During WWI she was a VAD nurse; later she became a journalist on the *Daily Herald* and a campaigner for peace and socialism. At thirty-five she married author-publisher (Thomas) Cecil Chisholm and they lived at 63 Pevensey Road, St Leonards, retiring in 1951 to Windrush Cottage, Warren Road, Fairlight. Her husband wrote *Retire and Enjoy It* (1954), which sold 20,000 copies, and died in 1962. He left £200 to Fairlight Village Hall, and it is assumed that she lived at Windrush Cottage until her death four years later. [Related image p275.]

THE VENERABLE CORNELIA CONNELLY née Peacock (1809–1879) founder of the CHCJ.

She was born in Philadelphia, where she married Episcopalian priest Pierce Connelly in 1831. They converted to Catholicism and moved to England. When she was pregnant with their fifth child he announced his intention to become a celibate priest. In 1844 the church granted a decree of separation, provided they each promised perpetual chastity. Mrs Connelly became a nun and music teacher and settled into her new life. In Derby in 1847 she co-founded the Convent of the Holy Child Jesus (HCJ) to educate factory girls and to train women as teachers.

Her husband then changed his mind. He renounced the priesthood, abducted their three surviving children and started legal proceedings to force his wife to break her holy vow, cohabit with him and submit to his 'conjugal rights'. A faction of highly-placed gentlemen, including the Earl of Winchelsea, funded his legal expenses. He won his case in the ecclesiastical court and, although the judgment was overturned on appeal, the case dragged her name publicly through the mud, as did her husband's series of defamatory pamphlets insulting both her and Catholicism. When she did not return he exercised his legal rights over the children [9]. She never saw her elder son again, and was reunited with her daughter only near the end of her life.

The convent moved from Derby to St Leonards before 1851, with Mother Connelly as superior. In 1863 Louisa, Duchess of Leeds, bought the ruins of the Old Palace at Mayfield, former synod hall of the archbishops of Canterbury, and after ten years' renovation donated it to be the mother house to HCJ schools all over the UK. Mother Connelly died at St Leonards and was buried in the chapel at Mayfield. In 1992 she received the title Venerable, the first step towards canonisation. A school in California and a centre in Manhattan are named for her.

Further reading: Flaxman, R. (1991) *A Woman Styled Bold: the Life of Cornelia Connelly.* [Related image p16.]

MARGARET COSTA (1918–1999) cookery writer.

A Rhodesian and graduate of Lady Margaret Hall, she was a food writer on *The Sunday Times* for twelve years. Her London restaurant, Lacy's, was worshipped by gourmets on both sides of the Atlantic and her legendary *Four Seasons Cookery Book* topped the bestsellers' list in 1972, 1996 and 1999. In later life she fell victim to Alzheimer's disease and went to live at Bryher Court Nursing Home, 85 Filsham Road, St Leonards, where she died.

MARY ELIZA FRERE (1845–1911) writer.

The daughter of Sir Henry Frere, later to be Governor of Bombay and a baronet, she was born in Gloucestershire and moved to India aged eighteen. She transcribed the tales and fables told by her ayah (servant), which had passed down the generations, publishing them in 1868 as *Old Deccan Days: Hindoo Fairy Legends Current in Southern India*, illustrated by her elder sister Catherine. By 1889 it was into its fourth edition and had been translated into three European and three Indian languages. When her father became High Commissioner of South Africa she studied the customs and traditions there. She wrote a play, *Love's Triumph*, and some poems for *The Spectator*. After learning Hebrew in order to read the original Old Testament she travelled to Palestine and Egypt to buy ancient texts and manuscripts. She left this collection to Girton (it is called the Mary Frere Hebrew Library).

She came to Sussex to recuperate from illness but died in her sleep in the Edinburgh Hotel, Warrior Square, St Leonards. She was buried at Brookwood Cemetery. *Old Deccan Days* was reprinted in 2006.

SELINA HADLAND (1838–1919) pioneering educationist.

A London cheesemonger's daughter she was for sixteen years 'lady principal' of Milton Mount College, Kent, which educated the daughters of Congregational ministers. When she took the post in 1873 only men headed such establishments and as a woman she had to prove herself (and her sex) capable of managing it. She succeeded. Under her leadership it became the first technical school for girls and was one of the first to install a gymnasium.

She visited the USA and Canada and wrote several books on education and occupations for women on both sides of the Atlantic, including *Education and Life in the United States* (1895). She was vice-president of the Association of Headmistresses, co-founder of the Teachers' Guild and of the Canning Town Women's Settlement, and a governor of Battersea Polytechnic. With her sister she moved to Miltolino, 2 Combermere Road, St Leonards, in 1898, where she died twenty-one years later.

ISABELLA ELIZA DARENT HARRISON née Tait (1855–1943) novelist and tax resister.

Born in Scotland, by 1887 she was living in London, where she married artist and sculptor (William) Darent Harrison. They lived at St Paul's Studios in Hammersmith, a community of artists, and in 1899 Fisher Unwin published her novel *Master Passions*. Set in the world of artists that she knew well, it was described as 'fascinating, well-constructed and thoughtful' and sold well. A second novel, *The Stain on the Shield*, appeared in 1906 and in 1912 she published a short biography of John Hampden.

During the women's suffrage campaign she was secretary of the Hastings and St Leonards Women's Propaganda League and a leading light in the local branch of the TRL. In 1912, aged fifty-seven, she withheld her Inhabited House Duty as a political protest and, when Hastings Borough Council's bailiffs came to seize her goods in lieu of payment, barricaded herself inside her home at 1 St Paul's Place. The outside doors being firmly bolted against the authorities, her food and supplies were raised up to the window in a basket on a rope. However, the seige fell when a careless visitor left the pantry window open after climbing out to gather flowers from the garden. The bailiff slipped in via the open window and served the official notice.

Her goods were taken away to be auctioned on 10th March, coincidentally her silver wedding anniversary. Local tax-resisters and suffragists organised a great banner-procession from St Paul's Place to the Albert Memorial, Hastings, returning to St Leonards along the seafront and finishing outside the auctioneers at 60 Norman Road, a busy shopping street, where a demonstration would be held.

Scores of suffragists came from Bexhill, Eastbourne and Brighton to join the procession. Before it even started a crowd of anti-suffragists collected and began grabbing and tearing at the banners. Despite this, the procession set off, and was repeatedly 'rushed' by unruly mobs of hostile men all the way to Hastings and back. 'The march was a continual struggle, varied by a free fight between the Antis and the Police and male friends of the Suffragists. The police did their best to hold back the crowd and prevent actual rough handling of the Suffragists, who showed considerable courage in continuing their march under the circumstances', reported the *Hastings & St Leonards Pictorial Advertiser.* In Norman Road the violence reached its peak. Antis again seized and tore the marchers' banners, ripped off their hats, overturned a carriage and engaged in fist-fights with male supporters. Women were physically attacked by roughs who tried to rip off their clothing. They fled, some taking refuge in a nearby forge; others in stables. When all was calm, they held a meeting in the Public Hall, Robertson Street (now Yates's).

Mrs Darent Harrison's goods were auctioned at a later date, bought by a sympathiser and returned to her. She lived the rest of her life peacefully at 1 St Paul's Place, where she died in her eighties. [Related image p274.]

ELLEN JULIA HOLLOND née Teed (1822–1884) philanthropist and author.

Of English parentage, she was born in India and raised in Middlesex. At seventeen she married wealthy, thirty-two-year-old barrister Robert Hollond, a man obsessed with ballooning, who had financed and participated in a pioneering, eighteen-hour flight from London to Germany in 1836. He became MP for Hastings, and also its mayor and a magistrate, and was not above giving bribes for votes: in January 1838 he gave three-hundredweight of coal to each working man in Hastings — but only if he was registered to vote in the constituency.

They moved into Allegria, a villa on Quarry Hill, St Leonards, in 1837 and resided there for fifteen years, maintaining also homes in Paris and Cannes, where Mrs Hollond hosted literary and political salons, becoming friends with all the great liberals of Europe and the Russian novelist Turgenev. Her husband concentrated on aeronautics; he took no part in salon life and had no interest in politics, either: in fifteen years as an MP he made only one speech — about ballooning!

Mrs Hollond wrote her first two books anonymously: *Channing: sa vie et ses Oeuvres* and *La vie de Village en Angleterre, ou, Souvenirs d'un Exilé* and, under the name E.J. Hollond, *Les Quakers* (1870) and *A Lady's Journal of her Travels in Egypt and Nubia*, which was published by the feminist printer Emily Faithful in 1864.

Widowed in 1877, she inherited for her lifetime use a sum today's equivalent of several million pounds and three fine mansions. She founded a home for English nurses at Cannes and left it a huge bequest, providing handsomely also for her twelve faithful house-servants.

LEONORA ISON née Payne (1904–1996) architectural illustrator.

The daughter of a barrister, she was born in Buckinghamshire and educated at St Paul's School for Girls and the Bartlett School of Architecture in London, where she was the first woman to win the Owen Jones Travelling Scholarship.

Considered to be the best architectural draughtsman of her generation, in 1931 she married fellow architect Walter Ison and illustrated several of his books, including *The Georgian Buildings of Bath* (1948, reprinted 2004), whose publication she funded from an inheritance, and *English Architecture Through the Ages* (1966); both went into several editions. She also illustrated John Betjeman's *Men and Buildings* (1960).

The Isons lived at Buckinghamshire, Essex, Bath and London but on retirement in 1970 settled in a flat at 10 The Mount, St Leonards. Mr Ison became chairman of the Burton's St Leonards Society, which later introduced Walter Ison Memorial Lectures. After sixty-five years of happy marriage, they died within a year of one another.

ANNA KINGSFORD MD née Bonus (1846–1888) physician and mystic.

She grew up in Kent but from the 1850s her family spent long periods in lodgings in St Leonards and she was educated in Brighton, where at age thirteen she wrote a novel, *Beatrice: a Tale of the Early Christians* (published 1863). She competed with the Queen's St Leonards Archers, winning a bouquet for Best Shot in the Gold in 1863. Two years later her family moved permanently to Dudley House, 56 Warrior Square, where her father died, leaving her wealthy. Although she married in 1867 (at nearby St Mary Magdalen Church), she was determined to pursue her own interests. The Revd Kingsford became vicar of Atcham, Shropshire, but she was more frequently found at St Leonards, where her daughter Eadith was born in 1868. She converted to Roman Catholicism in 1870, thereby permanently evading the usual duties of a vicar's wife.

She advocated equal access to education and careers, married women's property rights and women's suffrage, publishing *An Essay on the Admission of Women to the Parliamentary Franchise* in 1868. She wrote to both Hastings' MPs asking them to support votes for women (they refused), and in 1872 was co-organiser and speaker at Hastings' first women's suffrage meeting. Ten years later she was, owing to her sex, forbidden to read her paper on anti-vivisection at a meeting of the Hastings Philosophical Society (a man had to read it out on her behalf). She bought and edited the London-based *Lady's Own Paper;* although it closed after a few issues.

After spending six years studying medicine, mainly in Paris, she qualified in 1880 and for six years had a medical practice in London, where she was a fiend of Arabella Kenealy [171] and Florence Fenwick Miller [165]. She wrote books, poetry, short stories, political tracts and articles on health issues and vegetarianism, and was passionately against vivisection and vaccination, becoming sufficiently well-known to be lampooned in various publications (especially after she let it be known that she was trying to find some boots not made from animal skin), though *Le Folet* magazine described her as 'one of the cleverest and most scientific women of her age'.

While collecting signatures in Hastings in support of the Married Women's Property Act she had met a woman who introduced her to spiritualism. She became a mystic and gave lectures on 'The Perfect Way'; her book on that theme led to her presidency of the British Theosophical Society in 1883 and to her co-founding the Hermetic Society in 1884. In 1886 she contracted tuberculosis, died in London and was buried at Atcham. Nine of her books were published in her lifetime and four posthumously. [Related images pp16, 280.]

EVA LANCASTER MBE (1912–2004) military nurse.

Born in Bedford, she trained for five years before joining QARANC, serving in India and Egypt and, during WWII, on hospital ships, one of which was torpedoed off Sicily in 1943. She trained nurses in Egypt then worked for the Red Cross in dangerous, war-torn locations, among them the Malayan jungle, Kenya, Cyprus, the Seychelles and the New Hebrides in the Pacific. Her worst posting was in 1966, when she served in Vietnam. She was appointed MBE in 1954 and in 1969 received the coveted and prestigious Florence Nightingale Award for nursing. In retirement she lived for many years in St Leonards, where she died.

GRACE MCDOUGALL née Smith (1887–1963) officer of the FANY.

An international fencer and the first winner of the Empire Cup for rifle shooting at Bisley, she joined the FANY in 1910, becoming sergeant-major by 1912. Lilian Franklin [61] was her second-lieutenant. During WWI she drove an ambulance in Belgium and rescued wounded soldiers from the trenches while under fire. She married Ronald McDougall in 1915 (she was reputedly the first bride to marry in khaki) then returned to war, performing three more years of hard slog in France and Belgium, opening and running field and base hospitals, and being shelled, bombed and shot at. A letter she wrote to FANY HQ in 1917 reveals the personal danger under which the women worked: 'Baths and kitchen gone. Robertson had a very narrow shave. A piece of bomb came through the wall, passed across her bed and tore her skirts to ribbons and is now firmly embedded in her door. Cadell got her wall pierced and a bit of bomb under her bed. Moses [Miss Mosely-Williams] was thrown down on the ground and I got a bit of bomb in my coat'.

After her two brothers were killed in action, in 1916 she persuaded Belgian gunners to let her fire two shells at the Germans, and brought back the cases as souvenirs. She wrote to her mother: 'I am going to try and blow up their aerodrome with dynamite ... if this [letter] falls into their hands I shall be shot!' Because the British War Office was about to abolish it in 1917, she persuaded the Belgian Army to make her corps of the FANY (Calais Belgian Convoy) soldiers of their corps of transport. Risking capture, when the British Army withdrew she courageously remained to nurse one of its officers, arranged a military funeral for him, read the burial service, and was taken prisoner by the Germans. Somehow she escaped to London via the Netherlands and went to Lamarck, a makeshift hospital opened in Calais to deal with the 8,000 men wounded at Ypres.

For her countless heroic deeds she was lavishly decorated by the grateful French and Belgians, receiving the Ordre de la Couronne, the Ordre de Leopold II, the Mons Medal, the 1914–18 Service Medal, the Victory Medal, the Croix de Guerre (Silver Star), the Médaille d'Honneur, the Médaille des Epidémies, the Médaille Secours des Blessés Militaires, the Médaille de la Reine Elisabeth and the Rosette to the Mons Star. The British gave her nothing.

In peacetime she and her husband were farmers in Southern Rhodesia (Zimbabwe) and had three children. She wrote (anonymously) *Nursing Adventures: a F.A.N.Y. in France* (1917) and a novel, *The Golden Bowl* (1926). In later life she moved into Filsham House Nursing Home, Filsham Road, St Leonards, where she died.

MOTHER AGNES MASON (1849–1941) founder of the Community of the Holy Family.

Welsh-born Miss Mason was from a religious family and performed social and educational work before graduating in moral sciences at Newnham (she later also earned the Lambeth Diploma in Theology). She lectured in mental and moral science at Bedford College and was secretary to the Guild of the Epiphany. In 1895, supported by the Archbishop of Canterbury, she founded and was first mother superior of the Anglican Community of the Holy Family, dedicated to the religious teaching of female scholars and artists of all ages, worldwide. The Community opened premises in London, Leeds, Cambridge, Peakirk and India. Its mother house, Holmhurst St Mary, The Ridge, St Leonards, was opened in 1913 and Mother Agnes was its superior for twenty years. She died there and was interred in its private graveyard.

Holmhurst, a Grade II listed building, was sold by the Mother Agnes Trust to a property developer, who turned it into a gated development of luxury residences too expensive for the average local. The funds raised were used to create the Magnet Centre (from 'Mother AGNEs Trust') on London Road in 2003, where the Holmhurst Theological Library of 20,000 books is now housed.

MURIEL MATTERS-PORTER née Matters (1877–1969) suffragette.

Born in Australia, she took a degree in music and became an actress and elocution teacher. She came to Britain, joined the WSPU and TRL and in 1908 participated in a suffrage caravan tour of Kent, Surrey and Sussex, holding meetings at many towns. That autumn she and another suffragette held a protest in the ladies' gallery of the House of Commons, chaining and padlocking themselves to the grille. After being forcibly removed she joined another protest outside, was arrested for disorderly conduct and imprisoned for a month. (The grille, now classified as a historical artefact, is preserved in the Museum of London.) On 17th February 1909, in a now-legendary publicity stunt, she hired an airship, had it painted with the slogan 'Votes for Women' in gigantic lettering, and hovered over Westminster, showering the area with suffragette propaganda leaflets. Her campaigning for feminism, peace and socialism took her to Scotland, Wales and Australia.

In 1914 she married dentist William Porter, adding his surname to hers. A friend of Mrs Montefiore [226], she was a member of the Women's Guild of Empire [see Elsie Bowerman, 247] and stood unsuccessfully as the Labour candidate for Hastings in 1924. She retired to the Hastings area, was widowed in 1949 and died twenty years later at St Anthony's, 82–4 West Hill Road, St Leonards. She was buried at Hastings Cemetery in the presence of members of the Suffragette Fellowship.

MURIEL PEMBERTON RWS, FRCA (1910–1993) artist and designer.

A friend of Alison Settle [85] and of Pearl Binder [122], who described her as 'spectacularly gifted', she was born in Staffordshire. After winning scholarships to Burslem School of Art and the Royal College of Art, where she gained the first-ever Diploma in Fashion in 1931, having devised the course herself, she taught for many years at St Martin's School of Art. Here she became head of Britain's first faculty of fashion and design (one of her students went on to head Christian Dior) and in 1941 married the head of graphics, John Rowe.

She painted in watercolours, created stage costumes, designed cards for Fortnum and Mason and fabrics for Liberty. She was the fashion artist on *News Chronicle* (1945–52) and *Vogue* (1952–56), a fellow of the Royal Watercolour Society and the Chartered Society of Designers, and a Senior Fellow of the Royal College of Art.

By the mid-seventies she was living at St Leonards and teaching at both Brighton and Hastings art colleges. Her final exhibition was in 1993; she died soon afterwards at her home, 56 Vale Road, St Leonards.

Further reading: Taylor, R. (1993) *Muriel Pemberton: Art and Fashion.*

MARY WEBB née Meredith (1881–1927) novelist and poet.

A sufferer of Grave's disease, she was born in Shropshire. Her first novel was *The Golden Arrow* (1916); her sixth and last *Precious Bane* (1924), which won the 1926 Femina-Vie Heureuse Prize. She was not yet well known, and her life was cut short when, was staying with her close friend and former governess Miss Lory at St Leonards, she was suddenly taken ill and admitted to Quarry Hill Nursing Home. She later died there, aged just forty-six. Prime Minister Stanley Baldwin wrote the preface to the 1928 reprint of *Precious Bane* but she and her work remained obscure.

When, seven months after her death Mr Baldwin praised her work during his speech to a host of influential persons at a Royal Literary Fund Dinner, nobody present had heard of her. *The Times* scrambled to write an obituary, Thomas Moult wrote a biography (published in 1932) and her stories were reprinted, broadcast on radio, dramatised for the stage and BBC TV, and her style parodied by Stella Gibbons. A Mary Webb Society was founded in 1972 and her books are still available today, including in large print and on cassette.

Further reading: Barale, M.A. (1986) *Daughters and Lovers: The Life and Writing of Mary Webb.*

SALEHURST

KITTY MUGGERIDGE née Kathleen Dobbs, (1903–1993) author.

Leaving her birthplace, Switzerland, she was educated at Bedales and was British junior ski champion in 1923. In 1925 her aunt Beatrice Webb, co-founder of the LSE, enrolled her onto a social science course there, but she failed the exams. In 1927 she married journalist Malcolm Muggeridge. They broke up and reunited several times, once for several years, and for long periods she raised their four children alone.

During the 1930s and 1940s their address was Mill House, Whatlington Road, Whatlington; subsequently they lived in Manchester, Moscow, Switzerland and, for five years in the 1950s, at Salehurst Park farmhouse. In 1963 they settled at the seventeenth-century Park Cottage, Salehurst, their home for nearly thirty years. The house was modest, having only five rooms, but within its 1.5 acres they built an annexe and a private chapel. She grew sunflowers, kept chickens and bees, and wrote or co-wrote several books, including *Beatrice Webb: A Life* (1972) and *Gazing on Truth: Meditations on Reality* (1985).

The family converted to Catholicism in 1982 at Hurst Green chapel. Widowed in 1990 she put the house up for sale. She died in Canada four years later and is buried alongside her husband at St Mary Magdalene churchyard, Whatlington.

SANDHURST

PRIMROSE CUMMING (1915–2004) children's writer.

Born in Kent and educated by a governess, she began writing as a teenager. She was a keen equestrian and her first novel, *Doney* (1934), was about ponies. She used the royalties to buy a horse and continued writing in order to feed him. By the time she was twenty-two she had three books in print.

After working on a farm during WWII (and almost being killed when a bomber crashed close by) she wrote *Owl's Castle Farm.* She joined the ATS and while serving in an anti-aircraft battery wrote *The Great Horses.* After the war she returned to live with her family, who had moved to Sandhurst. Here, she devoted herself to writing short stories for magazines, and to gardening. Her most popular novel, *Silver Snaffles* (1937) was reprinted in 1960, 1976 and 2007.

SEAFORD

AVRIL COLERIDGE-TAYLOR (1903–1998) composer and conductor.

The daughter of a noted black composer and a white mother, she was born in London. Her first composition, the song *Goodbye Butterfly*, was published when she was fourteen and she later studied music at the Guildhall School and at Trinity College. Her début as a conductor was at the Royal Albert Hall in 1933. She founded and conducted several orchestras and ensembles, including a symphony orchestra bearing her name, and composed large-scale orchestral works, chamber music, keyboard pieces, songs and a march to celebrate Ghana's independence.

In 1979 she wrote a biography of her father, Samuel, but it was criticised as 'wayward' and 'slipshod'. She lived most of her life in London and Kent, spending five years from 1946 at Wyndore, a house in Buxted (Wyndore was the name of her 1939 'song without words' which used only 'ah' and humming). She died in Seaford.

MONIKA DANNEMANN (1946–1996) figure skater, painter and author.

A German-born championship figure skater and artist, she met rock guitarist Jimi Hendrix in 1969 and followed him to London, where he died in her flat in 1970. She was accused by some as being implicated in his death but revered by those who believed her presence at his 'passing over' gave her a mystical connection with him. Although his close friends recalled her association with him as brief and casual, she claimed they were secretly engaged and for many years acted the role of bereaved fiancée, giving dozens of media interviews and making guest appearances at Hendrix conventions. She also created and sold numerous paintings of him. From 1981 she lived with her mother at Little Thatch, Seaford, which became a shrine to him and was featured in a spread in *Hello!* magazine.

Hendrix's former girlfriend Kathy Etchingham was among those who disputed Miss Dannemann's claims and, when the latter called her a liar, she sued her for libel and won. Although ordered by the court not to repeat the libel, she did so in her 1995 book *The Inner World of Jimi Hendrix* (described in *The Times* as 'guff accompanied by revolting "cosmic" paintings'). Found guilty of contempt of court, two days later she killed herself by carbon monoxide poisoning in her Mercedes-Benz in the garage of her Seaford home.

JANET LANE-CLAYPON MD, JP Lady Forber (1877–1967) physiologist and co-founder of the science of epidemiology.

Educated privately at home and later at the LSMW, she gained a BSc with first-class honours in physiology in 1902, DSc in 1905, MB in 1907 and MD in 1910. She researched reproductive physiology and epidemiology and became a senior government scientist on hygiene matters, specialising in the health and welfare of women and children. She published three related books and thirty scientific reports, one of which was her 1926 landmark study of breast cancer for the Ministry of Health. For seven years she was dean of the Household and Social Service Department of King's College for Women and in 1920 was among Britain's first female magistrates. At the age of fifty-two she married Sir Edward Forber. Despite her renown and senior position in the civil service, owing to the marriage bar [8] she was required to resign.

Between 1929 and 1967 the couple lived at Ragged Lands, Glynde; Flat 3, Ravenhurst, St John's Road, Eastbourne (1940s); the middle house at The Manor, Bishopstone (1950s) and finally The White House (now the White Lion Hotel), Claremont Road, Seaford. Widowed in 1960, Lady Forber died in a nursing home, St Mary's House, St Peter's Road, Seaford, and was buried with Sir Edward under a single headstone in Bishopstone Cemetery. [Related image p274.]

(FRANCES) ROSALIE HARVEY (1855–1932) medical missionary.

One of the seven children of a curate, she was born in Seaford and by the time she was six her family had moved to Cheshire. In 1882 she went to India with the Zenana Bible and Medical Mission. After two years in Poona she was moved to Nashik, where she initially looked after sick animals, then rescued 1,500 unwanted children. She opened a babies' home and adopted a little boy herself. Turning her attention to wandering lepers, she built them an asylum of corrugated iron where, as superintendent, she employed only female doctors. In 1927 she was awarded the Kaisar-I-Hind Gold Medal for her work. She died at Nashik, having lived abroad for fifty years without once returning home.

DAME MARGARET RUTHERFORD DBE (1892–1972) actress.

An Oscar-winning character actress of stage and screen, she boarded for several years at Raven's Croft School for Girls in Seaford. Of her hundreds of film and stage roles, she is best known for playing Miss Marple. She has a blue plaque in London.

DAME BARBARA SALT DBE (1904–1975) pioneer diplomat.

A boarder for several years at the Downs School, Seaford, she pioneered women's entry into the higher echelons of the diplomatic service, becoming, in 1962, the first woman appointed ambassador to another country. Illness struck just as she was to take up her post in Israel and both her legs were amputated. She spent the rest of her career at the Foreign Office training new recruits in international diplomacy.

SEDLESCOMBE

PATIENCE STRONG née Winifred May; Mrs Williams; Mrs Cushing (1907–1990) poet.

An amateur pianist, devout Christian and countryside lover, she was a shorthand typist in a music publisher's office when she began to write lyrics for popular music, including the tango *Jealousy*. She is best known for her sentimental poems, which appeared in the Quiet Corner of the *Daily Mirror* from 1935 until the late 1940s, in *The Pictorial* (which became the *Sunday Mirror*), in *Woman's Own* and in *This England*, and on greetings cards and calendars. She also made sound recordings and published anthologies of her poetry.

Married and widowed twice, she was made a Freeman of the City of London in 1970. She died at her home, Sunnyside, The Street, Sedlescombe. Her book *Thoughts for Every Day* was reprinted in 2004.

SOUTHEASE

F.O. (FRANCES OLIVE) UNDERHILL MBE (1884–1973) labour reformer.

The daughter of a prosperous grocer, she was born in Oxford and won a scholarship to Royal Holloway College in 1902, graduating in mathematics in 1905. She was universally known as 'Stalky'; her hobby was folk-dancing; her passion, women's rights, and she became a suffragette.

She was a delegate to the 1919 International Labour Conference in Washington, USA (provided for in the Peace Treaty of 1918), for which she was appointed MBE. After a brief spell at the Ministry of Food, she moved to Geneva to work in the International Labour Office of the League of Nations, were she influenced labour reform in many countries. According to one source she then became the first woman to work at the Bodleian Library, Oxford. During WWII she was deputy warden of the Mansfield House University Settlement, Canning Town, east London (established as a base for students of Mansfield College, Oxford, to live in the slums while carrying out social work).

In retirement she built Field Edge, a house at Southease, and lived there for at least fourteen years. When arthritis set in she added an outdoor swimming pool, using it into her eighties.

STUNTS GREEN

ANNE SHELTON OBE real name Patricia Sibley (1923–1994) singer.

A clerk's daughter, she was born in south London and at sixteen was appearing on BBC radio. She replaced Vera Lynn as singer with a big band at London's Mayfair Hotel. Known as the 'forces' favourite', during the war she recorded her signature tune, *Lili Marlene*, and appeared frequently on radio entertaining troops in North Africa and Malta with her morale-boosting songs. Bing Crosby requested her specially when he appeared in London in 1942 and she sang with many famous bands. She appeared on television and in four films, had a few hit records, topped the bill in variety theatres across the UK and toured Europe and the Commonwealth. In 1958 she withdrew from a BBC broadcast after finding herself billed second to Alma Cogan [95], which she felt was an affront. She appeared in three Royal Variety Shows and had her own TV show in 1958-9.

In 1967 she married her long-term boyfriend David Reid; he died in 1990, the year she was appointed OBE for her work with the Not Forgotten Association for disabled former servicemen. After fifty years in London she moved to Glendower (now Dragon Lodge) in Stunt's Green, in February 1994, gave her final performance (at Buckingham Palace) on 27th July and died at home in her sleep four days later. Her memorial service was held at Corpus Christi, Covent Garden and she was buried in south London.

TELSCOMBE CLIFFS

DAME GRACIE FIELDS DBE (1898–1979) singer and comedian.

A working class lass from Rochdale, she made her first London music hall appearance in 1915 and by the 1930s was the richest working woman in the world. A star of stage, screen, television and radio, she was known to every British household as 'Our Gracie' and during a stay in hospital in 1939 was deluged with over 100,000 letters from well-wishers.

She memorised over 300 songs, among them her most famous: 'Sally in Our Alley'. Her records sold in their millions, she signed the most remunerative contract ever issued and became Britain's highest-paid performer when she received £6,500 for eight appearances at the Empress Hall. In her late sixties she toured three continents and was still recording albums in her seventies. She sang at ten Royal Command Performances, was appointed CBE and DBE and given the Freedom of Rochdale, where a theatre was named for her.

Her association with Sussex began in 1935, when she bought a house for her parents at 127 Dorothy Avenue, Peacehaven. Later she gave this to the Theatrical Ladies' Guild [see Kitty Carson, 156] as a home for the children of impoverished actresses (it is now the offices of a housing association). Later she bought The Haven, 29 Telscombe Cliffs Way, for herself (it is now a nursing home). She married Italian film director Monty Banks in 1940 and after 1952 lived mainly in Capri, where she died. There is a Gracie Fields Room at the Meridian Centre at Peacehaven.

Further reading: Moules, J. (1999) *Gracie Fields: A Biography.* [Related plate 49.]

TICEHURST

IDA COPELAND MP née Fenzi (c1875–1964) politician.

Italian-born Mrs Copeland became the twenty-fifth woman to be elected to the House of Commons and the sixth female Conservative MP when she won Stoke-on-Trent by a massive majority in 1931. Despite her excellent work in representing the potteries' interests, she lost her seat to Labour in 1935.

Married with two children, she was godmother to Dorothy Crisp's daughter [186]. She served on the Council of Girl Guides, was recipient of the Polish Gold Order of Merit in 1952 and in 1956 donated Trelissick Gardens, Truro (which she had inherited from her stepfather in 1937) to the National Trust. In later life she resided in Ticehurst, where she died at The Highlands, Vineyard Lane.

UCKFIELD

MARY HOADLEY DODGE (c1861–1934) philanthropist.

A fabulously wealthy New York heiress, her family made its immense wealth from railways, forests, coal, copper and motor cars and she was a childhood friend of Theodore Roosevelt. She suffered from a degenerative form of arthritis, which began to disable her by 1914, and spent most of her life in a wheelchair.

Moving to London in 1910 she was welcomed into high society and made many aristocratic friends, including Muriel Sackville [260], with whom she lived for several years. She was a generous benefactor to many causes, donating valuable works of art to the Tate Gallery as well as supporting the *Daily Herald*, a left-wing national newspaper. She gave an expensive Wolseley car to the WSPU and settled a life income on Annie Besant [246].

She had several residences in England, including an historic mansion, Westside, at Wimbledon Common; a rented house in Crowborough and Old Lodge, Nutley [283]. She also leased the splendid Warwick House, 25 St James's Place, overlooking London's Green Park. Little

17. Dame Ellen Terry

18. Agnes Zimmermann

19. Mary Chavelita Dunne

20. Mrs Martindale

21. Marguerite Radclyffe Hall by Howard Coster

22. Zoë Brigden

23. HRH Princess Beatrice

24. Dolly Collins

25. Cora Goffin

26. Lydia Lopokova

27. HRH Princess Amelia by Ann Mee

28. Viscountess Wolseley

29. Alice Dudeney

30. Ray Strachey

31. Maud Arncliffe-Sennett

32. Emily Davies by Rudolph Lehmann

33. Rosamund Dale Owen

34. Mabel Constanduros

35. Mother Mary Garson

36. Virginia Woolf

37. Elsie Randolph

38. Diana Petre

39. Elinor Glyn

40. Kitty Marion

41. Binnie Hale by Dorothy Wilding

42. Hilda Leyel

43. Nancy Price

44. Margaret Bondfield CH

45. Victoria Liddiard

46. Decima Moore OBE

47. Marie Löhr

48. Dame Anna Neagle

49. Dame Gracie Fields

50. Clare Sheridan

51. Edna Best

52. Ethel Irving

53. Edna Thornton

54. Vesta Tilley

55. Elsie Waters OBE (top) and Doris Waters OBE

56. Muriel George by Yevonde

57. Brenda de Banzie

58. Ida Lupino

59. The Hon. Ursula Wyndham

60. Daisy and Violet Hilton

61. Marie and Charles Corbett

62. Fanny and Johnnie Cradock

63. Winifred Emery

is known of her later life, other than that she owned a racehorse and was embroiled in a legal battle with Muriel Sackville in 1929. About 1931 she bought the Decimus Burton house Wick Hall, Hove, where she died. It was demolished soon afterwards and a block of flats covers the site.

UPPER HARTFIELD

SADIE BONNELL (1888–1993) first female recipient of the Military Medal.

A upper-class Surrey 'gel', she was educated at Bedales and during WWI drove an ambulance for the Canadian Army. Later she joined the FANY in France, driving field kitchens, mobile bathing facilities and supply lorries, and later a motorised ambulance with 'a rudimentary windscreen, no self-starter, and tiny, oil sidelights' to ferry a never-ending stream of wounded soldiers to field hospitals. On the night of 18–19 May 1918 she was evacuating casualties from near an ammunition dump and poison gas shell store when the enemy attacked from the air. 'There was imminent danger of a catastrophic explosion, quite apart from the shrapnel from bursting projectiles. When Sadie Bonnell arrived on the scene the only ambulance for evacuating the wounded had been destroyed. Getting hold of three more, she returned to the scene, again and again, and would not give up the task until all the wounded had been taken to safety' (*The Times*, 9 September 1993). The British Army recognised her bravery with the Military Medal.

Back in England she performed voluntary work in hospitals. In 1919 she married Major Herbert Marriott, but within two years she was widowed. At the age of sixty she married Charles Talbot and had a cottage built for them at Cotchford Lane, Upper Hartfield, calling it Thrushling. Here she befriended a neighbour, the author A. A. Milne, and his young son, Christopher Robin, now immortalised in Milne's books. Widowed again when she was eighty, she lived another quarter-century, dying at Droitwich. The Conservative politician Julien Foster is her great-great nephew.

MARGIAD EVANS real name Peggy Whistler (1909–1958) novelist and poet.

Although born in Middlesex she grew up in Ross-on-Wye and moved to Wales after marrying Michael Williams. She wrote four novels, a volume of verse and two autobiographies and made radio broadcasts. Her novel *Country Dance* (1932, reprinted 2005) gained her a high reputation, while her verse received the Poetry Award of the Welsh Committee of the Arts Council.

Her husband's teaching career took them to Upper Hartfield sometime before 1949, where they raised a daughter. She died at Tunbridge Wells aged just forty-nine, and her papers were donated to the National Library of Wales.

KATE HARVEY née Felicia Catherine Glanvill (1863–1946) suffragette and philanthropist.

A native Londoner, she married merchant Frank Harvey and later, as a widow with three daughters, took in and raised disabled children at her Kent home and practised as an unqualified physiotherapist. She was a close friend and personal assistant of well-known suffragist and socialist Charlotte Despard and, despite being profoundly deaf, was press secretary for the WFL. As a member of the TRL she had twice barricaded herself into her house, was sent to Holloway in 1913, and was later awarded a suffragette medal.

In 1916 she and Mrs Despard bought a large house, Kurundai, three small ones (1 and 2 New Cottages, and Woodhatch) and twelve acres overlooking Ashdown Forest near Gallipot Wood, Upper Hartfield. They equipped Kurundai as a thirty-one-bedroomed hospital for women and children. By 1921 it was in the sole hands of Mrs Harvey, who ran it as a home, hospital and school for disabled children. From 1923 until 1928 the school was operated by the Invalid Children's Aid Association as Brackenhill Home School Ltd, for children suffering from rheumatic afflictions of the heart. While retaining ownership, Mrs Harvey moved to a nearby house called Wroth Tyes.

In 1928 she reinvented Brackenhill as an open-air, vegetarian boarding school with a heavy emphasis on physical exercise. The children lived a Spartan way of life, wearing shorts and living and playing outdoors as much as possible. They even slept in the open air, in covered shelters whose shutters were put up only in bad weather. Mrs Harvey was intensely pious. She wore sandals and a headscarf, told the children to call her 'Godmother', installed a chapel and undertook their religious instruction. The headmistress was Helen Smith, who lived with Mrs Harvey at Wroth Tyes, and to whom she bequeathed the house. The school closed because of WWII, when the estate was used by the government for other purposes. Mrs Harvey died at Wroth Tyes. In 2005 her Holloway medal was sold at auction for £840.

WADHURST

MARY CHAMOT (1899–1993) art historian and author.

Of English and Dutch parentage, she was born in Russia and studied fine art at St Petersburg Academy and the Slade School, leaving with a diploma in 1922. After training in art history she worked as an exhibition organiser and lecturer at the National Gallery, the V & A and London University. She wrote several books, including *English Medieval Enamels* (1930) and *Russian Painting and Sculpture* (1963) translated others, and wrote articles and reviews for *Apollo* and *Country Life*.

Fluent in English, French, Russian and German, during WWII she worked in postal and telegraph censorship and as an interpreter for the Allied Control Commission in Vienna. After the war she was assistant keeper of the Tate Gallery, sharing a London house with Lulette Gerebzov. In old age she moved to a nursing home, Weald Hall, Mayfield Lane, Wadhurst, where she died. Her books are now out of print.

C.A.F. RHYS DAVIDS née Caroline Augusta Foley (1857–1942) Pali language scholar and translator.

Born at Wadhurst vicarage, where she lived for at least a quarter of a century, uniquely for a woman she studied economics, philosophy, psychology and Sanskrit at University College, London, gaining a BA in 1886 and MA in 1889, the year she won the John Stuart Mill Scholarship in Philosophy of Mind. She became a prolific writer, translator and campaigner for poverty relief, children's rights and women's suffrage, and was interested in psychic communication with the dead via séances.

After marrying in 1894 she had three children by 1900 and lived in south London, where two resident nursemaids, a cook and a housemaid made it possible for her to continue her career. She researched Buddhist psychology and women in Buddhism, and translated and published *A Buddhist Manual of Psychological Ethics* (1900), the first of her twenty or so books. In addition she published four translations and produced dozens of learned articles and academic papers. She was lecturer in Indian philosophy at Manchester University 1910–13, lecturer in the history of Buddhism at the School of Oriental Studies, London, 1918–1933, and secretary of the Pali Text Society from 1907; after her husband's death in 1922 she replaced him as president until 1942. She died in Surrey and her books are now out of print.

WINCHELSEA

FRANCES HELEN ANDERSON (1912–2005) musician.

Born and raised in Winchelsea, she studied music and history at Lady Margaret Hall and the RCM. In 1938 she joined Bernard Robinson's Music Camp and during WWII the Council for the Encouragement of Music and Arts appointed her music traveller for Northumberland, Durham and North Yorkshire, and later for the south-west. This was a very usual job for a woman: it involved travelling hundreds of miles alone in the blackout in a clapped-out, unheated Austin Tourer, organising musical events to boost wartime morale.

When the war was over she sang in the Glyndbourne chorus, founded the Chelham Quartet, was music adviser to the Townswomen's Guild, warden of the Women's Institute Adult Education Centre, Denman College [see Lady Denman, 32] and a music teacher in Oxfordshire.

VERA MAY ATKINS CBE née Rosenberg (1908–2000) SOE officer.

The daughter of Ukrainian Jews, she was born in Transylvania and worked as a top-class secretary in Bucharest. She was driven out of Romania by anti-Semitism, and in 1937 moved in with her aunt at Winchelsea and adopted her mother's surname, Atkins.

An ARP warden during WWII, she joined the SOE as an intelligence officer in 1941, staying at her mother's London flat. Her work was so secret that even her mother was not told about it: she excused her absences by claiming to be having a secret affair with a married man. She became a British citizen in 1944, and at the end of the war was given the rank of squadron officer in the WAAF and detailed to travel across a devastated Europe and search for 118 missing secret service agents, discovering that all but one had been killed [see Diana Rowden, 221].

In peacetime she worked for UNESCO, organising exchange schemes for schoolchildren. In 1996, aged eighty-eight, she became vice-president of the Special Forces Club, living between Winchelsea, Kensington and South Africa and lecturing on the dangers of tyranny. Appointed a Chevalier de Légion d'Honneur in 1995 and CBE two years later, she died at The Laurels, a nursing home at 71 Old London Road, Hastings. She was cremated and, after a funeral service at St Thomas the Martyr, Winchelsea, her ashes were buried in Zennor, Cornwall.

Further reading: Helm, S. (2006) *A Life in Secrets, Vera Atkins and the Lost Agents of the SOE.*

SARA MELHUISH (1861–1939) academic and author.

Educated at University College, Liverpool, not far from her Cheshire birthplace, she achieved first-class honours in history in 1890 and in 1905 was among the first women ever to gain an MA. She took increasingly senior posts lecturing in education, eventually becoming head of the Training Department at Bedford College. She wrote *English History Illustrated from Original Sources from the Earliest Times* (1911) and was a contributor to the *Victoria County History* on the ecclesiastical history of Lincolnshire. She died at her home, Gable, Hiham Street, Winchelsea, and was buried at Conduit Hill, Rye.

DAME ELLEN TERRY DBE (1847–1928) actress.

The second of nine children, she was born in Coventry into a touring theatrical family (Sir John Gielgud was her grand-nephew.) She did not go to school, but was taught theatre skills by her parents. Her highly-celebrated career spanned sixty-six years, with few breaks, and included in the early days singing and dancing, though it is for her Shakespearean roles that she became most famous. Her first appearance was in a West End production at the age of eight, in which she gave 102 consecutive performances. By the 1880s she was the UK's leading actress; she was painted by eminent artists and Oscar Wilde wrote a sonnet about her.

Although she married thrice (the first time at seventeen, to a man of forty-six), both her children were fathered by her lover. In 1896 she moved to Tower Cottage, High Street, Winchelsea, and four years later to Smallhythe Place, Kent. From 1903 she and her son Edward Craig managed the Imperial Theatre. She lectured on Shakespeare's female characters in the UK and USA, made recordings of readings from Shakespeare and, between 1918 and 1922, also appeared in films.

Appointed DBE in 1925, she died at home and was cremated. Her ashes were buried at St Paul's, Covent Garden (known as the actors' church) and she has a blue plaque in London. Smallhythe Place is now run by the National Trust as an Ellen Terry museum.

Further reading: Melville, J. (2006) *Ellen Terry.* [Related plate 17; image p270.]

WITHYHAM

HILDA MATHESON OBE (1888–1940) founder of radio journalism.

She was born in London, but her family moved to Oxford, where she studied history as a university home student. In WWI she was initially a VAD nurse in a military hospital but her superior intelligence and fluency in French, German and Italian led to her being recruited by MI5. The nature of her work is unknown, but when war ended she was in the British Military Control Office in Rome. She became political secretary to Nancy Astor MP and in 1926 was head-hunted by John Reith, head of the BBC, for a high-ranking post at £900 a year. Lady Astor encouraged her to take the position and even gave her a golden handshake.

She created the BBC news department in 1927 and rose to be director of talks, pioneering the concept of broadcasts by eminent people. In 1928 she invited Harold Nicholson and his wife Vita Sackville-West to give talks and the two women began a three-year affair [see Virginia Woolf, 243]. Managerial interference caused her to resign in 1932, and she was replaced by Grace Goldie [135]. She moved to Rocks Farm, Withyham, a house on the estate of her lover Dorothy Wellesley [261], wrote a book, *Broadcasting* (1933), then worked for the Carnegie Trust. In 1938 she produced a 2,000-page report, *The African Survey*, for which she was appointed OBE.

During WWII she was again recruited by military intelligence to co-found the Joint Broadcasting Committee, a rival organisation to the BBC, responsible for broadcasting British information and opinions to eleven neutral countries worldwide (her staff included Isa Benzie, 246). To supplement this propaganda, she began a journal called *Britain in Pictures*, to counteract a similar German publication. Mrs Wellesley was a co-director, and the first of the 140 editions were published from Rocks Farm.

Miss Matheson was a member of the Bach Choir, enjoyed foreign travel and was an experienced mountaineer. She died unexpectedly, after an operation, at a nursing home in Surrey, and Mrs Wellesley erected a memorial to her at Penns-in-the-Rocks. The first high-ranking woman in the BBC, she laid the foundations of radio journalism and her *African Survey* was consulted by policy-makers until the 1960s. Nevertheless, she has almost been forgotten. Michael Carney's self-published book *'Stoker': The Life of Hilda Matheson OBE, 1888–1940*, her only biography, is already hard to find, just nine years after its publication in 1999.

LADY MARGARET SACKVILLE FRSL (1881–1963) poet and writer.

The daughter of Baron Buckhurst, rector of Withyham and the future 7th Earl de la Warr, she was born in Mayfair and grew up at Buckhurst Park, south of Withyham, where she was educated by governesses. Her life was entirely dedicated to literature. She was involved in many local writing groups, wrote reviews and poems for numerous popular magazines (including *Country Life* and *The Spectator*), and produced twenty-one books, including *The Travelling Companions and other Stories for Children* (1906) and *A Book of Verse by Living Women* (1910). A pacifist, during WWI she published poems criticising women for sending their sons to war. She was a fellow of the Royal Society of Literature and winner of the Schroeder Foundation Medal for Services to Literature. In adulthood she lived mainly in Scotland, then Cheltenham, where she died.

LADY MURIEL SACKVILLE née Brassey; Countess de la Warr (1872–1930) suffragist and benefactor.

The daughter of Earl Brassey, MP for Hastings, and Annie, Lady Brassey [195] she was born at Buckhurst Park, near Withyham. She had an elder sister, Mabel, a younger sister, Marie and a brother, Thomas. When she was fifteen the whole family went on a trip on their yacht, *Sunbeam*, to Ceylon, Rangoon, North Borneo and Australia. While in mid-ocean her mother died and was buried at sea. Her father later married Sybil de Vere [195].

In 1891 she married Gilbert Sackville, who became 8th Earl de la Warr five years later. He built the Bexhill Kursaal and organised the first motor-car races in Britain, which were held nearby. The couple lived in the thirteenth-century Manor House at Bexhill (demolished in 1968, its remains can be seen at Manor Gardens) and in 1896 they played host to the Duchess of Teck, mother-in-law to the future King George V. When his daughters were five and one, Earl de la Warr was unfaithful to his wife. She forgave him, because he was suffering terrible financial troubles; helped him, and they were reconciled. A year later, when Lady Muriel was pregnant with her son, her husband went on military service to South Africa, returning for the boy's birth. Six months later he started another affair, this time with Miss Turner, an actress appearing at the Kursaal. Just before the baby's first birthday he walked out, leaving his wife with three children under nine, and wrote her a letter admitting his adultery. The whole town was scandalised by the revelations that were splashed all over the local and national newspapers. The countess was granted a divorce and sole custody of the children, whom she raised at her father and stepmother's mansion, Normanhurst Court, Catsfield. (Despite his iniquitous conduct Earl de la Warr was elected mayor of Bexhill 1903–4. He remarried in 1903 but his second wife also divorced him for adultery in 1914 and the same year he was declared bankrupt. He died on active service in 1915.)

The countess became involved in politics and social issues. She initially supported the Liberal Party, which was in power at the time, but when it refused to give women the vote she changed her allegiance to the Labour Party. She joined the militant WSPU, switched in 1912 to the NUWSS and co-founded and was president of the East Grinstead Women's Suffrage Society, working with her daughter Lady Idina Sackville, her stepsister Lady Helen Brassey, and Margery Corbett [202].

Although she played a very important financial role in the feminist and socialist movements, most of the time she insisted on remaining in the background. She also gave large sums, usually anonymously, to support trade unionism, self-rule for India, animal welfare and striking London dockers, and several times saved the ailing *Daily Herald,* a left-wing national newspaper, from collapse (it was bought by the *Daily Mirror* in 1960 and later became the *Sun).*

From 1910 the countess shared her life with a fabulously wealthy American heiress, Mary Dodge [256] residing between each others' homes at Old Lodge, Nutley; Westside, Wimbledon,

and Warwick House, an opulent London residence. Both women were close friends and supporters of Annie Besant [246].

Muriel Sackville died in Wimbledon. She lived to see her son Herbrand (Lord Buckhurst, the 9th Earl de la Warr, for whom the present pavilion is named) become the first hereditary peer to take his seat in the House of Lords as a supporter of the Labour Party. Her daughter Idina was notorious for being married and divorced five times, a record then unmatched among the English aristocracy. Famed for her physical courage and bravery, she was a big-game hunter in Kenya. Idina's daughter Diana succeeded to her father's titles, becoming Countess of Errol and Lord High Constable of Scotland, and was among the peeresses who demanded the right to sit in the House of Lords. [Related image p283.]

DOROTHY WELLESLEY née Ashton; the Duchess of Wellington (1889–1956) poet.

Privately educated, she wrote poetry from childhood. Her first publication was *Early Poems* (1913) and several more appeared but she was far from prolific, producing ten volumes in forty years. She also edited for the Woolfs' Hogarth Press [243].

Although she married Lord Gerald Wellesley in 1914, they lived separate lives after the birth of their second child in 1918 and he became the 7th Duke of Wellington in 1943, long after they parted. She had affairs with men and women. Vita Sackville-West, future lover of Hilda Matheson [259] and Virginia Woolf [243], dedicated her book *The Land* (1926) to her and together they travelled to Egypt, India, Russia and Persia. In 1928 she purchased Penns-in-the-Rocks at Withyham, where the dining room was designed by Vanessa Bell [214] and Duncan Grant, and where she and her girlfriend Hilda Matheson entertained a glittering array of literary folk. She wrote her autobiography (which she called a 'commentary on a lifetime') *Far Have I Travelled,* in 1952 and died at home.

Mary Mantell's former home in Lewes

Isabel Sieveking once lived in this house at 1 Exmouth Place, Hastings

Pelham Crescent, Hastings, where Barbara Bodichon and Bessie Rayner Parkes lived in the 1840s

Blackboys, Rye, once the residence of
Radclyffe Hall and Una Troubridge.

Jeake's House, Rye, former home of
Joan Aiken and later, Mary Aiken.

Windydene, Mark Cross, once the home of Dr Sophia Jex-Blake and Dr Margaret Todd

Gospels, Ditchling, former residence of Ethel Mairet

The graves of Lilian Clapham (left) and Caroline Spurgeon. Professor Spurgeon placed the memorial headstone to her companion Lilian Clapham in 1935 and her ashes were buried beside it in 1945. The home they shared is behind the trees. The memorial reads: *'In loving memory of Lilian Mary Clapham, of the Old Postman's Cottage, Alciston, a good friend to this village, who died 21st December 1935, aged 64 years. This stone is placed here by Caroline F.E. Spurgeon in grateful remembrance of forty years of steadfast friendship and of happy life together.'*

Southover Grange, Lewes, once the home of Isabel Thorne and, later, of Violet Gordon Woodhouse

Windlesham, birthplace and former residence of Dame Jean Doyle

The Sanctuary, Alice Gregory's house on the Downs above Alfriston.

The enormous wooden crucifix she commissioned and placed on the perimeter wall, facing the road.

A close-up of the plaque

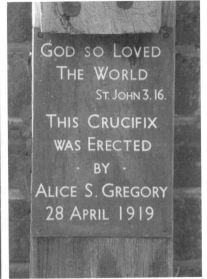

GOD SO LOVED
THE WORLD
ST. JOHN 3. 16.

THIS CRUCIFIX
WAS ERECTED
· BY ·
ALICE S. GREGORY
28 APRIL 1919

6 College Road, Eastbourne, once the residence of Ada Bayly and Hendrina Bentley

Irving's Ghyll, Joyce Hicks's retirement cottage in Mayfield

St Peter's Rectory, St Leonards, childhood home of Noël Streatfeild; a plaque can be seen between the gates

Monk's House, Rodmell, the world-famous but modest home of Virginia Woolf

Batchelors, Cowbeech Hill, once home to Elsie Bowerman

Red Lodge, 6 Devonshire Place, Eastbourne, former residence of Lady
Goldsmid and Agnes Zimmermann (photo: A.C. Hancock).

Tower House, Dame Ellen Terry's former residence in Winchelsea

Asheham House, Southease, once the home of Vanessa Bell and Virginia Woolf (from an old photograph)

The Hurst, 124 Hoadswood Road, St Leonards, once the residence of novelist Dame Catherine Cookson

Farley Farm, Muddles Green, former home of Lee Miller

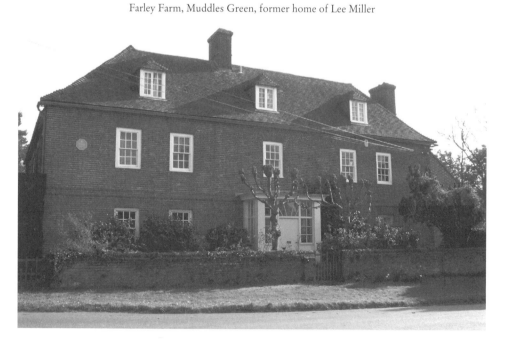

Rock House, Exmouth Place, Hastings, formerly the residence of Dr Elizabeth Blackwell, the world's first qualified female physician. The memorial plaque (below) can be seen on the side wall to the left of the window.

In 1914, Hastings held a Pageant of Heroes, during which twenty-four plaques were unveiled to 'historical and literary heroes'. On 6th June a huge procession of girls and women in their Sunday best greeted the suffragist leader Millicent Garrett Fawcett at Hastings station and proceeded to Exmouth Place, where more people had congregated, including a deputation of suffragettes. Mrs Fawcett gave a speech and unveiled this memorial plaque. Nearly forty years later, Dr Effie Evers, wife of the rector of Guestling, happened to upturn a white marble slab that lay in her pantry and had been used for years for rolling out pastry. She discovered it was a commemorative tablet inscribed to Elizabeth Blackwell, with just the barest amount of information and the Hastings Coat of Arms. The riddle of how and why it came to be there is, as yet, unsolved. Perhaps it was the original one, and the inscription was later considered to be inadequate; perhaps it was removed for safe keeping during WWI. The Guestling Tablet was donated to the Royal Free Hospital in London in 1953 where it was set into the archway to the Dean's office.

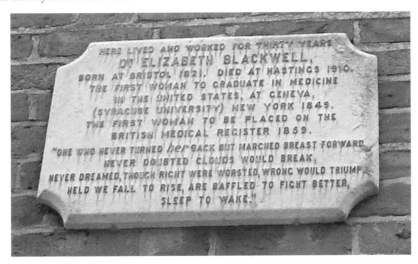

1 St Paul's Place, St Leonards, once the home of Mrs Darent Harrison and site of a siege

The Manor House, Bishopstone, one time residence of Dr Janet Lane-Claypon (photo: Kevin Gordon)

A signed photograph of Mabel Capper, dated 1911, wearing her suffragette medal; her former home, 63 Pevensey Road, St Leonards.

St George's Retreat, Ditchling, where Victoria Drummond, Lady Herringham and Dame Marjorie Maxse ended their days.

HOUSE BURNED AT ST. LEONARDS.

An outrage, supposed to be the work of woman suffragists, was perpetrated at St. Leonards yesterday morning by the burning of Levetleigh, a house until recently tenanted by Mr. Arthur Du Cros, M.P. The damage to the house, which was empty, is estimated at nearly £10,000.

The fire was discovered between 1 and 2 o'clock yesterday morning by a policeman, and before the fire brigade arrived the whole building was well alight. Investigations showed that paraffined paper had been used to make a trail of fire, and that an entry was gained through a window which was broken after being covered with paper and jam. All but two rooms were "gutted," and during the operations of the fire brigade several explosions occurred, and it afterwards appeared that fires had been lit in every room of the house. In the grounds were found a hatchet, a card with the words "Votes for Women," and other suffragist literature. The entire loss, it is stated, will fall upon the trustees of the Eversfield estate.

Mr. A. Du Cros stated last night:—"As usual the suffragists have aimed at one person and hit another. I am neither owner nor lessee of the house at St. Leonards which has been burnt down, and the loss is not mine." Mr. Du Cros added that he had received many covert threats, and was not altogether surprised when he heard what had been done, as he was a consistent opponent of women's suffrage.

I did not really mind — though my family did — when I was accused of burning down Levetleigh, the Borough Member's house, which stood opposite ours.

It was destroyed one night, almost certainly by Suffragists, and I remember the bitter disappointment with which, on waking the next morning, I realized what a spectacle I had missed. I had never seen a fire, and this by all accounts had been a specially splendid and satisfactory one ... Therefore great was my surprise when I heard that I myself had done the deed.

For a time things looked unpleasant, and might really have been so if my father had not succeeded in establishing my innocence ... I believe that there are still people who think that I burned down Levetleigh. It is just the sort of thing a novelist would do.

Cutting from *The Times,* April 1913

Extract from *Three Ways Home* by Sheila Kaye-Smith (1937)

Dane Lodge, 9 Dane Road, childhood home of Sheila Kaye-Smith, which bears a blue plaque (photo: A.C. Hancock).

The smouldering remains of Levetleigh, Dane Road, St Leonards, burned by suffragette Kitty Marion.

Marine Mansions, Bexhill, where Clara Mordan ended her days (from an old photograph)

Letter from Clara Mordan to the *Pall Mall Gazette*, 1889

ANOTHER WOMAN'S GRIEVANCE.

To the EDITOR *of the* PALL MALL GAZETTE.

SIR,—I wish to call the attention of your female readers to the habit of certain societies, whose committees, composed entirely of men, see no incongruity in appealing for funds to the women whom they exclude from their counsels. In the appeal they virtually say :—" Women's money is worth using, not their co-operation." If every woman whose pecuniary aid is thus solicited would write a few lines of reply expressive of her indignation at what is nothing less than an impertinence, certain societies would reconsider their constitutions. The incongruity reaches its height when a society calling itself the " Female Mission to the Fallen " is managed exclusively by men. That every one should mind his or her own business is an axiom which cannot be too strongly insisted upon. If men would look at home and concentrate their attention on the fallen of their own sex, women would be found quite able to undertake the management of the fallen of theirs Trusting these remarks will fall naturally into their place in the columns of a newspaper which always goes to war for the weak,—I remain, Sir, faithfully yours,

CLARA MORDAN.

THE ROKEBY VENUS.

SUFFRAGIST PRISONER IN COURT.

EXTENT OF THE DAMAGE.

The famous Rokeby Velasquez, commonly known as the "Venus with the Mirror," which was presented to the National Gallery in 1906, was mutilated yesterday morning by the prominent militant woman suffragist Mary Richardson. She attacked the picture with a small chopper with a long narrow blade, similar to the instruments used by butchers, and in a few seconds inflicted upon it severe if not irreparable damage. In consequence of the outrage the National Gallery will remain closed to the public until further notice.

Mary Richardson: a police photo dated 1914; cutting from *The Times*, 1914.
Her final home, 46 St James's Road, Hastings, in which she had a flat.

Woodgate, Danehill, once the home of Marie Corbett and her daughters Margery Corbett Ashby and Cicely Corbett Fisher; a press cutting from the *East Grinstead Observer,* 26 July 1913.

SUFFRAGE DISTURBANCE AT EAST GRINSTEAD

The main streets of East Grinstead were disgraced by some extraordinary proceedings on Tuesday evening. The non-militant section of the advocates of securing women's suffrage had arranged a march and public meeting on its way to the great demonstration in London. The 'procession' was not an imposing one. It consisted of about ten ladies who were members of the Suffrage Society. Mrs. Marie Corbett led the way carrying a silken banner bearing the arms of East Grinstead. The reception, which the little band of ladies got was no means friendly. Yells and hooting greeted them throughout most of the entire march, and they were the targets for occasional pieces of turf, especially when they passed through Queen's Road. In the High Street they found a crowd of about 1,500 people awaiting them.

Edward Steer had promised to act as chairman, and taking his stand against one of the trees on the slope he began by saying, 'Ladies and Gentlemen'. This was practically as far as he got with his speech. Immediately there was an outburst of yells and laughter and shouting. Laurence Housman, the famous writer, got no better than Mr. Steer. By this time pieces of turf and a few ripe tomatoes and highly seasoned eggs were flying about, and were not always received by the person they were intended for. The unsavoury odour of eggs was noticeable over a considerable area. Unhappily, Miss Helen Hoare of Charlwood Farm, was struck in the face with a missile and received a cut on the cheek and was taken away for treatment.

Some of the women were invited to take shelter in Mr. Allwork's house, but as they entered the crowd rushed the doorway and forced themselves into the house. The police arrived and the ladies were taken out the back way and escorted to the Dorset Arms Hotel, their headquarters, and this was for a long time besieged by a yelling mob... Mrs. Marie Corbett slipped away and took up a position lower down the High Street on the steps of the drinking fountain. A young clergyman who appealed for fair play was roughly hustled and lost his hat. Mrs. Corbett had began to speak from the fountain steps but the crowd moved down the High Street and broke up her small meeting.

Mrs Georgina Weldon, *Illustrated London News*, 1887. Cuttings from *The Times*: Anna Kingsford, 1889; Mrs
Nisbett (Lady Boothby), 1837; Annie Keary, 1869; Agnes Zimmermann, 1868. Cuttings from the *Pall Mall
Gazette*: Alice Dudeney, 1900; Isabella Harwood (Ross Neil), 1874.

Cuttings from *The Times*: D.K. Broster, 1926; Virginia Woolf, 1928; Marguerite Radclyffe Hall, 1928;
Ada Bayly, 1893; Esther Meynell, 1948. Matilda Betham-Edwards, from *Hearth and Home*, 1892.

Woman's Pictorial

The highest value in weekly Magazines for Women.   3d.   *ON SALE TO-DAY.*

SPECIAL ATTRACTIONS IN THIS WEEK'S NUMBER.

SUCCESS IN LOVE
by SHEILA KAYE - SMITH

This is the first of a series of articles on "What Makes a Woman a Success" by the brilliant authoress whose two later novels, "Joanna Godden" and "The End of the House of Alard," have placed her in the forefront of women writers. Miss Sheila Kaye-Smith sees life from an entirely feminine point of view and her definition of the goal at which women should aim is one to be read by every mother and every daughter.

Saints in Sussex
by
SHEILA KAYE-SMITH

Just Published   *7s. 6d. net*

An exquisite collection of poems and plays in which the inwardness of Sussex life is revealed by this gifted and versatile author.

CASSELL'S   LONDON, E.C.4

The Story of Lady Eleanor Butler and Miss Sarah Ponsonby, known as the Ladies of Llangollen.

CHASE OF THE WILD GOOSE

MARY GORDON

The Observer: "The delicate and lively reconstruction of a great romance, remarkably blending judgment, knowledge, taste, and imagination . . . The ultimate charm of the book is that it is a rhapsody in praise of friendship by one who understands the technique of friendship."   *Illustrated 10s. 6d.*

THE HOGARTH PRESS
52, Tavistock Square, London, W.C.

Cuttings from *The Times*: Sheila Kaye-Smith, 1924 and 1926; Mary Gordon, 1936.

Houses for sale in *The Times*: Tylehurst (Violet Needham), 1936; Little Douce Grove (Sheila Kaye-Smith and Rumer Godden), 1956; Old Lodge (Muriel Sackville), 1921; The Corner (Winifred Emery) 1924.

Appendix

Silk banner of the AFL

ABBREVIATIONS AND GLOSSARY

AFL — Actresses' Franchise League; a group working for votes for women [293]
ARAM — Associate of the Royal Academy of Music
ARP — air raid precautions during WWII
ARRC — Associate of the Royal Red Cross. A military nursing medal, second class
ATA — Air Transport Auxiliary [295]
ATS — women's section of the army during WWII [295]
BA — Bachelor of Arts degree
Backset/Backsettown — a convalescent home for women [299]
Bedales — an co-educational school [289]
Bedford College — women's college [289]
BEM — British Empire Medal
Black Friday — see WSPU [294]
Bishop Otter — a college for women [289]
BMJ — British Medical Journal
BSc — Bachelor of Science degree
Bt — baronet
CB — Companion of the Most Noble Order of the Bath [15]
CBE — Commander of the Order of the British Empire [15]
CD Acts — Contagious Diseases Acts (anti-woman laws to combat venereal diseases)
CH — Companion of Honour [15]
CI — Lady of the Imperial Order of the Crown of India
DBE — Dame Commander of the British Empire [15]
DStJ — Dame Commander of the Most Venerable Order of St John of Jerusalem [15]
DL — deputy lieutenant to the Lord Lieutenant, who is the monarch's representative in a county
DNB — *Oxford Dictionary of National Biography*
FANY — First Aid Nursing Yeomanry [297]
FRCS — Fellow of the Royal College of Surgeons
FRGS — Fellow of the Royal Geographical Society
FRS — Fellow of the Royal Society
FRSL — Fellow of the Royal Society of Literature
Girton — a women's college [289]
GCStJ — Dame Grand Cross of the Most Venerable Order of St John of Jerusalem [15]
GCVO — (Dame) Grand Cross of the Royal Victorian Order [15]
GBE — (Dame) Grand Cross of the British Empire [15]
GPO — General Post Office
Guildhall School — a music and drama school in London, founded 1880
Holloway — a women's prison [301]
IFUW — International Federation of University Women [301]
JP — Justice of the Peace; a magistrate
KGB — Russian secret police and intelligence agency
Lady Chichester Hospital — a hospital for women, based in Brighton [299]
Lady Margaret Hall — a women's college [289]
LAMDA — London Academy of Music and Dramatic Arts
LCC — London County Council
LG — Lady Companion of the Most Noble Order of the Garter [15]
LCStJ — Lady (formerly Dame) of Grace of the Most Venerable Order of St John of Jerusalem [15]
LFP&S — Licentiate of the Faculty of Physicians and Surgeons of Glasgow
LKQCPI — Licentiate of King's and Queen's College of Physicians of Ireland
LNSWS — London National Society for Women's Suffrage [293]
LSE — London School of Economics
LSMW — London School of Medicine for Women [289]
LRAM — Licentiate of the Royal Academy of Music
LRCP — Licentiate of the Royal College of Physicians of London
LRCS — Licentiate of the Royal College of Surgeons of London
LSWS — London Society for Women's Suffrage [293]
MA — Master of Arts degree

MBE — Member of the British Empire [15]
MD — Medicinae Doctor: a doctor of medicine
MP — Member of Parliament
Newnham — a college for women [289]
New Sussex Hospital — a hospital for women [299]
NHS — National Health Service
NPG — National Portrait Gallery
North London Collegiate School — a girls' school [289]
NUWSS — National Union of Women's Suffrage Societies [293]
NUWT — National Union of Women Teachers
NUWW — National Union of Women Workers [301]
OBE — Officer of the British Empire [15]
OM — Order of Merit [15]
PNEU — Parents' National Education Union, now the Bell Educational Trust
QAIMNS — Queen Alexandra's Imperial Military Nursing Service [297]
QARANC —The Queen Alexandra's Royal Army Nursing Corps [297]
Queen's College — an early college for women [290]
RADA — Royal Academy of Dramatic Art, London
RAF — Royal Air Force
RAM — Royal Academy of Music, London
RCM — Royal College of Music, London
Roedean — a girls' school [290]
Royal Holloway College — a college for women [290]
RRC — Royal Red Cross. A military nursing medal, first class [15]
RSC — Royal Shakespeare Company
St Hugh's — a college for women [290]
Six Point Group — a women's rights group [301]
SOE — Special Operations Executive [295]
Somerville — a college for women [290]
SWH — military hospitals run by women during WWI [297]
TD — Territorial Decoration, a military award
TES — *Times Educational Supplement*
TG — Townswomen's Guilds [301]
TGLC — Theatrical Ladies' Guild of Charity
TRL — Tax Resistance League [293]
TUC —Trades Union Congress
V & A — the Victoria and Albert Museum, London
VA— Royal Order of Victoria and Albert
VAD — Voluntary Aid Detachments [297]
WAAC — women's section of the British Army during WWI [295]
WAAF — Women's Auxiliary Air Force [295]
WFL — Women's Freedom League [294]
WI — Women's Institute [301]
WLA — Women's Land Army [295]
WPPL — Women's Protective and Provident League [301]
WPS — Women's Police Service [295]
WRAC — Women's Royal Army Corps [295]
WRAF — Women's Royal Air Force [296]
WRNS — Women's Royal Navy Service [296]
WSPU — Women's Social & Political Union [294]
WTUA — Women's Trade Union Association [301]
WTUL — Women's Trade Union League [301]
WVS — Women's Voluntary Services [296]
WWI — the Great War, or First World War, or 1914–18 war
WWII — the Second World War, or 1939–45 war
Wycombe Abbey — a girls' school [290]
YWCA — Young Women's Christian Association

Educational Establishments

BEDALES

A co-educational, experimental school. Founded near Lindfield, Sussex, in 1893, it moved to Hampshire in 1899. Three notable Sussex women were pupils there.

BEDFORD COLLEGE

Founded by Mrs E.J. Reid in 1849, primarily to educate women to teach in girls' schools. The first higher education college for women, it had male tutors and, therefore, chaperones for the students. Fifteen women in this book either studied or taught there. In 1900 it became part of the University of London and in 1985 merged with the Royal Holloway.

BISHOP OTTER COLLEGE

A small, Anglican, teacher-training college for women founded in 1873 by Louisa Hubbard [66] as Bishop Otter's Memorial College, using the buildings of a former men's college. It became co-educational in 1957 and is now part of the University of Chichester.

GIRTON COLLEGE

In 1869 Emily Davies [39] and Barbara Bodichon [193] opened Benslow House in Hitchin, moving it in 1872 to a site two miles from Cambridge and calling it Girton. It took nine years to obtain permission for Girton's students to take degree examinations at Cambridge University, and even then they received certificates instead of degrees. Eventually, after sixty-eight years, Girton received the status of a college of the university and women were awarded degrees from 1947. Twelve women in this book attended or taught there.

LADY MARGARET HALL

A college for women, founded at Oxford in 1878, when Oxford University did not admit women. It admitted women to exams from 1884 but, if they passed, refused to give them degrees. This was finally changed in 1920. Ten women in this book were among its students.

LONDON UNIVERSITY

London University was empowered to grant degrees to women in 1879. Edith Creak [158] was one of the first three women to gain its BA.

LSMW   The London School of Medicine for Women

Founded in 1874 [see Sophia Jex-Blake, 236], in 1877 Isabel Thorne [234] was elected honorary secretary. Sixteen women in this book studied or taught there. In 1902, as The London (Royal Free Hospital) School of Medicine for Women, it became part of London University.

NEWNHAM COLLEGE

Founded by Henry Sidgwick in 1871 as a residence for five women attending the recently-inaugurated 'Lectures for Ladies' at Cambridge University. By 1879 it had become a college with its own tutors. It differed from Girton, where students studied the same subjects as men, by having special ladies' courses which excluded Greek and Latin. Fifteen women in this book attended or taught at Newnham.

NORTH LONDON COLLEGIATE SCHOOL

A girls' school opened in 1850 by Frances Buss at Camden Town, it became public in 1870.

QUEEN'S COLLEGE

Founded in 1848 by Frederick Denison Maurice in Harley Street, London, to provide training for governesses and schoolteachers, it was Britain's first higher education college for women, securing a royal charter in 1851. Initially, all the tutors were men, and students were chaperoned by aristocratic ladies. It had male principals until 1932. In 1881 Camilla Croudace [96] became lady resident and the college's dominant influence for a quarter of a century, and four women in this book were among its students.

ROEDEAN

A girls' public school near Brighton, opened by the Lawrence sisters [139] in 1899.

ROYAL HOLLOWAY COLLEGE

A women's college founded in 1886 at Egham, Surrey, by Mr Holloway with money he earned from selling quack medicines. Seven of our notable women studied there, and it is now part of London University.

SLADE SCHOOL OF FINE ART

Founded in 1871 with a bequest from Felix Slade it is the art school for University College, London, part of the University of London. Six women in this book studied there.

ST HUGH'S COLLEGE

Founded in 1886 by Elizabeth Wordsworth, the principal of Lady Margaret Hall, as a Church of England college for women who could not afford the fees levied by the women's colleges in Oxford and Cambridge. By 1910 it had educated 225 women, of whom nineteen had become headmistresses and 106 schoolmistresses.

SOMERVILLE COLLEGE

A college for women, founded at Oxford in 1879 [see Lady Margaret Hall, 289] and attended by eight of those in this book.

WYCOMBE ABBEY

An independent girls' school in Buckinghamshire attended by three women in this book. Founded in 1896 by Frances Dove and later supported by Elsie Bowerman [247], it is academically the best girls' school in the UK.

N.B. This glossary does not include all relevant organisations, only those mentioned in the biographies.

Barbara Bodichon: woman of Sussex and a founding mother of the women's rights movement

NATIONAL POLITICAL LEAGUE.

GREAT DEMONSTRATION

QUEEN'S HALL, TUESDAY, JULY 8th, at 8 p.m.

To Protest Against Government's Extreme Coercion Policy

Whereby WOMEN ARE FACING DEATH

through the Administration of the CAT AND MOUSE ACT, and to Demand the Only Statesmanlike Alternative,

THE VOTE, as
THE END OF IT ONCE FOR ALL.

SPEAKERS, representative of Opinion in all parts of the Country :

LORD COWDRAY.

W. LYON BLEASE, Esq. (Barrister-at-Law), Author of "Emancipation of English Women," "History of English Liberalism," &c.

SIR VICTOR HORSLEY, F.R.S.

Rev. LEWIS F. DONALDSON, Vicar of St. Mark's, Leicester.

Rev. T. GOBAT, Darlington.

Miss MARGARET MILNE FARQUHARSON, M.A.

And others.

Supported by

Mrs. HERTHA AYRTON
"AN EMINENT LAWYER"
Mrs. AGNES ANSTRUTHER
Miss MARY ABBOTT
Rev. H. O. ALLBROOK, Hackney
Miss LENA ASHWELL
Miss JANIE ALLAN
Dr. L. GARRETT-ANDERSON
Rev. W. E. BOTT, Grimsby
Mrs. LUCY RE-BARLETT
Mrs. S. BONWICK, Women's Liberal Federation
The EARL and COUNTESS BRASSEY
Rev. W. H. BRIDGE, Edinburgh
Rev. C. BAUMGARTEN, London
Hon. Mrs. BLYTH
SIR EDWARD BUSKE, M.A., LL.D.
Lady BUSK, B.Sc.
Rev. J. S. BURN, Middlesbrough
Rev. FRANK BUTTLE, Cambridge
Rev. J. F. BETHUNE-BAKER, D.D., Cambridge
Mr. H. N. BRAILSFORD
Rev. R. J. BRYANT, Birmingham
Mrs. PERCY BOULNOIS
Mrs. CAVENDISH-BENTINCK
The LADY COWDRAY
Professor S. J. CHAPMAN, M.A., Manchester
Mr. EDWARD CARPENTER
Dr. MAUDE CHADBURN
Rev. ALBERT CORNIBEER, Salford
Rev. JOHN CALLEN, D.D., Radcliff-on-Trent
Dr. STANTON COIT
Mr. WALTER CRANE
Dr. E. DAVIS-COLLEY, London
Mrs. CHAPMAN-CATT (U.S.A.)
Rev. G. HERBERT CHAPMAN, Manchester
Rev. Dr. COBB, D.D.
Rev. IVORY CRIPPS, B.A., Swindon
Rev. HUGH B. CHAPMAN, London
The Misses COLERIDGE
Mrs. CECIL CHAPMAN
Mrs. JACK DALE
Canon HERBERT J. DAVIES, Hereford
Mr. ALBERT DAWSON
Mr. A. C. FOX-DAVIS (Barrister-at-Law)
Mr. and Mrs. JOSEPH FELS
Sir JOHNSTON and Lady FORBES-ROBERTSON
Miss SARA FALCKE
Hon. Mrs. FORBES
Rev. A. F. FENNS, Norfolk
Mrs. BEDFORD FENWICK
Mr. PERCY GRAINGER
Rev. PHILIP P. W. GENDALL, London
Dr. L. HADEN GUEST
Mr. EDWARD HOUNSLOW
Colonel H. B. HANNA

Lady HEMPHILL
Professor W. D. HALLIBURTON, D.Sc., F.R.S., &c.
Mr. LAURENCE HOUSMAN
Miss HORNIMAN
Mr. HENRY HOLIDAY
J. KEIR HARDIE, M.P.
Rev. H. K. HOPE, M.A., Bexhill-on-Sea
Miss BEATRICE HARRADEN
Mrs. CHARLES HANCOCK
Rev. J. CARNEGIE MULLIN, Stoke-on-Trent
Rev. BERNARD HEYWOOD, Manchester
Rev. W. LLEWELYN HERFORD, Manchester
Mr. HENRY HARBEN (Barrister-at-Law)
Mrs. HENRY HARBEN
ALFRED H. HOUGH, Esq.
Rev. CYRIL ISHERWOOD, Little Ilford
Rev. VIBERT JACKSON, Newcastle-on-Tyne
Mr. ATHERLEY-JONES, K.C., M.P.
Lady LELY
Lady EMILY LUTYENS
Mrs. BELLOC LOWNDES
Mr. GEORGE LANSBURY
Lady MUIR MACKENZIE
Dr. FLORA MURRAY
FELIX MOSCHELES, Esq.
Professor BENJAMIN MOORE, F.R.S.
Miss CONSTANCE MAUDE
Dr. L. MARTINDALE, Brighton
Mr. AYLMER MAUDE
Alderman R. R. MEADE-KING, Liverpool
Mr. F. J. MARQUIS, University Settlement, Liverpool.
Mr. MANSELL-MOULLIN, M.D., F.R.C.S.
Mrs. MANSELL-MOULLIN
Hon. MALCOLM MACNAGHTEN, K.C.
Rev. H. S. MILNER, Stockton-on-Tees
Rev. W. H. MARION, Melton Constable
Mr. D. M. MASON, M.P.
A "Monk"
Miss CLARA E. MORDAN
Mr. H. W. MASSINGHAM, Editor of *The Nation*
Miss WINIFRED MAYO
MURIEL COUNTESS DE LA WARR
Mr. THEOBALD MATHEW (Barrister-at-Law)
Mr. RONALD McNEILL, M.P.
Rev. A. M. MITCHELL, Newton-le-Willows
Rev. E. A. MOULD, Barrow
LADY MEYER
Rev. E. A. MORGAN, London
LADY ONSLOW
Mr. ROWLAND PROTHERO
Mrs. ROWLAND PROTHERO
REGINALD POTT, Esq.
Rev. W. H. PAINE, London
Mrs. GERALD PAGET

JOHN RUSSELL, Headmaster of King Alfred Schools
Mrs. BAILLIE REYNOLDS
Miss ELIZABETH ROBINS
Mrs. RAYMOND ROBINS, U.S.A.
Rev. L. D. ROBERTS, London
Rev. W. C. ROBERTS, Rugby
Rev. CLEMENT F. ROGERS, King's College
Rev. E. de M. RUDOLPH
Rev. J. E. ROBERTS, Manchester
Mrs. JANE ROBINSON, Manchester
Mr. HALSEY RICARDO
Professor SIR E. A. SCHAFER, F.R.S.
Mrs. FLORA ANNIE STEELE
Miss MAY SINCLAIR
Dr. ETHEL SMYTHE
Dr. MARIE STOPES
Rev. E. S. SHUTTLEWORTH
Mr. JOHN SCURR
LADY SYBIL SMITH
Dr. AGNES SAVIL
GEORGE BERNARD SHAW
Rev. H. M. STEPHENSON, Derby
Dr. AMY SHEPHERD
Mr. J. KEIGHLEY SNOWDEN
LADY KATHARINE SOMERSET
Dr. ETTIE SAYER, London
Rev. E. VERNON SHAW, Lewisham
Dr. MARGARET TODD.
Miss ELLEN TERRY
Dr. TCHAYKOWSKY
Mrs. AGNES COBDEN TAYLOR, Norwich
Rev. F. R. TENNANT, Brandon
Rev. JOHN M. TAMPLIN, Kent
MAJOR-GENERAL SIR ALFRED TURNER, K.C.B.
WILL THORNE, M.P.
Rev. E. H. TAYLOR, M.A.
Mrs. TAYLOR of Chipchase
Mr. H. BAILLIE-WEAVER, LL.B.
J. C. WEDGWOOD, Esq., M.P.
Mr. CHARLES J. WILLCOK (Barrister-at-Law)
Rev. RHONDDA WILLIAMS
SIR HENRY J. WOOD
Dr. JANE WALKER
Mr. BEN WEBSTER
Mr. A. J. WEBBE and Mrs. WEBBE
Dr. ALBERT WILSON
Mr. SIDNEY WEBB, LL.B.
Mr. FISHER UNWIN
Mrs. JANE COBDEN UNWIN
Mr. ALLEN UPWARD
Dr. MARION VAUGHAN
Mr. ISRAEL ZANGWILL
Mrs. AYRTON ZANGWILL
Mr. J. S. ZIEGLER, J.P., Chairman of the Birkenhead Liberal Association

An earnest appeal is made for names and generous donations in support of the Demonstration, offices of the League, Bank Buildings, 14, St. James's Street, S.W. Telephone, 334 Gerrard.

TICKETS: Reserved, 5s., 2s. 6d.; Unreserved, 1s. and 6d., and Free.

Apply, Miss Broadhurst or Miss Farquharson, at the

ADMISSION BY TICKET ONLY.

The involvement of thirteen notable women of Sussex (and five of their partners) in the suffrage movement is immortalised in this poster which lists supporters of a great demonstration in 1913: Hertha Ayrton, Countess Brassey, Lady Cowdray, Eleanor Davies-Colley, Marie Belloc Lowndes, Dr Martindale, Clara Mordan, Muriel Sackville (Countess de la Warr) Elizabeth Robins, Margaret Todd, Ellen Terry, Jane Cobden Unwin and Mrs Zangwill. The partners were Lord Cowdray (one of the speakers), Earl Brassey, Dr Maude Chadburn, Mr Fisher Unwin and Israel Zangwill.

SUFFRAGE SOCIETIES

The organised campaign for votes for women began about 1865 and continued for over sixty years. When John Stuart Mill presented the first bill for women's suffrage to parliament in 1867 it was received 'almost with horror and commonly treated with derision' *(Women's Penny Paper*, 1889); however, from 1869 women rate-payers could vote for local councillors and serve as churchwardens, poor law guardians and on school boards. From 1888 women could vote for county and borough councillors and they could stand for election to those offices from 1907. The big struggle was for the right to vote for MPs. Anti-suffragists claimed that voting would take a woman away from her 'proper sphere'[6].

After nearly forty years of campaigning with peaceful methods, the movement was brought out of the doldrums by the WSPU. In March 1917, the House of Commons voted 341 to 62 to give the parliamentary vote to women over thirty who were householders, wives of householders, occupiers of property with an annual rent of £5 or graduates of British universities. This became effective in February 1918 and also meant that women on the electoral register could serve on juries. In 1928 the Equal Franchise Act reduced the age to twenty-one, the age at which men could vote. From 1918 women over twenty-one could stand for parliament and the first to win an election was Countess Markievicz. However as a Sinn Feiner she refused to take the vow of loyalty to the King and could not take her seat, and so the first female MP was Nancy, Lady Astor [48, 53, 261]. Female life peers were admitted to the House of Lords in 1958 and hereditary peeresses in 1963.

AFL   Actresses' Franchise League
A group of actresses campaigning for votes for women. Founded in 1908, a branch was opened in Eastbourne in 1911. Members included Maud Arncliffe-Sennett [66], Decima Moore [143], Elizabeth Robins [56], Eva Moore [144], Kitty Marion [222] and Ellen Terry [259]. Membership in 1914 was 900.

LSWS   London Society for Women's Suffrage
(Also LNSWS, the London National Society). Founded in 1867 after the failure of the Kensington Society's suffrage petition. Its honorary secretary was Mentia Taylor [167]. Similar groups opened all over Britain and in 1887 seventeen of them joined forces to form the NUWSS.

NUWSS   National Union of Women's Suffrage Societies
Founded in 1887, Millicent Fawcett, sister of Agnes Garrett [75] was its president from 1897. Its newspaper *The Common Cause* was at one time edited by Clementina Black [123]. Members held public meetings and marches, organised petitions, wrote letters, distributed literature and sent deputations to parliament. They did not use violence and were called suffragists. It was allied to the Liberal Party, which won the 1906 election. When it failed to give women the vote, from 1912 the NUWSS allied itself with the Labour Party. By 1914 the NUWSS had 500 local branches and a membership of over 100,000 (at least sixteen women in this book were members). It supported the war effort and suspended its activities during WWI. After the vote was won many members joined the Six Point Group [301].

TRL   Tax Resistance League
Founded in 1909, it was based on the principle that taxation without representation is tyranny. More than 220 of its members withheld their tax in protest at women being denied the vote, including the Beck sisters [42], Isabel Harrison [249], Kate Harvey [257], Dora Montefiore [226] and Minnie Turner [150].

WFL Women's Freedom League
A breakaway group founded in 1907 by seventy members of the WSPU, it was non-militant and law-abiding (though some members withheld taxes). Eventually it had sixty branches, 4,000 members and a weekly publication, *The Vote*. Muriel Matters [252] and Mrs Cobden-Sanderson [57] were among its members. It was pacifist during WWI.

WSPU Women's Social & Political Union or 'suffragettes'
Founded by NUWSS member Emmeline Pankhurst in 1903 because, despite decades of campaigning, women still did not have the parliamentary vote. Members held marches and demonstrations and sent deputations to parliament, but from 1905 became progressively more militant, beginning with interrupting meetings, progressing to window smashing and culminating in acts of arson, during which private homes, railway stations, cricket pavilions, racecourse stands and golf clubhouses were set ablaze. Suffragettes also cut telephone wires and destroyed letters by pouring chemicals into post boxes. Over 1,000 women were imprisoned, many of whom went on hunger strike and were force-fed by tubes forced into the throat or nose. The WSPU's official newspaper 1907–1912 was *Votes for Women* and from 1912 it was *The Suffragette*. In 1914 the WSPU had about 2,000 members, known as 'suffragettes', a perjorative term invented by a journalist on the *Daily Mail* in 1906 and later adopted by the women themselves to distinguish them from the law-abiding suffragists, who mainly joined the older and far bigger NUWSS.

When WWI began the WSPU suspended militancy and all suffragettes were released from prison; most joined the war effort. Thirty-three women in this book were known to be WSPU members. In 1918 two of the leading suffragettes, Annie Kenney and Grace Roe, spent the winter in St Leonards studying theosophy.

Cat and Mouse Act
Officially the Prisoner's Temporary Discharge of Ill Health Act, it allowed hunger-striking suffragettes ('mice') to be released when they became very ill, so they would not die in prison. Once restored to health they were re-arrested (by the 'cats') and returned to prison.

Census Resistance
As a protest against not being treated as full citizens, an unknown number of women refused to be counted in the census in 1911, staying out all night so they would not be recorded as resident anywhere at 2am, the official census-taking time. Several places of public entertainment in London, including an ice-rink, stayed open all night to accommodate and amuse them.

Black Friday
A violent clash in Parliament Square, London, on 18th November 1910, between about 300 suffragettes and a great number of police, after the Liberal government failed to pass a law that would allow women to vote. Women were deliberately roughed up, about 200 were arrested and two died later, almost certainly from injuries sustained. One of them, Mary Clarke, had once been WSPU organiser for the Brighton area and was Mrs Pankhurst's sister.

N.B. This glossary does not include all relevant organisations, only those mentioned in the biographies.

Wartime Organisations

ATA   Air Transport Auxiliary
A WWII civilian organisation that employed women as pilots to ferry planes between airfields but not on combat missions. In 1940 there were twelve female pilots; by 1945 there were 166.

ATS   Auxiliary Territorial Service
Founded in 1938, it was the women's branch of the British Army during WWII. In 1941, when 65,000 were women working as drivers, mechanics, despatch workers, ammunition inspectors, cooks, clerks and storekeepers, the ATS was given full military status and members were no longer volunteers. Some ATS women operated searchlights, barrage balloons and anti-aircraft batteries.

SOE   Special Operations Executive
A handpicked corps of 9,000 men and 3,200 women formed in 1940 to 'co-ordinate, inspire, control and assist the nationals of the oppressed countries'. Trained in combat, they forged documents, transmitted coded messages and performed dangerous undercover work as couriers and wireless operators for the French Resistance. Two hundred lost their lives, most being executed.

WAAC   Women's Auxiliary Army Corps
Founded in 1917, when women were needed to replace men in non-combat army jobs to release more men for fighting. By November 1918, 57,000 women had served as clerks, signallers, telephonists, motorcycle despatch riders, cooks and gas-mask instructors. Dame Helen Gwynne-Vaughan [86] was the chief controller (Overseas). The WAAC was disbanded in 1921 and reformed in 1938 as the ATS.

WAAF   Women's Auxiliary Air Force
Formed in 1939, by 1943 it had 180,000 members, including aircraft mechanics, radar plotters, flight engineers and signallers (female pilots were in the ATA). It became the WRAF in 1949.

WLA   Women's Land Army or 'Land Girls'
Women who replaced male agricultural workers when they went to war in 1914. By 1917 over 260,000 women were in the WLA, and without them the population would have starved. The WLA was revived in 1938 and by 1943 was 80,000-strong [see Lady Denman, 32; Dame Meriel Talbot, 68].

WPS   Women's Police Service
Founded in 1914 by Margaret Damer Dawson [159], it was called the Women's Police Volunteers until 1915 and its first recruit was Mary Allen [223], who replaced Miss Dawson as commandant in 1919. Its main mission was to protect women and children from prostitution. Officers patrolled garrison towns and searched female war workers serving in munitions factories. In peacetime the regular police forces began to recruit and train their own female officers, who took over the work of the WPS.

WRAC   Women's Royal Army Corps
Formed in 1949, it was the women's branch of the peacetime army. It was headed by Brigadier Dame Mary Colvin [76] 1957–1961 and Brigadier Dame Jean Rivett-Drake [166] 1961–1964. It disbanded in 1992 because women were absorbed into the regular British Army.

Margaret Damer Dawson OBE   Mary Allen OBE

WRAF Women's Royal Air Force
Formed at the same time as the (men's) RAF, in 1918, Dame Helen Gwynne-Vaughan [86] became its commandant. The WRAF recruited thousands of women as clerks, fitters, drivers, cooks and storekeepers. From 1939 and during WWII it was called the WAAF, reverting to WRAF in 1949. Women were employed as fighter pilots in the RAF from 1991.

WRNS Women's Royal Naval Service or 'Wrens'
Formed in 1917 to replace men as cooks, clerks, wireless telegraphists, code experts and electricians, by 1918 it had 5,000 ratings and 450 officers. During WWII members repaired ships and worked in coastal mine spotting. Since 1990 Wrens have served on warships.

WVS Women's Voluntary Services
Founded in 1938 [see Elsie Bowerman, 247], during WWII its members ran canteens and advice centres, distributed forty-five million ration books, evacuated the civilian population and took on fire-watching duties. They dealt with the aftermath of bombing raids, administered first aid and sheltered and re-homed people who were bombed out. By 1941 there were a million members.

WARTIME MEDICAL ORGANISATIONS

During WWI military nurses, doctors and non-medical orderlies were unpaid volunteers. They witnessed horrific sights and frequently worked under shell-fire. The drivers were entirely responsible for the maintenance and repair of ambulances and lorries at a time when society disapproved of women merely driving ordinary cars on British streets. As a writer in *The Times* (9 September 1993) explained: 'They transported endless streams of wounded men from the advanced dressing stations, close to the lines, to field hospitals and the Channel ports. Bumpy roads and ambulances whose tyres frequently punctured made these journeys a nightmare for the wounded, many of whom died in agony.'

FANY   First Aid Nursing Yeomanry
Founded in 1907, it was a voluntary organisation of wealthy women who organised field hospitals and canteens for fighting men in the battle areas of France and Belgium during WWI. In 1938 the FANY became part of the ATS and was the only female military unit permitted to carry arms. It still exists, working in military communications under the name the Princess Royal's Volunteer Corps or FANY (PRVC).

QAIMNS Queen Alexandra's Imperial Military Nursing Service
Founded by Royal Warrant in 1902, it replaced the Army Nursing Service and absorbed the Princess Christian's Army Nursing Service Reserve. All recruits had to be 'of impeccable social standing' and must have trained as nurses for three years. They nursed sick and wounded soldiers at home and abroad. During WWI the 297 regulars were supplemented by 10,000 reserves. It was renamed QARANC in 1949 on becoming part of the British Army.

QARANC Queen Alexandra's Royal Army Nursing Corps
See QAIMNS, above.

SWH   Scottish Women's Hospitals
WWI field hospitals, created by Scotswoman Dr Elsie Inglis in 1914 so that women doctors could volunteer for war work and care for the wounded. Initially opposed by the War Office, the SWH was funded by private subscription, the NUWSS [294] and the American Red Cross. The hospitals and dressing stations treated wounded soldiers and civilians caught up in the war in France, Corsica, Salonika, Romania, Russia, Malta and Serbia. Women volunteers, many of them former suffragettes, served as doctors, nurses, cooks, ambulance-drivers and orderlies. Some were captured by the enemy (but released). Katherine North [82], Elsie Bowerman [247], Mary Gordon [199] and Dr Louisa Martindale [141] served with the SWH, Lady Cowdray [88] was treasurer and Countess Brassey [195] was chairman of the London unit.

VAD   Voluntary Aid Detachments
Formed in 1909 to provide medical services to fighting men, during WWI it had 74,000 members, of whom 50,000 were women, working as auxiliary nurses, ambulance drivers and caterers in field hospitals in Britain, France, the Western and Eastern Fronts, Mesopotamia and Gallipoli.

N.B. This glossary does not include all relevant organisations, only those mentioned in the biographies.

The sum needed at once
IS

£50,000.

Will you
send to us
£100 to-day?
We say 'to-day' because
the need is so urgent

Can we acknowledge
your help to-morrow?

SMALLER SUMS WILL ALSO BE
MOST GRATEFULLY RECEIVED.

FOR THE
LONDON UNITS
SCOTTISH
WOMEN'S
HOSPITALS
(L.S.W.S.).

PLEASE
HELP QUICKLY

SEND A CHEQUE
TO

The Lady Cowdray
Honorary Treasurer,
16, Carlton House Terrace,
London, W.
OR TO

The British Women's
Hospital Committee,
21, Old Bond Street,
LONDON,
W

(The 'Star & Garter' Head-)
(quarters kindly lent by)
(Messrs. Duveen.)

Elsie Bowerman [247] in her uniform as an SWH volunteer orderly

Annie, Lady Cowdray [88] appealing for funds for the SWH, *The Times* 1916

PEACETIME MEDICAL ESTABLISHMENTS

BACKSETTOWN

A convalescent nursing home for women co-founded by Dr Octavia Wilberforce [152] in 1927 at Backset, a fifteenth century farmhouse in Henfield owned by Elizabeth Robins [56]. By 1963 Backsettown became a trust and the nursing home closed in 1988. The house reverted to a private home, which it remains today. [Related image p300.]

LADY CHICHESTER HOSPITAL

The LCH began life as the Lewes Road Hospital for Nervous Diseases of Women and Children at 101 Roundhill Crescent, Brighton, having grown from a dispensary for women and children at Islingword Road. It moved to 70 Brunswick Place under the name Lady Chichester Hospital, Hove Branch, then became the Lady Chichester Hospital after moving to Aldrington House in New Church Road, Hove, in 1921. Helen Boyle [155] was the consultant psychiatrist. The building is now an NHS day centre which, at the time of writing, is under threat of closure. [Related image p300.]

NEW HOSPITAL FOR WOMEN

Located in Marylebone, it was originally a dispensary for women and children, operative by the 1870s. In 1918 it was renamed the Elizabeth Garrett Anderson Hospital. It later became part of the University of London and has since closed. The building has been demolished.

NEW SUSSEX HOSPITAL

A women's hospital for medical and surgical cases, it grew from a dispensary for women and children in Islingword Road, Brighton, and upon moving to 4–8 Ditchling Road was named the Lady Chichester Hospital, Brighton Branch. In 1921 the hospital moved to Windlesham House, Hove, and changed its name to the New Sussex. Louisa Martindale [141] was honorary senior surgeon and physician. The building is now a block of flats.

[Further reading: Brown, V. (2006) *Women's Hospitals in Brighton & Hove*]

N.B. This glossary does not include all relevant organisations, only those mentioned in the biographies.

Lady Chichester Hospital, Aldrington House, in the 1920s (from an old photograph)

Backsettown, Henfield, former residence of Elizabeth Robins (from an old photograph)

Miscellaneous women's organisations

HOLLOWAY A prison in London.
Opened in 1852 it had men's and women's sections until 1902, when it became women-only. Many hundreds of suffragettes were imprisoned in Holloway. Joy Kinsley [39] and Mary Gordon [199] held senior postions there.

IFUW International Federation of University Women
Founded in 1919 by Hertha Ayrton [63] and Caroline Spurgeon [185], by 1932 its annual conference drew 400 academic women from thirty-six countries. It is currently administered from Geneva.

NUWW National Union of Women Workers
A Christian federation of charitable and social reform groups that had its origins in the rescue work of Ellice Hopkins [136], it held its first national conference in 1889. It was renamed the National Council of Women and still exists.

SIX POINT GROUP
Founded in 1921 to campaign for satisfactory legislation to combat child assault; for the widowed mother, the unmarried mother and her child; for equal rights of guardianship for married parents; equal pay for teachers and equal opportunities for women in the civil service. Its journal was *Time and Tide*. Its goals having been achieved, it was dissolved in 1983.

TG The Townswomen's Guild
Originally formed in 1865 to campaign for equal rights, Eva Hubback and Margery Corbett Ashby [201] re-founded it as the first organisation for women that was not linked to any religion or political party, to educate women in the principles of good citizenship. The first meeting took place in Haywards Heath in January 1929. Today there are 55,000 members in 1,300 branches, organised into 111 regional federations.

WI Women's Institute
Founded in Canada in 1897, the first UK meeting took place in 1915 and focussed on encouraging rural women to produce food during WWI. When Lady Denman [32] was appointed head in 1917 it had forty branches; by 1919 this had grown to 1,400 and by the 1950s to over 8,000, with a total membership of 450,000. It flourishes today as a campaigning, social and educational organisation.

WPPL Women's Protective and Provident League. Founded 1874, it was the first women's trade union.

WTUA Women's Trade Union Association. Founded 1889.

WTUL Women's Trade Union League. A later name for the WPPL.

N.B. This glossary does not include all relevant organisations, only those mentioned in the biographies.

WOMEN OF VICTORIAN SUSSEX
Their Status, Occupations & Dealings with the Law, 1830~1870

First published 2003; second edition, 2008

This groundbreaking book shatters many myths about the lives of working women in nineteenth-century England. We move amongst publicans and pew-openers, pickpockets and poisoners, taking in courtroom dramas and domestic battles, as the social and legal status of women is examined in a wide-ranging overview that is constantly enlivened by fascinating local detail.

As the story unfolds we find women at work in 180 occupations. We meet some memorable characters trying to survive in the male-dominated world of Victorian society. Some beat the system; some are destroyed by it; others live outside it. Their stories are told in this absorbing study, richly illustrated with newspaper reports and advertisements, providing a unique historical resource.

"Well researched, scholarly and immensely readable. This book is a classic."
Rt. Hon Tony Benn

"Reveals a forgotten world of daily struggles against appalling injustice – tragic, brave, stubborn, desperate and comic. It is an untold story of English society brought to life in vivid and shocking detail. A rich canvas swarming with life: surprising, fascinating, heart-warming and above all, very, very readable."
Richard Elmore

"A passion for accuracy and an eye for detail that will keep the reader spellbound ... a fine reference book and worthy of a place on any historian's book shelf. Compulsive reading for anyone with an interest in local and regional history."
Ray Hatley

"Helena fills her pages with real, live women, not always chaste and subordinate but often tough and resourceful, and always interesting. A delightful read as well as an informative one."
Open History magazine

"Rather splendid ... scholarly, but decidedly attractive. Fascinating stuff."
Sussex Express

A valuable historical resource ... meticulously researched ... an engrossing study of women trying to survive in a male dominated world."
Brighton Argus

ISBN 978–1–904–10905–1 ~ £12

TO OBTAIN A SIGNED COPY BUY DIRECT FROM THE PUBLISHER ~ SEE P304

CAPTAIN SWING IN SUSSEX & KENT
Rural Rebellion in 1830
by Mike Matthews

The year is 1830. A state of anarchy terrorises Sussex and Kent. Panic-stricken landowners cower behind bolted doors. Cottagers tremble for their lives as farm machinery is smashed to smithereens. Petrified farmers receive blood-chilling, anonymous letters, threatening to roast them alive in their beds. The search is on for the bandit leader Captain Swing — Wanted: Dead or Alive!

ISBN 978–1–904–10913–6 ~ 128 pages ~ £7.99

CLARE SHERIDAN
by Betty Taylor

A cousin of Sir Winston Churchill, her family home was Brede Place, Sussex. She was a sculptor, a journalist, a suspected spy and an adventurous traveller who stayed on a reservation with the Blackfoot Indians. Among others she sculpted Lenin, Trotsky, Churchill and Charlie Chaplin. In later life she lived in Hastings.

Gloss colour booklet ~ 44 pages ~ £3.99

MATILDA BETHAM-EDWARDS
by Joan Rees

"One of the most remarkable of the group of distinguished women whom we now call Mid-Victorian." This comment, by the nineteenth century novelist and feminist Sarah Grand, is an apt summary of the life and career of successful novelist, travel writer and Francophile Matilda Betham-Edwards, who lived in Hastings Old Town for many years.

ISBN 978-1-904-10901-2 ~ 144 pages ~ £9.99

WOMEN'S HOSPITALS IN BRIGHTON & HOVE
by Val Brown

The story of the Lady Chichester Hospital and the New Sussex Hospital. In 1898 two young women doctors arrived in Hove and nervously set up in general practice. Twenty eventful years later Brighton & Hove had two women's hospitals.

ISBN 978–1–904–10909–9 ~ 208 pages plus 16 pages of plates ~ £7.50

POOR COTTAGES & PROUD PALACES
The Life & Work of the Revd Thomas Sockett of Petworth
by Sheila Haines and Leigh Lawson

~ ISBN 978–1–904–10916–7 ~ £14.99

RAILWAYWOMEN
Exploitation, Betrayal and Triumph in the Workplace
by Helena Wojtczak ~ ISBN 978–1–904–10904–4 ~ Hardback £20
Winner of the 2007 DSJT Prize for Best Non-Fiction

ALF COBB: MUGSBOROUGH REBEL
The Struggle for Justice in Edwardian Hastings
by Mike Matthews ~ ISBN 978–1–904–10911–2 ~ £7.99

THE DECLINE OF HASTINGS AS A FASHIONABLE RESORT
Some Edwardian Explanations
by Mike Matthews (Booklet) £2

Forthcoming in 2009

FOOTPLATE TO FOOTPATH
A Guide to the Lost Railways of the Isle of Wight
by Adrian C. Hancock ~ ISBN 978–1–904–10912–9

NOTABLE HAMPSHIRE WOMEN
by Helena Wojtczak ~ ISBN 978–1–904–10920–4

NOTABLE KENT WOMEN
by Helena Wojtczak ~ ISBN 978–1–904–10918–1

How to purchase

- ✪ By credit card via our website www.hastingspress.co.uk
- ✪ By cheque/PO to Hastings Press, PO Box 96, Hastings TN34 1GQ
- ✪ From Amazon.co.uk or any online bookshop
- ✪ On order from any bookshop
- ✪ Enquiries: orders@hastingspress.co.uk

~ Books bought direct from us are post-free ~